Mastering Software Architecture

A Comprehensive New Model and Approach

Michael Carducci

With Daniel Tippie

Apress®

Mastering Software Architecture: A Comprehensive New Model and Approach

Michael Carducci
Parker, CO, USA

ISBN-13 (pbk): 979-8-8688-0409-0 ISBN-13 (electronic): 979-8-8688-0410-6
https://doi.org/10.1007/979-8-8688-0410-6

Managing Director, Apress Media LLC: Welmoed Spahr
Acquisitions Editor: Celestin Suresh John
Development Editor: James Markham
Coordinating Editor: Kripa Joseph

Cover designed by eStudioCalamar

Cover image designed by R. Buckminster Fuller and adapted from US Patent 2,682,235 *Building Construction/Geodesic Dome*
filed December 12, 1951 SN 261,168 granted June 29, 1954
Pursuant to 37 CFR 1.71(d) & (e) and 1.84 (s) this image is not subject to copyright restrictions.

Distributed to the book trade worldwide by Springer Science+Business Media New York, 233 Spring Street, 6th Floor, New York, NY 10013. Phone 1-800-SPRINGER, fax (201) 348-4505, e-mail orders-ny@springer-sbm.com, or visit www.springeronline.com. Apress Media, LLC is a California LLC and the sole member (owner) is Springer Science + Business Media Finance Inc (SSBM Finance Inc). SSBM Finance Inc is a **Delaware** corporation.

For information on translations, please e-mail booktranslations@springernature.com; for reprint, paperback, or audio rights, please e-mail bookpermissions@springernature.com.

Apress titles may be purchased in bulk for academic, corporate, or promotional use. eBook versions and licenses are also available for most titles. For more information, reference our Print and eBook Bulk Sales web page at http://www.apress.com/bulk-sales.

Any source code or other supplementary material referenced by the author in this book can be found here: https://www.apress.com/gp/services/source-code.

If disposing of this product, please recycle the paper

For Kaden, may your creative philosophy live on.

BROTHER MIKE . . .
GROW YOUR SKILL SET
MAKE COOL SHIT

7/5/15

Table of Contents

About the Author

Michael Carducci is a seasoned IT professional with over 25 years of experience, an author, and an internationally recognized speaker, blending expertise in software architecture with the artistry of magic and mentalism.

Michael's career spans roles from individual contributor to CTO, with a particular focus on strategic architecture and holistic transformation. Notable roles over the past 15 years include being named the chief architect at a Fortune 100 company you have certainly heard of and being named chief architect of a social media startup you certainly have *not* heard of.

As a magician and mentalist, Michael has captivated audiences in dozens of countries, applying the same creativity and problem-solving skills that define his technology career. He excels in transforming complex technical concepts into engaging narratives, making him a sought-after speaker and emcee for tech events worldwide.

In his consulting work, Michael adopts a holistic approach to software architecture, ensuring alignment with business strategy and operational realities. He empowers teams, bridges tactical and strategic objectives, and guides organizations through transformative changes, always aiming to create sustainable, adaptable solutions.

Michael's unique blend of technical acumen and performative talent makes him an unparalleled force in both the tech and entertainment industries, driven by a passion for continuous learning and a commitment to excellence.

About the Contributing Author

Daniel Tippie has been a software architect, software engineer, systems architect, systems engineer, and technical lead with over 17 years of experience working in both commercial and DoD software development.

He has a passion for taking computer science theory, software engineering practices, and systems engineering principles and converting that knowledge into practical application. He has also spent years designing, building, and integrating complex projects of various sizes and phases of development. Daniel applies methodical and flexible approaches to everything that he does.

Daniel loves to discuss computer science, math, physics, ballistics, astrodynamics, science fiction, and dogs. He has a very supportive wife, kids, parents, and in-laws.

About the Technical Reviewer

Darrell Rials is an accomplished software and enterprise architect, helping teams deliver worthwhile solutions for over 25 years in the manufacturing, building automation, financial services, and telecommunications industries. A lifelong learner, writer, and teacher, Darrell maintains an abundance mindset, believes that the way we treat people matters a lot, and is grateful to be able to experience this mystery we call life.

Acknowledgments

If I have seen further, it is by standing on the shoulders of giants.

—Sir Isaac Newton

As I look at this long and dense manuscript that I have spent the past two years writing, I cannot help but remain surprised. Honestly, I never thought I would ever have enough to say to fill a book, let alone the ability to sit down and write one. Yet here we are. Life, sometimes, surprises us.

My entire adult life I have juggled dual careers in magic and technology with an intention to retire from software and focus completely on magic. In fact, I did just that in 2014.

Just when I thought I was out, they pull me back in!

—Michael Corleone, *The Godfather Part III*

I have Jay Zimmerman, founder of the No Fluff Just Stuff (NFJS) conference series, to thank for pulling me back in. In 2008 or 2009, he found me online and booked me to perform a magic show at his flagship conference, ÜberConf. At that time, nobody knew that software engineering was my "day job"; however, my domain knowledge was clearly evident in the show that I wrote, and that performance was exceptionally well received by the audience. Well, almost.

As I was leaving the ballroom, I heard a voice bellow "You're wrong, by the way!" I turned to the source of the comment, and the volunteer critic expanded on his statement, pointing out a factual error in my script. OK, the show was well received except by that one guy. You can't please everyone.

On the success of the show at ÜberConf, Jay booked me for another conference that year, this time in Florida where I delivered a similar performance. Once again, the show was exceptionally well received. While I was packing up to head to the evening reception, a member of the audience approached me to say "Kudos! You fixed your script!" It was the volunteer critic I met at ÜberConf, six months earlier. The critic was not an attendee, as I had first assumed, but rather was Brian Sletten who was—and is—a regular speaker at NoFluff events. It is Brian Sletten to whom I owe an enormous debt of gratitude.

Despite a rather gruff initial interaction, Brian and I have grown to be good friends, and he has contributed enormously to my philosophy and collection of mental models. Brian is a deep thinker who is a master of critical thought and possesses the rare ability to see things as they really are.

Brian is not the only NoFluff speaker who has had a profound impact on my personal and professional growth. In fact, many subsequent conference performances allowed me to meet and befriend many brilliant thought leaders. I cannot name them all; however, at a minimum, I want to thank the tour regulars. Venkat Subramanium, Ken Kousen, Raju Gandhi, Ken Sipe, Danny Brian, Daniel Hinojosa, Jonathan Johnson, Doug Hawkins, Tim Berglund, Craig Walls, Chris Maki, Nate Schutta, Scott Davis, and Llewellyn Falco have all supported me and inspired me to become who I am today.

I also owe a particular debt to Mark Richards and Neal Ford. For years, these towering intellects dominated the architecture tracks at most of the conferences I have participated in. Although they are no longer regulars at NoFluff events, their friendship and influence live on. It is no surprise that I cite and quote these individuals and their work frequently throughout this book.

I'm also extraordinarily grateful to Roy Fielding, both for his contributions to the Web and for his dissertation which introduced me to a new model of software architecture that has informed my thinking ever since.

There is, of course, more to the story than just doing magic tricks at conferences. As the NFJS resident magician, my software bona fides were not widely known. The speakers and crew, however, welcomed me into the fold without question. Jay always recognized that there was more to me than meets the eye, and, within a year or two of giving shows, he invited me to speak. At that point, the two worlds that I fought so hard for so long to keep separate irrevocably collided. Like it or not, I was back in the game.

History repeats itself. I met Martin Anderson, an early mentor and my first employer in the tech industry, when I was the resident magician at TGI Friday's back in the late 1990s. Through sheer luck, I learned of Martin the night before we met. His name had come up as someone I should approach for an internship or junior developer role, and subsequent research turned up a personal home page he had built as an exercise to learn HTML. The website laid out his, and his family's, whole life story. Such inside information is particularly valuable when giving mindreading demonstrations. I can only imagine that the "insight" I displayed was nothing short of astounding. When I had finally deployed every fact at my disposal (and, thus, finally time to conclude my extended performance), I mentioned that I was *"a keen amateur programmer"* who might be in the market for an entry-level software development position. Martin responded by saying *"If you're half as good at that as you are at this, you're hired"* and gave me a job on the spot.

I suppose I should have come clean to Martin, but the timing never seemed right. In the beginning, it seemed too soon to confess and pull the rug out from underneath the first impression I had created. Before long, the optimal window for sharing the truth had passed. Consequently, the story never came up. Martin, if you are learning this for the first time, let me take this opportunity to say both "Thank you" and "I'm sorry."

Another notable employer is Robert Harris, a standout boss, friend, and mentor who instilled a sense of ruthless pragmatism into me and taught me how to navigate the complex human element of software engineering. I also owe a debt to another manager, Ståle Veipe, who encouraged me to refine and sharpen my unique perspective on software architecture.

Of course, I must go even further back to thank my parents, Bob and Jackie, for somehow acquiring an Apple IIgs in the 1980s, where I first learned to program. I also owe a debt to Jim Rogers, my neighbor growing up, for mentoring me during my early programming journey and who first connected me to the Internet in 1993, allowing me to participate in the dawn of the Web. Also, my sister Sara who lit the spark of magic in me at an early age, which led me to where I am today.

Michael Lewis, my stepfather, also helped me greatly during my formative years exploring technology and facilitated many opportunities that were not yet commonplace.

As I enumerate the names of those who have been instrumental in my journey, I realize a list of acknowledgments will never be complete. In truth, I owe a debt to so many people who have helped me along my journey. Even if you do not see your name in this section, it is not a reflection of the extent of your contribution, but rather a reflection of the challenges inherent to writing an "acknowledgments" section for a book that I know will always be incomplete.

Before I close, however, I want to personally thank a few more people. I am grateful to Celestin John and the team at Apress for their patience as they waited for me to finally respond to their requests for me to join the ranks of their authors (and their patience as they waited for a completed manuscript). Thanks to my good friend, Joshua van

Allen, who was always there for me with support, encouragement, and is a reliable sounding board. All my early reviewers and beta readers, who have provided invaluable suggestions and feedback as this book was taking shape. The most prolific reviewers are Darrell Rials, my official technical reviewer; Jerome Broekhuijsen, who has been reviewing chapters as fast as I can write them; Kevin D'Ornellas, a former colleague and good friend who has given me support and encouragement throughout this entire project; Schusselig, who provided much invaluable, unvarnished feedback; and Bill DeSmedt, another good friend and former colleague who voluntarily edited the entire first draft of Section 1.

I particularly need to call out Daniel Tippie, this book's contributing author. I originally asked Daniel to submit two chapters that he has unique insights on, but he sat next to me throughout the final editing process and provided incredible depth and feedback. He fearlessly challenged me on almost every line of this book. Without Daniel's tireless effort, this book would not be what it is today; it might never have made it to a final draft.

As valuable as all the reviewer and contributor feedback has been, good or bad, I take full responsibility for the quality of this book, but I promise you it wouldn't be nearly what it is today without these individuals' contributions.

For everyone I have met over the past decade+ of speaking at conferences, I thank you. You have given me purpose and drive to continue growing, learning, and polishing my talks and writing.

I especially want to thank my wife, Kate, who has been a source of unwavering support and encouragement for this and every project I undertake. Although writing a book is hard, *living with someone writing a book* is probably even harder.

Finally, I want to thank you. Yes, you. If you are reading this far into the off-topic minutiae, you and I are kindred spirits, and I hope the pages that follow reward you handsomely for your diligence and open-mindedness. One of the secrets to success in software architecture is looking at things from multiple perspectives, and you have demonstrated a willingness and aptitude to go much deeper than most in our industry.

Whether I have named you explicitly or not, I sincerely hope that life repays you tenfold for the joy and support you have given me over the years.

For all of you, from the bottom of my heart, I thank you.

Foreword

It's not every day you get asked to write the Foreword to a book that points out that you can occasionally be a bit of an asshole. *Yet here we are. Life, sometimes, surprises us.*

If you don't know what I am talking about, please go read the "Acknowledgments" section. I encourage you to read the whole thing as it is genuine and heartfelt, but specifically the first part. I'll wait.

Back? I don't dispute his claims, but here's my side of the story. When I heard there was going to be a magician at ÜberConf, my first thought was, *"Oh, the balloon animal guy must have been busy."* Look, I know who I am. I own it. I made sure to go check out his show with the full expectation of Hate Watching it, but within minutes I realized that I was completely wrong. Not only was he a great showman, his magic was good. Really good. A perfect fit for the conference.

I didn't go out of my way to track him down afterward. He walked by and I felt compelled to say what I said not to demean him, but to very modestly improve an otherwise exceptional show. To his credit, he listened patiently, accepted the ding, and absorbed the feedback into his performance.

The other reason I said what I said was because he was factually wrong, and I chafed at the idea that a room full of software people were given misinformation about password management. I couldn't fix that, but I could try to stop it happening again. Because of Michael's openness to feedback and thoughtful processing of what I said, we did.

Too much of what goes on in our industry involves people parroting what other people say without thinking about it (cf. current AI hype). This must change. Reality is often much more nuanced, contextual, and driven by forces that compel old ideas to fall by the wayside in time.

Our social, technical, commercial, geopolitical, and environmental contexts are rapidly changing how and where software is being used. This requires us to constantly evaluate what makes sense. The role of the architect is to make reality-based recommendations, to identify issues, correct for them, and to use their words to convey why certain decisions matter to both technical and nontechnical stakeholders.

It's a complex role that requires skills in multiple disciplines. It necessitates an openness to feedback and a willingness to change your mind when presented with new evidence. It requires honesty, rigor, and a compassion for your audience, whoever they may be. It also requires you to do the hard work. To think for yourself. You must listen to others, but you have to do research and understand history both within your organization and your industry. I don't know many people who embody all of these characteristics as well as Michael does. This is why when he felt incapable of producing a book as broad and deep and well researched as this one has become, I knew he would and told him so.

Good authors need good audiences. If you are reading this, you are very likely a good audience and have attributes that already set you apart from your peers. Michael doesn't tell you what to do in this book, he tells you how to think about what to do. Your work isn't done when you finish it. In fact, it is just beginning.

I'm convinced you'll be better prepared for having read this book.

Brian Sletten

Preface: Holism in Software Architecture

You never change things by fighting the existing reality. To change something, build a new model that makes the existing model obsolete.

—R. Buckminster Fuller

An undergraduate course on applied mathematics will focus on general principles and concepts, simplifying the complex by reducing the dimensionality of the problem space. We simplify for the sake of theory, overlooking the true complexity of reality. A mass might be attached to a "*light, inextensible string*." There are only perfect pulleys, frictionless planes, and systems always operating in a vacuum.

It has often been said that "*software architecture cannot exist in a vacuum*," yet that vacuum remains one that is notoriously difficult to escape. This fact is compounded by the common approach of many works in this field, focusing only on one or a small number of aspects of the field in the abstract. In reality, architecture forms part of a living, breathing ecosystem of humans, technologies, networks, machines, customers, dreams, and aspirations. Applying architecture requires making the abstract concrete and designing models that integrate all the fragments of architecture theory as well as the messiness of the reality that architecture must exist within.

Historically, it has only been possible to connect these discrete pieces into a much larger understanding over the course of a lengthy career with a checkered record of successes and failures. A more comprehensive and holistic look at this field is long overdue, and this integrated view is the ambitious goal of *Mastering Software Architecture*.

Of all the various engineering disciplines that have emerged over the course of human history, software is arguably the youngest by a substantial margin. Civil, mechanical, and military engineering evolved over *millennia*. Chemical and electrical engineering span centuries. In contrast, software engineering has only been around for a handful of decades. We still have much to learn and discover.

It was only as early as 1975 when the first notions of *structured software*[1] began to enter the industry lexicon. At that point, proto-architecture began to emerge as a unification of software engineering and systems engineering. In 1976, a handful of forward-looking individuals saw a future marked by increasingly complex software systems composed of numerous components built and maintained by multiple teams.[2] These pioneers in the software development space began to explore ideas around system components, modularity, and higher-level conceptual descriptions of software systems. A changing world also required changing software, so increasing effort went into novel approaches to optimally structure code for understandability, maintainability, and evolvability. By 1990, the first books with an explicit focus on what we now call software architecture[3] appeared, and the industry soon believed it had found its silver bullet.[4] Yet we seem doomed to discover again and again that, as Fred Brooks asserted in 1986[5] and Roy Fielding reiterated in 2000,[6] *there are no silver bullets*. Unfortunately, silver bullet thinking still permeates our industry.

In software architecture, there are no best practices; there are no universal and objective "right answers." There are only trade-offs. The weight of this fact is so significant that Neal Ford and Mark Richards codified this as their First Law of Software Architecture.[7]

Designing systems today requires practitioners to evaluate many decisions, weigh many trade-offs, and arrive at a *locally optimal design* for a given project, system, subsystem, or component relative to the time of decision (although a system's needs *will* change in the future). The decisions and trade-offs span many dimensions, from the technological to the human and from the environmental to the organizational. For the field of software architecture to continue to evolve, new models must be applied that

---

[1] Yourdon, E., Constantine, L. (1975). *Structured Design: Fundamentals of a Discipline of Computer Program and System Design*, Yourdon Press

[2] De Remer, F., Kron, H. (1976). *Programming in the Large Versus Programming in the Small.* In: IEEE Transactions on Software Engineering, pp. 312–327

[3] Best, L. *Application Architecture: Modern Large-Scale Information Processing*, John Wiley & Sons, 1990

[4] Cox, B. (1990). *There is a Silver Bullet.* Byte; Vol. 15, No. 10:209–218

[5] Brooks, F. (1986). *No Silver Bullet—Essence and Accident in Software Engineering.* Proceedings of the IFIP Tenth World Computing Conference: 1069–1076

[6] Fielding, R. (2000). *Architectural Styles and the Design of Network-based Software Architectures.* Doctoral dissertation, University of California, Irvine

[7] Ford, N., Richards, M. (2020). *Fundamentals of Software Architecture: An Engineering Approach* O'Reilly

take a more holistic perspective. The individual patterns, technologies, practices, and tools have value and continue to be necessary, but they have proven to be insufficient in isolation at making an architect effective.

Consider the headwinds today's architects face. Since Brad Cox first suggested there might be a "*silver bullet*," we have learned that many paths toward system design are available, and each path yields different outcomes. An outcome that is best for one project will be suboptimal for another. Different systems require different sets of architectural characteristics and inherent system capabilities. These capabilities must originate from business requirements and needs, which are never communicated in the domain-specific language and idiom of the architect or programmer. Moreover, where these capabilities are not expressed, they must be inferred. If we fail at this foundational task, it is impossible to be effective as an architect.

Even if an architect can correctly infer these architectural requirements, if the architect's metaphorical quiver only contains a relatively small number of patterns and potential implementations while lacking a more sophisticated and nuanced set of tools and mental models to *derive* architectures rather than shoehorning existing patterns into the problem, their efficacy will be severely constrained.

Assuming the architect can perfectly design a target architecture, this, too, is not enough. Their vision and architecture must be communicated with high fidelity, such that implementation teams may understand and execute effectively. If the most vital details of the design are lost in translation, even an optimal architecture for a system will be moot.

Executing architecture within an organization provides yet another challenge. Virtually every decision an architect makes will be challenged. Many knowledgeable and experienced individuals are responsible for implementing any given project. These individuals may have different ideas around how the system should be built. The architecture may not be compatible with existing organizational biases, preferences, norms, and conventions; yet the macro system must be cohesive which requires adherence to architectural standards and conventions. To be effective, the architect must not only be skilled in the art of requirements analysis and system design but also be an equally skilled communicator and change agent. If we are not able to build consensus that spans project stakeholders and teams, much of the design work will be for naught.

Finally, the architect must be aware of messy realities that can be easily overlooked in theoretical discussions of architecture yet cannot be ignored in the practice of delivering software. These are external factors such as the nature, structure, and maturity of the organization; the skills, maturity, and practices of the teams; and the factors governing the environment within which the project exists.

Architecture is no longer as simple as a set of best practices to organize complex codebases or modeling tools to describe a system at a high level. It is not just about the newest patterns that have emerged over the past 20 years. There are many crucial aspects of software architecture beyond the “what” and “how” that require further exploration. In short, for our field to continue to evolve, we must embrace the idea of holism in our approach to architecture. The work that follows is an ambitious attempt to do exactly that.

Introduction

All models are wrong, but some models are useful.

—George Box

This book, and the Tailor-Made Architecture Model described within, is an attempt to address myriad challenges today's architects face. Much of the body of literature in this space addresses these challenges in a piecemeal way or overlooks some of them entirely.

Mastery of software architecture requires an integrated approach that, historically, has required a great deal of experience, trial and error, and failures to grow into a truly effective architect. In other words, failure is an integral part of the learning process as we continue to grow and evolve. This book aims to accelerate your journey to mastery by providing a broad base of knowledge to build a career upon. Although many chapters could be expanded to fill an entire book, this work primarily aims to illuminate *unknown unknowns* to enable you to continue to pursue depth as needed in your future. This book is written to begin your learning journey rather than end it.

While many technical books are written as reference works, where individual chapters and subsections may be consulted in isolation in arbitrary order, as necessary, to fill specific knowledge or skill gaps, this work is designed to first be read sequentially. A holistic look at software architecture requires connecting many discrete and seemingly disjoint concepts. Each chapter introduces a number of these concepts and ideas, while each subsequent chapter builds upon the growing body of knowledge, connecting them in important ways. Furthermore, the structure of this work is designed to combat the effect of "*semantic diffusion*"[1] in the tech industry.

[1] Fowler, M. (2006). *Semantic Diffusion,* `https://martinfowler.com/bliki/SemanticDiffusion.html`

> *Semantic diffusion occurs when you have a word that is coined by a person or group, often with a pretty good definition, but then gets spread through the wider community in a way that weakens that definition. This weakening risks losing the definition entirely - and with it any usefulness to the term.*
>
> —Martin Fowler

In the technology space, a great many terms have succumbed to semantic diffusion. TDD, REST, agile, DevOps—even architecture patterns such as microservices—are examples of ideas that, today, have wildly differing definitions in practice. Semantics requires context; in addition to building upon and connecting concepts, the structure of this book is intended to set that context within the scope of the pages that follow. This is particularly true for the chapters in Section 1 and Section 2. The chapters in Section 1 build an important foundation for the remainder of the work, even if it may be tempting to skim or skip topics that appear familiar; holism requires comprehensive context. Likewise, in the chapters in Section 2 where we re-derive the common/mainstream architectural patterns, the defining constraints that are shared across multiple patterns are only introduced once and simply referenced wherever they reappear. It is important to remember that the patterns described in Section 2 are necessary for common understanding and communication; however, these are introduced in support of a more nuanced approach to system design.

Finally, this book incrementally introduces the Tailor-Made Software Architecture Model and its constituent concepts, practices, ceremonies, and motivations. The model itself is an integrated approach to software architecture from gathering requirements, to design, evaluation, documentation, communication, enforcement, and evolution. Given this model is repeatedly referenced throughout the book while individual aspects are being described, an advanced summary may be helpful to you, the reader.

The Tailor-Made Architecture Model in a Nutshell

This model consists of a number of ideas, some of which may be—or appear to be—familiar to the reader while others may seem new. It must be stressed that none of the ideas are revolutionary. Instead, they are simply *evolutionary* (Figure 1). The heart of this model is architectural design by constraint. One of the earliest explorations of this idea appeared in Fred Brooks' 1975 work *The Mythical Man-Month*,[2] while this same idea is central to *Foundations for the Study of Software Architecture*,[3] *Architectural Styles and the Design of Network Based Software Architectures*,[4] and *Software Architecture Constraint Reuse-by-Composition*.[5]

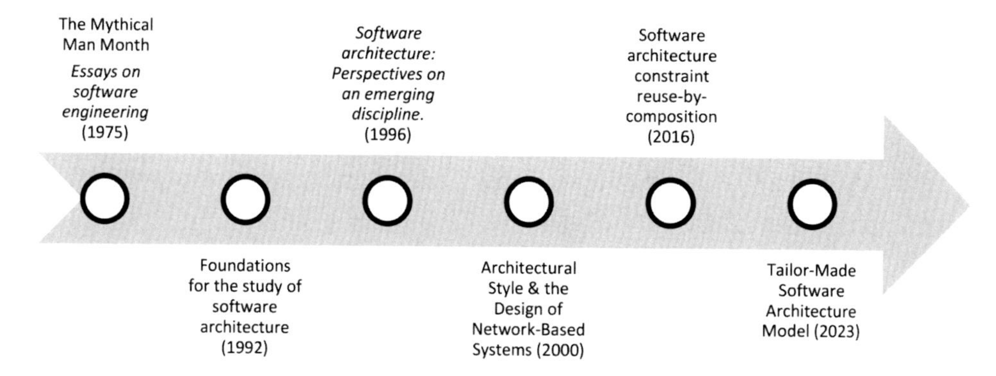

Figure 1. *Timeline of Architectural Design by Constraint*

The Tailor-Made Architecture Model (TMAM) begins with the understanding that there are no best practices in software architecture as every nontrivial software system is unique in both its needs and their measure. Every architecturally significant decision carries with it both positive and negative consequences, and, to be effective as an architect, the business impact of each consequence must be understood and weighed. Throughout this book, you are provided tools and techniques to navigate this complex space.

TMAM deviates from conventional architectural design approaches to address their numerous shortcomings. Rather, it embraces the long-standing (but largely forgotten) idea of design by constraint. The model extends the 30+ years of work in this area by defining both the trade-offs inherent in each constraint, but also associated numeric weighting for each trade-off. This replaces much of the trial and error currently necessary in many architecture practices with rich, design-time feedback on candidate architectures. Additionally, this approach results in much more deterministic outcomes.

[2] Fowler, M. (2006). *Semantic Diffusion*, `https://martinfowler.com/bliki/SemanticDiffusion.html`

[3] Perry, D., Wolf, A. (1992). *Foundations for the Study of Software Architecture*, ACM SIGSOFT, pp. 40–52

[4] Fielding, R. (2000). *Architectural Styles and the Design of Network-based Software Architectures*. Doctoral dissertation, University of California, Irvine

[5] Tibermacine, C., et al. (2016). *Software Architecture Constraint Reuse-By-Composition*. Future Generation Computer Systems, 61, pp. 37–53

Design by constraint has the side effect of solving endemic problems in communicating architectures to the organization. A key concept in TMAM is that of an "architectural style" defined by Fielding as *"a named, coordinated set of architectural constraints."* We will introduce (or, perhaps, reintroduce) the concept of an architectural style and show how it solves many architecture communication issues and addresses the inherent challenge of semantic diffusion within an organization.

While this work alone is valuable and has the potential to change the way many practitioners think about architecture and system design, architecture decisions must be made holistically. Beyond meeting the business and system needs, for an architecture to truly fit it must be compatible and within reach of the teams and organizations as well as the environments within which they operate. TMAM accepts that people are integral to the architect's success or failure. Thus, people and the organizations within which they exist form critical components to the model. Therefore, TMAM connects these architecture decisions to architectural X factors, thereby providing another dimension of design-time feedback on architectures that might look good "on paper" but will likely fail in practice.

TMAM rejects the idea that architectures must be rigidly defined by isolated and largely incompatible patterns. Our exploration of design by constraint will prove that architecture exists as a continuum rather than a finite set of discrete patterns. This aspect of the model forms a foundation for building truly agile and evolvable architectures that need neither be over- or under-engineered up front. Section 2 explores the common architecture patterns and their defining architectural constraints and how these patterns are modified or evolved by adding/changing constraints at design time (or modernization time). Ultimately, this section demonstrates the power and flexibility of the model as well as providing you with additional tools to reduce risk, confusion, and missed expectations.

TMAM emphasizes the importance of *holistic architectural fit*. Fit requires tailoring, tweaking, and customization (both up front and over time), and this model produces designs which are highly customizable to achieve this ideal fit.

Finally, TMAM is not just about design, but execution. The model includes processes, practices, and ceremonies around documentation, communication, and effecting meaningful change across teams and organizations. Additionally, mastery of software architecture requires a spectrum of skills to build strategic relationships, engender buy-in, and support the organization toward the optimal system design.

In short, TMAM is a total, integrated, holistic approach to software architecture that will provide you with many powerful tools and mental models to become more effective in your practice. A growing body of contributors are now expanding this model. If you would like to subscribe to updates or get hands-on training and experience for yourself or your teams, visit `https://MasteringSoftwareArchitecture.com/`.

SECTION 1

Foundations

CHAPTER 1

The Scope and Role of Architecture

You don't drive the architecture, the requirements do. You do your best to serve their needs.

—Richard Monson-Haefel

Like so many words in software development today, the term "architect" has become vague and overloaded. A quick survey of open architect roles along with their requirements and job descriptions underscores the diversity (and often incompatibility) of existing definitions. For some, rightly or wrongly, an architect is primarily a kind of super-developer (a *senior developer*++, if you will) responsible for the patterns and conventions adopted by the rest of the team. For others, an architect is just a cloud platform expert. There are enterprise architects, solution architects, system architects, and application architects, to name but a few. Many more definitions and variations exist in the wild. Some define the scope of an individual's contributions; others define the area of expertise within which the individual must specialize. This muddies the waters surrounding expectations of the role and may lead to impostor syndrome as it is easy to find a variety of "architect" jobs or positions that you or I am yet seemingly unqualified for.

Although many sub-specializations exist, leading to a variety of paths an architect may pursue over the course of their career, there remains an ongoing tension between the idea that an architect is yet another type of software development specialist and the idea that an architect is a type of "master generalist." As will be explored further, this work asserts that an architect is not simply another species of subject matter expert (SME), but rather a "master generalist" who trades depth of knowledge in a small

M. Carducci, *Mastering Software Architecture*, https://doi.org/10.1007/979-8-8688-0410-6_1

number of areas for breadth of knowledge across a spectrum of areas while deploying diverse mental models. In this practice, the architect will collaborate with SMEs while bringing a higher-level perspective to the solution.

Likewise, the definition of "architecture" has evolved considerably since the term was first introduced into the technology industry lexicon in the late 1980s. Architecture can exist in various scopes within a project, system, or organization. For the context of this book, these terms must be defined generally by exploring their common and unifying themes and ideas. We can deduce that "architects," at some level, are responsible for the decisions relating to "architecture," so perhaps it would be wise to begin by defining "architecture."

What Exactly Is Architecture?

Many definitions have been put forward in answer to this question. For example, in 2007, the International Organization for Standardization (ISO) published ISO/IEC 42010:2007 *Systems and software engineering — Recommended practice for architectural description of software-intensive systems* which defines software architecture as

> *The fundamental organization of a system, embodied in its components, their relationships to each other and the environment, and the principles governing its design and evolution.*

We see similar definitions across a host of other sources, including *Software Systems Architecture* by Rozanski and Woods who put forward this definition:

> *Software architecture is the discipline concerned with model-based description and analysis of software systems, with a particular focus on the system's highest-level components and their interaction.*

And in *Software Architecture in Practice* by Bass, Clements, and Kazman, we see software architecture defined as

> *...the set of structures needed to reason about the system, which comprise software elements, relations among them, and properties of both.*

as well as many others. The common themes relate to the organization of the system, its major components or elements, their interactions, and the decisions that drive the design and evolution of the system.

While all these definitions address the "what" of software architecture, we must also consider the *why*.

Why Architecture?

Why is more important than how-Second Law of Software Architecture[1]

"Why" is the operative word here. What value does architectural thinking contribute over that of a senior developer focused on building and delivering the features of the software system?

At its core, *architecture is the set of high-level decisions driving the essence of the software, transcending functional requirements and defining everything it can do beyond providing the defined features and functions.*

The ultimate success of a system is defined not only by delivering the right set of features, but those features must be implemented in such a way that crucial capabilities (e.g., scalability, elasticity, evolvability, agility, overall simplicity, etc.) are also present in the system. These *capabilities* (frequently referred to by many other names, including architectural characteristics, system quality attributes, nonfunctional requirements, or simply *-ilities*) are the heart of the "why" in software architecture. Architecture is much more than components and their interactions or a high-level description of the system; architecture must constrain the degrees of freedom in software development to ensure the macro system exhibits the necessary capabilities for the overall success of the system.

In pursuit of this goal, many approaches were developed, and, over time, *architecture patterns* began to emerge. A pattern is a general, reusable approach to solving common and recurring problems in system design or development. The common/recurring problems addressed in architecture patterns revolve around approaches to induce those crucial capabilities alongside delivery of desired features and functions. Architectural patterns describe the structure, components, and interactions of a software system, but, it must be reiterated, *architecture is much more than components and their interactions,* as will be seen in continued exploration of this topic.

[1] Ford, N., & Richards, M. (2020). *Fundamentals of software architecture: An engineering approach.* O'Reilly Media

Patterns

Early patterns simply focused on approaches to organizing code for maintainability, understandability, and reuse. As expectations of software evolved from monolithic desktop or mainframe applications, new problems arose that required innovative solutions. Both single-host and distributed client-server architectures emerged with the requirement to scale to support more users or decomposition to manage growing complexity (or both). This approach also provides *independent evolvability* by decoupling dependent components and allowing modifications to one component to take place without impacting others. These new capability requirements became particularly important as applications were increasingly deployed to the Internet. Architects discovered a new disparity between existing conventions, their relative strengths, and which capabilities the software had to support that, in turn, led to more patterns.

Patterns are often a product of their time and sometimes fall into disfavor as better alternatives appear. Consequently, some patterns may seldom be used for new development but remain relevant in architectural literature both for the legacy systems that still apply them and as teaching tools to learn lessons from both their successes and failures, thereby informing future architectural decisions.

At the time of this writing, most architecture literature focuses on one or more of several patterns prescribing a particular organization of the components to induce. These patterns promise expected strengths and weaknesses when it comes to desired system capabilities. An overview of these patterns can be seen in Figure 1-1 and will be explored in depth in Section 2 of this book.

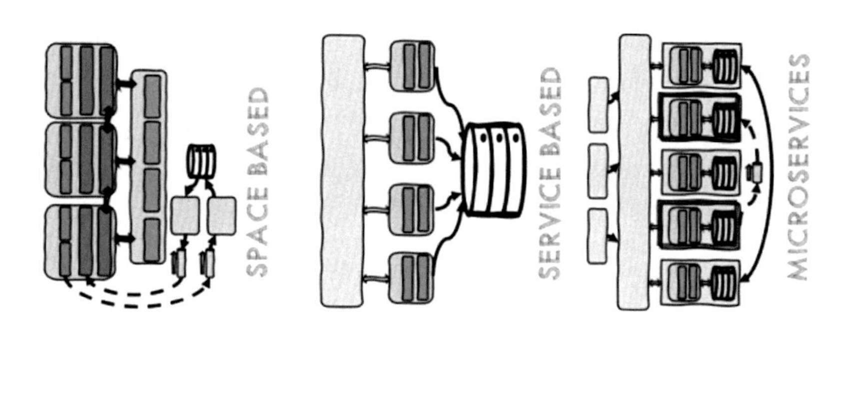

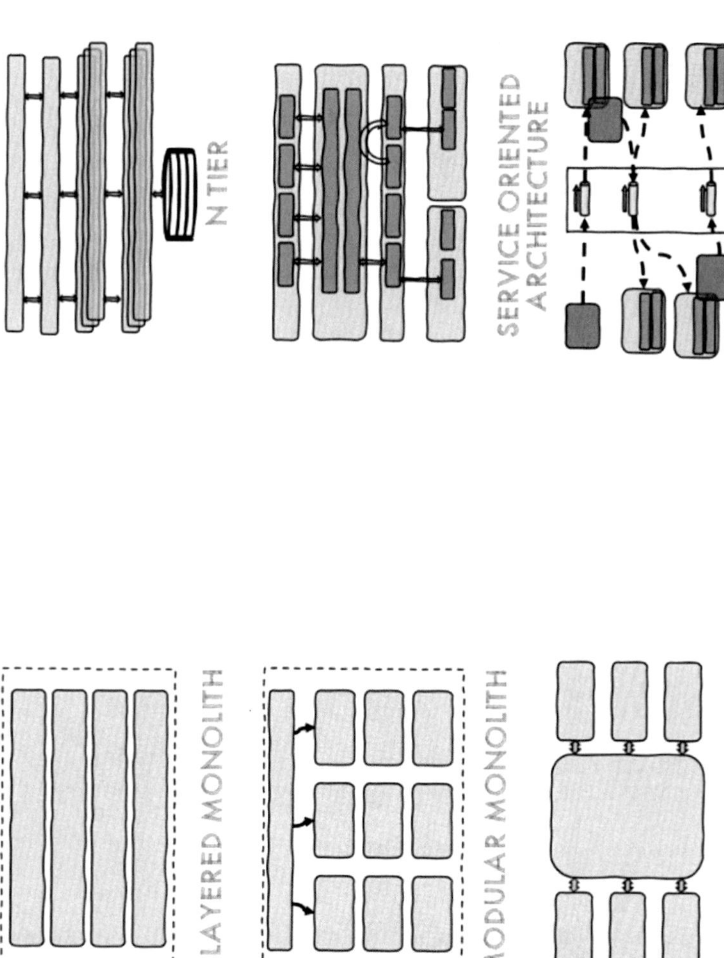

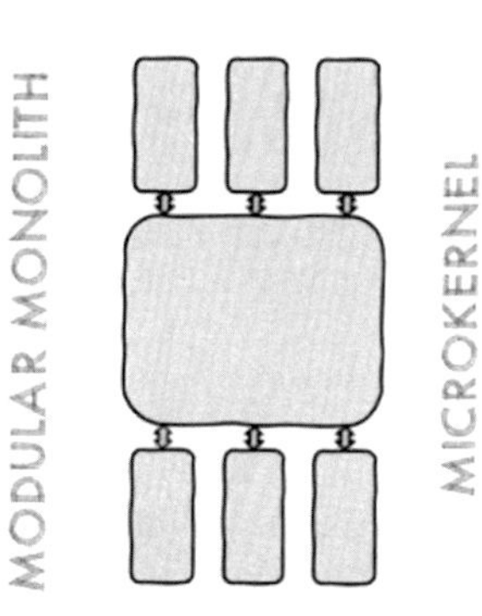

Figure 1-1. *A Depiction of Several Common Architectural Patterns*

At a high level, the architectural patterns in Figure 1-1 represent nine options for defining components, their boundaries, and their interactions. It is possible to build a software system with a given set of features/functions using *any* of the patterns. Remember, however, architecture transcends features and functions by providing a set of high-level design decisions that determine the overall capabilities of the system beyond the features.

> *If you do not have the right architecture in place—or you choose the wrong architecture for a given project—generally the functionality may work, but the application as a whole will not be a success.*
>
> —Mark Richards

This quote is exemplified by a study of the launch of Twitter in 2006/2007.[2] Twitter was launched on the hypothesis that people would find Twitter's concept of "microblogging" compelling. A set of features was built and deployed that were a hit. Within a few months, however, users began to see the infamous fail whale (Figure 1-2) indicating that the system was overcapacity and thus currently unavailable.

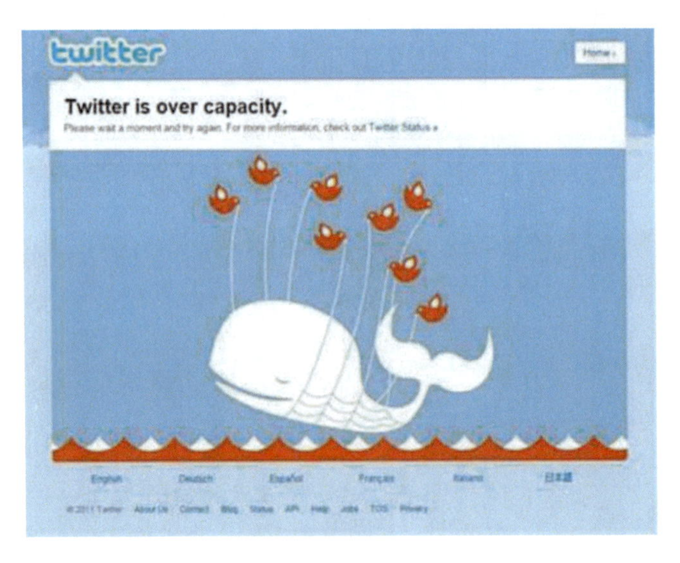

Figure 1-2. *The Infamous Twitter Fail Whale*

[2] Hoff, T. (2009). *Scaling Twitter: Making Twitter 10000 Percent Faster*. High Scalability. `https://highscalability.com/scaling-twitter-making-twitter-10000-percent-faster/`

While the functionality of Twitter worked, the system, as a whole, struggled. It lacked important capabilities that originated not from features and functionality, but from architecturally significant decisions. It lacked key *architectural capabilities*. Over the next five to six years, Twitter evolved their architecture to elicit these crucial capabilities like scalability, elasticity, and reliability. Although the features remained largely static during the transition, the capabilities ensured the platform would continue to grow more successful over the next several years. Does that mean the architecture of 2006 Twitter was wrong? Not necessarily. The original architecture of Twitter likely fit in 2006, but it did not in 2008.

"Likely" is the operative word here. Based on the frequent, high-profile failures of early Twitter and the subsequent redesign, it would be natural for you or me to deduce that the architecture was a failure. Reality, as always, is far more nuanced. Architecture must be driven by *business value*, and the highest business value can—and will—change over time. This is exemplified in Eric Reis' book, *The Lean Startup*, which emphasizes the value of a *Minimum Viable Product* (MVP).

An argument can be made that, despite the limitations and outages, the initial architecture of Twitter was the locally optimal choice in 2006. For a startup with limited runway and an unorthodox idea, there is value in getting software released quickly to resolve market uncertainty. In fact, as Joe Yoder, who popularized the term "Big Ball of Mud"[3] to refer to a "*haphazardly structured, sprawling, sloppy, duct-tape and bailing wire, spaghetti code jungle*," reminds us, there can even be value in a big ball of mud.

It Depends

Designing for billions of monthly visits often makes little sense when the business does not yet know if there will be any interest in the project at all. That level of architecture and engineering leaves little room for pivoting and creates excessively long feedback cycles. At the same time, there is value in building something scalable out of the gate to avoid considerable growing pains. Each approach has pros and cons; each approach involves trade-offs. Which is best? As is so often the case in software architecture, the answer is *it depends*. There is no objective "right" answer; there are no "best practices," only *trade-offs*. Tools and techniques to help you navigate this tension and move toward an optimal solution will be introduced later in the book.

[3] Foote, B., & Yoder, J. (1997). *Big Ball of Mud*. Presented at the 4th Conference on Patterns, Languages of Programs (PLoP)

This reality, however, makes our job challenging, but it also makes effective architects increasingly valuable. In late 2022, large language models (LLMs) rocketed into the collective consciousness with the introduction of ChatGPT. These models quickly began to demonstrate proficiency in generating code from natural language requirements which was previously the exclusive domain of humans. Largely through inductive learning, these models can connect the concepts expressed in a prompt with the syntax rules of a language to produce what is often working code and even evaluate different implementation options. At this level, however, generating code distills down to an admittedly complex set of best practices and rules to follow. Conversely, they tend to perform poorly in problem spaces that are not so cut and dried and often require explicit prompting from an experienced practitioner to account for security, performance, documentation, reuse, conventions, etc. In other words, they might be able to write code, but are a long way from being able to design systems as the decision contexts go well beyond what can be inferred and deduced from the training corpus. They lack the kind of thinking, reasoning, and navigation of nuance that we, as good architects, must exhibit. Currently, indications continue to suggest that level of reasoning remains a long way off. A further exploration of architectural reasoning is needed.

Thinking, Reasoning, and Navigating Nuance

There is currently no direct, academic path to becoming an architect. Consequently, most architects grow into the role from an individual contributor (IC) developer role after a number of years.

Imagine, if you will, the hypothetical path of a self-taught developer entering the industry with the ability to cobble together some code to make the computer do something. Over time, this developer begins to see that their approach of hacking together code to ship features may be an expedient means to an end, but the resulting codebase is becoming unwieldy and difficult to maintain. Also, over time, they begin to adopt design patterns that make the code more maintainable and robust. This process continues over the years, and this developer gains increasingly more long-term perspective. Eventually, if they have had to live with—and learn from—their decisions, they develop a broad base of knowledge and a sense of what good code and good systems look like. It is this experience that yields fertile soil for becoming a burgeoning architect. The transformation, however, is not complete.

Since architecture is, at its core, grounded in decisions that elicit capabilities in a system—and given there are many different paths to achieve said capabilities—each fraught with trade-offs and pitfalls—architecture decisions should originate from thinking about capabilities, not code. This is not always easy. Take the ongoing debates about REST vs. graphQL vs. gRPC vs. *whatever*. The *function* of all these things might reductively look like different approaches to simply move data across the wire, yet the *capabilities* of each can be massively different. gRPC trades performance for tight coupling and highly constrained clients. graphQL brings speed to market, developer productivity, and some flexibility at the cost of long-term evolvability, scalability, performance, and security. "REST," in the form of RPC over HTTP, provides common and well-supported protocols for integration along with the convenient mental model of exposing functionality over the wire. Conversely, "REST" that more closely aligns to the REST Architectural Style as defined by Fielding[4] allows a system to be completely decoupled enabling significant long-term evolvability, abstraction, and longevity, but that trade is made in exchange for increased up-front design work and potentially reduced network efficiency. An average developer might argue that one of these options is objectively superior, but thinking like an architect means realizing that none of these are inherently good or bad, superior or inferior, nor necessarily an either/or proposition; they are different approaches that involve different trade-offs. The best choice is the one with the optimal set of trade-offs based on the needs of the business and the actual problems being solved.

> *There are no best practices, only trade-offs.*
>
> *Every decision involves trade-offs. Every. Single. One.*

True perfection is often far too elusive to be obtainable within reasonable time and budget constraints. Because there will always be trade-offs, it is frequently said architects do not aim to produce the "best" architecture, just the "least worst" architecture. This looks different for every project, every time. It will even look different for the same project over time (e.g., the earlier Twitter example). This is not an easy space to navigate. Effective architects aim to define an architecture that holistically aligns with the specific product needs and the nature of the business.

[4] Fielding, R. (2000). *Architectural Styles and the Design of Network-based Software Architectures.* Doctoral dissertation, University of California, Irvine

Understanding Business Drivers

Capabilities alone are not enough; they must be the subjectively "right" capabilities. Capabilities must be aligned with business drivers, and every architectural decision must be made in the context of the business value being provided (and, potentially, the business value being sacrificed). No capability comes for free, and every decision is a trade-off that must be made deliberately and mindfully. Far too many architecture decisions are made first based on preferences, biases, resume skill gaps, or the architect's comfort zone. Ultimately, no matter how cool, how shiny, how trendy, how good *technology X* will look on the architect's resume, if it does not directly solve a business problem and provide relative business value it has no place in their architecture. In short, architects cannot have a conversation about architecture until they have had the *business/customer value conversation.*

Beyond the current problem set, the architect brings a different and/or broader perspective. Interpreting business drivers requires a certain visionary quality, to look at the present with an eye toward the future (without overengineering the solution) and often reading between the lines. As the saying goes in jazz, *"you've got to listen to the notes that aren't being played."*

The typical business problem space is complex. There are often many competing priorities and several interrelated and cross-dependent problems to solve. It would be wonderful if the business spoke the language of developers and architects, but that fantasy has no basis in reality. The business is going to speak the language of the business. They will talk about things like feasibility, cost, compliance, user satisfaction, and domain challenges.

Communication failures often account for a significant portion of product failures. A core skill of an architect is to be able to speak the language of the business and translate business requirements, vision, marketing materials, and pitch decks into the language of the architect. Further, architects must communicate with the development teams (as well as other organizational areas) in *their* language. In short, as architect and speaker Nate Schutta often says, architects must become the *Organizational Rosetta Stone* (Figure 1-3).

Figure 1-3. *The Rosetta Stone*[5]

This is all, of course, part of developing a new set of "soft skills" that do not always come naturally.

Architects Bring Breadth of Knowledge

In addition to shifting focus from functions to capabilities, architects must possess vision, wisdom, and problem-solving skills. This shift represents a stark contrast between the role of developer and the role of an architect. The core value proposition of a developer is often largely a function of their technical depth. Developers must bring deep knowledge of the specific technologies they work with. Transitioning from developer to architect requires inverting focus to breadth rather than depth, which can

[5] Hillewaert, H. (November 21, 2007). *The Rosetta Stone in the British Museum* [Photograph]. Wikimedia Foundation. `https://commons.wikimedia.org/wiki/File:Rosetta_Stone.JPG`. Licensed under CC BY-SA 4.0

be a challenging shift. It often means letting go of a certain amount of depth to focus on a broader foundation of knowledge. This is necessary as architects must make room for additional tools in their professional toolbox.

At a minimum, architects must have a broad awareness of various technologies and ideas, including ones that do not seem relevant to any current project. This provides what author David Epstein calls "range."[6] The *range* concept champions breadth of knowledge to power our ability to connect diverse ideas in novel ways. This prevents practitioners from overreliance on a small number of solutions and opens our perspective to creative and innovative potential solutions. In short, range vastly expands the domain of potential options in various pursuits.

> *...breadth of training predicts breadth of transfer. That is, the more contexts in which something is learned, the more the learner creates abstract models, and the less they rely on any particular example. Learners become better at applying their knowledge to a situation they've never seen before, which is the essence of creativity.*
>
> —David Epstein, *Range*

An architect's technical (and nontechnical) breadth is the toolbox from which they work. If an architect only possesses depth in a handful of areas, they too easily fall into the trap of solution space thinking (e.g., *this is what I know how to do, therefore this is what I will do*). Depth still matters, but balancing depth in some areas vs. breadth in others is a tightrope that we architects must constantly walk. Naturally, this requires yet another mindset shift as well as letting go of some degree of depth (which has been many technologists' core value proposition throughout most of their careers).

Therefore, we must also continuously refine our skills in broad learning and abstract thinking. This requires understanding the broader technology ecosystem, the available tools, the problems they solve, and their relative strengths and weaknesses.

[6] Epstein, D. (2019). *Range: How Generalists Triumph in a Specialized World.* Macmillan

The Scope of Architecture

The scope of architecture varies by the role and the individual. An enterprise architect might drive organization-wide architecture constraints, but there is no one-size-fits-all blueprint at that level. The needs of individual subsystems, applications, and components might necessitate deviation from prescribed conventions. Solution or systems architects may need to work with an enterprise architect to negotiate variances, or they may have free reign over the system(s) they oversee. The same is often true of application architects working under solution architects. Typically, architects with more focused scopes will work more closely with the developers to assist in adhering to architectural guidelines and guardrails, while architects tasked with broader scopes will often work more closely with the business (Figure 1-4).

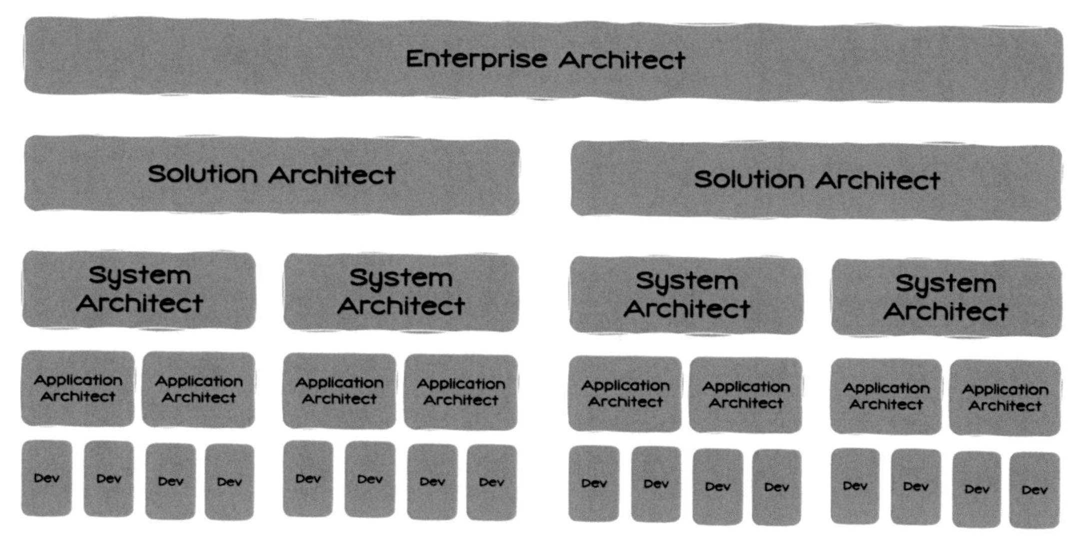

Figure 1-4. *Example Architecture Scopes*

Although not all levels of architecture will require detailed interfacing with the business, the business drivers and business value must be understood at all levels.

Summary

Architecture may be about components, their interactions, and the rules governing their interaction, but it is so much more. The architectural decisions must be driven, first and foremost, by business value. Business value is achieved by identifying the right capabilities for the system and making decisions that induce those capabilities.

In addition to some level of technical prowess, architects must possess many "soft" skills. Communication, business domain knowledge, analyst skills, and a broader perspective are all crucial. While breadth resolves many cognitive biases, it introduces a new one; "the curse of knowledge," a concept popularized by economists Colin Camerer, George Loewenstein, and Martin Weber.[7] As we develop breadth and range, we risk a new cognitive bias where we assume other people know what we know.

For developers moving into an architect role, many shifts in how they work, think, and learn are necessary. Those transitioning are encouraged to enter the space with "the beginner's mind" and the necessary willingness to be "new" at something again (which can be uncomfortable 10+ years into a career). It can be daunting, but it can also be rewarding. We must adopt and maintain a mindset of continuous learning with an emphasis on *understanding* to support application of what we learn. We must also be cautious of many marketers and industry pundits who peddle their wares as "silver bullets."

> *Data is not information, information is not knowledge, knowledge is not understanding, and understanding is not wisdom.*
>
> —Cliff Stoll

Also, note that the role of "architect," like "leader," is not necessarily constrained to specific titles. Just as an individual can embody the virtues and attributes of a leader without a formal title, many thoughtful developers can perform the role of a great architect without ever possessing the formal title or occupying a specific box on the org chart.

[7] Camerer, C., Loewenstein, G., Weber, M. (1989). *The Curse of Knowledge in Economic Setting: An Experimental Analysis.* Journal of Political Economy 97(5)

CHAPTER 2

Breadth of Knowledge: The Architect's Superpower

The ideal engineer is a composite ... not a scientist, not a mathematician, not a sociologist, or a writer; but [one who] may use the knowledge and techniques of any or all of these disciplines in solving engineering problems.

—N. W. Dougherty

In 1932, a young Claude Shannon entered the University of Michigan with the intention of building depth in the fields of engineering and mathematics, but Shannon was a passionately curious individual who prized breadth as much as depth. Despite the considerable academic load of a dual major, Shannon made time to pursue many tangents. He participated in the Junior Math Club, the Radio Club, the gymnastics team; he taught himself to juggle and ride a unicycle. He would also take elective classes on subjects outside of his majors.[1] Through the narrow lens of that time, it might appear that Shannon lacked focus and was squandering his chance at an academic career, but it was his breadth of knowledge and diversity of thought that paved the way for Shannon to fundamentally change the world.

The seemingly inconsequential decision that would define the course of much of Shannon's life was to take Philosophy 33 as an elective. According to the University of Michigan General Register, Philosophy 33 taught students "*the general principles of both inductive and deductive logic.*"

[1] Soni, J., & Goodman, R. (2017). *A Mind at Play*. Simon and Schuster

M. Carducci, *Mastering Software Architecture*, https://doi.org/10.1007/979-8-8688-0410-6_2

It is important to note that, while mathematics and philosophy have a concept of logic, those concepts—and how they are applied—differ in key ways. Philosophy takes a broader view of logic, with a particular emphasis on rhetoric and syllogisms, what makes a valid argument, how arguments may be classified, and how arguments function in language. This education undoubtedly armed Shannon with new mental models to bring to his core academic focus, but, more importantly, it introduced Shannon to new ideas to which he might not have otherwise been exposed, including the work of a relatively obscure mid-19th-century philosopher, George Boole, who explored a unique approach to symbolic logic.

> *1st. To express the Proposition, "The proposition X is true."*
>
> $x = 1$
>
> *2nd. To express the Proposition, "The proposition X is false."*
>
> $x = 0.$
>
> *3rd. To express the disjunctive Proposition, "Either the proposition X is true or the proposition Y is true;" it being thereby implied that the said propositions are mutually exclusive, that is to say, that one only of them is true*
>
> $x(1 - y) + y(1 - x) = 1$
>
> *An Investigation of the Laws of Thought (1854)*[2]

This idea of performing logic with ones and zeros found their way into Shannon's postgraduate thesis on electronic switching circuits, and later his ideas grew and blossomed with the publication of his landmark paper "A Mathematical Theory of Communication"[3] which paved the way for information theory and our modern digital age. With Shannon's insight, entire classes of problems once thought intractable were solved. The linchpin originated from exposure to a broader set of ideas and mental models, including George Boole's work from 1847 and 1854, then connecting them. This is an example of *linchpin knowledge*. Facts, ideas, or patterns that single-handedly bring the whole solution together; the one dot that connects all the dots.

[2] Boole, G. (1854). *An Investigation of the Laws of Thought*

[3] Shannon, C. E. (1948). *A Mathematical Theory of Communication.* Bell System Technical Journal, 27(3)

It just happened that no one else was familiar with both those fields at the same time

—Claude Shannon[4]

There is an ongoing debate in the technology world, whether a technologist should focus on depth and specialization or whether they should focus on breadth. Like so many such debates, this need not be—and is not—an either/or proposition.

Certainly, early in one's career, depth in a particular skill is a key value proposition and often necessary for "breaking into" the industry. As one progresses in terms of seniority, often breadth—in addition to strategic depth—becomes increasingly valuable. Good, senior developers are often described as "T-Shaped" with depth in the small number of tools and technologies they work with on a day-to-day basis, but that depth is surrounded by shallow breadth. Different mental models, awareness of different technologies, etc.

At the level of architect, however, we are expected to have a much broader view of the world. Our metaphorical shape is often the "broken comb," vast breadth and varying amounts of depth in many areas. The areas of breadth and (limited) depth encompass everything from various business domains, human relations, various coding skills, and the state of the current technology landscape. Our breadth, consequently, relies on many diverse mental models. In the world of the architect, deep/narrow knowledge becomes a liability as it hampers our ability to connect problems with solutions. The *linchpin* to whatever problem we may face likely resides outside of a single, narrow view. Like everything in the field of software architecture, breadth and depth are trade-offs. The key, as always, is finding the optimal balance.

Balancing Depth vs. Breadth

Anything an individual knows (or does not know) will fall into one of four quadrants in the "Knowledge Matrix" (Figure 2-1).

[4] Horgan, J. (1992). *Claude Shannon: Tinkerer, prankster, and father of information theory.* IEEE Spectrum, 29(4), 34–411

	Known	Unknown
Known	Known-Knowns Information we are aware of.	Known-Unknowns Information gaps or risks we are aware of.
Unknown	Known-Unknowns Information we are unaware of or are biased towards.	Unknown-Unknowns Information or gaps we are unaware of.

Figure 2-1. *The Knowledge Matrix*

The fundamental and inescapable truth is there will always be gaps in any technologist's knowledge. Often, these gaps are merely tactical or syntactic: *"How do I do X with framework Y?"* or *"How do I apply construct A in language B?"* These are examples of *known unknowns* and are rarely linchpins. The *unknown unknowns*, however, are more insidious, and it is here that most linchpins lie. To become effective, architects must continually strive to move as much as possible from the *unknown unknowns* to the *known unknowns*.

The shift from depth toward breadth requires the architect to carefully choose which areas of depth should be allowed to atrophy to free up time and energy to build breadth and cognitive diversity. With this new capacity, the architect must spend more time exploring what Allen Newell and Herbert Simon referred to as the "problem space" and "solution space."[5]

In software engineering, the solution space is the domain of all the interesting technologies, tools, patterns, frameworks, languages, and libraries, including those that typically appear in certain roles (e.g., operations, security, and QA). Although we may never develop mastery or even proficiency with most of these tools, we should possess sufficient awareness to be able to answer questions like: *"What is this technology?" "What problem does this solve?" "What are its trade-offs?"*

[5] Newell, A., & Simon, H. A. (1972). *Human Problem Solving*. Prentice-Hall

There are several strategies to accomplish this. Live technology conferences generally present a broad spectrum of timely content and provide value both from the lectures and the "hallway track" where ad hoc conversations between attendees take place between sessions, during meals, or after hours. These conversations not only reframe and add context to new knowledge but also allow us to escape the echo chamber of our own team and organization.

Attending conferences consistently proves to be a valuable learning environment. At a live conference, the ad hoc conversations arm us with multiple contexts, but, additionally, the immersive learning environment is conducive to long-term retention. This is exemplified by the "Learning Pyramid" (Figure 2-2) that originated at the National Training Laboratories Institute in the early 1960s.[6]

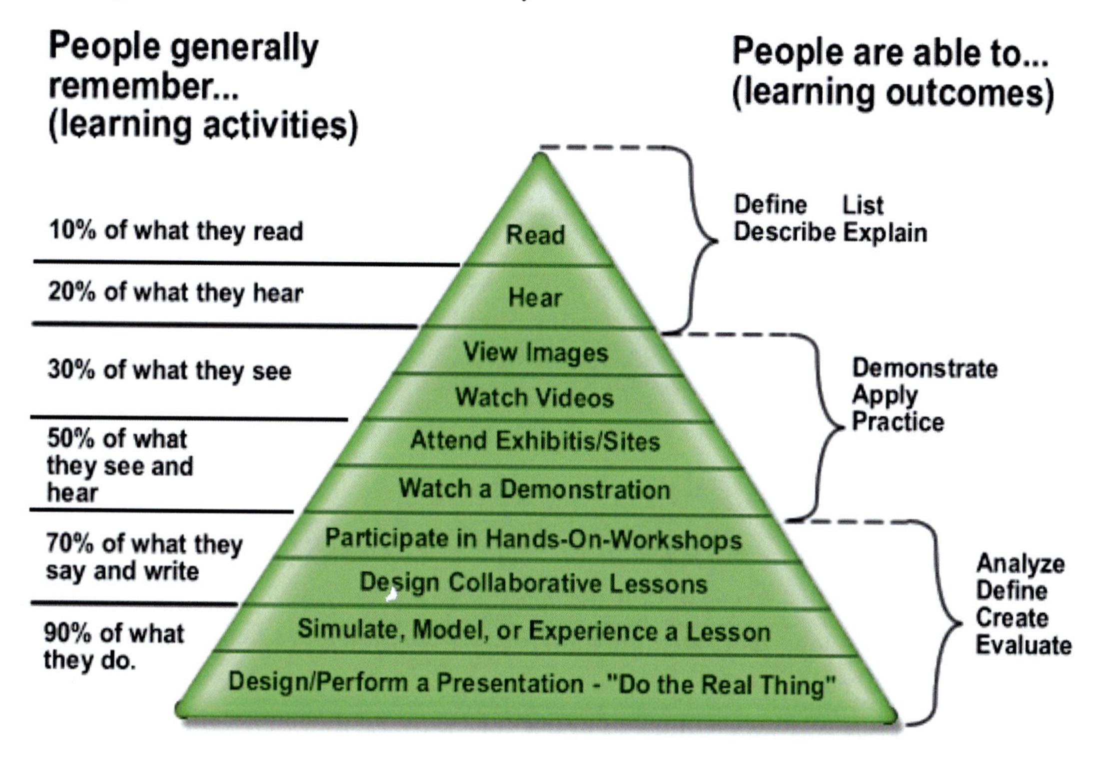

Figure 2-2. *Learning Pyramid or Cone of Learning*[7]

[6]Letrud, Kåre (2012). *A rebuttal of NTL Institute's learning pyramid.* Education (133): 117–124

[7]Anderson, J. (2012). *Learning Pyramid or Cone of Learning* [Illustration]. Wikimedia Foundation. https://en.wikipedia.org/wiki/Learning_pyramid#/media/File:Edgar_Dale's_cone_of_learning.png.https://commons.wikimedia.org/wiki/File:Rosetta_Stone.JPG. Licensed under CC BY-SA 3.0

Unfortunately, organizational responsibilities and realities often limit time for conferences. However, conference lectures are often published to video sharing sites. While the additional value of the immersive environment and hallway track may be absent, these videos provide valuable information and sufficient focus on new ideas and technologies to chip away at our *unknown unknowns*.

Another valuable source of diverse new ideas and technologies is the available collection of industry news aggregators on the Web. At the time of this writing, the technology consulting company Thoughtworks publishes a quarterly "Technology Radar" (`https://www.thoughtworks.com/radar`) and provides tools for practitioners to begin to create and cultivate your own technology radar.

In addition to Thoughtworks' technology radar, the TIOBE Index (`https://tiobe.com/tiobe-index/`) is also useful for navigating addition or inclusion of languages and/or technologies to your architecture.

Finally, Tiago Forte's Building a Second Brain methodology[8] prescribes a high-level filing system for knowledge that might not yet need to be top of mind but can be easily located and retrieved at a later date for review or expansion.

By cultivating and maintaining breadth of knowledge of the technology and solution landscape, you are better positioned to select the right solution for a given problem or, at the very least, to know where to begin exploring to build sufficient depth to tackle the problem at hand.

Discovering Linchpins

The solution space is interesting and valuable, but it does not provide enough to enable an architect to be effective. The solution space is the domain of *answers*. Perhaps, at one time, technology problems were so homogeneous that architects could leap directly into the solution space and enjoy a reasonable probability of success. Today, however, the problems we solve are much more complex. It is not enough for architects to simply understand the answers, they must also understand the *questions*.

The "problem space," while typically less interesting from an engineering perspective, is where the questions reside. Only by exploring the problem space can architects begin to ask the right questions, and only by asking the right questions can they consistently map problems to solutions. Discovering linchpin knowledge begins

[8] Forte, T. (2022). Building a Second Brain. Atria Books

with skillfully navigating the problem space. Understanding the problem, the business context, and asking the right questions at the outset of a project will often lead architects into surprising and unexpected places. Jumping directly to the solution space rarely yields new insights.

> *If I had only one hour to save the world, I would spend fifty-five minutes defining the problem, and only five minutes finding the solution.*
>
> —Albert Einstein

"Soft" Skills

The final area where architects must expand their knowledge is in the realm of the so-called "soft" skills. Architecture is more than designing solutions; those solutions must eventually make it into production. Tools to communicate with the business, approaches to build consensus, the ability to be "wrong" and course correct, relationship building, and the ability to inspire teams are all important.

Arguably, the greatest work in this area remains the timeless *How to Win Friends and Influence People* by Dale Carnegie. This comprehensive work teaches empathy, relationship building, communication and collaboration skills, and negotiation. I believe this book should be required reading for all architects because so much of an architect's role involves skillful communication, collaboration, negotiation, and building broad consensus across the organization.

Wisdom from Schusselig

Previously in my career I was on a team that was embracing Agile in the way programmers with limited experience do. We were accelerating our release schedule and feeling great. One release went out that resulted in an outage for several hours. The fix was not a rollback, but another release to fix the culprit bug. In the meantime, a manager of a certain ilk took the opportunity to convince the owners of the company to rein us in significantly. Granted, we eschewed things like comprehensive test suites, automated build and deploy, but worse we failed to honor the two "soft skill" values on the [agile] manifesto.

Had someone on the team had the breadth to nurture the relationships with the business side of the company, we could have avoided going from "release features when they're ready" to "once a month" releases (for bug fixes too—if the bug was big enough to warrant a release, then that meant rollback). Such a person could have proven the linchpin to get us to where we wanted to go (both the tech team and the business folks).

The Essential Unity of All Knowledge

Filling in linchpin gaps also requires looking at problems from new and unique perspectives. We gain these perspectives when we deviate from the course of deep specialization and explore ideas from outside of our core domain.

> *Specialization tends to shut off the wide-band tuning searches and thus to preclude further discovery.*
>
> —R. Buckminster Fuller[9]

Richard Hamming, a renowned mathematician and computer scientist, worked to instill a sense of holism in his students' approach to knowledge acquisition. He acknowledged that knowledge is taught as individual fragments but urged his students to embrace the connected nature of knowledge and value all knowledge equally.

> *In your future anything and everything you know might be useful, but if you believe the problem is in one area you are not apt to use information that is relevant, but which occurred [elsewhere]*
>
> —Richard Hamming[10]

Shannon could not have anticipated the impact of both taking the philosophy class and learning Boolean logic during his undergraduate program. Often, the value of some idea, fact, or mental model can only be realized in hindsight. Beyond the problem space and the solution space, an architect should possess a level of intellectual curiosity and be willing to let that curiosity and intuition drive continuous broader exploration.

---

[9] Fuller, R. B. (1969). *Operating Manual for Spaceship Earth.* Simon & Schuster

[10] Hamming, R. W. (2020). *The Art of Doing Science and Engineering: Learning to Learn.* Stripe Press

New Challenges

The landscape of software is changing. The development work of the coming decades will undoubtedly involve creating solutions to problems that currently seem impossible. There are almost certainly business problems one could begin to solve today with the help of a single linchpin fact, but the challenge is finding it. We are almost never aware of missing linchpin knowledge. These linchpins are particularly critical when tackling modern problems that reside in the complex Cynefin[11] domain (Figure 2-3).

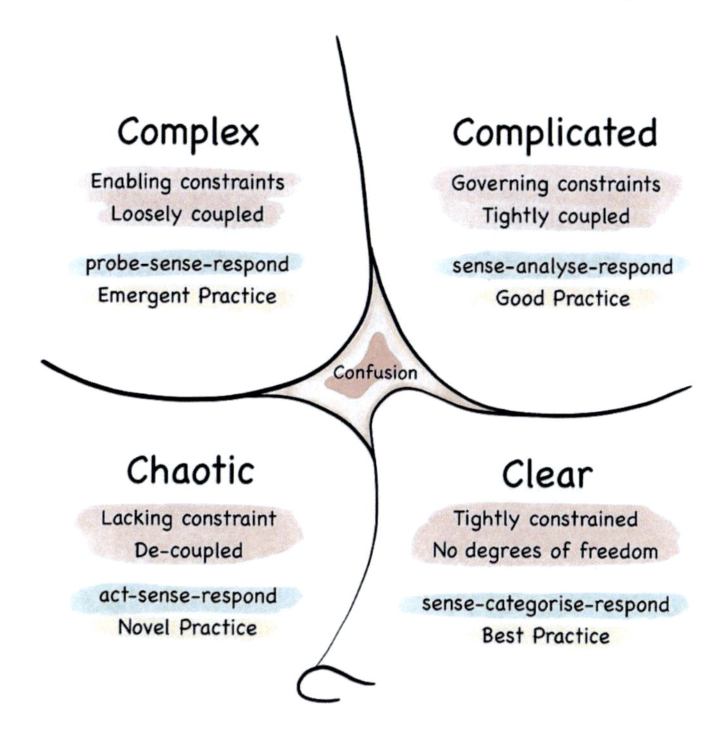

Figure 2-3. *Visualization of the Cynefin Domains*[12]

The Cynefin framework illustrates that a strategy or solution that works well in one domain is not necessarily transferable to another. Much of the low-hanging fruit in our field has been picked. We need to develop the skills and breadth necessary to operate effectively in the complex domain, as well as helping organizations escape the chaotic domain.

[11] Snowden, David (1999). "Liberating Knowledge," in *Liberating Knowledge*. CBI Business Guide. London: Caspian Publishing

[12] Cox, T. (September 22, 2022). *Cynefin framework 2022* [Digital image]. Wikimedia Foundation. `https://commons.wikimedia.org/wiki/File:Cynefin_framework_2022.jpg`. Licensed under CC BY-SA 4.0. Adapted from `https://commons.wikimedia.org/wiki/File:Cynefin_as_of_1st_June_2014.png`

Summary

Fundamentally, the transition from developer to architect requires a significant shift in focus and perspective. Perhaps architects could, at one time, coast on familiar patterns and tools, but today's emerging needs require diverse thinking and ideas. Breadth and range are the architect's superpowers. Illuminating *unknown unknowns* and transitioning them to *known unknowns* is ongoing work that builds a foundation for discovering future linchpin knowledge.

The real work of the modern architect takes place in the complicated and complex Cynefin domains. Navigating this space effectively is the value proposition of the 21st-century architect—how they think, how they solve problems, and how they connect diverse ideas into novel solutions. In short, the future of software development requires radically different thinking to that which is currently commonplace. The most valuable architects and engineers of the coming decades will be those who can discover the linchpins and translate these into a vision and a direction that teams and organizations can follow. Breadth and soft skills are the way.

CHAPTER 3

Capabilities: The Language of the Architect

Everything is vague to a degree you do not realize 'til you have tried to make it precise.

—Bertrand Russell

As you learned in Chapter 1, much of architecture is focused on design decisions that induce certain capabilities of a system that transcend its features and functions. If you were asked to name a few of these, capabilities like performance or scalability might immediately leap to mind. If you continued to think about it, many more would emerge. Eventually, you would run out of ideas. Have you missed any? How many are there?

At the time of this writing, Wikipedia lists 86 "System Quality Attributes"[1] which could be considered capabilities, and *that* list is certainly incomplete. Capabilities are often self-describing; thus, should a new capability be introduced, you could probably infer its meaning quickly.

Although capabilities are easily understood, we are faced with two challenges:

1. When considering the capabilities for a candidate architecture, we must ensure we're considering *all* relevant capabilities. It is easier to see what is unnecessary than to see what's missing.

2. Even self-describing capabilities can become overloaded or fall victim to semantic diffusion if effort is not made to ensure that everyone is using the same definitions.

---

[1] `https://en.wikipedia.org/wiki/List_of_system_quality_attributes`

M. Carducci, *Mastering Software Architecture*, https://doi.org/10.1007/979-8-8688-0410-6_3

While we cannot enumerate all possible capabilities in this chapter, we will focus on a subset that is most commonly top of mind for architects. By establishing a common context, we can ensure precise communication throughout the remainder of this book. This precision also enables a more mindful exploration of the trade-offs that permeate all of software architecture.

Architectural Capabilities of Key Interest

After examining a broad sample of projects spanning multiple domains, many practitioners, and countless person-decades, numerous capabilities appear with a consistently high frequency. Conventional architectural thinking often universally connects capabilities to architectural patterns. This kind of thinking is, however, overly reductive. While some capabilities emerge as a consequence of a particular topology, pattern, or prescribed modularity, others emerge from architectural decisions or guidance that may be applied to any pattern or style. Therefore, for the purposes of our work, we will break them down into two groups.

The first group encompasses capabilities directly influenced by the general definition of a given pattern. These include

- Abstraction
- Affordability
- Agility
- Deployability
- Elasticity
- Evolvability
- Fault tolerance
- Integration
- Performance
- Scalability
- Simplicity
- Testability
- Workflow

The capabilities above are among the primary attributes we will use to evaluate the relative strength of each pattern (style) in the abstract. This, however, only provides a partial view into the architectural process. Our work as architects requires our designs to holistically meet a broader set of needs that span the business, the customers, the users, the developers, and more. Consequently, operating effectively requires additional tailoring to induce the full set of capabilities needed for a given project. We must, therefore, consider this group of capabilities—induced by prescribing additional architectural constraints—in any of the abstract styles described in Section 2.

The second group of capabilities include, but are not limited to, the following:

- Availability
- Composability
- Customizability
- Feasibility
- Efficiency
- Interoperability
- Maintainability
- Multitenancy
- Observability
- Privacy
- Reliability
- Reusability
- Safety
- Security
- Visibility

Capabilities tend to fall into a natural taxonomy of closely adjacent and conceptually related attributes. The following sections will follow such a taxonomy, grouping capabilities into the higher-level categories: performance, agility, integration and interoperability, feasibility and manageability, and reliability.

> *Being clear on what you're trying to achieve through measurement is 100% essential and unavoidable. If you skip this crucial step, you only achieve your organizational objectives by accident.*
>
> —Bernie Smith[2]

Category: Performance

"Performance" is often an extremely overloaded term, with wildly varying definitions and implications depending on the communication context. In our context, performance refers to the responsiveness and efficiency with which a software system operates. Specifically, it gauges the system's ability to handle its tasks within an acceptable time frame and with appropriate use of resources. In some projects, "performance" may be a key capability; however, there are many elements of performance, and, as such, they represent individual capabilities that may need to be fine-tuned.

Network Efficiency/Network Performance

Network efficiency refers to how effectively a software system uses network resources to communicate and transfer data among various components or external entities. When evaluating or designing software architectures, ensuring efficient use of the network is often important, especially in distributed systems, cloud architectures, or any setup where components communicate over a network.

Network efficiency is largely driven by bandwidth usage, latency, protocol overhead, payload compression, connection management, and serialization efficiency. It is important to note that these factors often exist in tension with other capabilities.

Compute Efficiency

At a high level, compute efficiency refers to the amount of CPU time or energy needed to produce a given result (and many optimizations may be either-or when it comes to CPU time efficiency vs. power efficiency). Traditionally, compute efficiency has been informed by code optimization which is usually outside the scope of architecture. Times have changed significantly.

[2] Smith, B. (2013). *KPI Checklists: Practical how to guide templates included.* Metric Press

Distributed architectures occupy a larger hardware footprint, and, without careful architectural consideration, this can lead to runaway cost and underutilized hardware.

Modern software increasingly requires specialized hardware for specific tasks and will continue for the foreseeable future. This trend is particularly pronounced as demand for artificial intelligence (AI) and machine learning (ML) solutions increases. GPUs, for example, will significantly outperform CPUs by orders of magnitude for the linear algebra workloads underpinning many of the algorithms utilized by AI and ML.

Scalability

Scalability defines how easily resources can be allocated and put to use as those resources become needed. Once again, this requires careful architectural consideration and evaluation of the various dimensions.

How an architect might scale for *total users* might be different from *concurrent users* or even simply scaling for data/storage. Consequently, conversations around scalability should revolve around the idea of *"what is enough"* and which specific resources must be scalable.

Be aware that "scalability" has become overloaded. Some years ago, I was consulting on a project, and one of the stakeholders kept repeating that the system needed *"to be scalable."* This confounded me somewhat as the anticipated limits of storage, compute, and total/concurrent users were relatively low. Following several probing questions, I understood that this stakeholder was using scalability as a synonym for extensibility. At the time, I felt that "scalability" had become yet another industry buzzword. I have since come to understand that there are many dimensions to scalability. One could argue this stakeholder was not referring to *load scalability* (the ability for a system to expand to accommodate increased amounts of processing, memory, traffic, storage, etc.) but rather *functional scalability* (the ability to enhance the system by adding new functionality without disrupting existing activities).

Other dimensions of scalability[3] include *geographic scalability* (the ability to maintain effectiveness during expansion from a local area to a larger region), *administrative scalability* (the ability for an increasing number of organizations or users to access a system), *generation scalability* (the ability of a system to scale by adopting new generations of components), and *heterogeneous scalability* (the ability to adopt components from different vendors).

[3] El-Rewini, H., Abd-El-Barr, M. (2005). *Advanced Computer Architecture and Parallel Processing* John Wiley & Sons

Personally, I prefer the *extensibility* moniker over *functional scalability*, but, as you will see throughout this chapter, many terms overlap and there can be a great deal of nuance in their discussion. In the context of this book, we will use scalability primarily to refer to *load scalability* to avoid ambiguity.

Elasticity

Elasticity is another dimension of scalability that is often conflated with *load scalability* and used interchangeably. Again, we will break apart these two capabilities within the context of this book. Elasticity, as the name implies, is not only about "stretching" to adapt to a higher workload but also an ability to contract as load decreases to return to baseline. Fellow architect and friend, Jerome Broekhuijsen likes to point out there is also a cost factor motivating elasticity. Without elastic resources, we tend to over-provision static resources to prepare for bursts of peak loads, and most of the time those over-provisioned resources are spinning their wheels wastefully, which manifests unnecessary costs in multiple ways: financial (e.g., server rental/usage fees), server space, cooling, maintenance, etc.

Notably, certain decisions can afford some degree of elasticity to almost any architectural pattern; the question always comes back to "*what is enough*" as well as how well any given architecture will fit the organization and the problem as a whole.

User-Perceived Performance

> *Perception is reality to the one in the experience*
>
> —Toba Beta

While the raw metrics of performance have value, in some cases the *perception* of performance is enough. Architects can sometimes mitigate performance trade-offs with decisions that enhance *perceived performance*. Caching, asynchronous processing, careful user experience design, eager/speculative processing or prefetching, and more can dramatically improve the perception of performance to the end user, compensating for performance trade-offs elsewhere in the architecture.

It is also important to point out that it is not always about perception being "enough." There are aspects of optimizing the things that make sense to optimize. An example of this is when processing batches of data. If the user knows that it will take an hour to process the data, then they can go take lunch rather than sitting there watching the progress bar. They may not mind that some things take a while if they have control over *when* they take that one hour hit to their schedule and they understand what is being done is computationally or transactionally expensive. In this case, the perception is improved not because of caching or asynchronous processing but because the user is not actively waiting for a result (i.e., watching paint dry).

Category: Agility

> *The trouble with programmers is that you can never tell what a programmer is doing until it's too late.*
>
> —Seymour Cray

If scalability is approaching buzzword-level, "agility" has passed that point with such velocity that a sonic boom follows. Seemingly everyone wants to be "agile" (or, at least, everyone wants to be able to *say* they are agile).

What is "agility"? At its core, it refers to the ability of a system, process, or organization to quickly respond to change in an efficient and effective manner. Agility is defined by several enabling capabilities:

- **Evolvability**: The ability for a system to gracefully adopt and absorb both business and technical change. This is often accomplished through some combination of
    - **Extensibility**: The ability for a system *to be changed* to support functionality or behavior for which it was not originally designed
    - **Composability**: The ability for a system to *induce new functionality* in a system through the composition of components or modules with minimal additional code, adding new functionality or behavior in a system beyond what was originally designed
    - **Adaptability**: The ability for a system *to be used in novel ways* to support functionality or behavior for which it was not originally designed

- **Testability**: The ease, completeness, and confidence in an automated testing process.
- **Deployability**: The ease, completeness, and confidence in deploying changes to the system.

Let us examine these dimensions of agility in more detail.

Evolvability

This is an attribute that rarely materializes by accident. Building most software systems is like working with concrete—easy to pour, mold, and shape in the beginning, but once it hardens changes require a jackhammer and can be very disruptive. It is no wonder that often organizations would prefer to rebuild a system from scratch rather than try to make significant changes (although this almost never makes economic sense[4, 5]).

"Agile" methodologies accept the inherent uncertainty of initial requirements and inevitable change once the system is deployed. Or "Schrödinger's Spec," as my friend, mentor, and former boss, Robert Harris, calls it:

> *Schrödinger's Spec - you can know what the client wants, or what they actually need, just not at the same time.*[6]

Numerous decisions from the micro-architecture of code to the macro-architecture of a system can impact evolvability. A great case study on evolvability for architects is the World Wide Web. Some brilliant decisions were made that enabled the Web to grow and change radically from what was originally envisioned without ever stopping for a rewrite. Web resources were once simply coarse-grained hypertext documents and images forming an information-space that could be explored; today, the granularity has changed, enabling smooth, responsive document interactions enabling a new platform for application delivery and interaction with a rich set of first-class resources and bidirectional flows of data, audio, and video. I don't know of a single system that can compare with the Web in terms of its evolvability. There are many architectural ideas

[4] Spolsky, J. (April 6, 2000). *Things You Should Never Do, Part I.* Joel on Software. `https://www.joelonsoftware.com/2000/04/things-you-should-never-do-part-i/`

[5] Martin, R. (January 9, 2009). *The Big Redesign in the Sky.* Object Mentor. `https://www.luckymethod.com/2013/03/the-big-redesign-in-the-sky/`

[6] Harris, R. (April 19, 2020). *Simple rules for keeping dev teams out of trouble.* `https://robertnharris.com/2020/04/19/simple-rules-for-keeping-your-development-team-and-project-out-of-the-ditch/`

and lessons that can be taken away from this example. Evolvability is therefore another area where architects often need a certain amount of vision to anticipate the potential rate of change of a system and make sure decisions accommodate this.

Extensibility

Effectively, this describes how easy it is to extend the functionality of the system without breaking/disrupting what is already there. How architects think about modularity, interfaces, and abstraction at the system level is usually an important starting point. The microkernel architecture (Chapter 20) is an example of how to induce this capability architecturally. A common exemplar of this architecture at the time of this writing is Microsoft's open source editor, VS Code. At its core, VS Code is a simple text editor that can be expanded through the inclusion of various plug-ins. Plug-ins offer language support, syntax checking, highlighting, build-tool integration, and more. In this case, extensibility is achieved through composability.

Composability

Composability refers to the ability to create, adapt, and scale systems by combining existing, often reusable, components in various configurations to satisfy different requirements. Composability emphasizes the design of components in a way that they can be seamlessly and flexibly composed together to achieve desired functionality or behavior.

The centerpiece of UNIX is composability of simple tools through a uniform interface. This enables a wide array of small, self-contained, single-purpose tools that can be composed in any number of combinations and configurations to solve a wide variety of problems. This is exemplified by "The UNIX Philosophy" summarized as[7]

- Write programs that do one thing and do it well.
- Write programs to work together.
- Write programs to handle text streams, because that is a universal interface.

[7] Salus, P. (1994). *A Quarter-Century of Unix* Addison-Wesley

The Web adapted this idea for large, distributed systems, using the uniform interface constraint of the REST architectural style. The resource abstraction creates a flexible, stable mechanism to build highly composable systems.

Also notable are subsequent abilities to create a composable data fabric using ideas from the architecture of the Web and *linked data*. The core ideas and motivation are detailed in the data-centric manifesto.[8] As always, there are significant trade-offs associated with these ideas, but if long-term agility (or any subcomponent) is highly aligned with the business drivers, these are ideas worth exploring and adding to your technical breadth.

Adaptability

Best defined by asking the question: How easy is it to use a system in unanticipated ways without requiring code changes? Regardless of what we intentionally design into a system, there will always be users who will try to use a tool for a different purpose (think driving screws with a hammer). Sometimes, that is not a problem, but other times it can create unwanted side effects.

The popular spreadsheet application, Excel, offers a great deal of adaptability (whether or not any particular adaptations make the most sense). The tabular data structure and low-code mechanisms to define behavior cause many people to use Excel for database use cases, for displaying tabular data when tables in an application like Word might be more appropriate, or leveraging its VBA interpreter to use it in lieu of Matlab, Python, Mathematica, etc.

Contrast this with the text editor vim. Vim has been used for databases, programming, or its core use case of viewing and editing text. Vim is designed to be adapted to many use cases through robust configuration and extension mechanisms.

I think it is helpful at design time to imagine how a user may *creatively* apply the tool we are about to create and try to hem in the user to a safe range of purposes.

Testability

> *It's fragile because even the smallest of changes can break it down completely. Code doesn't degrade slowly. It crashes.*
>
> —Lasse Koskela[9]

[8] The Semantic Arts (n.d.). *The Data Centric Manifesto.* The Data Centric Manifesto. `https://www.datacentricmanifesto.org/`

[9] Koskela, L. (2013). *Effective Unit Testing: A Guide for Java Developers.* Manning

Change does not exist in a vacuum, and change necessarily involves risk. If an organization wishes to be agile—if they operate in a problem space where the risk of stagnation is greater than the risk of change—the business must be able to make changes confidently. How easily can developers test and validate changes before they are released?

Any time a developer wants to refactor code (separate from making a functional change or fixing a bug), they want to have confidence that the refactoring does not inadvertently break relied-upon functionality. Having a bank of tests in place gives them confidence when doing a refactoring by providing a contract of expected behavior.

The granularity of tests is also influential here. This is where architecture can directly influence the testability of a system. One architecturally significant decision is how we prescribe module boundaries/seams in the system. Domain-driven module boundaries tightly constrain testing scope and blast radius. This is also improved by how we think about component abstraction and API interfaces.

Bringing this back to the points already made, having a bank of good/useful tests is only possible if you have testability baked into your system. Generally, more modular architectures with clear boundaries and contracts for interactions produce more testable systems. The surface area of the risk becomes smaller as does the blast radius of a defect. We recently encountered two Big Balls of Mud that were so intertwined that they were deemed "untestable"—certainly unit tests were not possible without a LOT of brittle mocking, and higher-order tests were too hard (and time-consuming) to write. TDD as a philosophy often becomes a forcing function to help to bake in testability.

> *TDD helps you pay attention to the right issues at the right time so you can make your designs cleaner, you can refine your designs as you learn.*
>
> —Kent Beck[10]

Deployability

> *Releasing software is too often an art; it should be an engineering discipline.*
>
> *Continuous Delivery: Reliable Software Releases through Build, Test, and Deployment Automation*

[10] Beck, K. (2003). *Test-Driven Development by Example.* Addison-Wesley

Another component of agility is deployability—how quickly, easily, and confidently changes may be released. Generally, the more granular the architecture pattern, the easier it is to deploy changes, providing there exist clear module boundaries and well-defined interfaces. Patterns like microservices are considered to be more deployable due to their highly granular nature, strict module isolation, and resulting small deployment scope. It is worth emphasizing that this capability influences far more than initial releases but also changes, patches, upgrades, and other improvements.

This particular capability also influences horizontal scalability; if a component can be easily deployed, additional instances can be easily deployed. Notably, there are other implied decisions that are part of that pattern that are enablers for deployability.

Category: Integration

Integration as a capability is determined by measuring the ability of merging distinct systems or components, allowing them to function as one. It is not just about connecting A to B; it is about ensuring that A and B communicate effectively, efficiently, and seamlessly.

There are several distributed architecture patterns, and they are generally popular (even when the promised benefits rarely materialize for reasons that will be explored in a later chapter). While most literature on distributed architectures focuses on taking systems apart, remember that it will be necessary to "*put Humpty Dumpty together again*." Moreover, when building new systems, often they need to interact and interoperate with legacy and third-party systems. Finally, enterprises are not static entities. Mergers and acquisitions are often almost inevitable. Depending on the organization, it may be necessary to design systems that will be able to integrate with other, as-yet unknown systems in the future.

Integration can be a daunting task due to diverse technologies, but it can be valuable to foster a unified (or flexible) solution. Architecture decisions around tools, adherence to standards, and different approaches to APIs or messaging services can affect the amount of friction systems experience when cross-communicating. As always, there are many options, and each brings its own trade-offs. This can be an important area for architects to continue to build breadth of knowledge.

Like scalability and agility, this category of capabilities overlaps with several capabilities.

Interoperability

Interoperability goes deeper than just connectivity between systems—it is the ability of the systems to exchange, interpret, and cooperatively *use* information.

Often, we have many approaches to integration (e.g., the use of an application protocol such as FTP or SMTP to allow systems to seamlessly exchange data regardless of their implementation details); however, we often want to do more than simply connect these systems, we want them to work together without excessive intervention. The Microsoft Office suite consists of a number of independent applications focused on a particular set of functions, but the tools interoperate extremely well. A spreadsheet forms an effective data source for a mail-merge operation; shapes can be copied from a PowerPoint document and pasted into a Word document without loss of fidelity. They share a set of common standards.

As an alternative analogy, consider early trains and rail networks. Separate rail companies often operated independently, but at junctions, they rely on meticulously designed intersections to allow trains to switch tracks, combine routes, or operate side by side. Interoperability is achieved not through patterns or abstract architectural styles, but rather through the prescription of compliance with standards. In early, heterogeneous rail networks, the lack of standards (or the abundance of competing standards) made it enormously difficult to move rail cars from one rail network to another.

When designing a distributed, domain-partitioned system, architects quickly realize that, even in the same organization, different business units define terms and concepts in very different ways. One of the first and most important steps is to do the work to define each business domain's ubiquitous language (to use the DDD parlance).

Architects can try to build consensus between upstream and downstream components using the *conformist pattern*; we can "agree to disagree" and build an *anti-corruption layer* to translate terms across domains, we can define a *shared kernel*,[11] or we can think about the problem differently and exchange information (data with context) rather than mere data (e.g., JSON serialized decontextualized name/value pairs). Linked data, which was mentioned earlier, is perhaps one of the best options to achieve this. Linked data embraces the non-unique naming assumption and resolves the inherent conflicts and challenges surrounding global consensus. None of these approaches are easy, of course, and all of them involve trade-offs.

---

[11] Evans, E. (2003). *Domain Driven Design: Tackling complexity in the heart of software.* Addison-Wesley

Abstraction

When considering how two software components might interact and interoperate, there is often an overemphasis on integration mechanisms. We must, however, pay attention not only to which components must interact but also how we insulate portions of the components to ensure implementation changes do not introduce breaking changes outside of those components. When a change to one component requires a compensatory change to another component in order to maintain the broader system's correctness, these components are said to be *connascent* (a form of coupling). Abstraction is one of our primary tools to manage coupling.

There are many dimensions to coupling that are useful to understand. Equally, it is important to understand the concept of *cohesion* as well as the interplay between the two.

> *Finally, we suggest that the cost of modification of a system will be minimized when its parts are:*
>
> – *Easily related to the problem*
>
> – *Modifiable Separately*[12]

For *coupling*, two modules are considered completely independent if each can operate entirely without the other. This means there are no interconnections between the modules, whether they are direct or indirect, explicit or implicit, obvious or subtle. This establishes a baseline level of independence.

For *cohesion*, related things are kept "close" to one another, as was described in the 1975 book *Structured Design*.

> *What we are considering is the cohesion of each module in isolation—how tightly bound or related its internal elements are to one another.*
>
> —Edward Yourdon and Larry Constantine

Microservices, as an architecture pattern, deeply embrace the idea of cohesion by creating independent, standalone services that encapsulate everything necessary to complete a particular domain behavior within a single piece of working software. It is also important to note that structuring software as a set of highly cohesive modules

[12] Yourdon, E., Constantine, L. (1975). *Structured Design: Fundamentals of a Discipline of Computer Program and System Design.* Yourdon Press

with low coupling is not unique to fine-grained microservices but can also be achieved through medium-grained "mini" services or even monolithic component granularities.

Workflow

The above idea of cohesion suggests *"things that belong together are placed together."* There is, however, a practical limit to cohesion. Nontrivial software systems are constructed by many teams with differing organizational affinities. Therefore, they will tend to take different approaches to tackling their independent (but related) problems. Broader organizational business processes will often span multiple software components to cohesively execute a given domain workflow. The architecture of the system will influence how easily (or not) individual components can be composed into a broader business process or *workflow*.

In Ford and Richards' 2020 book, *Fundamentals of Software Architecture*, they assign a number of high scores to several architectural capabilities promised by the microservices pattern. These scores are a product of the pattern's topology of highly decoupled, independent components. The nature of this pattern also results in a very low score for the workflow capability. As soon as a domain workflow requires chaining together many microservices for a single domain behavior, we begin to erode those scores as the pattern's high independence is undermined by reintroducing dependencies in a distributed system. Mark Richards has introduced a concept of *"Domain to architecture isomorphism"* which asks us to consider whether the "shape" of the architecture matches the "shape" of the problem.

Consequently, we must evaluate the need for composing software components in such a way that we may execute domain workflows in a way that does not compromise other system capabilities.

Category: Feasibility and Manageability

Just as there exist many ways to write code to deliver a set of features, there exist many paths to design a system architecture. Thinking about system architecture is interesting and challenging in and of itself, but architects cannot escape two realities:

1. At some point, the software must be built and released.
2. Once the software is deployed, it must be able to be understood and maintained.

As systems grow, complexity can become a significant problem. With a distributed system, developers cannot simply set a breakpoint or step through the code anymore. Additional capabilities are necessary.

Visibility

Visibility refers to the ability to "see" into a system. It could be as simple as having an up-to-date map of microservices or what components are online/offline, healthy or not. Visibility focuses on what's happening but may not explain the *why* of the current state. Thus, while visibility provides crucial insights, it may not offer the depth required to understand complex issues, especially in distributed systems where problems might arise due to intricate interactions. An architect might select tools or standards around how the components produce metrics and logs or standardize how health checks are performed.

Observability

While closely related, visibility and observability differ in depth, scope, and application. Observability is a measure of how well you can understand the system's internal state based on its external outputs. It not only lets you see *what* is happening but understand *why* it is happening.

Observability is particularly valuable in environments where the system is too complex to predict all potential problems beforehand. Instead of trying to foresee every possible issue, teams build systems that can be interrogated for insights when unexpected situations arise. If this is an important concern, an architect might prescribe distributed tracing tools or logging solutions that can correlate data from various sources to provide a more complete picture. For example, some teams will employ technologies like Splunk or LogRhythm to be able to unify log sources from many services to improve a team's ability to debug complex issues that transcend a single service. Also, many cloud providers include tools like Datadog, Helios, Honeycomb, etc. for a similar ability to provide insight into the overall state of a system.

Affordability

Affordability typically refers to the total cost of ownership (TCO) of the system. What will it cost to build the proposed system? What will it cost to run and maintain the system?

Given a fixed amount of money, an architect will inevitably need to make trade-off decisions to place an upper bound on cost. This is a constraining reality of every project.

You may encounter situations where there are different categories or "buckets" of money for activities like research and development, development, operations and maintenance, etc. The design and the implementation will have changes funded in any phase of the project, so it is important to satisfy the needs of the phase while also accounting for the larger goals of the product. Prototype code will not be as refined as code that has been fielded and has accumulated operations and maintenance changes. You must become good at determining which changes should be funded at what phase. Picking which battles are fought is an important skill for anyone who wishes to effect change.

Maintainability

Nearly every system that is used will require patches for defect repairs, security vulnerabilities, performance enhancements, and new functionality. There are important decisions about architecture, data, and implementation that will influence how easy it will be to make changes, debug, upgrade, and alert users of issues. The overall architecture of the system will strongly influence maintainability.

> *We don't create things we change them. Development is a nested set of change cycles. Stop thinking about outcomes.*
>
> —Dave Thomas

Reusability

The software industrial revolution, as some call it, mirrors the previous industrial revolution in that much of what we build is composed of many reusable software components. The industrial revolution optimized the production of many instances of objects, whereas the software industrial revolution has all but eliminated any cost of the instances. This has led to interesting challenges with capitalization for businesses. A piece of software that is built once but can be used in many different contexts becomes an asset on the balance sheet and will be accounted for differently than a system with software that can only be purchased by one customer and cannot be adapted or resold to another. There is much more value in creating software that can service multiple customers or multiple users within an organizational unit to a customer. When software is made available outside of an organizational unit, it opens up the potential for new revenue opportunities, especially when licensing includes a repeated collection of fees per use or fees per unit of time.

Licensing for software has evolved from

1) Companies building the computer and the software for a client: 1940s–now
2) Shrink-wrapped software: 1980s–now
3) Shareware/Free and Open Source Software (FOSS): 1980s–now
4) Subscription-based software: 1990s–now
5) License server/shared licenses: 2000s–now
6) SaaS/PaaS/IaaS/FaaS: 2000s–now

No licensing scheme has ever fully displaced the other schemes. Different products will lend themselves to a particular scheme better than to others. The licensing will influence many of the software architect's decisions.

Multitenancy

When software is reusable, we must consider how it will be used. Particularly whether the instances will be shared or not. When shared, multitenancy provides a way for multiple users to concurrently access functionality within a single instance. Multitenancy leads to a series of trade-offs:

- Complexity added to handle the nature of having multiple users concurrently accessing the single software instance and the cost saving of not having multiple instances of the software (including the increased computing hardware)
- Decreased risk of loss of software IP against the ability for users to run offline
- Data isolation and security against cost
- Loss of control over the system or components of the system against lower total cost of ownership

- Etc. (the considerations will vary widely across industries and even applications within industries)

It is an important consideration that, again, will influence many of the architect's decisions.

Simplicity

Ultimately, there is a point where the solution space of a project becomes too hard. Microservices, for example, are quite possibly one of the most difficult architecture patterns to execute well. Breaking apart teams is difficult, breaking apart data is difficult, Domain-Driven Design (DDD) is difficult, reorgs are difficult, building the infrastructure and tooling to support development, deployment, and management of microservices is difficult. Perhaps one of the reasons so many microservice implementations fail is that organizations massively underestimate the complexity inherent in this pattern. It is important to look at architecture holistically and determine what level of complexity and disruption the organization can withstand. This kind of architectural intuition tends to develop with time and experience. Getting the level of simplicity wrong can make or break a project. It is often advisable to err slightly on the side of simplicity, it is much easier to add complexity than remove it.

Category: Reliability

Fault Tolerance

At some point, things will fail. Ultimately, failure is the only option. Sometimes systems can withstand the occasional service disruptions; other times it can literally be the difference between life and death. Most systems, however, operate somewhere in the middle. Generally, it is desirable to avoid small failures cascading into larger failures; thinking about the characteristic of fault tolerance can be helpful. Architecture decisions, choice of pattern, how inter-component communication is implemented, and how we coordinate/manage distributed transactions all impact the system's and component's level of fault tolerance.

Availability

Availability is a broader look at the concept of fault tolerance and is usually measured in uptime as a percentage of total time (e.g., 99.99% uptime). Generally, in discussion with the business, architects will determine how much downtime is acceptable for a system or component and make decisions to maintain that service-level agreement (SLA). There are many paths to ensure a minimum level of uptime.

Category: Safety and Security

One final category that must be explored is the capabilities that surround safety and security. These capabilities are rarely induced directly by a particular architectural topology, but rather stem from additional architectural constraints that define certain implementation details. These capabilities almost always have some baseline value, but we must determine the extent of these capabilities as well as whether a baseline achieved through adherence to a set of defined "best practices" is sufficient or whether additional architectural constraints must be prescribed to exceed the baseline.

Safety

Safety refers to managing the system's ability to cause harm to people, property, or the environment when the system is operating normally or under fault conditions. While commonly associated with industrial control systems, medical devices, weapon systems, or autonomous vehicles, safety is increasingly relevant to a broader range of software-driven contexts as systems integrate more deeply with the physical world. Safety considerations may span from ensuring that emergency shutdown procedures can execute reliably to guaranteeing that a data analysis error does not inadvertently mislead critical decision-making. Safety may be induced by architectural patterns that support isolation, redundancy, controlled failover mechanisms, and continuous monitoring of operational conditions.

Ultimately, safety is often achieved through a combination of deterministic system design, rigorous testing (including stress and chaos testing), formal verification of critical subsystems, and adherence to relevant industry regulations or standards.

Unfortunately, in this industry, unlike other engineering disciplines ethics considerations are not held in the same regard. Some of the trade-offs come in the form of increased complexity, higher development costs, earlier delivery, decreased quality, and potentially reduced performance. As always, we architects must work with the business and domain experts to determine what level of safety is "enough," balancing the substantial costs of increased rigor against the practical risks inherent in the system's domain.

Security

Security as a capability ensures that the system is protected from unauthorized access, tampering, data breaches as well as user data protections, and system monitoring or auditing.

A secure architecture typically includes multiple layers of defense—from network segmentation, encryption, and secure communication protocols to well-defined authentication and authorization mechanisms at the application level, static code analysis to decrease accidental introduction of security flaws, and penetration/exploitation testing to prevent delivery of products with known issues.

After delivery, security often includes protective measures like anomaly detection, intrusion detection/prevention systems, and secure coding practices.

However, perfect security is an illusion; there is always a spectrum of potential threats, and attempting to defend against all possible exploits can rapidly inflate costs and complexity beyond any reasonable level of benefit. The challenge, therefore, is determining what is "enough" security for a given scenario. We must consider the value of the protected assets, compliance requirements, the system's threat profile, and the organization's risk tolerance.

In short, secure software that is "good enough" optimally aligns the system's defense posture with business drivers, regulatory obligations, and practical limitations, without overengineering every software component and compromising business agility or affordability.

Privacy

Privacy, as a capability, focuses on protecting the personal data and sensitive information entrusted to the system. This involves ensuring that data is collected and processed according to privacy regulations (such as GDPR, HIPAA, or CCPA), as well as meeting user expectations regarding data handling. Privacy-preserving architectures incorporate mechanisms like data minimization, anonymization, and pseudonymization; they also enforce strict governance over data storage, retention, and sharing. Determining how much personal information should be collected, retained, and exposed to various system components is a delicate balance. Overly permissive data handling can result in loss of user trust, regulatory penalties, and reputational harm. On the other hand, collecting no data at all may render some desirable features or analytics impossible. Thus, privacy considerations must be thoughtfully integrated into the architectural design, often guided by legal counsel, compliance teams, and a clear understanding of user expectations.

Auditability

Auditability refers to the ability to trace actions within the system, from user interactions to machine-level operations, enabling investigators to understand historical events, detect fraud, analyze user or system behavior, and validate compliance.

Systems that value auditability often employ immutable logs, event sourcing, or cryptographically verifiable ledgers to produce tamper-evident records. You might prescribe architectural decisions that support fine-grained event logging, secure log storage, and correlation mechanisms that can integrate with monitoring or observability tools. However, achieving strong auditability can be at odds with privacy. Detailed audit trails that record which user performed what actions can be immensely helpful for compliance, forensic investigations, and governance—but the same granular tracking can degrade user privacy and raise the risk of regulatory noncompliance if sensitive data inadvertently leaks into logs or metadata. This creates a tension between transparency and discretion.

While they might seem to always be at odds, often auditing can also help protect user data and therefore privacy.

In practice, you must work closely with legal, compliance, and privacy experts to determine the right balance. Perhaps only certain user actions are logged, or sensitive fields are masked or encrypted in audit records.

> *The guiding principle should be to log and store 'just enough' information to accomplish the auditability goals—detecting illicit activity, complying with industry regulations, or providing transparency for stakeholders—without compromising user trust or violating privacy standards.*

Balancing these considerations ensures the system can both demonstrate accountability and uphold the data protection principles crucial to user confidence.

Summary

This chapter provides a set of high-level definitions and offers a few potential decisions around these capabilities as well as broader considerations that will enable you to navigate future architecture decisions effectively. These capabilities are summarized as follows:

Category	Capability	Brief Definition
Performance	Network Efficiency	Efficient use of network resources (bandwidth, latency, protocols) to enable effective communication.
	Compute Efficiency	Optimal usage of computing resources (CPU, energy) to produce results with minimal overhead.
	Scalability	The ability to increase or scale resource capacity to handle varying workloads.
	Elasticity	The ability to dynamically expand and contract resources as load fluctuates.
	User-Perceived Performance	Enhancing the end user's sense of responsiveness, often through caching, asynchronous operations, or careful UX design.
Agility	Evolvability	The ease with which a system can accommodate and adapt to both business and technical changes.
	Extensibility	The ability to add new functionality without disrupting existing features.
	Composability	The ability to build new capabilities by reusing and combining existing components and modules.
	Adaptability	The ease of using the system in new, unanticipated ways without code changes.
	Testability	The ease and confidence with which changes can be verified and validated through testing.
	Deployability	The ease and confidence in rolling out software updates, patches, and new releases.

(continued)

Category	Capability	Brief Definition
Integration and Interoperability	Integration	The capability to connect distinct systems or components so they function as a cohesive whole.
	Interoperability	The ability of separate systems to exchange, interpret, and cooperatively use shared information with limited intervention.
	Abstraction	Managing complexity and change by encapsulating details behind stable interfaces and contracts.
	Workflow	The ease of orchestrating and automating multi-step processes that span multiple components.
Feasibility and Manageability	Visibility	The capability to "see" into the system's state (e.g., health, status) at a basic level.
	Observability	The ability to understand the system's internal behavior from its external outputs and telemetry.
	Affordability	The total cost of ownership, ensuring the solution fits within budget constraints.
	Maintainability	The ease with which the system can be updated, fixed, and improved over its lifetime.
	Reusability	The ability to leverage components or modules across multiple contexts or applications.
	Multitenancy	Supporting multiple, distinct users or organizations within a single, shared software instance.
	Simplicity	Ensuring the architecture and design remain as straightforward as possible, minimizing unnecessary complexity.
	Customizability	The ability to tailor or configure the system to meet specific needs without extensive redevelopment.
	Feasibility	Ensuring that the architectural approach can realistically be implemented with given constraints and resources.

(*continued*)

Category	Capability	Brief Definition
Reliability	Fault Tolerance	The ability to handle failures gracefully without causing systemic breakdowns.
	Availability	Ensuring the system (or components) remains accessible and operational within agreed-upon service levels.
Safety and Security	Safety	Reducing or eliminating harm to users, property, or the environment under normal or fault conditions.
	Security	Protecting the system against unauthorized access, data breaches, and malicious activities.
	Privacy	Safeguarding personal or sensitive data in compliance with legal and user expectations.
	Auditability	The ability to trace and verify actions and changes, balancing the need for accountability with user privacy.

CHAPTER 4

Aligning on Vision and Architectural Requirements

> *...the architect is the interface between the business and the technology team, the architect must understand every aspect of the technology to be able to represent the team to the business without having to constantly refer to others. Similarly, the architect must understand the business in order to drive the team toward their goal of serving the business.*
>
> —Richard Monson-Haefel

Architecture does not exist in a vacuum, and we must avoid projecting our own biases and preferences into this work. As architects, we cannot begin architecture conversations and planning without first having business conversations; we must approach architectural requirement analysis deliberately and with rigor. Anything less is putting the cart before the horse, which many describe as architecture anti-pattern.[1]

> *The Cart Before the Horse Anti-Pattern*
>
> *The "cart before the horse" anti-pattern in software architecture refers to making architectural decisions without—or before—understanding the business needs. To avoid this anti-pattern, decisions should be based on business needs, system characteristics, and constraints.*

[1] Richards, M. (May 10, 2021). *Cart Before the Horse Anti-Pattern.* Developer to Architect. https://www.developertoarchitect.com/lessons/lesson113.html

M. Carducci, *Mastering Software Architecture*, https://doi.org/10.1007/979-8-8688-0410-6_4

It is tempting to believe that simply providing "a lot" of architectural capabilities is an adequate approach to delivering business value. *Too much*, perhaps, is better than *not enough*. Unfortunately, this often leads to enormous complexity and excessive cost up front while delivering little net business value. Let us look for a moment at how this type of thinking can emerge by looking at the respective capabilities of various architecture component patterns without context.

In their 2020 book,[2] Neal Ford and Mark Richards developed an architecture scorecard star-rating system, where a one-star rating indicates that particular capability is not well supported in the architecture, while a five-star rating denotes that characteristic is one of the strongest features in the pattern. The result of their work can be seen in Figure 4-1.

[2] Ford, N., Richards, M. (2020). Fundamentals of Software Architecture: An Engineering Approach. O'Reilly

	Layered Monolith	Microkernel	Modular Monolith	Microservices	Event-Driven	Space-Based	Service-Based	Service-Oriented
Agility	☆	☆☆☆	☆☆	☆☆☆☆☆	☆☆☆	☆☆	☆☆☆☆	☆
Abstraction	☆	☆☆☆	☆	☆☆	☆☆☆☆	☆	☆	☆☆☆☆☆
Configurability	☆	☆☆☆☆	☆	☆☆☆	☆☆	☆☆	☆☆	☆
Cost	☆☆☆☆☆	☆☆☆☆☆	☆☆☆☆☆	☆	☆☆☆	☆☆	☆☆☆☆	☆
Deployability	☆	☆☆☆	☆☆	☆☆☆☆☆	☆☆☆	☆☆☆	☆☆☆☆	☆
Domain Part.	☆	☆☆☆☆☆	☆☆☆☆☆	☆☆☆☆☆	☆	☆☆☆☆☆	☆☆☆☆☆	☆
Elasticity	☆	☆	☆	☆☆☆☆☆	☆☆☆☆	☆☆☆☆☆	☆☆	☆☆☆
Evolvability	☆	☆☆☆	☆	☆☆☆☆☆	☆☆☆☆☆	☆☆☆	☆☆☆	☆
Fault-tolerance	☆	☆	☆	☆☆☆☆☆	☆☆☆☆☆	☆☆☆	☆☆☆☆	☆☆☆
Integration	☆	☆☆☆	☆	☆☆☆	☆☆☆	☆☆	☆☆	☆☆☆☆☆
Interoperability	☆	☆☆☆	☆	☆☆☆	☆☆☆	☆☆	☆☆	☆☆☆☆☆
Performance	☆☆☆	☆☆☆	☆☆☆	☆☆	☆☆☆☆☆	☆☆☆☆☆	☆☆☆	☆☆
Scalability	☆	☆	☆	☆☆☆☆☆	☆☆☆☆☆	☆☆☆☆☆	☆☆☆	☆☆☆
Simplicity	☆☆☆☆☆	☆☆☆☆	☆☆☆☆☆	☆	☆	☆	☆☆☆	☆
Testability	☆☆	☆☆☆	☆☆	☆☆☆☆☆	☆☆	☆	☆☆☆☆	☆
Workflow	☆	☆☆	☆	☆	☆☆☆☆☆	☆	☆	☆☆☆☆☆

Figure 4-1. *Ford/Richards Architecture Pattern Score Matrix*

Reviewing these scores, it would be easy to proclaim microservices a "clear winner"—after all, it has the most five-star ratings of any of the patterns. In the absence of specific business requirements, selecting this pattern for its abundance of strong capabilities would be a meaningful potential hedge, right? As a hedge, *never*. The microservices architecture demands enormous technical and organizational complexity, as well as considerable cost. Consequently, adopting such a pattern must be a very deliberate decision in response to extremely specific business and system needs within a very mature development organization.

Assuming that the highest-scoring option must be the "best" option results in another anti-pattern known as the "Out-of-Context Scorecard Anti-pattern."[3] Anyone who has ever used an unpleasant piece of enterprise software will have experienced this. Regrettably, the customers of such software are rarely the users. Committees tasked with selecting and standardizing upon a piece of software or service will often decide based on a feature matrix, and whichever option has the most "check marks" will often win out. *Users* of the software would decide based on the context of the problems they are trying to solve, but *committees* often lack this context. More capabilities do not always equate to success—they must be the right capabilities.

The Out-of-Context Scorecard Anti-pattern

The "Out-of-Context Scorecard" anti-pattern occurs when architects or developers use scorecards or other matrices to compare options, like shared services vs. custom libraries, without considering the specific context of the system. While scorecards can be helpful for identifying trade-offs, they often lead to flawed conclusions if the context (such as operational or business needs) is not considered. The solution is to tailor the evaluation process to the specific needs and circumstances of the project or architectural decision.

An interesting example of how this anti-pattern manifests can be taken from a system developed in the 1970s that failed to be successful over lessor competitors in the following decades. Introduced in 1976, VHS won out over arguably superior alternatives and remained the dominant media format until the late 1990s, when it was supplanted by DVDs.

[3] Richards, M. (Oct 10, 2022). *The Out-of-Context Scorecard Antipattern.* Developer to Architect. `https://www.developertoarchitect.com/lessons/lesson146.html`

No, not Betamax.

Laserdisc was an optical media format patented in 1968 and brought to market in 1978, just two years after VHS. As Figure 4-2 shows, Laserdisc checked a lot of boxes for desirable features. Many of the features that made Laserdisc stand out were identical to those which led to the rise of DVDs decades later.

Capability/Feature	VHS	Laserdisc
Quality	Low	Medium
Random Access	No	Yes
Chapters	No	Yes
Special Features	No	Yes
Additional Audio Tracks	No	Yes
Digital Audio	No	Yes
Interactive Menus	No	Yes
Media Retail Cost in 1979	$80-100	$30-40
Player Cost in 1979	$999	$650

Figure 4-2. *Capability Comparison of VHS and Laserdisc*

By every metric above, Laserdisc was superior. Some still argue this fact should have led to Laserdisc supplanting VHS the same way DVD did two decades later. It was better, cheaper, and more capable than either VHS or Betamax. Yet we remember the Betamax vs. VHS war and not Laserdisc. This is because, at the height of their competition, one Laserdisc player sold for every 50 VCRs, but why was that?

Laserdisc Solved the Wrong Problem

Consider the context at the time. Building an at-home library of videos was not yet in the consumer collective consciousness. In that era, video content was consumed primarily through broadcast television. This meant that, to watch any given program, a viewer had to be at home and tuned to the correct channel when the content was broadcast. If the viewer was away, or someone was already watching a different program on a different channel, the viewer simply missed out and that was it. Maybe they would get another chance when the program entered syndication in a year, but they would still need to be in the exact right place at the right time to view the rebroadcast. The market had spoken; consumers were primarily interested in time shifting—the ability to record one channel at a given time for later viewing while they were away or while a different channel was being watched live. Although the cassettes were relatively expensive, they were highly reusable. Once a viewer had watched the program they did not want to miss, they were free to record over that content with a new program. It is right there in the name, Video Cassette Recorder (VCR). The idea of building a library of video content did not come until later, and by that time there was a large installed base of VCRs in the world. Despite its technical advantages, Laserdisc never stood a chance.

Architecture Must Solve the "Right" Problem

In Chapter 3, various architecture capabilities were defined, but which of these matter—and in what measure—must be inferred and derived from what the business needs (which is often distinct from what the business *says they want*).

Architecture patterns such as microservices currently remain very trendy. A highly evolved and advanced architecture is certainly something that can confer bragging rights as well as resume fodder, but if that architecture does not translate to real, tangible business value, it is moot. This is why architecture decisions must be made, not through bias or resume-driven design but based on the domain problems that need to be solved. While an architecture pattern such as microservices solves *many* problems (e.g., *extreme* scalability, elasticity, testability, deployability, agility, etc.), when the business truly only needs to solve a subset of those problems, the trade-offs are not warranted. Often, when clients inform me that they "want microservices," I usually respond that what they really want is something they believe microservices will provide to them.

To design an architecture that is a better fit, seek to uncover the true needs and desires (as well as their extent) and design an architecture that does not overengineer where it is not currently needed.

Another common pitfall that architects sometimes fall prey to is "waiting" for the business to give them the "nonfunctional" requirements or capabilities of the system. Given these capabilities form part of the language of the architect and not the language of the business, the architect will be waiting a long time.

Moreover, even if the business did somehow communicate needs in the language of architecture, this is not their native tongue, and what the business *says* and what they *mean* will rarely align. This misalignment is exemplified in the earlier case where the business has expressed interest in adopting microservices when they *really* want certain anticipated capabilities.

As the chapters that follow will show, there are many paths to various capabilities, each with radically different trade-offs. It is the responsibility of the architect to translate from the language of the business to concrete technical and architectural requirements, thereby teasing out which capabilities are actually needed.

In short, architecture is not just about building robust or scalable systems or "future-proofing" our designs—it is about aligning those systems with the business's core objectives. Too often, the allure of technical perfection can overshadow the real-world problems architecture aims to solve. As with VHS vs. Laserdisc and the pitfalls of the "Out-of-Context Trap," success does not always go to the technically superior. It goes to the solution that best addresses the underlying needs. Likewise, an optimal architecture is one that best addresses the business's needs and goals; it must solve the "right" problems. Determining what the "right" problems are often requires both requirement analysis (below) and objective measurement (Chapter 5).

The Tailor-Made Requirements Analysis Process

As you have read, architecture is as much about understanding the problem as it is about devising the solution—*"Why is more important than how."* We must ensure that every architectural decision that is made serves the larger goals of the business and user. Deep exploration and understanding of the "problem space" is paramount. The Tailor-Made model offers a foundational analysis framework for arriving at such an understanding that may be followed, adapted, or expanded as needs dictate.

Step 1: Preparing for the "Business Conversation"

The foundation of this process begins with exploring the domains of the business, customers, and users of the system. Identify the typical problems, pain points, and challenges they face on a daily basis. If available, a high-level business process flow or data flow diagram is also often useful.

Next, locate documents and decks detailing requirements, vision, existing contractual requirements or KPIs, as well as available marketing materials. It may require some search, but such artifacts frequently exist. Although some projects begin unexpectedly, in order for many planned projects to be greenlit, the business first had to outline a clear vision and make a compelling case to investors, leadership, customers, or budget committees. Notably, this will be true whether the project is a greenfield (brand-new development) or a brownfield (an existing, legacy application that will undergo modernization). In fact, inferring capabilities is often easier in a brownfield as there will also exist well-known challenges, key performance indicator (KPI) thresholds to improve, and objectives and key results (OKR) that can be measured. Although KPIs will be explored in depth in the following chapter, as a brief heuristic consider KPIs as akin to goals that a businessperson might use, while OKRs are akin to goals that a product owner might have.

As you review these artifacts, you may notice they are often vague and laden with buzzwords. For clarity of your understanding, consider involving a domain expert to provide context as well as define any terms that have unique domain-specific meanings.

Aim to read each line from multiple perspectives while determining how the ideas being described bring new value to others. Typically, these perspectives include

- The target customer(s)
- The user(s)
- Business actors

Ultimately, you are creating a mental draft of a vision and understanding of the project. The first draft is exactly that, *a first draft*. There will remain knowledge gaps, misunderstandings, market changes, and implicit assumptions that require correction.

After consuming the available material, write a document articulating your understanding of the project and its goals. Include open questions, enumerated assumptions, and identify areas for further exploration. If candidate architectural capabilities emerge, you should note them here, but the focus at this stage is understanding.

Next, we must aim to validate and align their vision to that of the business.

Step 2: Identifying Stakeholders

To validate and align your draft vision, key stakeholders must be directly involved in the process. To this end, stakeholders must first be identified. These will often include the authors of the documents studied, and these authors may be able to identify who else should be part of a conversation around the core goals of the project.

Since implementing architecture often requires technical and organizational change, those able to drive such change will also potentially be key stakeholders. Daniel Tippie, a seasoned software architect in Colorado and contributing author to this book, points to five components necessary to effect change in an organization. They are

- Authority
- Accountability
- Responsibility
- Knowledge (know-how)
- Will

It is exceedingly rare to find an architect (or any single individual) who possesses all five; however, a good architect knows which they possess and will gather the actors with the other components.

That said, know-how may also be lacking at this stage—this is okay and is not a failing. Once the problem is well understood, it will often illuminate the path to know-how (the important part is to start with the context of the problem to solve).

Authority and responsibility vary within the scope of a project. Executive leadership or a budget committee may have responsibility over spending and authority for approvals. Authority to direct development teams toward certain technologies and practices may be culturally or organizationally under the purview of architecture or may be the responsibility of a software engineering manager.

For every element missing, you may find an individual, team, or committee that controls that element. These people form the foundation for a list of key stakeholders. Without consensus, alignment, and buy-in from them, the effort is likely doomed to fail. A useful tool for this process is shown in Figure 4-3. Utilize this table for each discrete problem within the project's domain. As a tip, pay attention to overly complex or conjunctive problem statements as these may indicate composite problems that you must first break down into smaller, constituent problems.

Problem Statement	
Who has Authority	
Who has Responsibility	
Who has Accountability	
Who has Knowledge	
Who has Will	

Figure 4-3. *Stakeholder Identification Matrix*

Additional stakeholders may be individuals driving the project vision. Part of the process is to identify these people, along with who communicates the vision, either up or down the organization. Two common examples are the authors of the documents mentioned above and the lead product owner(s) who may already be at work translating the business vision to a road map of effort.

Some parsimony is important in compiling your list of stakeholders. While a broader hierarchy of stakeholders may be valuable, the meetings and discussions outlined in this requirements analysis process should be focused only on *key stakeholders*. For example, development team leads may possess some authority within the scope of their teams, but these leads may ultimately operate under the authority of the software engineering manager. The leads may be stakeholders, but the manager is the *key stakeholder*.

With this list of key stakeholders, the first discussion should be planned and scheduled. All key stakeholders should be invited and as many as possible should attend, or the meeting should be rescheduled to accommodate everyone's availability.

Step 3: The First Meeting

Agenda:

- Introductions and roles
- Align on project vision
- Questions and clarifications from architecture

Introduction and Roles

The goal of the first meeting is to build trust and alignment between architecture and business while fostering an atmosphere of cooperation and collaboration. To cultivate such an atmosphere, you will begin by first asking everyone to introduce themselves and their role/background on the project.

Beyond setting the stage for collaboration, these introductions are often helpful for both architecture and other participants. Once all other parties have been introduced, the architect will introduce themselves. Although you are leading this meeting, all who are present should be able to contribute, and this process sets the stage for ongoing participation.

It is important to limit everyone's assumptions. Participants in this meeting may or may not have worked with an architect before, or they may have differing ideas on the role of architecture. In light of this inherent uncertainty, it is a good habit to always explain your goals and role as part of this introduction.

> *My name is Michael and I'm an architect on this project. We've got a clear backlog of features to deliver, and my job is to think about the best way to deliver these features to minimize risk and maximize our chance of success. There is a near-infinite number of ways to write software to deliver features and I want to ensure that we choose the optimum path for the present and future of this project.*

This quick introduction accomplishes two key aims. First, it clearly outlines the role of architecture. Second, it reiterates that architecture and business are "on the same side." It should be clear that you want what the business actors want. If successful, this will plant a seed of trust and orient the entire relationship to one of collaboration.

Align on Project Vision

Following this introduction and framing, you will continue by detailing your business-level understanding of the project and its aims.

> *Before we get too far, I want to validate that our vision and understanding are aligned...*

At this stage in the process, you are operating on a first draft understanding which will almost always be incomplete. This conversation is an opportunity to flesh it out and address misunderstandings early. As stakeholders weigh in to add depth, color, or corrections, pause to listen carefully and capture these insights in your notes for further review and eventual incorporation into subsequent effort.

Questions and Clarifications from Architecture

After aligning on a shared vision and understanding, the next step is to probe deeper by exploring what has not yet been said and what remains architecturally ambiguous. We also seek to validate any identified assumptions on our part. Many of these questions and identified assumptions will originate from the list produced during step 1 that is based on your preliminary reading and research, but others may have emerged during the meeting. Others, still, may originate from your experience or architectural judgment.

For example, business actors will rarely express the importance of testability. However, you may perceive testability to be a high priority capability due to the numerous failures of systems within your current or past organization(s) that can be traced back to a failure to adequately test prior to production deployment. This is one of many areas where we must be guided by business requirements but exercise good architectural judgment. This means both validating our assumptions and biases while guiding the business as much as they are guiding us.

Pay particular attention to things like budget, timeline, and hiring plans. Important details to account for at this stage are immediate scope and goals; is this project focused on building a minimum viable product (MVP) or a proof of concept (POC)? What does the business hope to achieve with the first release (of either the new or "modernized" system)?

When it comes to identifying architectural requirements that are *not* stated, it is often helpful to a list to act as a prompt to identify that which is missing. From experience, your authors have compiled a checklist of commonly overlooked requirements in these discussions, shown in Figure 4-4.

Category	Sub-category	Actor /Component	Capability	Notes
Functional	User-Facing Capabilities	Administrator	Security	
			System	
			Application	
			Domain	
		Operator	Actor/User Roles	
			Accessibility	
			Device Support	
			Usability	
		Manager	Reporting and Status Dashboards	
		Logistics	License Management	
			Version Management	
			Artifact Delivery	
	Machine-to-Machine Capabilities	Services	Communication Channel(s)	
			Interoperability	
			Local/Remote	
			Schemas	
		Executables	PID/Name	
			Interface	
		Frameworks	Programming Language(s)	
			Interface	
			License Restrictions	
			Training Requirements	
		Libraries	Programming Language(s)	
			Interface	
			License Restrictions	
			Training Requirements	
		Hardware	Infrastructure	
			Sensors	
			Network	

Figure 4-4. *Example Requirements Checklist*

Architectural	System		Abstraction	
			Affordability	
			Availability	
			Compatibility	
			Configurability	
			Deployability	
			Fault-Tolerance	
			Evolvability	
			Performance	
			Portability	
			Reusability	
			Safety	
			Scalability	
			Security	
			Testability	
			Workflow	

Figure 4-4. *(continued)*

When using the checklist, it can be helpful to know your audience. For a technically savvy participant in this meeting, you may be able to ask about some of these aspects directly. For others, it may be better to attempt to tease out some of these details indirectly, by asking about related pain points or business challenges.

Throughout this entire process, strive to understand each stakeholder's friction and pain points. What "keeps them up at night?" Not only is this important in the context of the initial meeting, but continued exploration of friction and pain points will take place in many subsequent conversations. These conversations strengthen understanding, build trust and empathy, and enable better communication of decisions and proposals to these individuals in meaningful context. These conversations also arm you with the tools necessary to communicate more persuasively and contextually to stakeholders in subsequent interactions (i.e., "...and architecture arrived at this particular decision to make *your pain point X go away*").

In addition to pain points, it can be equally important to begin to compile a "not" list—things the customer, user, and management do not care about. This is often more important than most people realize.

During this initial conversation and subsequent meetings, you may also pick up on various biases and idiosyncrasies that stakeholders have which better prepare you for future meetings and interactions. One example from a past project is the use of the term "nonfunctional requirements" to describe architectural capabilities. The project stakeholders were heavily oriented toward functional requirements—what the system would *do*—which caused them to immediately "tune out" at the mention of anything *nonfunctional.* I quickly adapted my language to refer to "capabilities." In my case, I not only adapted my language in the context of that particular project, I continue to use this terminology to this day.

At this stage, resist the urge to jump into solutioning. This is not yet the time as this meeting is purely *problem focused*; here, we are focused on the "*why*" rather than the "*how*." If potential solutions jump mind, capture these in notes in the moment for future review and analysis. These potential solutions are often important and typically driven by a combination of what is being heard and implicit assumptions.

Stakeholders may also begin solutioning at this point. In such a case, it often makes sense to challenge the assumptions that may have led those things to be defined by the non-architect because they may be due to buzzword affinity and not practicality.

While solutioning is out of scope for this meeting, these sparks of ideas are often an opportunity to enumerate and validate assumptions. Ultimately, we should strive to ask questions centered around the problems being discussed, not any particular solution being imagined.

The only common exception to the "remain in the problem space" rule is identifying the boundaries of the solution space. Will this project run in the cloud or on premises (or both)? Are there restrictions on the use of open source software or libraries? Is there a target operating budget that architecture must remain within?

In architecture, the future is almost as important as the present. It is critical to consider solutions in a long-term context. To this end, close by asking the stakeholders how they imagine this system will look in five and ten years' time (will it be largely static or radically different?). Although we do not want to architect for the millionth user before we have our first, having an idea of the anticipated direction of growth allows us to design an architecture that fits the present while leaving doors open for future evolution. Despite Grady Booch's famous definition of architecture as "*the stuff that's hard to change*," the Tailor-Made model enables the design of highly evolvable and agile architectures (which we will explore in depth in Section 2).

As the meeting heads to a conclusion point, list the reading done to date and ask if there is anything else that should be reviewed. Depending on the scope of the project, this first meeting can take quite some time. Ensure adequate time is allotted for the conversation. Also, where possible, take copious notes as there is still much work to do, and the discussion will help identify what that work should focus on.

Step 4: Identifying Architecture Capability Requirements

Following this meeting, you will now go back and review your notes and any other documents line by line and try to tease out architectural capabilities. These capabilities may be a subset of those defined in Chapter 3, or they may include capabilities from the broader set of system quality attributes currently defined or yet to be discovered.

Each capability must be directly tied back to pain points, customer needs, or some statement the business made (either in the meeting from step 3 or in existing documents). These capabilities need not be in any particular order, but your initial attempt at prioritization is useful. This candidate ranking of capabilities and relative priority can be a useful metric to gauge architecture and business alignment. In subsequent meetings, the business will provide input on the relative importance of capabilities. If your hypothetical priorities are aligned with the business' actual priorities, this is a strong signal that you are in good alignment with the business. If the priorities do not align, you will receive early feedback on additional implicit assumptions or underlying divergence in vision. This divergence is bidirectional, and it is equally probable that the architect might be operating under a faulty assumption or that you see something the business does not.

With this initial list of capability requirements, you are ready for the next round of meetings with the key stakeholders.

Step 5: Qualifying and Quantifying Capabilities with Stakeholders

Agenda:

- Further alignment on business vision
- Review architectural requirements
- Prioritize "business-critical" system capability needs

Depending on the organizational dynamics and how aligned the key stakeholders are, this phase of the process may take the form of a single meeting with all key stakeholders. Alternatively, you may decompose this step into a series of meetings with one or more stakeholders in each. This alternative approach prevents any single stakeholder perspective from dominating the conversation. Should you decompose this step, it is good practice to conclude with a meeting among all stakeholders to communicate a synopsis of the decisions and conclusions.

Further Alignment on Business Vision

You will kick off these meetings by restating your understanding of the business vision. This need not—and should not—be exhaustive; a high-level summary is sufficient, unless any new questions have emerged since the first meeting described in step 3. This, once again, sets a collaborative framing for ensuing discussion. This framing is further strengthened by making a concerted effort to speak to the various participants using their language and articulating your understanding of the vision.

Review Architectural Requirements

The next step is to begin to work through the prepared list of candidate architectural capabilities. While these capabilities might be prioritized from the perspective of architecture, care must be taken to ensure the conversation is not influenced unduly by your hypothetical prioritization.

Your first aim is to *qualify* each capability (i.e., do we truly need this?). For each capability on the list, verify if that capability needs to be expressed as part of the architecture requirements or if it can be eliminated from the architectural requirements. This is not to say a removed capability does not remain a notable nonfunctional requirement, but maybe it is out of scope of architecture, significantly less important compared to most others, or addressable elsewhere by hardware or developer guidance. Some capabilities are business-critical, some are important, some are nice-to-have, others the business could take-or-leave, the rest can be eliminated.

You also aim to *quantify* capabilities by determining an upper bound on a capability requirement. For each qualified capability, you need to determine how much of that capability is necessary to satisfy the current business needs. When quantifying, the range "how much" is defined as extremely low, very low, low, below average, average, above average, high, very high, and extremely high.

Quantification is a crucial process as some capabilities are seen by business actors as "universally critical" and, if left unquantified, may lead to significant overengineering. Examples of these are availability, security, and scalability. The question is not whether these capabilities are important, but instead determining the extent of architecture and engineering necessary to deliver *enough* of these capabilities. To objectively determine *enough*, ask qualifying business value–focused questions.

For example, when speaking about availability as a yet-unqualified capability, you probably should not frame the question as *"Is high availability important?"* as this will rarely result in a useful answer. Instead, ask questions like *"How negatively would the business be impacted if we experienced six seconds of downtime per week? How about 60 seconds?"* and so on, until a target service-level agreement (SLA) is determined. This line of questioning allows you to both *qualify* and *quantify* availability into a percentage of uptime. As you will see in Figure 4-5, should you determine that a 99% SLA is adequate, the capability could be scored *below average*. Alternatively, if a 99.9999% SLA is necessary, this capability would be quantified as *extremely high*.

	Availability (uptime)	per year	per quarter	per month	per week	per day	per hour
Very Low	**90%**	36.5 days	9 days	3 days	16.8 hours	2.4 hours	6 minutes
Low	**95%**	18.25 days	4.5 days	1.5 days	8.4 hours	1.2 hours	3 minutes
Below Average	**99%**	3.65 days	21.6 hours	7.2 hours	1.68 hours	14.4 minutes	36 seconds
Average	**99.5%**	1.83 days	10.8 hours	3.6 hours	50.4 minutes	7.20 minutes	18 seconds
Above Average	**99.9%**	8.76 hours	2.16 hours	43.2 minutes	10.1 minutes	1.44 minutes	3.6 seconds
High	**99.95%**	4.38 hours	1.08 hours	21.6 minutes	5.04 minutes	43.2 seconds	1.8 seconds
Very High	**99.99%**	52.6 minutes	12.96 minutes	4.32 minutes	60.5 seconds	8.64 seconds	0.36 seconds
Extremely High	**99.999%**	5.26 minutes	1.30 minutes	25.9 seconds	6.05 seconds	0.87 seconds	0.04 seconds

Figure 4-5. *Availability SLA Table*

Around security: *"What would the impact of a data breach be to this project and organization? What are the most important assets?"* This helps us determine if security should be an expressed, focused capability or an implied capability (in other words, is a baseline of security and best practices enough or are there particularly sensitive data assets that must be secured beyond best practices?).

Around scalability: *"How many users (both total and concurrent) do we expect the system to support at launch, in a year, five years, and ten years? Do we have an anticipated rate of growth?"*

As you ask further qualifying questions, record in your notes who answered each. When you document the resulting architectural decisions, these ensure each decision is backed by solid source citations. Then, when you communicate these decisions to the rest of the organization, they have organizational "weight."

Prioritize Business-Critical Capabilities

When you have a list of *qualified* and *quantified* architectural capabilities, you must finally work to prioritize them. While it can be tempting to seek to prioritize every qualified capability in the context of this meeting, this often results in the participants going in endless circles as different stakeholders will inevitably disagree on some of the minutia. The target of this phase of the meeting is to build consensus on what is *business-critical.*

The upper bound of *business-critical* capabilities is four. If more than four business-critical capabilities are identified, we must guide the stakeholders through a process of determining relative ranking of each. Not every capability can be *business-critical.* If everything is *high priority, ipso facto* everything is *low priority*; when everything becomes of equal importance, there is no basis for choosing what to do first or last or where to apply architectural trade-offs.

Crucial to the success of this process is leadership. Deadlocks may occur that must be resolved, and biases and fears will creep in that can derail constructing an accurate set of capabilities. Even when focusing only on what is *business-critical,* different business actors bring different perspectives and priorities. There are tools, such as the weighted decision matrix described in Chapter 26, which allow you to quantify the options and can help resolve conflicts amicably.

By the conclusion of this meeting, you and your architecture team will possess a *qualified, quantified,* and partially *prioritized* list of target capabilities, each linked to some written requirement or in-meeting discussion with named stakeholders.

Step 6: Documenting and Scoring Capabilities

Following the meeting in step 5, you will now begin formally documenting these capabilities and their score using the workbook and templates available at `https://MasteringSoftwareArchitecture.com`.

Documenting these capabilities begins by enumerating each constraint, its target quantity, trade-offs, and driving motivations. This will later inform the creation of an *architectural style document*. Although Chapter 24 describes this artifact (and other supporting artifacts) in detail, an *architectural style document* first outlines a summary of the vision and then identifies the business-critical capabilities the system must exhibit to enable that vision while linking to individual architectural decisions and supporting constraints. Your notes in this process are instrumental in providing context. Consequently, whenever you are documenting the architecture or its constituent decisions, quote and link sources wherever possible.

Scoring these capabilities takes place in the Tailor-Made Workbook. Within this workbook, the architect will list target capabilities and begin to assign scores to each capability on a nonlinear scale of -5 to 5 with each step broken into quarters.

Qualified Capability	Score
Extremely Low	–4 to –5
Very Low	–3 to –3.75
Low	–2 to –2.75
Below Average	–1 to –1.75
Average	–0.75 to 0.75
Above Average	1 to 1.75
High	2 to 2.75
Very High	3 to 3.75
Extremely High	4 to 5

It must be understood that these scores are absolute. The scores introduced by Ford/Richards (Figure 4-1) indicate, in a relative sense, how well a given architectural capability is supported within an architecture. A common mistake made by architects is conflating the business importance of a given capability with the strength of support a candidate architecture is purported to offer. In other words, a score of 5 does not represent the relative importance of a capability, but rather the maximum extent possible this capability can exist in a system. Consider the capability of *scalability*. A score of 5 represents Netflix, Google, or Amazon levels of scalability. While many projects and applications may deem scalability to be *business-critical*, defining scalability by its maximum possible value (5) and deriving an architectural style targeting that value will often result in an overengineered and overly complex architecture with scalability capabilities far too high for most applications. A prototype tool for capturing these scores to evaluate candidate architectural styles is shown in Figure 4-6.

TAILOR MADE

ARCHITECTURE CAPABILITIES WORKSHEET

Candidate Capability	Qualified	Quantified	Category	Target	Actual
Agility			Business-(	4.25	
Abstraction					
Configurability			Nice-to-ha	1.75	
Cost			Nice-to-ha	1	
Deployability			Notable	3	
Elasticity			Important	3.75	
Evolvability			Business-(	5	
Fault-tolerance			Notable	2.75	
Integration			Business-(	4.75	
Interoperability			Business-(	4.5	
Performance			Notable	2	
Scalability			Notable	2.25	
Simplicity			Nice-to-ha	1.25	
Testability			Important	4	
Workflow			Important	3.25	

Figure 4-6. *The Tailor-Made Architecture Workbook*

Notably, this scale places a large theoretical upper bound on the total number of architecture capability requirements, although the practical limit is closer to ten.[4]

Provided the key capabilities are quantified, it should be clear from the meeting in step 5 how to score the *business-critical* capabilities. There can—and should—be gaps between the scores of the half-dozen or so that remain.

[4] Carducci, M. (2023), Tailor-Made Architecture Workbook, `https://masteringsoftwarearchitecture.com`

Although the ranking of the remaining capabilities did not take place in the meeting, you should possess a good, shared vision and a reasonable understanding of the problem space, the needs of the customer, and the goals of the project. As such, you should review the remaining capabilities and attempt to prioritize and score them.

While completing this exercise, remain cognizant of the answers received about the business's vision and expectations for the future. Architecture is not just about V1.0 or V10.0 (and, of course, there must be a V1.0 before there can be a V10.0). The rankings produced by the architect are not set in stone. This is simply another tool to strengthen understanding and evaluate what exists with an eye toward the future.

In subsequent conversations, we should verify our rankings of important, notable, and nice-to-have capabilities. It can be more efficient and productive to introduce these in pairs rather than present the entire list to the business. The entire list can be potentially overwhelming (and lead to relitigating previous discussions and agreements). The goal is simply to gauge relative importance for capabilities that are not identified as *business-critical.*

Once this process is completed, you may choose to communicate the results of your analysis. It is important that all relevant parties feel they have been heard, even if not every decision went the way they may have hoped. Transparency is key in building and maintaining trust and an atmosphere of collaboration.

Summary

At the conclusion of this process, architecture is no longer in a vacuum. Business needs are understood, vision is shared, and architecture has clear requirements to begin the design process. Along with the critical capabilities, the broader perspective provided by the scoring process reduces risk and assists architecture in solving the right problems and creating a highly tailored architecture that *fits*. This tailored "fit" is the result of the Tailor-Made Architecture Model's capability for fine-grained control of architectural capabilities. The business-critical capabilities may drive major architectural decisions, but the important, notable, and nice-to-have will illuminate additional decisions in the design process. Consequently, each score becomes a target, and it is often possible to get remarkably close to each of those targets. It is simple, but it is not easy.

CHAPTER 5

KPIs, Metrics, and Data-Driven Architecture Decisions

Without Data, you're just another person with an opinion.

—W. Edwards Deming

In Chapter 4, we introduced the Tailor-Made Requirements Analysis Process. Although there is much that can be learned from the research, analysis, and discussions outlined in that chapter, quantifying capabilities (i.e., how much is enough) as well as identifying unspoken nonfunctional requirements often remains challenging. Furthermore, as you will see in Section 3, metrics are helpful for improving the overall observability of your design. Metrics provide important tools for monitoring and evolving your architecture over time as the variables driving design decisions inevitably change, and the system's needs evolve. Consequently, business metrics often become extremely valuable for you as an architect.

Unlike the well-structured Tailor-Made Analysis Process, navigating business metrics often requires a more contextual approach. In this chapter, we will introduce various metrics, show how they might apply in various business contexts, and illustrate how we may utilize these to improve the design and evolution of the systems you will create.

M. Carducci, *Mastering Software Architecture*, https://doi.org/10.1007/979-8-8688-0410-6_5

What Is a KPI?

Key performance indicators, also known as KPIs, are quantifiable ways to gauge a company or project's performance for the business actors. Businesspeople view KPIs as a means of measuring and tuning their business and products because KPIs often identify strengths and weaknesses in both. Businesses also use KPIs to decide what should and should not be funded. Management might also use them to justify the projects to the various entities and stakeholders. Since a central concern of architecture is connecting technology strategy with business strategy, KPIs provide us with valuable data to drive and justify architectural decisions.

Good and Bad KPIs

Good KPIs will have several aspects that make them useful to collect. They will

- Quantitatively measure something in a more objective way
- Have a goal established by the leadership of the organization
- Have a data source where the KPI data may be collected consistently (preferably automatically)
- Be consistently collected at the same frequency (i.e., time interval or event frequency)
- Have a single individual responsible for collecting and reporting the KPI data regularly (there should be a backup assigned for when that individual is unavailable)
- Communicate how your business is succeeding or can improve

Unhealthy or bad KPIs will have one or more of the following traits:

- KPIs that are unclear on how they help the organization
- KPIs with difficult data collection mechanisms
- KPIs with thresholds that are not attainable without heavy reliance on external actors (e.g., not on your immediate team)
- KPIs that have no threshold indicating success or failure
- KPIs that are overly rigid such that collection frequency cannot be adjusted as business needs evolve

Each KPI offers a sliver of information which could be viewed as a facet of a diamond that provides a different perspective on the performance of the business. **No single KPI should be viewed in isolation, or it will likely be abused which leads to unhealthy outcomes for the business.** Consequently, your analysis of KPIs must also account for the various ways a single KPI can be "gamed."

When a metric becomes a target, it ceases to be a good metric.

—Charles Goodhart

LoC—A Terrible Metric for Developer Productivity

Some years ago, I was working for a company that sought to measure productivity. For many in the organization, there were reasonable metrics that could be collected; however, the business struggled with measuring developer productivity. Eventually, they settled on lines of code (LoC) as a suitable metric.

First, we in the development team were tasked with implementing this metric. Since some files used carriage returns for line endings and others used line feeds, we naturally counted each. Additionally, file minification skewed our metrics so we also counted semicolons. In most cases, each line was counted three times.

As the codebase evolved, optimization and refactoring would frequently reduce the LoC count which would negatively skew our metrics. The entire development team quickly adopted the convention of never deleting code. Instead, dead code was simply wrapped with

```
if(false) {
...
}
```

Although we found the local maxima for the metric, our codebase suffered immensely which adversely affected our long-term productivity. The moral of the story is, as Charles Goodhart famously said, when a metric becomes a target, it ceases to be a good metric.

As is often the case in architecture, there are typically many competing considerations and drivers. With this reality in mind, it is important to identify approximately five (plus-or-minus two) KPIs which are the most important to the part of the organization with which you are working. You may be producing artifacts for, reporting on, and designing based on a couple dozen KPIs but only reporting a selected handful to any single department as the system progresses.

There are a couple of mechanisms to evaluate how well defined a KPI is. First, by using the same criteria used for metrics as defined in *Beyond Requirements*[1]—*"Comparative," "Understandable," "Is a Ratio or Rate,"* and *"Changes Behavior"*—we can eliminate the temptation to add fuzzy or subjective metrics. Second, by using a subset of the criteria used for requirements as defined in *NASA Systems Engineering Handbook*[2]—*"Clarity," "Completeness," "Compliance," "Consistency," "Traceability,"* and *"Correctness"*—the KPI will provide additional informational value and not just be a low-value data input for the user that requires additional knowledge to evaluate its meaning.

What Motivates Organizations to Use KPIs?

Organizations have often realized that they needed information about their own products, processes, and people to make business decisions whether they were the producer or the consumer of the software products being measured. A great example is described in the book *Software Metrics: Establishing a Company-Wide Program.*[3] Hewlett-Packard invested significant resources to put together a "Software Metrics Council" and give the council the resources and the authority to specify what should be measured, how the data could be collected, and why it should be collected. The effort led to improved transparency, and the organization was influenced by both the process and the resulting metrics that were collected.

Another book that provides great insights into both the risks and potential benefits of applying metrics to software development is *The Mythical Man Month.*[4] The book describes lessons learned from development efforts at IBM via a series of essays. If you

[1] McDonald, K. (2016). *Beyond requirements: Analysis with an agile mindset.* Addison-Wesley

[2] Hershorn, S. *NASA systems engineering handbook* (SP-2016-6105 Rev2). NASA, 2016

[3] Grady R., Caswell, D. Software metrics: Establishing a company-wide program. Prentice Hall, 1987

[4] Brooks, F. *The Mythical Man Month.* Addison-Wesley, 1975, 1995

look at both the essay *Progress Tracking* and the essay *Communication*, the spirit of KPIs is present, even though the terminology had not yet been coined.

It is important to note that both books were the product of their era. Many developers today might consider them the deep past with metrics they might view as quaint, naive, or invasive. In both cases, the use of KPIs was motivated by a set of common organizational desires:

- To connect product development to the organization's success
- To detect and diagnose development issues as early as possible
- To make early, inexpensive changes rather than experience late, expensive changes or outright failure

There should be benefits that motivate the collection of the KPIs for the organization:

- Defining thresholds for taking business action
- Providing clear indications of how things are proceeding
- Providing a common understanding of what victory looks like to everyone in the organization

> *It is important to do things right. It is equally important to do the right things. We can be the best developers that money and technology allow, but if we are not meeting market demand, there is little hope for our survival as a business. We must be strategically aligned with the business objectives.*
>
> —*Measuring the Software Process*[5]

Evaluating KPIs in Relation to Architecture

Each KPI represents one or more requirements that will impact—or be impacted by—your project. Accounting for them can significantly influence the perception of your project and the success of your product by your own organization, customers, and users.

If you keep the KPIs in mind as you design your architecture, you may be able to identify services, tools, or artifacts that will help you report KPI findings to the business leadership, customer, and user. Each product is a revenue stream for the business, and

[5] Garmus, D., Herron, D. (1996). *Measuring the Software Process.* Yourdon

your management will view it that way. Most engineers and architects have a hard time seeing how their work impacts the business or the customer, and they benefit from knowing that their work is making a difference.

Some service calls or application actions may be able to log metrics automatically in a way that can help your organization consistently collect the KPIs. For example, tools like Jenkins, GitLab, Sonargraph, ArchUnit, and SonarQube could automatically notify a user and/or log when some action has completed. This can be useful as an automated mechanism for collecting data, but it is important to account for situations where someone performs an undo. In those cases, the undo should not count or be subtracted from the count following the undone action.

When possible, automatic collection is ideal because it will provide an unbiased and low-cost mechanism for data collection. Moreover, automatic KPI collection enables *continuous collection* which enables you to surface negative trends earlier.

Not all KPIs will need input from a software architect. There are business-level KPIs that have more to do with the performance of departments like marketing or sales, and there is not much that you, as the architect, can influence. Conversely, some KPIs provide an opportunity for you to better tie your efforts to business goals.

Some architectures will lend themselves to better alignment with your organization's business model than others. For example, if your business favors ongoing small payments over large single payout license sales, then a SaaS solution will be more successful than a shrink wrap monolith application.

As shown in the table below, we have broken down the KPIs into several business units: sales, marketing, finance, business management, and revenue stream. We have listed 23 sales KPIs, 34 marketing KPIs, 22 financial KPIs, 26 business management KPIs, and 121 revenue stream/product KPIs. Although this list is not comprehensive, it is a good starting point. To remain brief, later in this chapter, each section will have one or two examples of KPIs for different business units that you might directly influence through your work.

Sales	Marketing	Financial	Business Management	Product/Revenue Stream		
• Market share • Monthly sales growth • Monthly sales/new customers • Monthly new leads/prospects • Number of qualified leads • New business service enablement • Resources spent on single nonpaying customer • Resources spent on single paying customer • Customer lifetime value/customer profitability • Lead-to-sale conversion rate	• Monthly new leads/prospects • Qualified leads per month • Prospect to Qualified Lead conversion rate • Total Active Marketing Qualified Leads (MQL) • Sales-Accepted Leads (SAL) • Sales Qualified Leads (SQL) • Cost per lead generated • Net promoter score • Cost per conversion • Cost per conversion by channel	• Net Profit Margin • Operating Cash Flow (OCF) • Net Profit Margin • Working Capital • Current Accounts Receivable • Current Accounts Payable • Accounts Payable Turnover • Accounts Receivable Turnover • Accounts Payable Processing Cost • Accounts Receivable Turnover • Budget Variance • Budget Creating Cycle Time	• Planned value (PV) • Actual cost (AC) • Earned value (EV) • Cost variance (CV) (planned budget vs. actual budget) • Schedule variance (SV) • Schedule performance index (SPI) • Cost performance index (CPI) • Planned hours of work vs. actual • Currently overdue project tasks	• Lead Time • Epics/Features Delivered • Release Cadence • Customer/User Satisfaction • Response Time • Met objectives set by customers • Customer Ticket Volume • Incidents • Technical Debt • Production Support • Availability/Uptime • Defect Escape Rate • Defect Volume • Maturity (code committed + Code volatility) • Documentation Coverage • Application Performance	• Mean Time to Recover (MTTR) • Mode Time to Recover (MTTR) • Best Time to Recover (BTTR) • Worst Time to Recover (WTTR) • Mean Time to Acknowledge/Accept (MTTA) • Mode Time to Acknowledge/Accept (MTTA) • Best Time to Acknowledge/Accept (BTTA) • Worst Time to Acknowledge/Accept (WTTA) • Mean Time to Implement and Deploy (MTID)	• Mean Time to Test (MTTT) • Mode Time to Test (MTTT) • Best Time to Test (BTTT) • Worst Time to Test (WTTT) • Mean Time to Deliver (MTTD) • Mode Time to Deliver (MTTD) • Best Time to Deliver (BTTD) • Worst Time to Deliver (WTTD) • Mean Time to Verify/Validate (MTTV) • Mode Time to Verify/Validate (MTTV) • Best Time to Verify/Validate (BTTV)

(continued)

Sales	Marketing	Financial	Business Management	Product/Revenue Stream		
• Cost per lead by each product • Cost of a new customer by each channel • Hourly, daily, weekly, monthly, quarterly, and annual sales • Average conversion time • Customer turnover rate • Number of monthly sales demos • Customer engagement level • Number of monthly quotes/orders • Average monthly/quarterly/annual sales volume per customer	• Average time of conversion • Retention rate • Attrition rate • Traffic (foot, web, calls, etc.) • Returning vs. new visitors • Visits per product • Average time of customer to business exposure • Average time on page or in application • Click-through rate on web pages • Pages per visit • Conversion rate for call-to-action content	• Line Items in the Budget • Payroll headcount ratio • Vendor Expenses • Payment Error Rate • Internal Audit Cycle Time • Debt to Equity Ratio • Return on Equity • Cost of Managing Business • Resource Utilization • Total cost of financial business unit	• Crossed/missed deadlines • % of overdue project tasks • Percentage of projects completed on time • Percentage of canceled projects • Missed milestones • Number of budget iterations • Percentage of tasks completed • Percentage of projects on budget • Project resource utilization	• Test Coverage • Automated Test Pass Percentage • Merge Request/Peer Review Lag • Code Volatility • Code Complexity • Mean Time to Failure (MTTF) • Mode Time to Failure (MTTF) • Best Time to Failure (BTTF) • Worst Time to Failure (WTTF) • Mean Time Between Failure (MTBF) • Mode Time Between Failure (MTBF)	• Mode Time to Implement and Deploy (MTID) • Best Time to Implement and Deploy (BTID) • Worst Time to Implement and Deploy (WTID) • Mean Time to Detect and Communicate (MTTD&C) • Mode Time to Detect and Communicate (MTTD&C) • Best Time to Detect and Communicate (BTTD&C)	• Worst Time to Verify/Validate (WTTV) • Cost per Transaction • Cost per Change Request • Cost per Release (Deployment Time + Resource Cost) • Deployment Frequency • Deployment Failure Rate • Lead Time (Committed code ➤ Release)

• Average monthly sales volume per customer • Relative market share • Product/service usage every day • Percentage of total sales from existing customers	• Inbound links to website • Traffic from organic search • New leads from organic search • Number of unique keywords that drive traffic • Keywords in top 10 SERP • Rank increase of target keywords • Conversion rate per keyword • Google PageRank • Traffic from social media • Leads and conversions from paid advertising		• Overhead (cost of managing processes) • Return on investment (ROI) • Employee retention • Motivation morale • Responsiveness to change • Skills growth • Cross-team collaboration • Internal-team collaboration	• Best Time Between Failure (BTBF) • Worst Time Between Failure (WTBF) • Mean Time to Restore Service (MTRS) • Mode Time to Restore Service (MTRS) • Best Time to Restore Service (BTRS) • Worst Time to Restore Service (WTRS)	• Worst Time to Detect and Communicate (WTTD&C) • Found to Planned Work (FTPW) • Mean Time to Diagnose (MTTD) • Mode Time to Diagnose (MTTD) • Best Time to Diagnose (BTTD) • Worst Time to Diagnose (QTTD) • Mean Time to Implement (MTTI)

(continued)

Sales	Marketing	Financial	Business Management	Product/Revenue Stream
	• Cost per acquisition (CPA) • Cost per conversion (CPC) • Number of conversions from social media • Percentage of conversion for social media leads			• Mode Time to Implement (MTTI) • Best Time to Implement (BTTI) • Worst Time to Implement (WTTI)

Identifying Requirements from KPIs

Most organizations already have KPIs, whether they call them KPIs or not. You may be able to just ask for the KPIs for each department or pay attention during staff meetings and take note of what the organization measures to evaluate success.

If the organization does not have any explicit KPIs, then you may be able to provide the KPIs of your choosing when you present status for your project. This will help to show management or the customer how your project is benefiting them. Remember, it is important to show the KPIs that are relevant to the parties to whom you present. We recommend those be restricted to only the KPIs that are relevant and permitted to be presented to those parties.

Once you identify the KPIs relevant to the various parties, your focus should shift to determining the best way to collect the related raw data. Automating the collection and processing of data will be useful in ensuring that the KPIs are available for reporting. This will also minimize the cost and effort of subsequent report generation.

Some KPIs may not have a direct tie to application or system architecture, but you may, regardless, be the ideal person to provide materials and/or assist the organization with those KPIs. Although not directly KPIs, providing artifacts that *reflect* KPIs such as *feature internal comparison table* (Figure 5-1) and *external comparison tables* (Figure 5-2), product descriptions and selling points (for brochures, websites, advertising materials, or RFIs/RFQs/RFPs) (Figure 5-3), or product bill of materials (list of subcomponents used) (Figure 5-4) is frequently valuable. All of these will be helpful in engendering further alignment between the architect and organization. Additionally, these artifacts can help the marketing team be more of an "inbound marketing"-focused team (focused on high-fit customers) rather than trying to just be a general marketing team.

	Feature A	Feature B	Feature C	Feature D	Feature E
Product A	✓	✗	✓	✗	✓
Product B	✗	✓	✓	✓	✓
Product C	✓	✗	✓	✗	✓
Product D	✓	✗	✗	✓	✗
Product E	✓	✗	✗	✓	✗

Figure 5-1. *Example Product Comparison Table*

Product A					
	Feature A	Feature B	Feature C	Feature D	Feature E
Version 2.1.6	✓	✗	✗	✗	✗
Version 3.4.5	✓	✓	✗	✗	✗
Version 4.3.3	✓	✓	✓	✗	✗
Version 5.5.2	✓	✓	✗	✓	✗
Version 6.7.2	✓	✓	✓	✓	✓

Figure 5-2. *Example Version Comparison Table*

Figure 5-3. *Example Trifold Brochure*

Component Name	Version	License	Dependencies	Hash/Signature	Known Vulnerabilities	Vulnerability Solution (mitigate/avoid/transfer/accept)
Log4J	2.22.0	Apache 2.0	log4j-1.2-api, log4j-flume-ng, log4j-iostreams, log4j-jakarta-smtp, log4j-jakarta-web, log4j-jcl, log4j-jul, log4j-mongodb, log4j-slf4j-impl, log4j-slf4j2-impl, log4j-taglib, log4j-to-slf4j, log4j-web	apache-log4j-2.22.0-bin.zip.sha512, apache-log4j-2.22.0-bin.zip.asc	CVE-2023-6378, CVE-2023-34055, CVE-2023-30601, CVE-2022-23307, CVE-2022-23305, CVE-2022-23302, CVE-2021-4104, CVE-2020-13936, CVE-2019-17571, CVE-2018-8088	Accept

Figure 5-4. *Example Bill of Materials*

Connecting Architecture Capabilities to KPIs

Identifying which architectural aspects can be associated with a particular KPI is challenging. This is especially true when an architect has biases toward particular architectural patterns. To provide some examples, the following sections illustrate multiple KPI-to-architectural aspect mappings.

KPIs by Department

As a concrete example, we will define a hypothetical company that provides a product that comes in two licensed versions: a "community" edition that is free to use but limited in functionality and a "professional" edition that includes additional features for a monthly fee (e.g., the professional edition might integrate with other products that the company produces that increase team productivity).

Business Management

We will begin with business management, with whom you will often frequently interact. To help facilitate your future interactions, we will start by exploring KPIs germane to this audience.

Planned Work vs. Actual Work

Architectures that favor loose coupling and more fine-grained modularity (whether distributed or monolithic) are increasingly favored for three reasons: initial implementation effort, long-term maintainability, and cost predictability. While the initial implementation and maintainability are important, the cost predictability is more pertinent to the *planned work vs. actual work* KPI.

With highly modular architectures such as the Modular Monolith, Service Based, or Microservices—which we will explore in detail in Section 2—it will be easier to estimate effort for the individual services themselves, but keep in mind that there is also a cost associated with integrating those services.

Keep in mind that a very limited monolith may be easy to plan for; therefore, it is important that an architect constrains the scope to remain small. It is, however, easy for things to get out of hand whenever one requires developers to limit the scope of their own components. They will often feel that it is easier to just add a little more code than incur the cost and overhead required to create a whole new small module, but it is often worth it in the end. Human nature favors adding one more feature to an existing module when, in reality, it is often better to separate concerns and produce smaller modules that will be easier to maintain, test, and reuse.

Product

In addition to management, you will also frequently interact with the product development teams. Like business management, it is particularly important to measure architecture in alignment with the product's subjective worldview.

Service Stability

The development teams' ability to decrease operations and maintenance costs by maximizing reliability is key to the success of the business and customer. The most common KPIs related to reliability are Mean Time Between Failure (MTBF) and Mean Time to Repair (MTTR). Common from a business perspective, MTBF shows how much time the system operates without issue, is easy to measure, and can be a straightforward metric for use as a contract requirement. Contrast this with MTTR, which measures the average time to resolve a defect once it has been discovered.

For most of the history of software, optimizing for MTBF was seen as highly desirable as the cost (both in terms of time and currency) of updating software was significant. In the modern, cloud-native era, designing software for high MTBF rarely makes the sense it once did. With good DevOps practices and automation, releasing patches is often quick and painless. It ultimately depends on the consequence of a failure and the cost of remediation.

While we often aim to design the objective "best" systems, overengineering for excessive reliability typically comes at a cost that may be difficult to recuperate. This practice often slows organizational agility as much more engineering effort is necessary prior to releasing a feature for the all-important user feedback. Sometimes the highest value we can deliver is a bulletproof system; sometimes the highest value we can deliver is the answer to a question: *"Will this feature meaningfully improve the customer experience?"* As always, there are no best practices, only trade-offs.

It is common to have one KPI composed of multiple nested KPIs as is described as a KPI tree in *KPI Checklists.*[6] MTTR is really a composite of multiple KPIs which are Mean Time to Accept (MTTA) and Mean Time to Implement and Deploy (MTID) which are each composite KPIs as well. This is shown in both the KPI tree (Figure 5-5) and the KPI timeline (Figure 5-6).

[6] Smith, B. (2018). *KPI Checklists – Practical How To Guide.* Metric Press

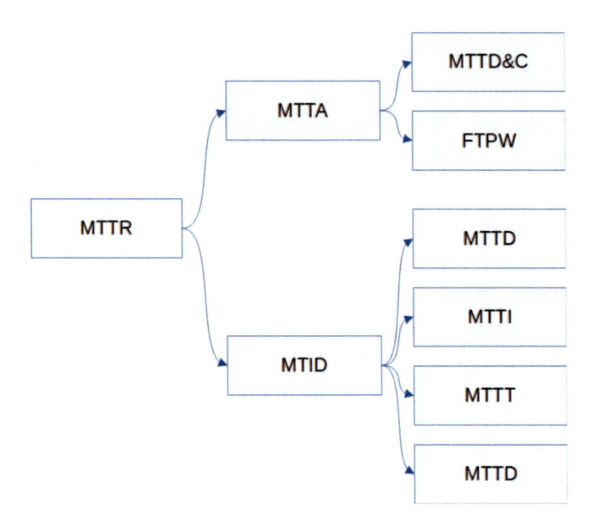

Figure 5-5. *Mean Time to Repair KPI Tree*

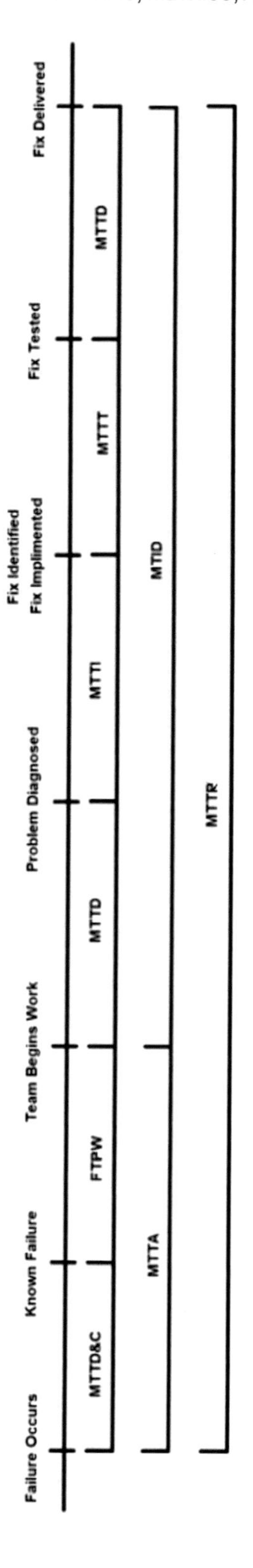

Figure 5-6. *Mean Time to Repair Timeline*

Mean Time to Acknowledge (MTTA) occurs between the time that a failure actually happens and when the company acknowledges that there is an issue to be resolved for the customer and user. There are two KPIs that define MTTA. The first is the Mean Time to Detect and Communicate (MTTD&C). The second is the Found to Planned Work (FTPW).

Mean Time to Implement and Deploy (MTID) measures the time between when the issue has been added to the maintainers' workload and when the fix is deployed in the production environment. It is composed of four components: Mean Time to Diagnose (MTTD), Mean Time to Implement (MTTI), Mean Time to Test (MTTT), and Mean Time to Deliver (MTTD). Each of these steps can represent a significant amount of time in the process of resolving the issue. If the time is tracked and managed for each step, then the time can be minimized significantly.

> *You can't improve what you don't measure*
>
> —Peter Drucker

An architect can do several things to decrease the cost of MTTR, and analyzing all the way down to the lowest phase of the repair process makes it easier. Building in observability and notification to detect failures and automatically notify the maintainers when failures occur—in addition to better system log aggregation and analysis that some Security Information and Event Management (SIEM) tools support—can dramatically decrease MTTA and help diagnose the issue. Additionally, having a high level of test coverage at unit, API/integration, and system levels decreases the time required for both diagnosis and testing while simultaneously decreasing the likelihood that a new fix causes some other regression in functionality. Finally, ensuring that all subcomponents can be patched by using either plug-in frameworks or container-based blue-green deployment strategies will drastically decrease the time spent delivering and deploying the patch to production.

The more modular your system, the harder it is to consolidate the logging; however, the easier it is to test and deploy fixes owing to the reduced regression surface area that such modularity introduces.

Sales

Although you will interact more frequently with business and product, it is helpful to expand the scope of audiences as project stakeholders often appear from all areas of the organization.

There are two KPIs that demonstrate how an architect can connect their work to business KPIs. The first is "Resources spent on a single *Nonpaying Customer*." This KPI represents a feature that the customer either gets for free to help marketing and sales sell other products, is part of a package that sweetens the sale, or gets the customer to use your other products. The second KPI is "Resources spent on a *Single Paying Customer*" and identifies aspects of the product or service that are worth spending resources on that truly add value to the customer, user, and/or your business to produce what is known as a return on investment (ROI) for using your product or service.

Resources Spent on Single Nonpaying Customer

Before continuing our exploration of this KPI, we will first define a few terms:

- A *Potential Customer* is someone who may be willing to buy in the future but has not yet.
- A *Hooked Potential Customer* is a customer who is spending—or about to spend—money and may be willing to increase their expenditure.
- A *Value-Added Customer* is one who has spent money but is willing to make further investment.
- A *Nonpaying Customer* is a user of the free products or services that the company provides.

While it is important that any expenses related to *Nonpaying Customers* are minimized, the sales department focuses their attention on the product's ability to add bonus features for the paying customers and to "hook" *Potential Customers.*

The sales department wants to see a low total Cost of Operations and Maintenance (COM) billed to their department but a high number of both *Hooked Potential Customers* and Value-Added Customers. This ratio is called *Cost Efficiency.*

Variables:

H = Hooked Potential Customers

VA = Value Added Customers

COM = Total Cost of Operations and Maintenance

CPC = Average Cost Per Customer

Functions:

*COM = (H + VA) * CPC*

CPC = (H + VA) / COM

The ideal is to identify aspects of the product or service that are so trivially inexpensive that there is effectively no cost to support/host a *Nonpaying Customer*, but sales may be willing to pay well above that if they see a high rate of conversion from *Nonpaying* to *Paying Customer*.

The easier that the product converts from the "community" edition to the "professional" edition, the better that conversion will be. In this scenario, we should design the architecture to make it easy for a user/customer to upgrade through the application itself (e.g., by adopting a plug-in architecture or prescribing feature toggling), contact the sales department via live chat, or support temporary licensing to get the user acclimated to the "professional" edition features.

Resources Spent on Single Paying Customer

The business sales department will be even more interested in the resources spent on a single *Paying Customer* than they are on the resources spent on a single *Nonpaying Customer* that they view as a *Potential Customer* because the customer has already shown that they are willing to spend money on products. That said, the *Nonpaying Customer* is still considered important because there is already a relationship and product familiarity that can be leveraged to convert them to a *Paying Customer*.

The calculations are very similar, but, in the case of *Nonpaying Customer* products, the low-level sales personnel will be very interested in the free products because they help them to make a sale. In contrast, the paid-for product is of more interest to sales leadership, as long as the for-profit product adds enough value.

It is less important that any expenses related to *paying customers* are minimized because the cost is absorbed by the licensing fees or monthly service fees. The sales department wants to see a low total COM billed to their department but a high number of both *Hooked Potential Customers* and *Value-Added Customers*. The ideal is to identify aspects of the product or service that are so valuable to the customer and user that they can easily see the *ROI*.

Marketing

Although *sales* and *marketing* are often conflated, they represent two distinct perspectives on customer acquisition. Consequently, they are often focused on different KPIs.

Prospect to Qualified Lead Conversion Rate

Before we begin this example, we will start with a couple definitions:

- A *prospect* is a potential candidate that seems to meet some criteria that the seller believes would make them a good customer.
- A *qualified lead* is a candidate that the marketing team has confirmed has met all the criteria to be a good customer.

There are a couple artifacts that an architect can provide to the marketing team to help them achieve their prospect-to-qualified-lead conversions. Providing a questionnaire or feature table to customers can help the marketing team tie the product features to the *prospect*. If the product features do not align completely with the *prospect's* needs, but the software architecture is flexible enough to allow for additional features or for turning off unwanted features in short time spans, the software changes can be made to help establish a *qualified lead*.

Ultimately, the business often aims to attract customer and user attention by providing features that not only overlap with the competition but exceed what the competition includes within their product.

While architecture is generally not responsible for defining these tantalizing features, this can inform architecture capabilities around agility, customizability, and deployability. Another thing to keep in mind is that it will help if your product can convert the data from competing products into your product's preferred format as a function of interoperability. This kind of compatibility being built into a product can be in and of itself what is known in the business world as a "moat."

> *The term 'economic moat,' popularized by Warren Buffet, refers to a business' ability to maintain competitive advantage over its competitors in order to protect its long-term profits and market share. Just like a medieval castle, the moat serves to protect those inside the fortress and their riches from the outsiders.*
>
> —Chris Gallant[7]

In short, being able to both completely overlap with the competition's feature set and being able to ingest the competition's data format will decrease the "barrier to entry" for your users transitioning to your product.

Financial

Sales and *marketing* are both focused on revenue and growth. In contrast, the finance department focuses on minimizing cost and risk. Consequently, their subjective worldview changes.

Vendor Expenses

Vendors supply parts, supporting products, and services that are used within a greater product offering or service offering that an organization can sell. This is a function of the affordability capability. As an architect, there are multiple things we can do to minimize the licensing costs and licensing risks associated with the use of third-party libraries and frameworks.

First, prescribing that third-party libraries are wrapped with suitable interfaces and abstractions can decrease overall financial risk. Such an abstraction will decrease the cost of swapping out libraries without impacting your own product's functionality should a change become necessary.

[7] Gallant, C. (2023). *How an Economic Moat Provides a Competitive Advantage.* Investopedia. Retrieved from `https://www.investopedia.com/ask/answers/05/economicmoat.asp`

Second, primarily using products whose licensing costs are extremely low or free is an excellent way to decrease vendor expenses, thus further improving affordability.

It is important to note that not all open source licenses are created equally. Open source software often comes with licensing agreements that dictate how you may use and distribute the code. Permissive licenses are generally more flexible, but some copyleft licenses require you to make any derivative works available under the same terms, which can conflict with closed source objectives. Many organizations have policies on which open source licenses are permissible; *you need to know what these are.*

Sometimes, the benefits of using a paid-for vendor product that will decrease development time or risk may overpower the motivation to decrease the vendor expense KPI. However, it is important to document this trade-off when doing a trade study or presentation in anticipation of any questions that the financial team will have because they will primarily be interested in minimizing vendor expenses. Tools for documenting such decisions will be discussed in Chapter 24.

Presenting KPIs to a Target Audience

When developing software, it is important to remember that there are multiple entities that will both influence and be influenced by the software being developed. The entities involved are the user, customer, business, development team(s), and the environment.

- The *user* is the actor who will directly interact with your product or service.
- The *customer* is the actor who will be writing the check to purchase your product or service. Notably, the customer and the user might not be the same individual or entity.
- The *business* is the organization that is paying the team(s) for their efforts and will collect the payments from the customer. It is important to remember that the business is made up of different internal organizations and that each one will have different KPIs.
- The *development team(s)* includes the initial developers and the maintainers of the product or service.
- The *environment* is anything else that will impact—or be impacted by—your architecture not covered by the previous four entities.

It is important to identify to whom each KPI is intended to inform and influence. Most target audiences will not be comfortable looking at raw data, so it is critical to turn data into meaningful information by providing context. This helps uncover trends or where the current state is relative to the target thresholds. Many businesses will be content with a PowerPoint presentation or a report, but some may want more real-time information using things like dashboards or dynamically updated web reports.

It is also critical to use the correct visualization when creating simple dashboards and reports. If, for instance, one wants to demonstrate a KPI that has a couple regions specified by thresholds yet they only show the data at a single point in time, then a dial may make sense for both a report and for a dashboard. However, if they want to see the trend over time, a line graph with highlighted thresholds would be more appropriate. As described in the paper "Dashboard design and its relation to KPIs,"[8] the process should follow the following phases: "*define the objective of the dashboard*," "*define metrics and identify the content (KPI)*," "*seek user input*," "*create initial prototype*," and "*launch and monitor*."

Make sure that the recipient knows how to interpret the information so that they do not over- or underreact to newly available information. It is very dangerous to assume that the other parties understand your metrics or the implications of the metrics that you present without first confirming that they are on the same page as you. It is advisable to set up a plan ahead of time for scenarios where KPI thresholds are not met and inform all relevant parties about these plans. Otherwise, they might attempt to "manage" the situation themselves, unaware that it is already being handled.

It is also important to define how often the KPI will be collected and how often it will be reported. For example, it does not make sense to report on the metric weekly when that metric is only updated quarterly. The additional output will just be noise. The rate of metric collection is more likely to be in the software architect's hands, whereas the reporting rate will be defined by the other management, users, or customers. If there is no way to collect or update KPI data between reports, it is important to differentiate between a lack of data collection and a value that was collected and happens to match the value from a previous report.

[8] Berglund, C. & Tenic. Dashboard design and its relation to KPIs: A qualitative case study on a software company. Linnaeus University Sweden. 2020

Summary

KPIs provide a valuable way to connect the management, customer, and user needs to the architectural decisions that must be made during the software development lifecycle. These KPIs can help you explicitly identify constraints that will influence future design decisions.

It is important to know which KPIs are of interest to the management, customer, and user. These should be the north star that guides decision-making rather than simply choosing KPIs based on how easy they are to measure or blindly selecting KPIs that are favored by the architect. The answer must not originate from the architect, but the architect must get the answer from the other parties.

You may have to produce artifacts that you are especially well placed to create but may not have been what you would typically consider a part of your traditional responsibilities. However, those artifacts will often give you even more insight into what is truly important to the business, development team(s), user, and customer.

While KPIs may feel onerous, in many cases knowing what they are will free you from having to guess what is important and needlessly overengineering or missing a crucial capability within your design.

This is a deep topic but valuable for our work as architects. Although it is not as exciting and creative as other aspects of our field, your knowledge in this area positions you to make better data-driven decisions and communicate more effectively to a wider audience. Your effort to make it this far will continue to pay dividends throughout your career. Kudos for making through what might be the least exciting chapter in this book!

CHAPTER 6

Architectures Are Not "Chosen," They Are Designed

Everything is designed. Few things are designed well.

—Brian Reed

Once a set of architectural requirements is identified, the natural and intuitive next step is to "choose" an architecture that best fits the requirements. This generally means selecting one of the nine or so common patterns. This conventional approach, however, may lead to disastrous consequences.

In the multifaceted world of software architecture, there is a tantalizing allure to architectural patterns promising a given set of capabilities. Architects often gravitate toward these seemingly well-structured models, expecting that by employing "Pattern X," their deployed system will exhibit "Capabilities A, B, and C." Others gravitate to a single pattern as their "golden hammer," anticipating that past success is a guarantee of future results. In both cases, reality often paints a different picture.

Despite an architect's sincerest intentions and methodical adherence to models, these expected capabilities can prove elusive, with few clues as to where and how the divergence occurred. This divergence is not just a hiccup in the grand scheme of system design, it is an essential reminder that patterns as architectural blueprints, foundational as they seem, often lack both context and completeness. This fundamental disconnect was one of the major drivers leading to formalization of the Tailor-Made Architecture

M. Carducci, *Mastering Software Architecture*, https://doi.org/10.1007/979-8-8688-0410-6_6

Model. Understanding why deterministic results from architectural patterns are so mercurial—and often more of a mirage than a milestone—requires a deeper exploration of this inconsistency.

The Limitations of Pattern-Driven Architecture

Any given set of architectural requirements in the form of qualified, quantified, and prioritized target capabilities will provide an excellent starting point for the architectural design process. The requirements provide a clear idea of what characteristics the system must possess. At this point, the architect *could* elect to simply select the pattern that appears to be the closest match. The Ford/Richards scorecard[1] introduced earlier in this book (Figure 6-1) provides a direct set of expectations for the capabilities of a given component pattern.

	Layered Monolith	Microkernel	Modular Monolith	Microservices	Event-Driven	Space-Based	Service-Based	Service-Oriented
Agility	★	★★★	★★	★★★★★	★★★	★★	★★★★	★
Abstraction	★	★★★	★	★★	★★★★	★	★	★★★★★
Configurability	★	★★★★	★	★★★	★★	★★	★★	★
Cost	★★★★★	★★★★★	★★★★★	★	★★★	★★	★★★★	★
Deployability	★	★★★	★★	★★★★★	★★★	★★★	★★★★	★
Domain Part.	★	★★★★★	★★★★★	★★★★★	★	★★★★★	★★★★★	★
Elasticity	★	★	★	★★★★★	★★★★	★★★★★	★★	★★★
Evolvability	★	★★★	★	★★★★★	★★★★★	★★★	★★★	★
Fault-tolerance	★	★	★	★★★★★	★★★★★	★★★	★★★★	★★★
Integration	★	★★★	★	★★★	★★★	★★	★★	★★★★★
Interoperability	★	★★★	★	★★★	★★★	★★	★★	★★★★★
Performance	★★★	★★★	★★★	★★	★★★★★	★★★★★	★★★	★★
Scalability	★	★	★	★★★★★	★★★★★	★★★★★	★★★	★★★
Simplicity	★★★★★	★★★★	★★★★★	★	★	★	★★★	★
Testability	★★	★★★	★★	★★★★★	★★	★	★★★★	★
Workflow	★	★★	★	★	★★★★★	★	★	★★★★★

Figure 6-1. *Ford/Richards Architectural Capabilities Scorecard*

[1] Ford, N., & Richards, M. (2020). *Fundamentals of Software Architecture: An Engineering Approach.* O'Reilly Media

For an architect adopting pattern-driven architecture, certain patterns that might otherwise be appropriate with tailoring will be immediately disqualified due to poor initial scoring in key areas. Of what remains, the architect will select the closest fit. The Tailor-Made Requirements Analysis Process detailed in Chapter 4 will provide a direct set of target capabilities which may be compared against these scores. Overlaying the capability scores of the closest pattern against the scored capability targets will, almost universally, show an imperfect fit. Figure 6-2 illustrates what this mismatch—*of the closest fit*—might look like at design time.

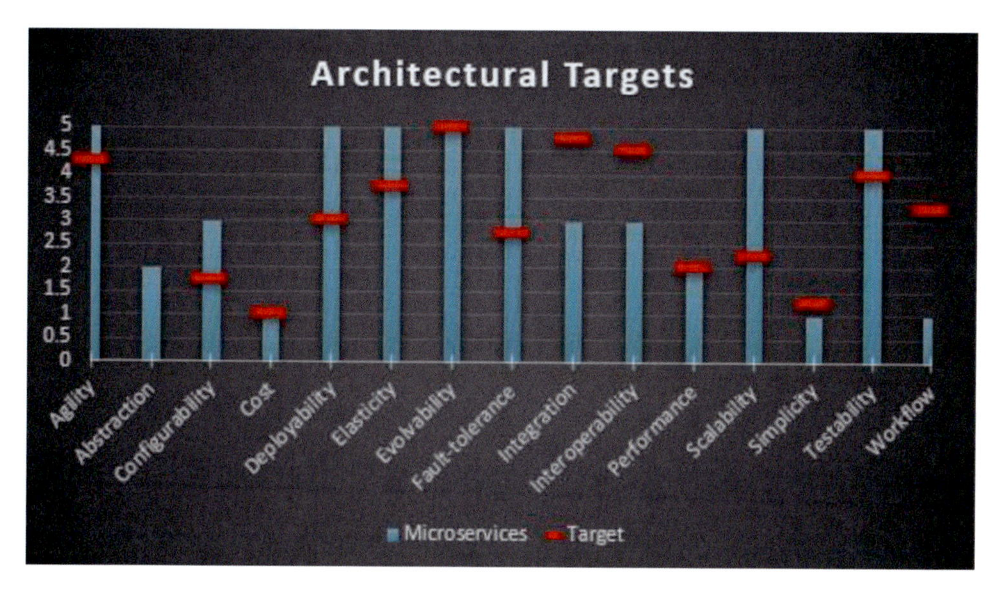

Figure 6-2. *Capability Targets vs. Pattern Capability Scores*

This mismatch underscores the first of two particularly important truths in software architecture—that **business and software challenges simply will not fit into just nine sizes**. To lean into the tailoring metaphor for a moment, if this were a suit it would be a bit wide in the shoulders, tight in the body, long in the sleeves, and bunching in the back. As it is, this suit will not be a great fit without some alterations, some tailoring. The scope and the consequences of this poor fit will manifest in tangible ways once the system is released to production and the next few years will consist of design tweaks in the form of costly trial-and-error changes. If the project survives this phase, either the design will have evolved to a point that the architecture is an acceptable fit, or the problems will have compounded to the point that many in the organization will be calling for a rewrite, but, without new approaches, there is little reason to expect the outcome of the rewrite will result in anything beyond more of the same.

You cannot solve a problem with the same thinking that created it.

—Albert Einstein

Assuming, for a moment, that the hypothetical system survives the period of growing pains and the implementation of that architecture pattern evolves to the point that it aligns much more closely to the desired characteristics, what might one now call this architecture? In all likelihood, those working on that project would still adopt the label of whichever pattern they started with or the one now most topologically similar. Alternatively, they may classify their architecture as a hybrid of two patterns.

Software architecture patterns exist in a regrettably flat taxonomy that has failed us for far too long. For any of the common architecture patterns, there are countless organizations who claim to have adopted that pattern, yet a closer look reveals almost as many variations on that pattern as there are adopters, and their ultimate experiences in production as well as macro system capabilities will vary wildly. Consequently, many will look at an architecture scorecard such as that introduced in the Ford/Richards book, proclaim "*these scores don't align with my reality*," and perhaps conclude incorrectly that software architecture is, and will always be, a crapshoot.

The flat classification scheme fuels this disconnect. With a vanishingly small number of classes to sort the near endless variety of pattern implementations that exist today, the definition of that class is reduced to the lowest common denominator of component topology, which leads to high imprecision in defining a concrete definition of any architecture pattern. While adept architects may take the time to deeply understand the details and nuances of any given pattern, communication becomes a major problem. Patterns are common in software engineering as a high-bandwidth mechanism to communicate shared ideas; however, the prevalence of innumerable variations of each pattern means, *at any meaningful scale, there are no shared definitions of an architecture pattern*.

The inescapable need for tailoring for any common pattern to fit, the untold number of variations that self-identify as an instance of a given pattern with widely differing capabilities, and the inevitable regression to the lowest common denominator definition result in the second important truth of software architecture: **the capabilities that patterns promise are not absolute**.

This is not to say that the Ford/Richards pattern scores are a fabrication; they are not. Instead, the takeaway is that architecture capabilities come from *decisions*, not patterns.

Summary

The lowest common denominator classification scheme that currently pervades software architecture, as we have seen, is deeply problematic; a new model is long overdue. The wealth of five-star ratings under the microservices pattern is a consequence of much more than the topology. Breaking an application into hundreds of tiny pieces will not magically make those capabilities appear, and, likewise, a monolithic build artifact does not automatically presage a big ball of mud.

The microservices pattern—like every architecture pattern—is, fundamentally, a set of design decisions. There are core design decisions that a practitioner should almost never deviate from, there are well-defined extension decisions that modify the pattern to better suit a given project, and there are optional decisions that might be outside the scope of any formal pattern but nevertheless modify the resultant system capabilities. Each individual decision is an atomic component of the architecture that modifies the capabilities of the system—with some capabilities strengthened and others weakened—each decision is a trade-off. *It is the decisions that matter*; the patterns are a side effect.

This is not to say you should throw out all the patterns and completely reinvent the wheel for every project. Instead, the Tailor-Made approach advocates a more holistic design approach that centers on the decisions and directly connects decisions to outcomes at design time, regardless of whether the project is greenfield or a brownfield development. The patterns hold a valuable place in this model, not as an end but as a starting point. In Tailor-Made Software Architecture, an architecture pattern is simply a foundational set of decisions that may be modified or built upon. By assigning positive and negative numeric weights to the capabilities impacted by each constraint, the Tailor-Made Architecture Model provides design-time feedback on the side effects of each decision. The consequence, as you will see in the coming chapters, is an approach that

- Reduces risk
- Yields significantly more deterministic results
- Gives us tools to surgically tailor an architecture without costly trial and error

- Eliminates ambiguity
- Clearly communicates architecture descriptions

The next chapter introduces this foundational approach to architectural design: design by composition of architectural constraints.

CHAPTER 7

Architectural Constraints: Designing for Deterministic Capabilities

Constraints are not limitations; they are insight.

—Steve Sanderson

In the world of software architecture, very little is black and white; the answer to almost any question is, invariably, "it depends." But "depends" on what?

The Tailor-Made Software Architecture Model champions a design/decision-driven approach to architecture. Chapter 6 introduces this concept, but more precision is required. "Decision" is far too broad. Some decisions absolutely do impact system capabilities, others do not. There exists a set of things called decisions, and within that set, there exists a subset of those decisions that modify system architectural characteristics. To identify that subset, the question of where capabilities ultimately come from must first be answered.

The Origins of Architecture Capabilities

Counterintuitively, *architectural capabilities are elicited through constraints.* Constraints in this context are architecturally significant decisions that reduce the degrees of freedom of implementation, thus driving the attributes of the system toward a desirable

M. Carducci, *Mastering Software Architecture*, https://doi.org/10.1007/979-8-8688-0410-6_7

state. As a concrete example, take the infamous "Big Ball of Mud" pattern.[1] The Big Ball of Mud emerges when unlimited degrees of freedom exist for implementation; UI concerns, business logic, and data access may be freely mixed. The resulting code is difficult to test, difficult to maintain, and difficult to understand. Constraining the degrees of freedom by prescribing separation of concerns and modularity materially impacts the resulting system capabilities.

The software industry at large may not typically think about their designs that way or use that precise terminology (constraints may, instead, be called design principles, "paved roads," or simply "design decisions"), but they exist. One of the most explicit explorations of the direct relationship between constraints and capabilities was in the year 2000 by Roy Fielding.[2] While this paper has been widely read, most readers skipped ahead to Chapter 5 where Fielding begins to talk about REST, which has historically received more attention than the core thesis of this paper. Fielding's work was neither the first nor last to explore the relationship between constraints and architectural capabilities. Many scholars and practitioners in both software engineering, design, and architecture have touched upon this idea. *Software Architecture: Perspectives on an Emerging Discipline*[3] also explores this idea of design by constraint and how these constraints influence architectural styles. In *The Mythical Man-Month*[4] and other writings, Fred Brooks touches on the idea that constraints, both in terms of software and project management, influence the architecture and design of systems. More recently, the paper "Software Architecture Constraint Reuse-by-Composition"[5] by Tibermacine et al. further explored how constraints are also useful for more precise definition and documentation of software architecture and how constraints are reusable and composable architectural design elements.

---

[1] Foote, B., & Yoder, J. (1997). *Big Ball of Mud*. Presented at the 4th Conference on Patterns, Languages of Programs (PLoP)

[2] Fielding, R. T. (2000). *Architectural styles and the design of network-based software architectures* (Doctoral dissertation). University of California, Irvine

[3] Shaw, M., & Garlan, D. (1996). *Software architecture: Perspectives on an emerging discipline.* Prentice Hall

[4] Brooks Jr., F. P. (1975). *The mythical man-month: Essays on software engineering*. Addison-Wesley

[5] Tibermacine, C., Sadou, S., Ton That, M. T., & Dony, C. (2016). Software architecture constraint reuse-by-composition. *Future Generation Computer Systems, 61*, 37–53

Perhaps the most widely known and tangible example of how constraints may be applied to realize desirable system qualities are the SOLID principles introduced by Robert C. Martin[6] (with the SOLID mnemonic coined by Michael Feathers[7]). The SOLID principles are widely considered to be a set of design principles or best practices for object-oriented software development. One could equally say they are design constraints, and, by adhering to those constraints, certain desirable characteristics emerge in the codebase. Although SOLID is code/language level, it provides a tangible microcosm that most developers and architects are already familiar with (but are briefly summarized below).

The Single Responsibility Principle introduces a constraint that, informally stated, constrains each class to have a single purpose. The consequence of adopting this constraint is code that is easier to reuse, understand, and reason about with a reduced test surface area, which also makes the code easier to maintain.

The Open/Closed Principle introduces a constraint that declares classes open for extension but closed for modification. One consequence of this constraint is that code becomes more extensible while remaining easy to maintain and test. Another is that, by making classes closed for modification, backward compatibility is maintained, resulting in both stability and evolvability.

The Liskov Substitution Principle is a constraint that formally describes the idea of "design by contract." This constraint induces improvements in the code's modularity and testability (among others).

The Interface Segregation Principle constrains code to prefer client-specific interfaces rather than general ones. Consequently, any concrete implementation only requires what is necessary without needing to implement every conceivable method. This results in code that is more modular, decoupled, and easier to refactor, change, and redeploy.

Finally, **the Dependency Inversion Principle** defines a set of constraints, namely:

- All member variables in a class must be interfaces or abstracts.
- All concrete class packages must connect only through interface or abstract class packages.

[6] Martin, R. C. (2000). Design principles and design patterns. Objectmentor.com

[7] Martin, R. (2017). *Clean architecture: A craftsman's guide to software structure and design.* Prentice Hall

- No class should derive from a concrete class.
- No method should override an implemented method.
- All variable instantiation requires the implementation of a creational pattern such as the factory method or the factory pattern[8] or the use of a dependency-injection framework.

Most notably, this improves testability, extensibility, and adaptability.

By adopting these constraints in code, developers can deliver the same features with significantly improved adaptability, evolvability, extensibility, maintainability, simplicity, testability, and understandability. Each constraint moves the needle on these characteristics and others. Architectural constraints mirror this methodology. In fact, some SOLID constraints are frequently applied, albeit in varied forms, to distributed architectures. For example, in the microservices architecture, some champion IDEALS[9] defined as Interface segregation, Deployability (is on you), Event-driven, Availability over consistency, Loose coupling, and Single responsibility. Notably, while the SOLID constraints are considered a set of best practices for object-oriented software development, in architecture there are no best practices, only trade-offs; nothing comes for free. Every constraint that strengthens one architecture capability will weaken another.

> *Care must be taken to recognize when the effects of one constraint may counteract the benefits of some other constraint.*
>
> —Dr. Roy Fielding

Constraints provide a robust set of atomic architectural primitives that may be composed in numerous ways to design and define an architecture. It is through the careful and thoughtful composition of constraints that a target architecture may be derived or, through the addition and modification of constraints, that a pattern may be heavily tailored and fine-tuned at design time or redesign (modernization) time. This is a powerful idea that has been overlooked for far too long.

---

[8] Gamma, E., Helm, R., Johnson, R., Vlissides, J. (1994). *Design Patterns: Elements of Reusable Object-Oriented Software.* Addison-Wesley

[9] Merson, P. (2021). Principles for microservice design: Think IDEALS, rather than SOLID. *The InfoQ eMag, 91*

Closing the Capability Gap

Historically, many architectural constraints are implicit. Neal Ford and Mark Richards are seasoned architects and have worked together collaboratively for close to two decades. They are undoubtedly very consistent with their various approaches in the projects on which they consult. The wider industry, however, is a different story. Books, videos, lectures, blog posts, and implementations of various architecture patterns fluctuate significantly. Likely every architect practicing today has been exposed to architecture descriptions from different sources that include implied constraints in their description and implementation. In working with architecture teams, a common exercise involves asking them to define the set of constraints inherent to a given pattern. At the outset, they believe they have an aligned and precise definition of the pattern, but upon completing the exercise, the team realizes their differing interpretations (Figure 7-1). No team has universally agreed on a full definition of an architecture pattern to date.

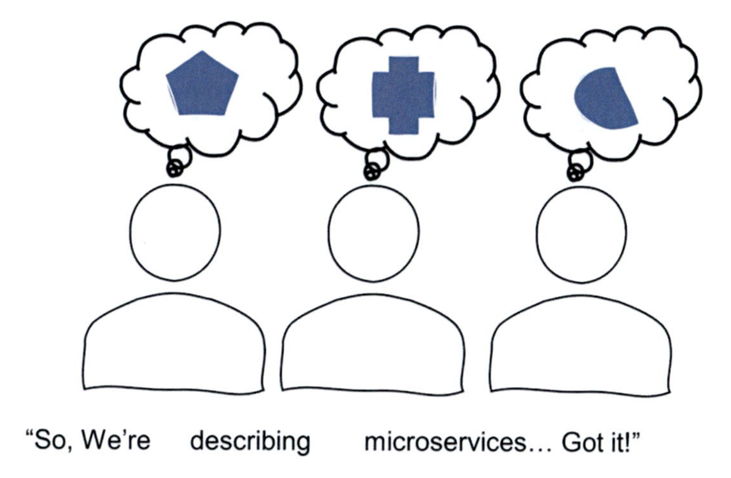
"So, We're describing microservices... Got it!"

Figure 7-1. *A Team of Architects or Developers with No Common Definitions of a Common Pattern*[10]

It is no wonder practitioners seem to get varying results from architecture patterns. This underscores the problems with a flat taxonomy of architecture patterns and applying the same label to different collections of constraints that are only superficially or topologically similar.

[10] Artwork inspired by Rasmusson, J. (2010). *The agile samurai: How agile masters deliver great software*. Pragmatic Bookshelf

Through explicit specification of the underlying constraints of an otherwise overloaded and ambiguous label, we can now begin to see more deterministic and consistent results. Undoubtedly, given more time in sessions discussing capability discrepancies with architects between the Ford/Richards scores and their experiences, the group would identify the delta between the Ford/Richard scores and their observed results in the field. Additionally, almost every pattern includes core, nonnegotiable constraints, but without thinking explicitly in this way, it can be easy to miss them. Consider the case of any of the numerous microservice mega-disasters discussed in blog posts and at conferences. Many stem from absent core constraints (the absence of clearly defined bounded contexts, domains, and domain-aligned teams or violation of the independent deployability constraint appears quite often) while overfocusing on irrelevant metrics like lines of code. By evaluating these underperforming architectures through the lens of constraints, a better path forward is almost always obvious.

Constraints for Deterministic Outcomes

Although Fielding's work on layering constraints to induce a set of architectural capabilities was groundbreaking, metrics to precisely quantify the impact of each constraint on the architecture properties they affect were not available, leaving the architect to work by their intuition. Since then, Ford and Richards took important steps to remedy this by quantifying the relative strengths and weaknesses in each pattern when implemented as described in *Fundamentals of Software Architecture*. It is by building and extending upon their work that the trade-offs of each constraint may now be numerically weighted, providing architects with a new heuristic to visualize the result of each decision at design time, using a common scale, and ultimately fine-tune architecture to better fit the needs of the organization.

Another addition to this model of architectural constraints is formally expressing relationships between constraints. There are constraints that are dependent on each other, in that applying one constraint requires that its dependent constraint be applied. Other constraints are mutually exclusive, in that selecting "Constraint A" or "Constraint B" is a binary either/or proposition. A contribution of the Tailor-Made model is a formal, logical expression of each constraint, its description, and any axiomatic rules that govern it.

The Tailor-Made model not only formalizes a process based on the work of Fielding and others but offers great power to simulate many candidate architectures at design time with relative accuracy while also receiving immediate feedback on logical model violations.

Summary

As Tibermacine et al. show in their research, "*constraints can serve as a documentation to better understand an existing architecture description, or can serve as invariants that can be checked after the application of an architecture change to see whether design rules still hold.*" In Dr. Fielding's dissertation, he shows, "*Since properties are created by the application of architectural constraints, it is possible to evaluate and compare different architectural designs by identifying the constraints within each architecture, evaluating the set of properties induced by each constraint, and comparing the cumulative properties of the design to those properties required of the application.*"

Ultimately, constraints form the foundation of an architectural model that allows for both precise definition of architectural design and fine-grained control of architectural capabilities with deterministic results. The model applies both at design time as well as throughout the life of the project.

As stated in Chapter 6, patterns are simply collections of design decisions in the form of architectural constraints that may be taken individually and applied to a candidate architecture or applied *en masse*.

For now, understand that there are many possible constraints and that ultimately, by getting through the remaining chapters, you will have a firm understanding of how to select and tune constraints to align with business requirements. Section 2 will define each of the nine common architectural patterns by the core constraints necessary to achieve rough parity with the Ford/Richards scorecard. Section 3 will expand on how to tweak the capabilities in the base pattern or in your custom, derived architecture as well as how to clearly document, communicate, and execute it. These sections will illustrate that many constraints are germane to several patterns. Within these sections, a catalog of reusable, composable constraints will emerge empowering you to fine-tune architectures for any set of capability targets. Equipped with this knowledge, you will be better positioned to implement the entirety of the Tailor-Made model and process.

CHAPTER 8

Architectural Styles: The Tailor-Made Pattern Language

> *An architectural style is a named, coordinated set of architectural constraints.*
>
> —Roy Fielding

As noted in previous chapters, the business problems architects tackle seldom align perfectly with just nine sizes (the common/conventional architecture patterns). More often than not, any system's architecture that adheres to a named pattern tweaks it significantly while leaving the label unchanged. This deviation brings forth two critical challenges that the Tailor-Made approach seeks to address.

Firstly, the prevalent tendency to oversimplify diverse and distinct systems filled with numerous modifications into a single pattern label leads to miscommunication and ambiguity in portraying the architecture's intricacies (as illustrated in Figure 7-1 in the previous chapter). Secondly, as we also explored in the previous chapter, relying on a pattern-based language holds value only if there's a unanimous consensus regarding the pattern's definition.

In short, the "flat taxonomy" of architectural patterns is overdue for replacement with a new, more comprehensive model; that model is the *architectural style*. This concept is not new to the Tailor-Made model. Although architectural styles factored

M. Carducci, *Mastering Software Architecture*, https://doi.org/10.1007/979-8-8688-0410-6_8

heavily in Roy Fielding's influential postgraduate work,[1] architectural styles were first explored in 1992 by D. E. Perry and A. L. Wolf[2] who defined an architectural style as an abstraction comprising element types and formal aspects from an assortment of specific architectures.

The significance of this concept lies in its ability to encapsulate key architectural decisions directly tied to the style's label, rather than one of countless variations that share a common name. Such an adaptation ensures clearer definitions and more transparent architectural communication. Moreover, it unlocks a vast spectrum of architectural styles, moving beyond the confines of the common nine patterns.

> *An architectural style is a coordinated set of architectural constraints that restricts the roles/features of architectural elements and the allowed relationships among those elements within any architecture that conforms to that style.*
>
> —Dr. Roy Fielding

Architects adopting the Tailor-Made model are no longer "choosing" an architecture. Instead, starting with target capabilities, architects are composing architectural constraints (or *abstract styles*—more on that later!) to derive new, tailored architectural styles. The axioms, heuristics, and weighting introduced within the Tailor-Made model make this approach even more powerful.

Architectural Styles and Architectural Patterns

The architectural patterns known today emerged as common solutions to recurring problems in business and system design, and, as such, they are known to have value. Architectural patterns represent hard-earned lessons in software architecture that should not be forgotten. Yet, with this focus on constraints and styles, where do patterns fit into this model?

---

[1] Fielding, R. T. (2000). *Architectural styles and the design of network-based software architectures* (Doctoral dissertation). University of California, Irvine

[2] Perry, D. E., & Wolf, A. L. (1992). Foundations for the study of software architecture. *ACM SIGSOFT Software Engineering Notes, 17*(4), 40–52

An architectural style is simply a named composite of architectural constraints—those key, architecturally significant decisions that act as the smallest atomic architectural primitive which act as building blocks of a given candidate or selected architectural design.

As a named, coordinated set of constraints, any architectural style may function as a more coarse-grained building block providing similar composability to individual constraints. Chapter 6 notes that a named architectural pattern is simply a set of implicit architectural constraints in the form of design decisions. If each pattern is explicitly described in terms of core constraints that are common across most mindful implementations, that pattern becomes a formal architectural style in its own right—at least in the abstract sense.

The key to using patterns as architectural styles lies in precise definition of the underlying constraints. In Section 2, the common patterns will each be defined by their core constraints in alignment with the decisions from which the scores were derived.

Why "Style"

Although formally defining architecture patterns by their constraints brings much needed semantic clarity to the realm of architecture patterns, "style" has the potential to introduce new ambiguity. Before closing this chapter, it is worth addressing the potential confusion this term may introduce.

In the technology industry today, "style" tends to refer to an individual's or community's preferences, biases, or adopted conventions. Developers are often said to have a "coding style"; certain languages and frameworks will prescribe a style to provide consistency within a respective community. Based on common usage, the two usages are at odds. Although "style" in the context of architecture may share similar roots to "style" as it is used in most contexts, the two carry different meanings.

Fielding adopted the use of "architectural styles" as he was building on the work of Perry and Wolf, who first coined the term. In doing so, he scrutinized the term "style" noting that this term might insinuate that a particular style emanates from individualistic stylistic choices. However, a deeper understanding of "style" emerges when we delve into architectural usages from diverse eras and locales. Here, styles reflect design constraints—be it available resources, construction methodologies, societal norms, or even the specific requirements or whims of local leadership. In essence, in building architecture, the emergent styles are the manifestation of design constraints. Numerous scholars have further accentuated this perspective, viewing this convention as a tool to interpret architectural descriptions and defining an architectural style.

> *Since referring to a named set of constraints as a style makes it easier to communicate the characteristics of common constraints, we use architectural styles as a method of abstraction, rather than as an indicator of personalized design.*
>
> —Dr. Roy Fielding

Summary

In the Tailor-Made context—as in Fielding's—any distinct mix of constraints leads to the creation of a novel architectural style. Architects will be crafting novel architectural styles by blending constraints, other architectural styles, or even a mix of both. This new style would be christened and documented formally, enabling crystal-clear communication regarding its definition. Although "style" may be ambiguous to outsiders, your styles—and the architectures you design that implement them—will not be.

CHAPTER 9

Architectural X Factors: Environment, Organization, and Teams

> *When I write software, I know that it will fail, either due to my own mistake, or due to some other cause.*
>
> —Wietse Venema

Today, software projects continue to fail (or at least fail to live up to their potential) at alarming rates. Architectures regularly fall short of promised capabilities. The underlying causes of such failures are manifold. Certainly, some—if not many—failures in the architectural realm are due to a lack of constraints or the wrong constraints. Yet even the perfect set of constraints, the ideal architectural style provides vanishingly few guarantees of success. There exist X factors outside the intellectual space of architectural design that must be understood and addressed in order for an architect to become truly effective in their work. The Tailor-Made model emphasizes the concept of "fit" in architecture, but "fit" is a concept with a deceptively vast scope. At this stage, a deeper exploration of our couture metaphor is necessary.

The Many Dimensions of "Fit"

A gentleman's suit is a marvelous garment that offers incredible range and versatility to adapt to numerous body types. Short, tall, athletic, rotund, slim, or broad, a well-tailored suit will result in a dapper presentation and flattering silhouette. Shifting fashions notwithstanding, the core elements of a suit have remained relatively unchanged over

M. Carducci, *Mastering Software Architecture*, https://doi.org/10.1007/979-8-8688-0410-6_9

the past 150+ years due to this quality of versatility of fit. The tailor must balance many measurements, choices, and other variables to produce an optimum fit for the wearer. This is difficult but crucial work as an ill-fitting suit will never look good regardless of cost, material, label, or any other single detail. Fitting the body, however important, is but the first dimension of fit. Beyond sizing, the color and fabric of the suit must complement the skin tone and accessories of the wearer. The style of the suit must fit the environment in which it will be worn. The suit must fit within the wearer's broader wardrobe. It must fit the style of the time. The overall cost must be within means. The relative value of purchasing a suit is a function of many other considerations, and "fit" when viewed holistically is so much more than just physical measurements.

Architectural fit, in many ways, is analogous. Thus far, the Tailor-Made model has examined only the first dimension of fit, aligning business needs with architectural capabilities. More precise measurements and tools have been introduced to reduce risk and uncertainty in this process, but architecture, like a suit, must fit holistically. Before we close this section, the nature of these additional dimensions must be examined along with how these might be integrated into the Tailor-Made model. Consider the frequent failures of the microservices architecture.

X Factors and the Road to Microservices

The Ford/Richards architecture scorecard awards the microservices pattern extremely high marks across several capabilities. Based on these scores, an architect might expect their reality to mirror those scores (Figure 9-1), but anecdotally the reality often falls far short of these lofty expectations (Figure 9-2). Rarely are organizations able to manifest the full scope of the benefits this approach promises, and industry analyst Gartner once predicted 90% of the organizations who attempt to adopt microservices will struggle to such an extent that they pivot to a different architectural approach.[1] One of the most high-profile shifts this prognostication predicted happened in 2023 when a team at Amazon announced they were pivoting from microservices back to a monolithic architecture.[2]

[1] Cope, R. (July 3, 2019). Multigrain services: Micro vs. mini vs. macro. *The Software Development Times.* `https://sdtimes.com/devops/multigrain-services-micro-vs-mini-vs-macro/`

[2] Jackson, J. (May 4, 2023). Return of the Monolith: Amazon Dumps Microservices for Video Monitoring. *The New Stack.* `https://thenewstack.io/return-of-the-monolith-amazon-dumps-microservices-for-video-monitoring/`

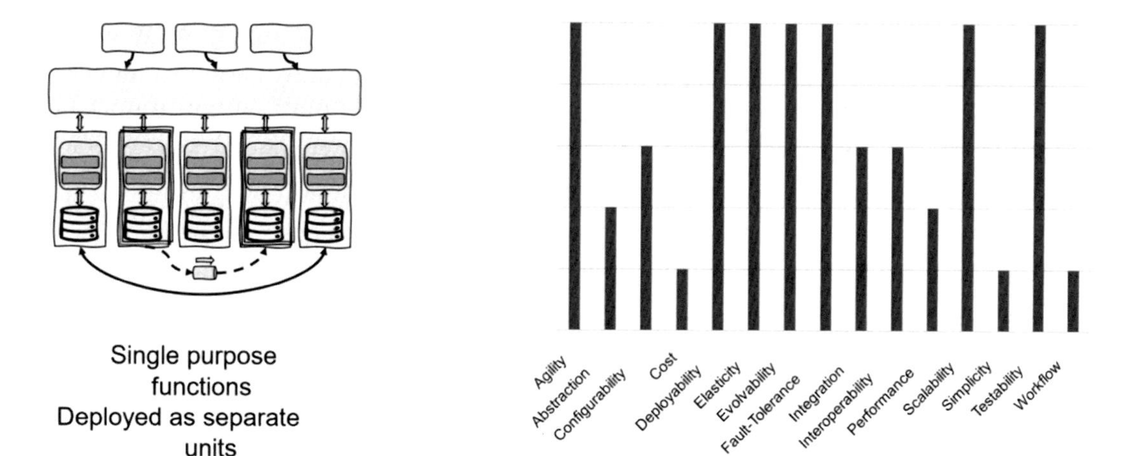

Figure 9-1. *The Promised Capabilities of Microservices Architecture*

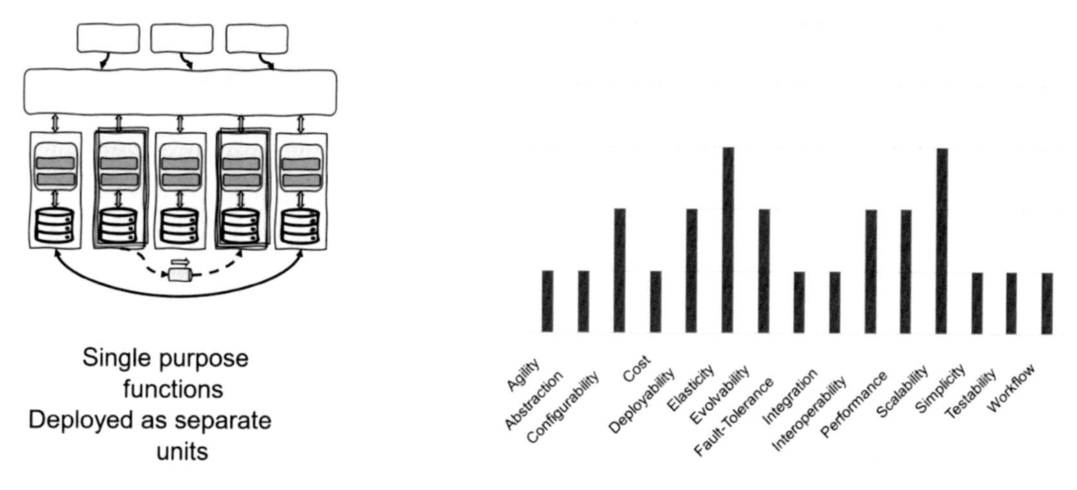

Figure 9-2. *The Anecdotal Reality of Many Microservices Implementations*

While it is true that many microservices architectures are prescribed without specifying many of the constraints that would otherwise elicit these capabilities, those constraints represent only part of the story; the challenges facing potential adopters extend far beyond the technical and design concerns.

The microservices pattern was not the result of a sudden flash of insight in the mind of some architect who realized that tiny, distributed components were a panacea for architecture problems. It was not simply an idea that was just waiting to be discovered. If an architect were to travel back in time a decade before the first microservices as we know them went into production to encourage early adoption of this pattern, they would be considered crazy. It is not that, at the time, the ideas were radical; they were *impossible*. The pattern was not discovered, it *emerged* over time due to changing cultures, technologies, practices, and organizational theory; these are the X factors, the hidden variables necessary for success. The pattern itself, and its defining constraints, cannot operate effectively without the X factors instrumental in driving the development and success of this approach. What were some of these X factors?

The Agile Manifesto, signed in 2001,[3] was more than just an acknowledgment that change is inevitable so it must be embraced; it was a call to the industry to work in new ways that facilitate change. Practices like Test-Driven Development (TDD) developed by Kent Beck,[4] a signatory on the original Agile Manifesto, provided developers with new tools for fast feedback on the correctness of software and the relative safety of a given change. This enabled more widespread adoption of the ideas surrounding continuous integration, paved the way for continuous delivery, and ultimately the DevOps movement from which many operational automation capabilities were born.[5]

Continuous Integration, Continuous Delivery, and Continuous Deployment

We see the effects of semantic diffusion in our industry surrounding these concepts and terms. Throughout this book, we will define these terms as defined by Jez Humble and David Farley in their 2010 book.

Continuous Integration

A team is practicing continuous integration (CI) only when the following statements are true:

- Every team member commits to main/trunk at least once per day.
- Each commit results in both a build and a full execution of all relevant test suites/quality gates.
- If the build breaks, resolution is top priority (typically the build is fixed within 10–15 minutes).

[3] Beck, K., Beedle, M., van Bennekum, A., Cockburn, A., Cunningham, W., Fowler, M., ... & Thomas, D. (2001). Manifesto for Agile Software Development. Retrieved from `http://agilemanifesto.org/`

[4] Beck, K. (2003). *Test-Driven Development: By Example*. Addison-Wesley

[5] Humble, J., Farley, D. (2010). *Continuous Delivery: Reliable Software Releases through Build, Test, and Deployment Automation*. Addison-Wesley

Although often considered to be an agile "best practice," true CI is seldom practiced. More accessible practices like GitFlow and feature branches delay integration to later in the development lifecycle. One of the primary challenges is the commit cadence of work in progress. Practices like feature toggling (where features in progress can be disabled until the feature is fully ready) are often necessary, enabling practices for CI.

Continuous Delivery

Continuous delivery builds on the practice of continuous integration by prescribing that, at the end of the CI stage, an artifact is produced that is in a ready-to-deploy state. Notably, a team cannot practice continuous delivery unless they are already practicing continuous integration. The essence of continuous delivery is described by Martin Fowler[6] as

- Your software is deployable throughout its lifecycle.
- Your team prioritizes keeping the software deployable over working on new features.
- Anybody can get fast, automated feedback on the production readiness of their systems any time somebody makes changes to them.
- You can perform push-button deployments of any version of the software to any environment on demand.

The key point of continuous delivery is your system is always in a ready-to-deploy state. This does not necessarily mean every build is deployed; rather, every build *can be* deployed.

Continuous Deployment

In highly agile environments where release velocity is considered a very high priority, continuous deployment dictates that *every commit* is released (once all tests and quality gates pass) automatically. In other words, your code's main branch and the production environment are *always* in sync.

---

[6] Fowler, M. (2013). *Continuous Delivery*. Retrieved from `https://martinfowler.com/bliki/ContinuousDelivery.html`

Other impediments to achieving the level of modularity prescribed by microservices are determining appropriate module boundaries and enabling teams to operate effectively within those boundaries. The influence of organizational communication structures on the systems those organizations produce (commonly known as Conway's Law) has been known since the late 1960s,[7] but it was not until 2003, when Eric Evans published *Domain-Driven Design*[8] (DDD), that organizational structures could truly evolve to support such an architecture.

We can define the microservices architecture pattern by architectural constraints, but the X factors enumerated above form subtle dependencies necessary for success. These dependencies roughly fall into three categories: team constraints, organizational constraints, and environmental constraints.

Team Constraints

These constraints will define skills, practices, behaviors, and habits the implementation teams must possess to effectively adhere to and implement the system's architecture. Team constraints will also dictate how they balance short-term priorities against long-term vision and the teams' incentives for each. The incentives and motives of the team must be aligned with those of architecture; otherwise, architecture will be seen as an impediment rather than an asset. One additional facet of some team constraints that blur the line between team and organizational constraints is the development teams' hierarchy.

Architects may produce the blueprints, but it is the teams that perform the actual construction. Without consideration of this fact, the blueprints become little more than a suggestion.

Organizational Constraints

These constraints will define the nature of the organization, process maturity, structure, and additional variables the architect must consider. While architecture and business may be aligned on vision, it is uncommon for alignment to extend beyond that. For example, organizations tend to be very risk-averse and will often equate change to risk. Consequently, architectural decisions that require sweeping organizational change

[7] Conway, M. E. (1968). How do Committees Invent? *Datamation*, 14(5), 28–31

[8] Evans, E. (2003). *Domain-driven design: Tackling complexity in the heart of software.* Addison-Wesley

(such as embracing DevOps or DDD) may be an uphill struggle to implement effectively. The initial delivery timeline and budget also represent organizational constraints that must be considered.

Environmental Constraints

These constraints not only define the runtime and development environments of the system, infrastructure maturity, and deployment maturity but also encompass other factors. One notable factor is the complexity of the problem space. Another is the complexity of the solution space. The cognitive load of solving challenging domain problems may necessitate simplicity elsewhere. Likewise, operating at the bleeding edge of technology is unavoidable at times, but, as always in software architecture, trade-offs may be necessary. Finally, if the environment is not one of innovation but stagnation, architects may be limited in what architectural constraints may be available in their toolbox.

Constraint Dependencies

A microservices implementation will consist of many constraints which will vary from project to project and implementation to implementation. The core constraints that nearly all will share may be summarized as "*Highly decoupled, independently deployable, fine-grained components that each control their own independent database, and are grouped by domain and partitioned at the bounded context with communication facilitated by some kind of API interface and running in an environment with high operational automation.*" In essence, seven architectural constraints. Although that is by no means a complete set of constraints for any implementation, it provides a solid foundation.

These architectural constraints have profound implications on the teams, organization, and operational environment. Decomposing a monolithic system into microservices calls for more than untangling code; it requires determining understanding domain boundaries which typically requires an investment into properly exploring, understanding, and defining the business domains by way of the practices prescribed in DDD. This effort, however, is insufficient. The organization's structure and team focus must morph into a domain-aligned structure to better conform to these domains; otherwise, the design will fall victim to Conway's Law. This type of organizational structure is not typical in most software environments ("feature" teams and teams that are focused on a particular technology are more common) and generally only exists as a result of deliberate analysis and change. The Domain Partitioning constraint—where module boundaries are defined by domain boundaries, rather than technical boundaries—requires the organizational constraints of Well-Defined Domains (we must know the domains and their boundaries) and Domain-Aligned Teams (as "*Organizations, who design systems, are constrained to produce designs which are copies of the communication structures of these organizations*").

To achieve a high degree of decoupling of components, many points of coupling are aggressively severed. Where many implementations might opt to reuse code where possible, following the adage of "Don't Repeat Yourself" (DRY),[9] microservices often favor the principle of "Please Repeat Yourself" (PRY) to decouple individual microservices from one another or shared libraries. This practice flies in the face of a career's worth of "best practice" for many developers; consequently, there is a team constraint that development teams must operate at a level of sophistication to understand why the "rules" exist and when they should be broken.

Further constraints dictate that developers must not only produce functional code but must produce it in a manner aligned with the agile principles emphasizing mature testing strategies and a high degree of automation. Often, these are secondary skills in many developers, and adopting these practices will cause team friction. The up-front investment in testing and automation often feels like impediments slowing their "coding flow" or productivity. Without a strong team and organizational commitment to these values, the practices will be short-lived.

Teams must be able to work independent of each other, requiring yet another shift in how software is traditionally built. Teams must define and publish message schemas, API interfaces, and contracts early in the development lifecycle, so other teams focused on building neighboring services may code to that interface in parallel. In mainstream practice, it is much more common for these interfaces and contracts to emerge while the code is being written. However, this practice will introduce frequent blockers for teams that must wait for the other services to be fully developed.

Mature and sophisticated pipelines must be created and managed by development teams for whom such work might be outside of their current core skillset. In short, development teams must embrace the practices and philosophies of DevOps.

[9] Hunt, A. Thomas, D. (1999). *The Pragmatic Programmer: From Journeyman to Master*. Addison-Wesley

Long-term delegation of this work to dedicated "DevOps" teams is a strong indication that the adoption of DevOps has failed and that the wall between "Dev" and "Ops" remains alive and well (except, in this case, "Ops" has been renamed "DevOps," ensuring the organization remains buzzword compliant for a thin veneer of technical sophistication).

Finally, the environment must be one that supports a high degree of operational automation and flexibility. Although with great care such an environment may be constructed using on-prem hardware, cloud providers offer Infrastructure as a Service (IaaS) and Platform as a Service (PaaS) that generally provide better flexibility and capabilities. Again, embracing these necessitates additional skills and practices of developers as much operational automation support must be baked into the microservices themselves. The broader environment must also be one that supports independent, autonomous development by teams.

Architects cannot operate effectively in a vacuum, and, while the underlying business needs fill part of that vacuum, the reality of the teams, organization, and environment must also fill important parts of that void. These team, organizational, and environmental constraints are prerequisites for adopting many of the architectural constraints central to microservices. Because the non-architectural constraints are dependencies on their architectural constraint counterparts, ignoring these non-architectural constraints results in the architecture violating architectural constraints. The result is a loss of key capabilities and the emergence of undesirable system characteristics. Architectural styles are defined by their constraints; remove any constraint and the resulting system will have adopted a different architectural style and perhaps one better avoided if it becomes an anti-style. Just as removing some constraints from the Layered Monolith style results in an anti-style—the Big Ball of Mud—subtracting the independent deployability constraint of microservices also results in an anti-style—the distributed monolith. Remove more and the system becomes the Distributed Big Ball of Mud.

Summary

Unlike architectural constraints, which constrain the degrees of freedom for implementation teams, team, organizational, and environmental constraints constrain the degrees of freedom for the architect. Any architectural constraint that carries dependent constraints of this type put the architect in a quandary. Ultimately, we must either perform the prerequisite work of driving organizational change up front, or they must accept our current reality and derive what may be a suboptimal architectural style when viewed through the lens of a single dimension for the sake of broader fit. At design time, these are truly the only available options.

A suboptimal architecture is never the goal of an architect, but a given set of circumstances may dictate certain compromises. To reiterate what was said in Chapter 1, "*Often it is said architects don't aim to produce the best architecture, just the 'least worst' architecture*," or, as the saying goes, engineering is never about perfect solutions, but rather it involves doing the best with what is available at the time.

Although we often need to become comfortable with designing suboptimal architectures for the sake of holistic fit, it is also important to recognize these compromises need not be permanent. Perhaps the pain an architect might foresee is theoretically avoidable; however, change often only happens when the risk of inaction becomes greater than the risk of action. Ultimately, architectural change and evolution is inevitable—even for "optimal" architectures. Architects must put the project on the best available course and always keep an eye toward the future.

Fortunately, as we shall explore in Section 2, architectural evolution need not be nearly as challenging as conventional wisdom dictates.

CHAPTER 10

Abstract Styles: A New Look at Patterns

> *The main lesson here is that not every problem can be solved at the level of abstraction where it manifests.*
>
> —Michael T. Nygard

We have established in this section that *Architectures Aren't Chosen, They're Designed.* On the surface, this statement might seem to suggest that patterns are irrelevant in this model; however, I do not advocate throwing away the established patterns and reinventing the wheel for many projects. There are many paths to a candidate architecture, and each has their trade-offs. Let us briefly return to the suit metaphor to provide context to how patterns can be selected, designed, and adapted.

First, it must be noted that "fit" (both in suits and architecture) is of the utmost importance. The extent of the fit is proportional to both the care of selection and the amount of tailoring or customization of the garment or its underlying measurements and design. When fit is a secondary concern to time or cost, the most expedient option is to purchase a "ready-to-wear" garment. This essentially means finding the closest fit and rolling with it, as is. We will start with why this is often a suboptimal approach and explore how various levels of tailoring or design can yield an increasingly optimal fit.

M. Carducci, *Mastering Software Architecture*, https://doi.org/10.1007/979-8-8688-0410-6_10

Ready-to-Wear

Ready-to-wear suits come in many sizes, all of which are denoted by just two components—a chest measurement and a height component of "short," "regular," or "long." How do these height modifiers translate to body length, sleeve length, and inseam? It depends on the manufacturer and their base patterns, but these are based on an average of the measurements that fall into the short, regular, and long buckets.

In Todd Rose's book, *The End of Average,*[1] he recounts a story where an increasing number of noncombat aviation incidents and accidents were found to be caused by designing the cockpit of a complex aircraft to fit the "average pilot." Even after putting a policy in place to only recruit pilots that, on paper, fit the average, accidents remained alarmingly high.

> *Using the size data he had gathered from 4,063 pilots, Daniels calculated the average of the ten physical dimensions believed to be most relevant for design, including height, chest circumference and sleeve length. These formed the dimensions of the "average pilot," which Daniels generously defined as someone whose measurements were within the middle 30 per cent of the range of values for each dimension. So, for example, even though the precise average height from the data was five foot nine, he defined the height of the "average pilot" as ranging from five-seven to five-11. Next, Daniels compared each individual pilot, one by one, to the average pilot.*
>
> *Before he crunched his numbers, the consensus among his fellow air force researchers was that the vast majority of pilots would be within the average range on most dimensions. After all, these pilots had already been pre-selected because they appeared to be average sized. (If you were, say, six foot seven, you would never have been recruited in the first place.) The scientists also expected that a sizable number of pilots would be within the average range on all ten dimensions. But even Daniels was stunned when he tabulated the actual number.*
>
> *Zero.*
>
> —Todd Rose, *The End of Average*

[1] Rose, T. *The end of average: Unlocking our potential by embracing what makes us different.* HarperOne 2017

Averages may provide ranges of measurements suggesting generalized fit, but, in any individual case, the probability of a good fit is close to zero. Consequently, if our notation of architecture is simply *selecting* a pattern, the results will not be great. This is the approach we continue to take with traditional pattern-driven architecture. When an architect looks at the relative capabilities of one pattern (such as the Ford/Richards scores), it is naturally assumed that those scores represent the best case for that pattern in practice. In reality, however, those scores simply communicate the base expectations of the pattern in the abstract.

Ultimately, the US Air Force discarded averages as their reference standard and embraced the new guiding principle of *individual fit*. At first blush, manufacturers proclaimed this new philosophy as wildly impractical, bordering on impossible. Eventually, manufacturers uncovered novel approaches that were both inexpensive and easy to implement; they designed cockpits that were easy to tailor to the individual from the baseline. They designed adjustable seats, adjustable foot pedals, adjustable helmet straps and flight suits, providing a foundational design that can be adjusted to optimize for individual fit. To quote Rose's book:

> *Once these and other design solutions were put into place, pilot performance soared, and the U.S. air force became the most dominant air force on the planet. Soon, every branch of the American military published guides decreeing that equipment should fit a wide range of body sizes, instead of standardized around the average.*
>
> —Todd Rose, *The End of Average*

Even ready-to-wear suits can—and should—be tailored (as illustrated in Figure 10-1). The same is true of any predefined architecture pattern. The Tailor-Made model provides practical guidance to architects to perform such tailoring based on the needs and realities of the project, the business, the teams, and the organization. The performance of a candidate architecture will similarly benefit from a philosophy of *individual fit*. This is accomplished by treating the mainstream architecture patterns as *abstract architectural styles*. In other words, an abstract style is one that is—like all architectural styles—defined by a common and well-defined set of architectural constraints. An abstract style, like an abstract class, cannot (or should not) be directly instantiated; rather, it is a blueprint from which the optimal implementation is derived and extended. In the Tailor-Made model, *this is the place for patterns*.

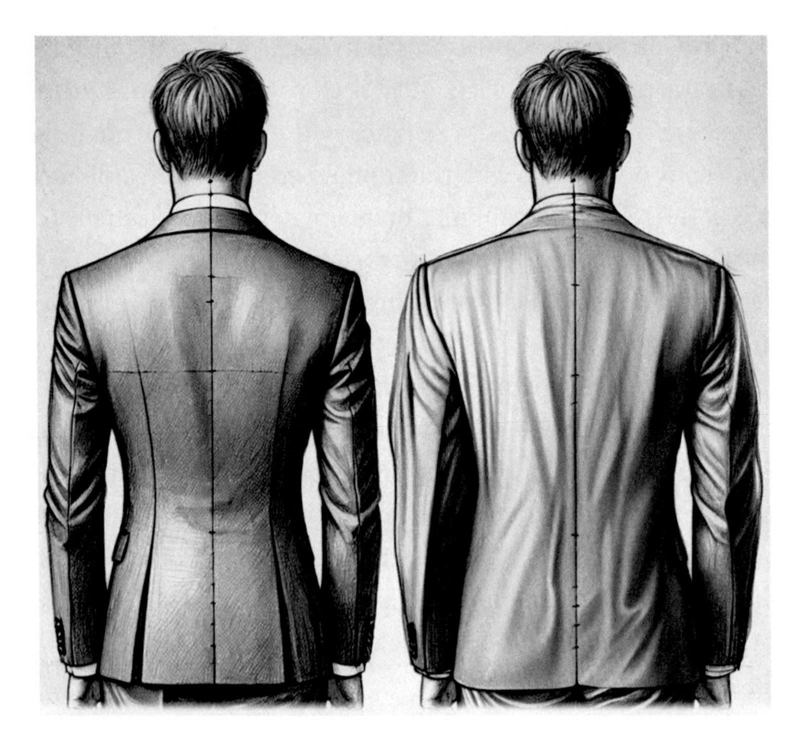

Figure 10-1. *Tailored vs. Ready to Wear*

Tailored Off-the-Rack

A reasonable fit may be achieved by beginning with the closest fit and making some quantity of changes and adjustments to the garment to achieve improved *individual fit* at a low cost. Your author typically wears a tailored instance of a 42S suit. Most base patterns for a 42S suit make assumptions about how the "short" height is composed (legs vs. torso), overall body girth, and sleeve length. Consequently, *my* individual fit typically requires hemming trousers to an inseam length of 30", taking in the waist to around 32" (a 10" *drop*) and taking in the body of the jacket. The result is an inexpensive path to an acceptable fit.

This is the de facto approach to architecture today, albeit with caveats. Architects or developers often begin with pattern selection and, upon deployment, begin to learn all the areas where the architecture is deficient and make multiple adjustments over time. Since these traditional approaches lack the granular controls and detailed design-time feedback of the Tailor-Made model, this process typically requires extensive (and costly) trial and error. This is analogous to purchasing a ready-to-wear suit, wearing it to a function, then returning for tailoring after receiving comments that the suit does not fit very well. It is preferable to tailor the garment or the architecture in the beginning. A much better fit can be achieved at comparable cost by modifying the pattern at design time. This is known in the field as "made-to-measure."

Made-to-Measure

These days, most custom suits follow an approach that optimizes both cost and individual fit. In the same way we begin with a detailed requirements analysis process to identify target fit, the tailor will begin with a more robust consultation process that results in not only significantly improved fit on day one but also provides improved *holistic fit*.

Many measurements are taken, which are used to modify one of several generic patterns. Since the garment is made to order, a closer *holistic fit* may now be realized as the tailor will collaborate with the customer to select from a broader range of fabrics, styles, features, etc.

In most cases, this is the recommended path when following the Tailor-Made model. In essence

- Begin with a standard reference pattern.
- Modify the pattern at design time based on true requirements for fit.
- Work closely with implementation teams to apply further customizations, variances, or implementation guidance, as necessary.
- Build the software.

Made-to-measure architecture provides a much richer set of tools to achieve optimal fit right out of the gate. Of course, once the system is in production, changing and evolving needs will necessitate additional tweaks and tailoring; however, these are typically much smaller in scope and, consequently, typically lower in risk. Notably, while fit inevitably changes over time, a well-designed architecture or suit provides many opportunities and paths for ongoing tailoring which is key for long-term business-value capture.

Made-to-measure architecture provides a balance between individual fit, cost, design effort, and time to production; however, this is not the only path to improved fit. The rarest, most expensive, but most comprehensive approach is bespoke tailoring.

Bespoke Tailoring

There remain a handful of skilled craftspeople in the world who specialize in bespoke tailoring. Unlike made-to-measure, the bespoke process begins from scratch, providing the client with complete control over every detail. Suits made this way will not only fit every contour of the client's body perfectly, but they will also equally fit the client's personality, identity, and environment. This truly holistic fit is a result of the deep collaboration between the tailoring house and the client and the house's precision and attention to detail. The cost of such a holistic fit is high; the process is labor-intensive and expensive.

Holistic fit always begins with understanding the client's needs and requirements. Accordingly, bespoke tailoring begins with a salesperson who collaborates with the client to understand their unique needs and advise as appropriate. The cutter is the architect of the garment, collaborating with both the client and the salesperson to understand the vision and infer unstated requirements. The cutter takes the necessary measurements and, in concert with the requirements, constructs a unique pattern for the suit. The cutter then cuts the fabric according to the pattern. The tailor, who acts as the implementation team, then assembles the garment.

Early fittings are the feedback loops in the construction process. Following the first fitting of the work-in-progress suit, the cutter will disassemble the suit and recut the fabric to refine the fit during construction. These feedback loops are important to validate early assumptions and course correct along the way.

We should strive to approach architecture with the same rigor and utilize feedback loops to validate we are on the right path, even if our approach to architecture more closely resembles made-to-measure or tailored off-the-rack. As for determining when to take a bespoke approach, the answer, unsurprisingly, is "it depends."

Architectural Styles and the Design of Network-Based Architectures[2] introduces the reader to architecture design by constraint. In Chapter 5, Fielding describes and formalizes the *REST Architectural Style*, which is architecture of the World Wide Web.

---

[2] Fielding, R. (2000). *Architectural Styles and the Design of Network-based Software Architectures.* Doctoral dissertation, University of California, Irvine

In the early to mid-1990s, when the Web was still in its formative stages, there were no patterns or well-known solutions for such a system that could scale from one user to billions. There were no patterns that promised the kind of evolvability the Web required. The *REST Architectural Style* was, consequently, a bespoke architecture derived from scratch (or, as Fielding described it, the *null architectural style*) based on the domain problems and requirements of the World Wide Web, expressed in Chapter 4 of the dissertation.

While deriving truly bespoke architecture may be uniquely interesting and challenging, this is rarely necessary. The diversity of software systems running today has led to numerous common problems with known solutions from which we may profit.

Summary

In Chapters 6, 7, and 8, we explored the problems surrounding the current "flat taxonomy of patterns" and how each pattern has devolved into vague umbrella terms that encompass many diverse implementations that share superficial topological similarities. In this section, we aim to remedy this disconnect between terminology and explicit meaning by redefining each of the nine common patterns by their *core constraints*. Remember that constraints, at their core, are named, codified, reusable, architecturally significant decisions capable of both effecting and affecting a system's architecture capabilities. When precisely defined, each pattern becomes an abstract style, making explicit what is often implicit (and potentially overlooked) and providing a valuable starting place for our work. A derived architectural style will thus extend an abstract style with additional or modified constraints as necessary to achieve optimal fit.

As you will see in the upcoming section, not only does this approach reduce risk, improve fit, and ultimately result in true clarity of architectural communication, a *constraint-driven* (or *decision-driven)* approach unlocks an unprecedented path for architectural execution and evolution.

One final note, although the next section is ostensibly about patterns, it is really about the constraints that make up those patterns and elicit their capabilities. Remember, *patterns are not architecture, they are a side effect of architecture*. In the following chapters, as each architectural constraint is first introduced, we will discuss considerations, trade-offs, and implementation details. The constraint descriptions, considerations, and implementation details will form the foundation of your work as you go from defining a style to designing an architecture (a blueprint for a concrete implementation of a style for a given system). As familiar constraints are subsequently referenced in additional styles, rather than repeat the trade-offs and implementation guidance, the chapter where that constraint is first introduced will be referenced.

SECTION 2

Patterns, Abstract Styles, and Architecture As a Continuum

CHAPTER 11

Architecture As a Multifaceted Continuum

> *When you change the way you look at things, the things that you look at change.*
>
> —Eugene Burger

For too long, we have regarded architecture the same way Martin Fowler once observed: *"...things that people perceive as hard to change..."*[1] which has resulted in a great deal of overengineering up front in countless projects, thus introducing significant risk. Mature and sophisticated architectures require equally mature and sophisticated development teams, environments, and organizations. Significant, rapid cultural change is extremely difficult to execute. That said, generally, practitioners see the risk of premature optimization as preferable to a downstream rewrite (where decomposing a monolithic system into a well-factored distributed system can take many years of effort). In truth, however, this is a false dichotomy.

As a practicing, independent software architect, my clients often express a desire to move in the direction of microservices. I am frequently known to respond to such statements with ***"No, you don't want microservices, you want something that you believe microservices will give you. Why don't we talk about what that is, then we can figure out the best way to get there."***

There are many architectural capabilities that microservices promise, all of which are a consequence of the style's underlying constraints. If a system requires any subset of those capabilities, typically only a corresponding subset of the constraints is required.

[1] Fowler, M. (2003). Who Needs an Architect? *IEEE Computer Society*

M. Carducci, *Mastering Software Architecture*, https://doi.org/10.1007/979-8-8688-0410-6_11

Looking at architecture as a multifaceted continuum will illuminate new evolutionary paths. Change becomes much less daunting, and a promise of increased architectural agility materializes as a result.

Agile Architecture

> *Once you let go of the fantasy of software development as delivering what the customer wants, and embrace the reality of software development as helping them to figure that out, it gets a lot easier*
>
> —Jason Gorman

The Agile Manifesto grew from repeated confirmation that all software begins as a hypothesis. When we blindly accept a hypothesis as fact, we rob ourselves of the opportunity to confirm our assumptions. Teams invest significant effort in the direction of unquestioned assumptions and untested hypotheses. It is only when we begin to get real feedback on *working software* that we learn if our efforts produced value or waste. This late-stage feedback will often shatter our assumptions and incinerate development budgets. Agile approaches, in their purest form, center on setting up feedback loops to quickly determine what is value, what is waste, and how development should pivot based on feedback.

We tend to think about agility in terms of product evolution. However, if the product and market are evolving, so too are the necessary architectural capabilities. We tend to think about *overall* agility as a product of design. Martin Fowler expressed this very well in his *Design Stamina Hypothesis*[2] illustrated in Figure 11-1.

[2] Fowler, M. (2007). *The Design Stamina Hypothesis*. Retrieved from: `https://martinfowler.com/bliki/DesignStaminaHypothesis.html`

Figure 11-1. *The Design-Payoff Pseudo-Graph*

Fowler's pseudo-graph illustrates how *"putting effort into the design of your software improves the stamina of your project, allowing you to go faster for longer"*; however, this is only a high-level illustration, leaving the reader to determine what is "good design." If Fowler's hypothesis is correct, it would appear our choices are "no design" (such as the *Big Ball of Mud Style* described in Chapter 12) and "good design" which could arguably be *any* abstract or intermediary styles described later in this section. Moreover, like features in a software system, the definition of "good" changes over time. Ultimately, any notion of "good design" is elusive, subjective, and mercurial. As a result, architecture efforts either frequently fail or fail to reach their true potential.

Following a multi-year, root-cause analysis, I have uncovered common themes. In the order I have typed them, these partial or total failures are often caused by some combination of

- The wrong pattern
- The wrong capabilities
- The right capabilities, but in the wrong measure
- Architecture decisions incompatible with the realities of the organization
- Communication failures
- Leadership failures
- Premature optimization

Notably, this list seems to parallel many of the problems the Agile Manifesto sought to address.

It is okay to outgrow architecture—As long as you know when and how to evolve it.

When to Evolve Architecture

Architecture should evolve when you can show that the system no longer meets the needs of the business or that the change will otherwise materialize meaningful and concrete business value. The analysis tools introduced in Chapter 4 and the metrics introduced in Chapter 5 arm you with tools to make these determinations.

Most practitioners only acknowledge outgrown architecture after there has been a period of pain; this is human nature. Recognizing this early is key to a project's successful growth. As a system's architecture becomes more sophisticated and capable, the underlying constraints make increasing demands on the environment, teams, and organizations. Some constraints, such as domain-driven module partitioning or switching from monolithic to distributed component granularity, can come with significant cost and/or organizational friction. It is important to undertake such efforts only when there is a clear, net-positive return on investment from the business perspective. This suggests that there is more than one "payoff line," and, more importantly, not every project will reach every payoff line, nor will every project follow the same trajectory. An example of a possible trajectory and evolution can be seen in Figure 11-2.

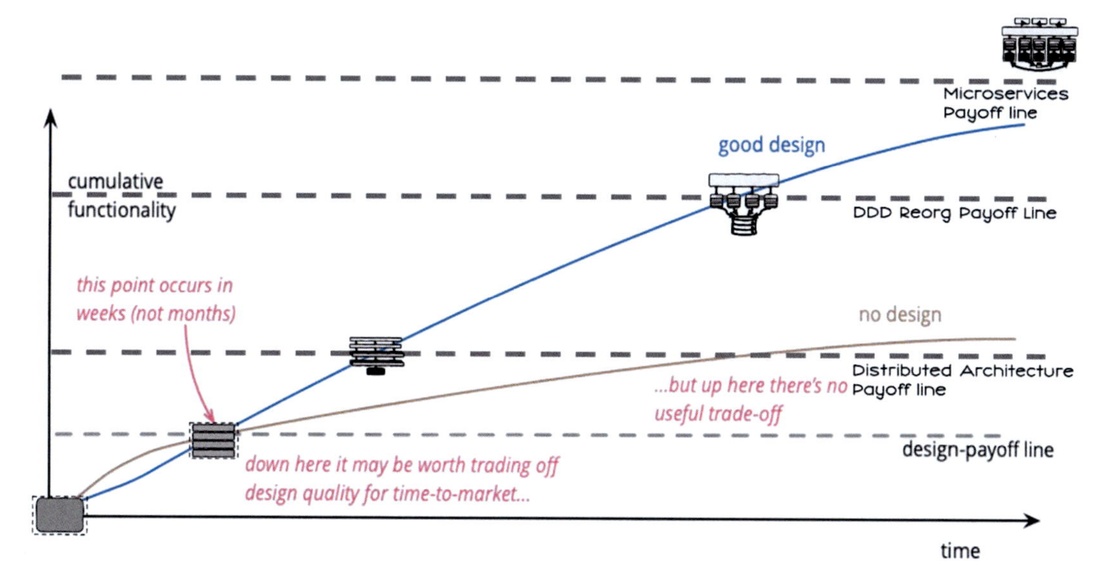

Figure 11-2. *Multiple Payoff Lines for Architecture Evolution*

We can see that a more data-driven, agile approach will reduce risk, waste, and provide clarity around the subjective definition of "good" over time. Far too often, architectural evaluation only takes place up front and after the fact. This is insufficient; architecture is often as much about monitoring as it is about design.

Both architectural oversight of the system's components' alignment with the prescribed constraints and iteratively reviewing runtime feedback to ensure ongoing fit should be a near-constant activity.

How to Evolve Architecture

The false dichotomy of *overengineer now or rewrite later* is a consequence of the prevailing pattern-based way of thinking. Pattern-driven architecture suggests the capabilities of each pattern are static, and changing capabilities will require changing patterns. Realizing the truth that patterns are not a set of discrete options but rather waypoints along a vast, multifaceted continuum of possibilities annihilates this notion. Constraints are atomic primitives that comprise architectural styles and induce architectural capabilities. If a monolithic system is insufficiently evolvable and agile, in addition to wholesale pattern replacement, we can individually apply relevant constraints from a more agile style (e.g., microservices) to increase agility. Every addition or modification of constraints moves the system along the architecture continuum.

The architecture of a system is not, in and of itself, difficult to change. The evolution of one architecture style to another through mindful addition or modification of architectural constraints gives us powerful tools. However, all constraints are not created equal. Some architectural constraints are trivial to change and adapt to while others remain enormously difficult. One of the more difficult constraints to change is that of how module boundaries are defined. The Layered Monolith Abstract Style, described in the next chapter, prescribes module boundaries defined by a technical area (UI, API, business logic, persistence, etc.) producing large, horizontal slices of a system. Each layer encapsulates a technical concern, offering a measure of abstraction, yet coupling *within* a layer is typically out of scope from the standpoint of architecture. This coupling becomes enormously problematic when attempting to switch to a domain-based module partitioning strategy, which prescribes dividing the system into vertical slices that entirely encapsulate a subdomain, or bounded context (depending on prescribed granularity).

DDD Definitions

Domain In the realm of Domain-Driven Design (DDD) and software architecture, a *domain* refers to a core area of expertise or business activity that your software is designed to address. This provides a conceptual space where your software solutions are applied to solve specific problems. For example, in an ecommerce application, one domain encompasses everything related to online shopping, such as product listings, orders, payments, and customer interactions. Understanding each domain deeply is crucial because it guides how you design, build, and evolve your software.

Subdomain Within a larger domain, *subdomains* are distinct areas of functionality or expertise that can be isolated and understood independently. They represent smaller, more manageable pieces of an overall domain. In our ecommerce example, subdomains might include inventory management, user authentication, and shipping logistics. Each subdomain has its own set of rules, logic, and complexities. Identifying subdomains helps in breaking down a problem space into more digestible parts, making it easier to design and implement solutions.

Bounded Context A *bounded context* is a crucial concept in DDD that defines boundaries within which a particular model is valid. It is a specific, well-delineated part of a domain where a certain set of concepts, rules, and relationships apply consistently. Each bounded context has its own *ubiquitous language*—a set of terms and definitions understood uniformly by all stakeholders within that context. For instance, the term "order" might mean different things in the context of inventory management vs. customer service. By clearly defining bounded contexts, you prevent the confusion and complexity that arises from overlapping or conflicting interpretations of the same terms and concepts.

These definitions help streamline communication and design processes, ensuring everyone on the team has a clear, shared understanding of each domain and its subdomains. Consequently, it can be helpful to build a dictionary/glossary of ubiquitous language terms within a bounded context.

Decomposing a technically partitioned system into subdomain modules or bounded contexts is a tedious and expensive process. As you shall soon see, however, this is not the only way to decompose a monolith. The path to *low-friction* architectural evolution involves introducing new architectural constraints or changing the constraints that are easier to change. With each change to the prescribed constraints, a new architectural style emerges. Once again, architecture is a multifaceted continuum and not a finite set of discrete choices that demand major rewrites or rework to switch from one to another.

Moving along your system's continuum in small steps results in tractable architectural evolution. However, the next steps available to us—and their subsequent adoption effort magnitude—will depend on the system's current position within the continuum, as defined by the current architectural style with its underlying constraints. This is true whether the design exists in production or on paper. Consequently, understanding both current and anticipated future needs, combined with the Tailor-Made model, will arm you with the ability to design for the optimum fit now while leaving the door open to ongoing architectural evolution.

In short, you will be able to clearly see multiple paths of evolution to align architecture to current or future needs. Moreover, this new perspective enables deliberate and mindful choices.

Summary

When we view architecture not as a finite set of discrete patterns but as inestimable possibilities within a continuum, the prospect of designing an architecture that is optimal for the current point in time with sufficient flexibility and evolvability for ongoing tailoring is now in reach. We no longer need to overengineer up front which often introduces significant risk and friction to a project. Additionally, this model enables us to practice architecture with a greater degree of precision and reliability, all while reducing risk.

In the subsequent chapters in this section, we will look at hypothetical systems and, through the introduction, addition, and modification of constraints, derive nine common patterns as new abstract styles while deriving “intermediary” styles that enhance each pattern along the way. You will understand the “how” and “why” behind each constraint along with its impact on capabilities and inherent trade-offs. Finally, you will see the Tailor-Made model in action.

CHAPTER 12

The Layered Monolith Abstract Style

> *With the growing emphasis on microservices and other distributed architectures, there is this idea that monoliths are inherently bad. 'Monolith' is not a pejorative; there are many monoliths that are well designed. Moreover, not every system should be a distributed system.*
>
> —Jeff Scott Brown

The humble layered monolith, an architecture that has stood the test of time, remains relevant and popular to this day. Variations of this style are known by different names. The "Clean Architecture"[1] describes a variant of this style that follows the structured, modular, testable, and maintainable approach to system design this style prescribes. The "Onion Architecture"[2] is another variation, with its choice of name a reflection of the system's composition of layers, with each layer depending only on the layers beneath it. Even the "Hexagonal Architecture"[3] (alternatively named "Ports and Adapters") can describe a variation of this style.

Many software projects, in the absence of a prescribed architecture, naturally gravitate to this style as a sensible starting point for modularizing and organizing the codebase. For this reason, architects might refer to this style as "the de facto architecture."

In general, this style and its numerous variations are widely understood, inexpensive, easy to implement, easy to deploy, and offer reasonable testability and maintainability. Unlike many of the styles that will follow, this style (and certain other monolithic styles)

---

[1] Martin, R. (2017). *Clean Architecture: A Craftsman's Guide to Software Structure and Design*. Pearson

[2] Palermo, J. (2008). *The Onion Architecture.* Jeffreypalermo.com

[3] Cockburn, A. (2005). *Hexagonal Architecture.* Alistair.cockburn.us

M. Carducci, *Mastering Software Architecture*, https://doi.org/10.1007/979-8-8688-0410-6_12

lends itself well to offline operation which can be helpful for systems that must continue operation in environments with tenuous network availability. Examples of these types of environments include—but are not limited to—spacecraft (e.g., satellites, probes, and even manned spacecraft), commercial aircraft transport, remote field operations, military applications, cargo shipping, remote scientific infrastructure (e.g., weather stations in places like Antarctica or mid oceanic buoys), and disaster response where communications are likely to be intermittent at best.

Like all abstract styles, there exist countless minor—and major—variations in production today, with the monolithic component topology being the single unifying attribute. Consequently, developers and architects often erroneously conflate this style with the Big Ball of Mud. The flat taxonomy strikes again.

To draw a contrast between the titular abstract style of this chapter and the Big Ball of Mud Style, we will begin by defining the latter. From this foundation, we will incrementally derive abstract and intermediary styles through addition and modification of constraints over the chapters that follow in this section.

The Big Ball of Mud Style

> *A BIG BALL OF MUD is haphazardly structured, sprawling, sloppy, duct-tape and bailing wire, spaghetti code jungle. We've all seen them. Their code shows unmistakable signs of unregulated growth, and repeated, expedient repair. Information is shared promiscuously among distant elements of the system, often to the point where nearly all the important information becomes global or duplicated. The overall structure of the system may never have been well defined. If it was, it may have eroded beyond recognition. Programmers with a shred of architectural sensibility shun them. Only those who are unconcerned about architecture, and, perhaps, are comfortable with the inertia of the day-to-day chore of patching the holes in these failing dikes, are content to work on such systems.*
>
> —Brian Foote and Joseph Yoder

The Big Ball of Mud[4] is an architectural style characterized by few architectural constraints. It is a free-for-all where anything goes. The absence of any prescribed architectural constraints results in a system that exhibits few architectural capabilities

(Figure 12-1). The Big Ball of Mud abstract style is defined by only two architectural constraints (both of which are implicit, not prescribed). They are

- Monolithic Component Granularity
- Monolithic Deployment Granularity

Breaking down this style by capabilities of key interest reveals the following.

Abstraction

The lack of architectural constraints defining this abstract style results in zero abstraction. UI concerns, data access, and business logic may comingle. Abstraction is **Extremely Low**.

Affordability

The initial cost of developing a Big Ball of Mud is low. Over time, however, the lack of structure, testability, maintainability, and scaling overhead will significantly increase total cost of ownership. These forces exist in tension with one another. The net result of these forces is an affordability quality that is **Below Average**.

Agility

The lack of any kind of structure or any prescribed modularity results in a system that is enormously difficult and risky to change, let alone change quickly in response to market demands. It is often extremely challenging to locate all the areas in the code that must change, and, without clear interfaces and interaction contracts, it is even more difficult to predict where regression may occur. Agility is **Extremely Low**.

[4] Foote, B., & Yoder, J. (1997). *Big Ball of Mud.* Presented at the 4th Conference on Patterns, Languages of Programs (PLoP)

Deployability

The monolithic component granularity results in a straightforward deployment process. Since the entire system is deployed all at once, in a single step, little—if any—additional work is necessary. The lack of constraints defining this style, however, introduces other challenges surrounding deployment confidence, patching, and deployability at scale. Deployability of such a system is **Average**.

Elasticity

Although many modern hosting environments provide an auto-scaling option that will respond to bursts in demand, all monolithic architectures exhibit weaker-than-average elasticity. A sudden spike in demand that triggers auto-scaling will, ideally, allow requests to be load balanced to the new instance right away.

Large, monolithic codebases often exhibit a slower start time due to the overhead of loading the application, performing Just-In-Time (JIT) compilation, processing annotations at startup, and other startup/warm-up tasks. Start times are measured in seconds (often dozens of seconds), and, during this time, some number of requests will typically time out. Scaling an entire monolith in response to demand provides a very blunt tool; the entire system must be scaled even when the burst in demand is very tightly scoped to a smaller subset of functionality.

Finally, the lack of constraints will often result in a system that is highly stateful which results in additional complexity in load balancing requests. While a monolith can usually demonstrate a degree of elasticity, the overall elasticity of this style is **Very Low**.

Evolvability

The lack of structure and abstraction results in a high degree of coupling across the entire codebase. The code is often highly *connascent*. Connascence is a software quality metric developed by Meilir Page-Jones[5] that measures complexity caused by dependency relationships. Two components are connascent if a change in one would require the other to be modified to maintain the overall correctness of the system.

[5] Page-Jones, M. *Comparing Techniques by Means of Encapsulation and Connascence*, Communications of the ACM, Volume 35, Issue 9, 1992

Changes become increasingly difficult and risky with this style. The overall evolvability of this style is **Extremely Low**.

Fault Tolerance

Another aspect of monolithic architectures in general, and poorly factored monoliths specifically, is a low degree of fault tolerance. In most cases, the entire system is either up or down, with little room in between. The lack of modularity inherent to this style, which precludes any form of bulkheads which might arrest cascading failures, compounds this problem. Furthermore, as mentioned in the section on elasticity, stateful systems introduce complexity when attempting to fail traffic over to a healthy instance. The overall fault tolerance of this style is **Very Low**.

Integration

The ad hoc and haphazard approach to building a Big Ball of Mud results in no well-defined interfaces necessary to improve the capability of integration. Integration might be possible, but APIs are typically inconsistent, incomplete, and the lack of strong interfaces and abstraction results in APIs that often introduce breaking changes. The overall integration of this style is **Below Average**.

Performance

Monolithic architectures generally exhibit reasonable performance owing to code invocation taking place on the stack rather than over the network. Abstractions will often trade performance for structure and modularity; thus, removing these more generalized interfaces in favor of tight coupling may further modestly improve performance. The ceiling of performance will often be governed by the combination of resources on the host machine and the required resources for your application. The challenges with scaling will limit overall performance. The performance of this style is **Above Average**.

Scalability

As we established in the section on elasticity, a monolith *can* scale. One way to accomplish this is by *scaling up* the hosting environment, a *vertical* scaling operation to increase the total amount of resources available to an instance of the system. Additionally, a monolith may be *scaled out*, a *horizontal* scaling operation accomplished by spinning up additional instances of the system. As you have already seen, the mechanism for scaling—loading the entire system in a second instance—is blunt. Moreover, in the absence of other constraints, load balancing across instances can be challenging. The scalability of this style is **Low**.

Simplicity

The initial development of a Big Ball of Mud asks little of a developer; write whatever code you want and put it wherever you feel like. The lack of governing constraints makes the act of writing code simple. However, the fact remains that any kind of maintenance and evolution will become increasingly challenging over time. This offsets overall simplicity. The complexity of this style has a nonlinear relationship with the code volume. Doubling the application's codebase may increase the complexity by parabolic or hyperbolic rates. Consequently, the overall simplicity of this style is **Below Average**.

Testability

The high degree of coupling, the lack of modularity, interfaces, and abstraction result in a system that is incredibly difficult to test. Little—if any—functionality can be tested in isolation. Typically, every change will require a comprehensive regression test, encompassing many potential code paths. Unstructured and ungoverned codebases often have exceedingly high *cyclomatic complexity*. Cyclomatic complexity is a metric that quantifies the number of linearly independent code paths through the source code.[6] Excessive use of branching statements will negatively impact cyclomatic complexity and will often increase the potential code paths beyond what can be manually tested (or even known). The testability of this style is **Extremely Low**.

Workflow

While any system can model and implement business workflows, this style offers few paths to orchestrate such a workflow resulting in a preference for hardcoded

[6] McCabe, T. (1976). *A Complexity Measure.* IEEE Transactions on Software Engineering SE-2

implementations that often lack observability and flexibility. The workflow capability of this style is **Below Average**.

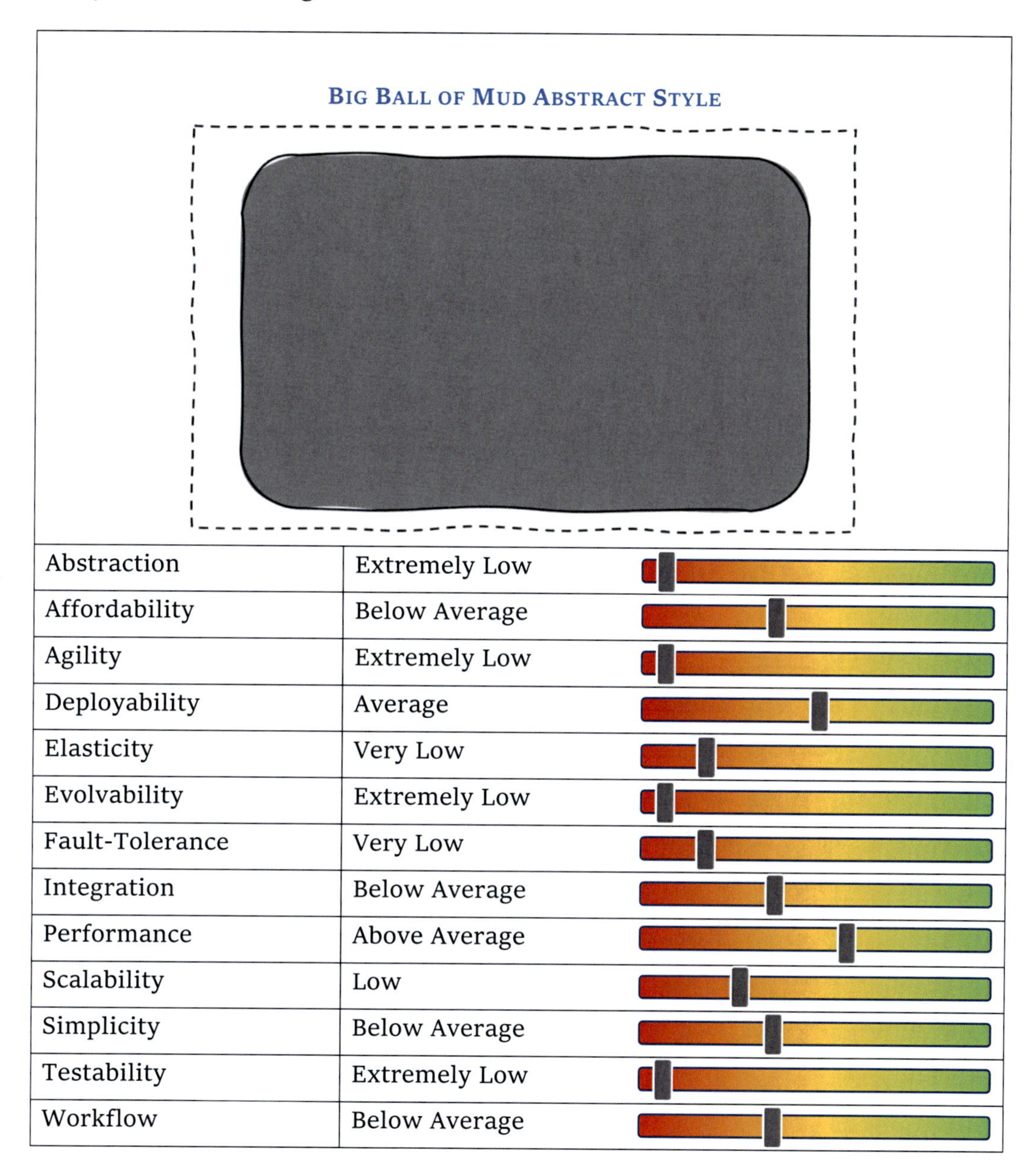

Abstraction	Extremely Low
Affordability	Below Average
Agility	Extremely Low
Deployability	Average
Elasticity	Very Low
Evolvability	Extremely Low
Fault-Tolerance	Very Low
Integration	Below Average
Performance	Above Average
Scalability	Low
Simplicity	Below Average
Testability	Extremely Low
Workflow	Below Average

Figure 12-1. *Architectural Capabilities of the Big Ball of Mud*

The Semi-structured Big Ball of Mud Style

The Big Ball of Mud Style has few strengths and many weaknesses. It may be suitable for a simple system that exhibits very low code volatility and runtime requirements. It may be equally suitable for a proof of concept, but be cautious of business pressure to quickly release a proof of concept as a production system. The capabilities of such an architecture begin to change when you define additional rules for the system in the form of additional architectural constraints.

We can derive a new architectural style by extending the defining constraints to include a degree of *separation of concerns*. For example, let us separate the UI from the rest of the application. Since the underlying constraints have changed, we now have a new architectural style, the Semi-structured Big Ball of Mud Style (Figure 12-2), defined by the following constraints:

- Monolithic Component Granularity
- Monolithic Deployment Granularity
- (Limited) Separation of Concerns

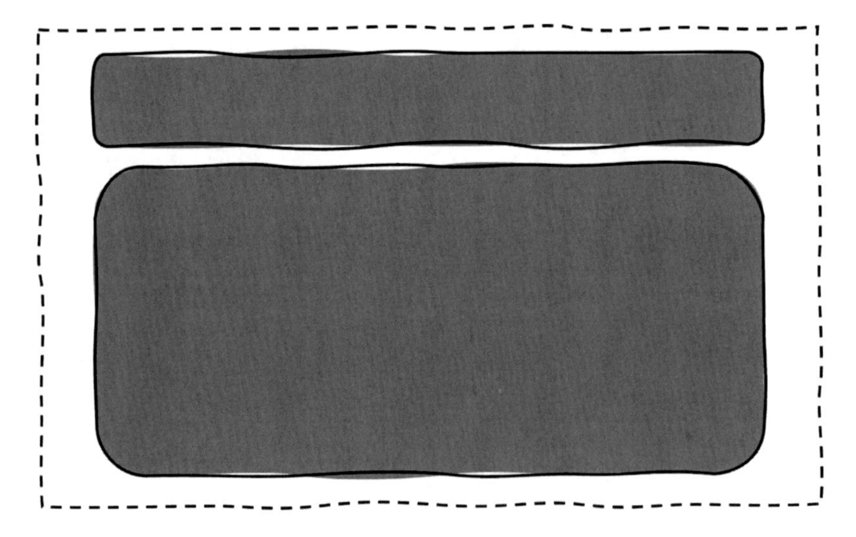

Figure 12-2. *The Semi-structured Big Ball of Mud Style*

This additional constraint will modestly improve total cost of ownership, evolvability, simplicity, and testability. The only perceptible improvement on our scale of extremely low to extremely high occurs with testability (which now scores **Low**). If there is a data storage component to this system, we might prescribe some form of shared data persistence such as a *shared database*.

The Semi-structured, DB-Backed, Big Ball of Mud Style

By prescribing a shared, persistent storage mechanism such as a relational database, there is an additional separation of concerns that takes place further improving simplicity. The database exposes a standard interface and offers possibilities to perform certain tasks (such as joining records) closer to the data itself which will often reduce bandwidth, I/O, and computation cost (improving total cost of ownership and performance). Stored procedures can be defined independently of the application code which can improve maintainability, performance, and potentially testability. The **Semi-structured, DB-Backed, Big Ball of Mud Style** (Figure 12-3) is defined by the following constraints:

- Monolithic Component Granularity
- Monolithic Deployment Granularity
- Separation of Concerns
- Shared Database

A Word on Databases

While virtually all databases provide similar functionality (the ability to store and retrieve data using a standardized query language and interface), they do not all offer similar architectural capabilities. NoSQL databases such as MongoDB are generally easier to scale out as structure naturally lends itself to sharding—distributing data across multiple nodes—while this is generally more difficult with relational databases. NoSQL databases can also offer improved raw query speed as many queries do not require joins to retrieve a representation of a complete object. This does not mean that NoSQL databases are objectively superior to relational databases, only that the trade-offs are different. Relational databases were not created to simply optimize storage cost (which was admittedly quite high when Ed Codd first created the relational paradigm[7]), but rather, they were designed to embrace the reality that many data entities are inherently related. By decoupling shared relations through the process of database normalization, the relational database provides better consistency with less overall overhead to keep state consistent.

The choice of database type will depend not only on the required architectural capabilities of the overall system or component but also on the shape of the data. Inherently relational entities will often benefit from a normalized, relational model, whereas entities that have few—if any—logical relations will perform better in document or object databases. Other systems will benefit from key-value stores.

The lines that separate these different database types have been steadily blurring. NoSQL databases increasingly offer join capabilities, and many modern relational databases can not only be denormalized as required but are also progressively becoming multi-model. A multi-model database can comprise of relational tables, JSON object stores, graphs, and more, all stored within a single Database Management System (DBMS). These discrete storage models will often interact seamlessly.

Choice of database technology depends on the shape of the data, storage and hosting costs, licensing costs, team or organizational skills, and the required degree of identified architectural capabilities. In short, it depends.

---

[7] Codd, E. F. *A Relational Model of Data for Large Shared Data Banks*, IBM Research Laboratory, 1970

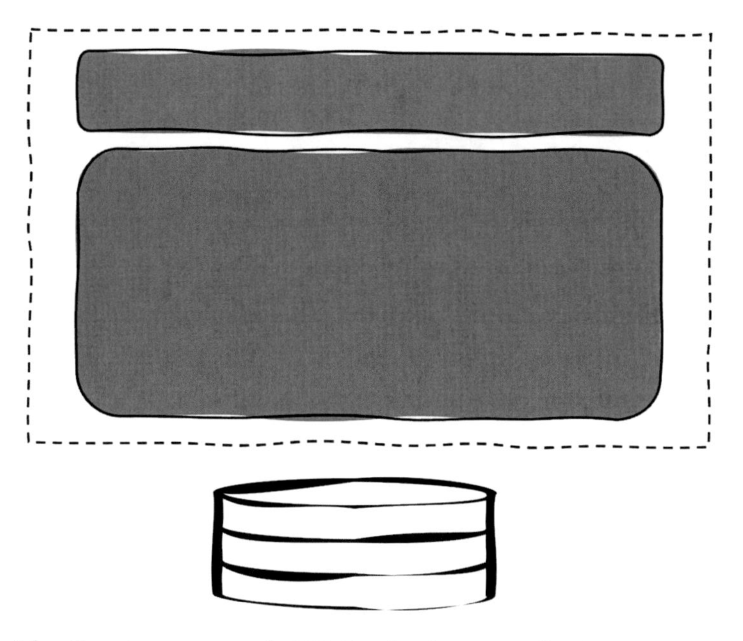

Figure 12-3. *The Semi-structured, DB-Backed, Big Ball of Mud Style*

The **Semi-structured, DB-Backed, Big Ball of Mud Style** offers **Low** *testability* (an improvement over the **Very Low** testability of the Big Ball of Mud), **Average** *performance*, **Average** *affordability*, and **Above Average** *simplicity*. The next phase of evolution of this style requires replacing the remaining ball of mud component with something a little more structured. By adding two additional constraints, we arrive at the **Layered Monolith Abstract Style**.

The Layered Monolith Abstract Style

Escaping the **Big Ball of Mud** family of architectural styles begins by prescribing some form of modularity. The **Layered Monolith Abstract Style** (Figure 12-4) prescribes the layered system constraint. The layered system constraint dictates a hierarchical organization of the system, with each layer providing services to the layer above it and serving as a client to the layer below. The precise boundaries of these layers are controlled by the technical partitioning constraint which dictates that layer boundaries are defined by technical area. In total, the defining constraints of the **Layered Monolith Abstract Style** are

- Monolithic Component Granularity
- Monolithic Deployment Granularity

- Separation of Concerns
- Shared Database
- Layered System
- Technical Partitioning

It is through the composition of constraints that we move from the *accidental architecture* of the **Big Ball of Mud Style** to a deliberately designed abstract style that represents a formal, foundational definition of the **Layered Monolith** pattern. However, as we explore this abstract style, we will derive many concrete styles by exploring the impact of additional constraints.

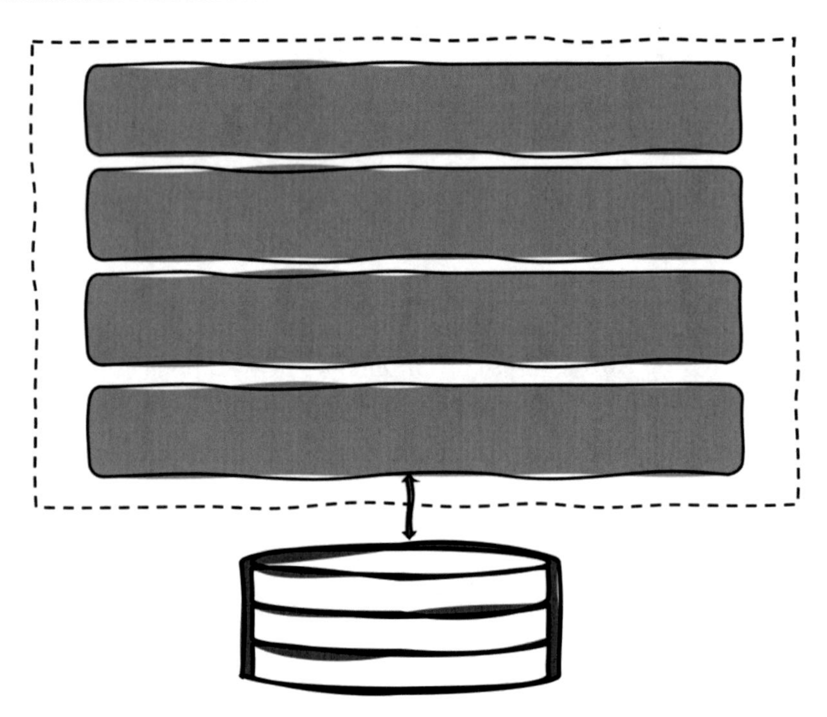

Figure 12-4. *The Layered Monolith Abstract Style*

This pattern, as an abstract style, acts as one of our primary starting points for a tailored or made-to-measure architectural style designed to fit the business, the project, the teams, the organization, and the environment holistically. Let us take a deeper look at this foundational, abstract style.

Inside the Monolith

In this style, the first layer of modularity occurs in the form of coarse-grained layers that provide both functional cohesion and clear roles and responsibility models (Figure 12-5). For example, a UI-focused team might own the presentation layer, while DBAs or DB developers might own the persistence and database layers. One or more backend teams might own the services or business logic layers. From an organizational standpoint, this structure aligns with many extant organizational structures. This is important as Conway's Law dictates that "*Organizations that produce systems, are constrained to produce designs which are copies of the communication structures of these organizations.*"[8] In other words, regardless of the architecture we design, we will ship the org chart. For organizations structured around technical teams or feature teams, we must either design architectures that mirror that structure or we need to change the structure of the organization to mirror the design. This is an example of a nonnegotiable *organizational constraint.*

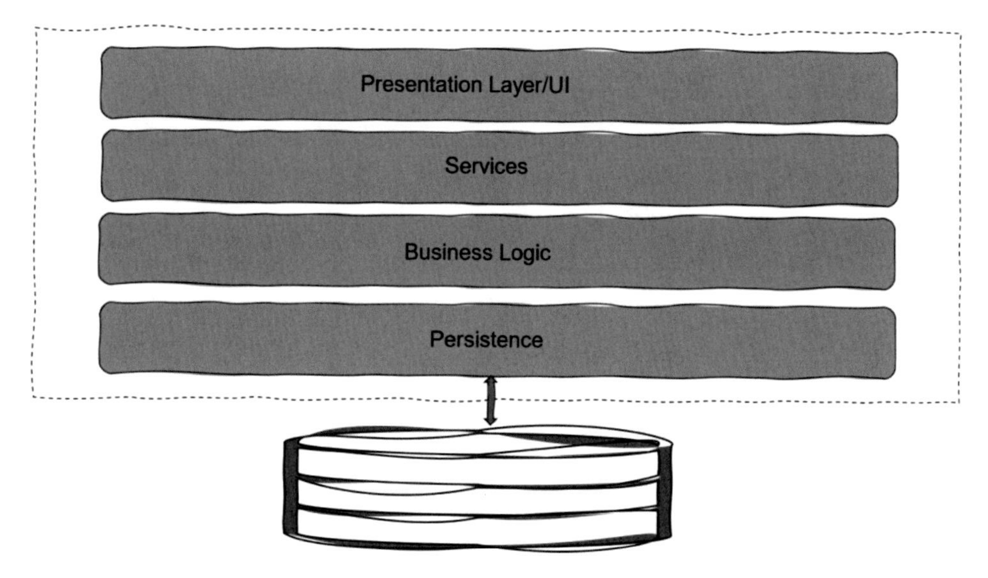

Figure 12-5. *Example Layers Inside the Monolith*

Inside this monolith, the number and nature of the layers is often an implementation detail which the architecture may, or may not, prescribe. Layers may be combined (e.g., business logic and persistence) or may be further decomposed in a manner consistent with additional architectural constraints (when prescribed) or by developer preference

[8] Conway, M. E. (1968). How do Committees Invent? *Datamation,* 14(5), 28–31.

(when left as a decision for the implementation teams). For example, by including a Model-View-Controller (MVC) constraint, the presentation layer may look like Figure 12-6.

The Presentation Layer

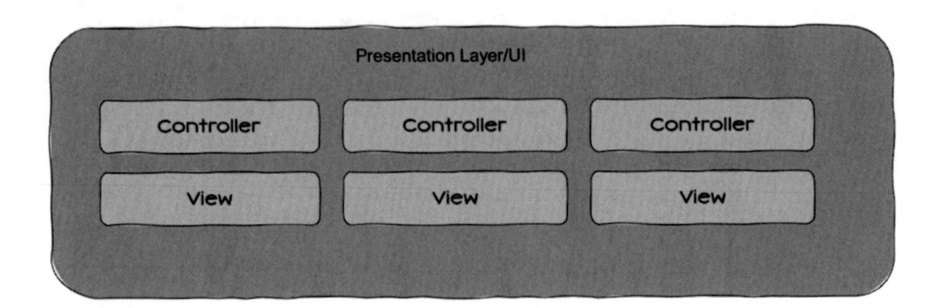

Figure 12-6. *Illustration of an MVC Presentation Layer*

In the MVC-Layered-Monolith style, the presentation layer will contain controllers which marshal user requests and views that present responses. One key aspect of this style is the abstraction afforded by these layers; the controllers and views do not need to know anything about the database, just how to handle requests and format responses. This layered approach has the added benefit of decomposing a complex application into smaller, approachable components.

The addition of the MVC constraint prescribes additional modularity within the presentation layer which improves testability, agility, maintainability, abstraction, evolvability, and simplicity.

The MVC pattern and its descendants are not the only way to design the presentation layer. In a forms-style application, the UI layer is comprised of forms and the "code-behind" the forms (Figure 12-7).

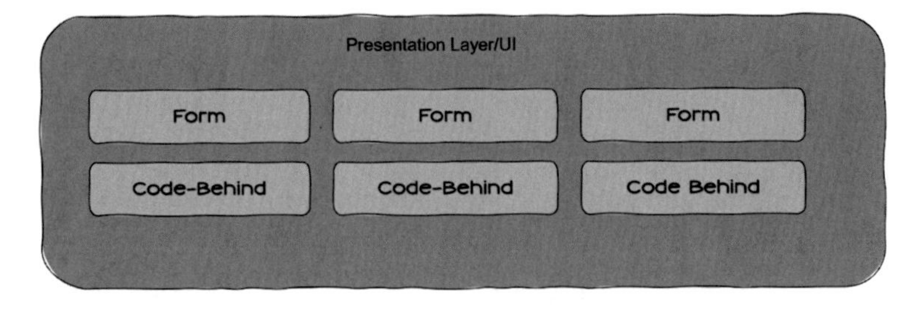

Figure 12-7. *Illustration of a Forms-Style Presentation Layer*

The entire presentation layer can also be sliced off the monolith, which is accomplished by prescribing the Client/Server constraint in a concrete/derived style. In this tailored style, the exposed layer on the backend is typically some sort of API (which may be yet another prescribed architectural constraint) and a standalone client which might be in the form of a fat-client application, a native mobile app, or a web-based single-page application (SPA). These are all derived variations of the abstract style forming a new concrete style. While there is significant ambiguity attached to a generic pattern label, a defined architectural style is precise and leaves little room for misunderstanding.

The Services Layer

The purpose of the services layer is to expose defined use cases to the presentation layer while providing an abstraction between the presentation and business logic layers. This layer may be a mini ball of mud, or it might be extremely well factored, with modular business services that are typically grouped by entity or domain workflow. An example depiction of this can be seen in Figure 12-8.

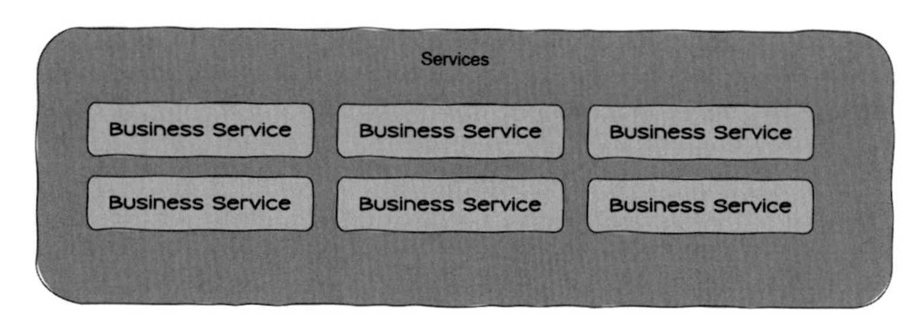

***Figure 12-8.** Illustration of an Example Services Layer*

The services layer typically provides specific domain or subdomain workflows through the composition of more general business logic components, which reside in the next layer, the business logic layer.

The Business Logic Layer

As we traverse down the layers of the onion, we get closer to the application core, this time focusing on the business logic (Figure 12-9). Isolating the business logic from the services layer allows for better reuse of business logic modules. Once again, generally business logic components are broken up by business entity.

In theory, as business logic components evolve, their module boundaries provide natural bulkheads to scope changes to a single component. They might be shared across other applications or exist as standalone modules within the system. There are trade-offs to both approaches. Reusable business logic components tend to require broad consensus and will often involve some amount of coupling with the consumers of these components. This will introduce challenges in attempting to evolve a single business logic component shared across multiple systems without introducing some kind of breaking change. Building truly general interfaces can often impact overall efficiency of the system since these core components are not optimized for any specific implementation. Notably, it is also possible to use a combination of custom components and shared components (Figure 12-9). Custom interfaces or optimized business logic components might simply extend generic, shared interfaces or components.

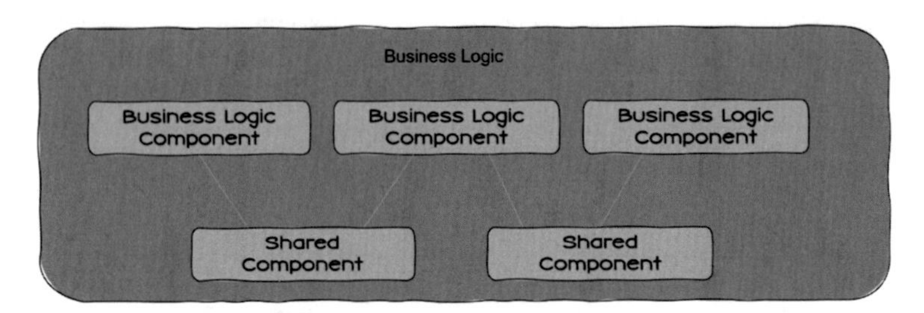

Figure 12-9. *Illustration of an Example Business Logic Layer with Shared Components*

As a general guideline, business logic exists independent of data storage concerns, which suggests another layer, the persistence layer.

The Persistence Layer

This layer is responsible for connecting the application to the underlying storage system. The classic depiction of the layered monolith architecture (Figure 12-5) suggests this is the innermost—or lowest—layer of the system. However, the mental model afforded by the hexagonal architecture suggests the core is the business entities, surrounded by the business logic, with the UI being a user-facing "port" (with controllers as the "adapters") on the surface. Likewise, the persistence layer being a technology-facing "port" with the persistence layer being its respective "adapter" (Figure 12-10). In the depiction below, the left half represents user-facing ports, and the right half represents technology-facing ports.

The key to the "ports and adapters" approach to modeling a system lies in dividing a system into several loosely coupled, interchangeable components. The ports represent where these components are "plugged in" to the system, and the adapters provide the standard interface, which powers the subsequent interchangeability. The Layered, Hexagonal, and Onion models are similar but different ways of describing, depicting, and reasoning about a system.

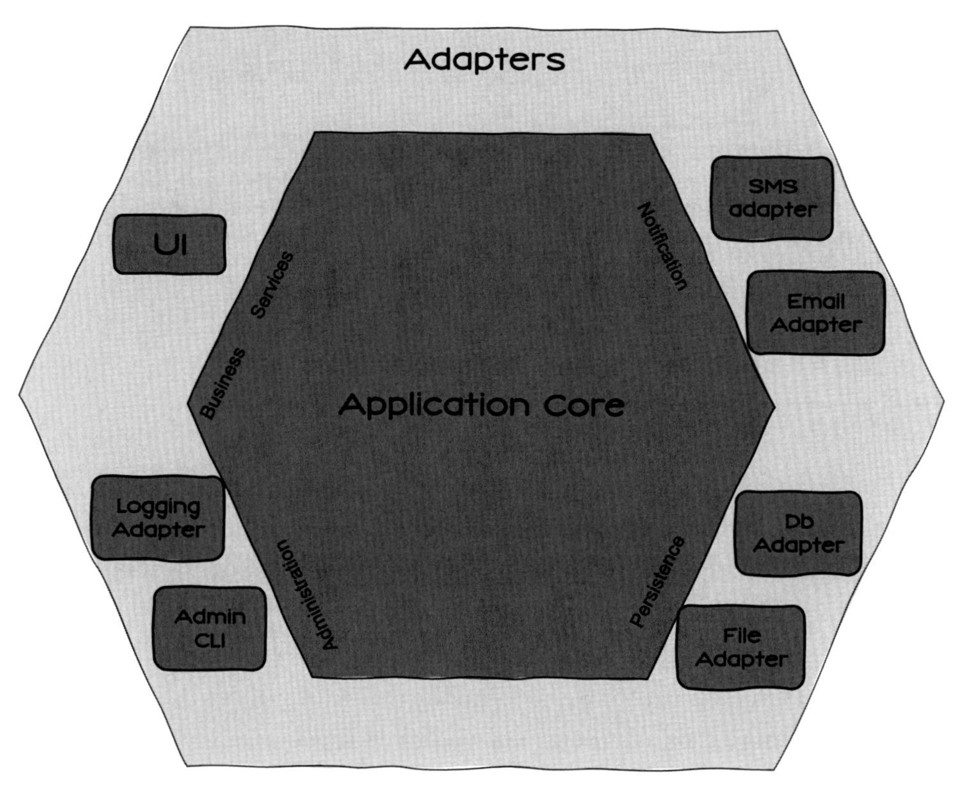

Figure 12-10. *Layered Architecture Described by Ports and Adapters*

The Layered Monolith Abstract Style prescribes a single, shared database. Consequently, all transactions can be atomic, even when a specific domain workflow modifies multiple entities. Adapters often take the form of the repository pattern, where each component is responsible for a single business entity (which may occupy one or more tables in a relational database or an external service), orchestrated by a single Unit of Work (Figure 12-11).

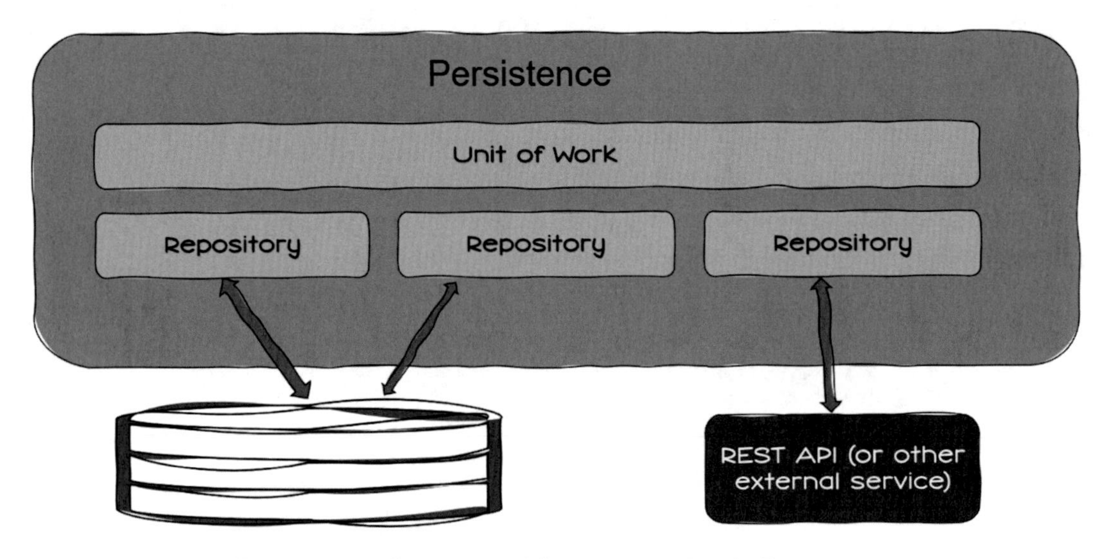

Figure 12-11. *Illustration of an Example Business Logic Layer*

Layer Encapsulation and Abstraction

Each layer in this family of styles provides some amount of abstraction, encapsulating a well-defined category of behavior. Lower layers do not have dependencies on any of the layers above them. In many cases, one layer cannot "see" beyond the next layer below it. When this is true, the immediate lower layer is said to be "closed."

We can explore this concept using the metaphor of a restaurant. The customer represents the user interacting with the system, the waiter or waitress (a.k.a. server) is the **presentation layer** (taking orders and serving up the food as it's ready), the restaurant point of sale (POS) is the **services layer**, the kitchen is the **business logic layer**, the walk-in fridge/freezer is the **persistence layer.**

In the normal flow of events, the customer interacts with the server, the server enters the orders into the POS, and the kitchen receives these orders and prepares the food, retrieving ingredients from the walk-in as needed. When the food is ready, the server takes the food from the kitchen and delivers it to the customer.

It would be highly unusual for the server to perform the actual cooking, and the customer should not be interacting with the restaurant's POS. All these layers can be considered "closed" (Figure 12-12).

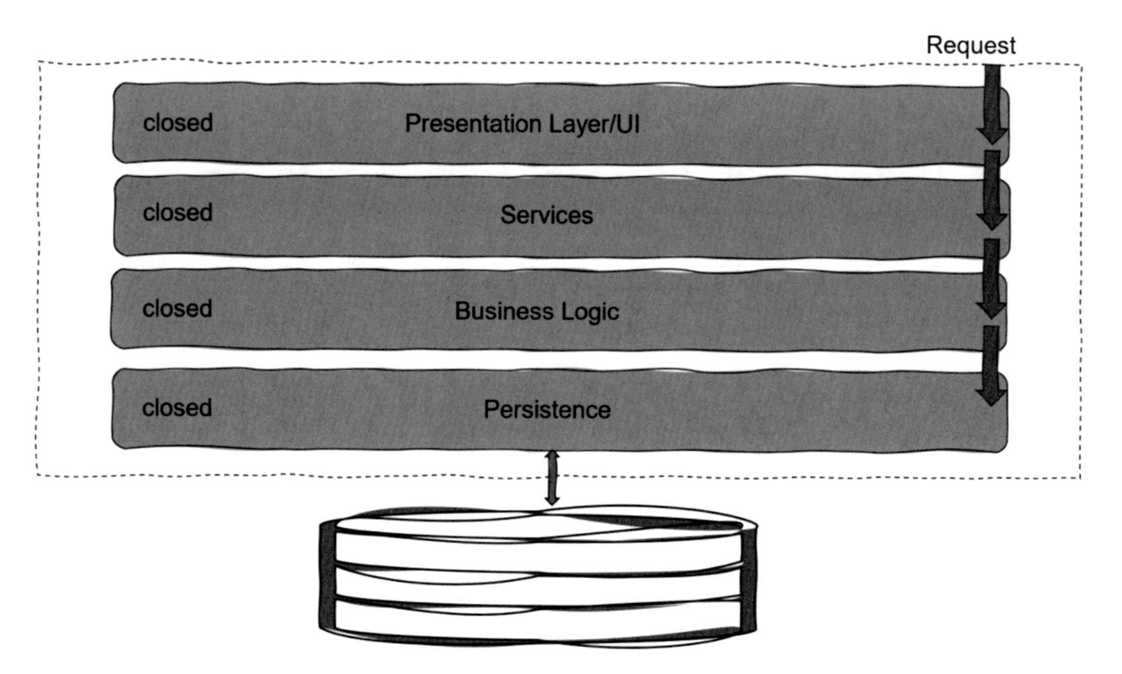

Figure 12-12. *Closed Layer Request Flow*

The ability for each actor in this system to specialize in a small number of scoped tasks will result in a smooth operational experience most of the time. A server does not need to know how to grill, sauté, prepare sauces, create desserts, etc. The kitchen can focus on this without the overhead and distractions that come with handling customer interactions. Having all kitchen requests flow through the POS streamlines communication between front-of-house and back-of-house following a first-in/first-out (FIFO) flow. Our software systems may benefit from similar encapsulation/abstraction.

What about exceptions? Imagine the server delivers the prepared food to the table but an item is missing or prepared incorrectly. Entering a correction into the POS, placing it in the back of a FIFO queue is a suboptimal action to take. In this scenario, it would be preferable if the server could bypass the POS and simply walk directly into the kitchen to request the missing item or the remake "on the fly." To account for this scenario, the services layer might be defined as an "open" layer, a layer that *should* be used for the common case but may be bypassed when necessary (Figure 12-13).

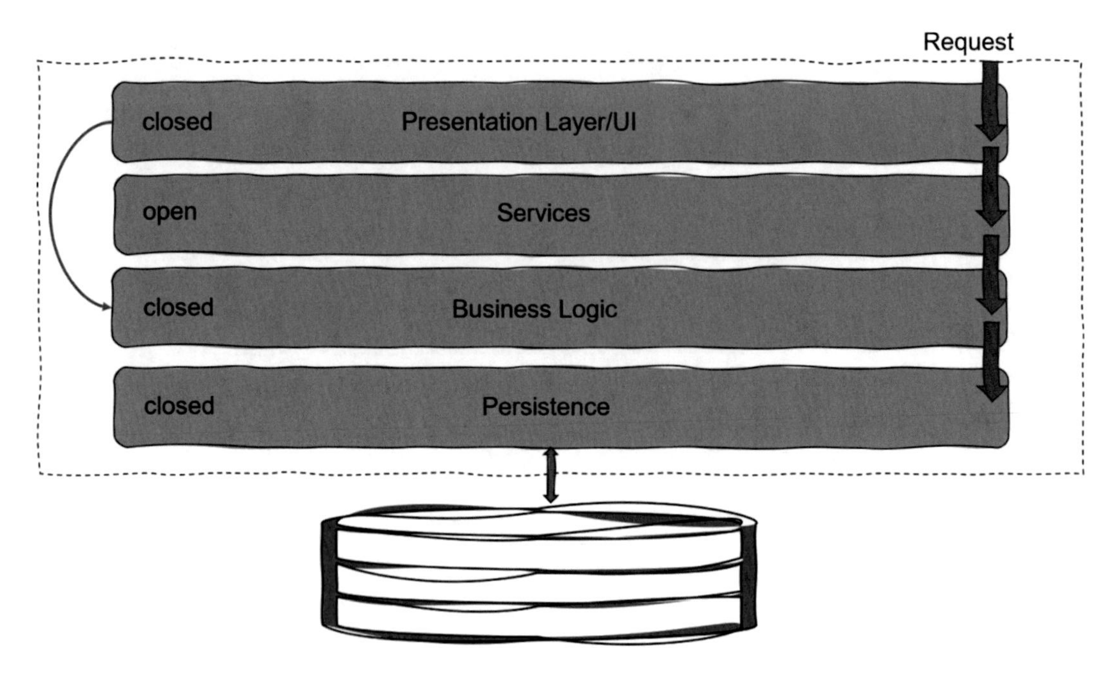

Figure 12-13. *Open Services Layer*

While exceptions and deviations from the "happy path" are examples where an open layer can be useful, there are also often situations where intermediary layers add no value, they simply accept input and then turn around and directly forward that input to the next layer. In such cases, intermediary layers add zero value, just overhead. This is referred to as the *Architectural Sinkhole Anti-pattern*[9] and is another case where open layers may be warranted to decrease accidental complexity.

Summary

This is a relatively long chapter to describe such a simple architecture pattern, but remember, this chapter has covered not one but numerous architectural styles. The *pattern-driven* architect might see all these styles as identical, but the *holistic* architect sees each distinct architectural style as a unique architecture with various strengths and weaknesses.

[9] Ford, N., Richards, M. (2020). *Fundamentals of Software Architecture: An Engineering Approach.* O'Reilly

Beyond the core constraints that define the abstract style, we introduced the following additional, optional architectural constraints:

- Stateless constraint
- MVC
- Forms UI
- Fat client-server
- Web client-server
- API constraint
- Additional database constraints
- Constraints around code reuse
- Modularity within individual layers
- Open/closed layer constraints

We also discussed an organizational constraint that requires that system component boundaries align with organizational structure in the context of Conway's Law.

Because none of these additional constraints define the core abstract style but rather exist as additional options available to us for tailoring or fine-tuning, we will not include them as part of our abstract style definition. Therefore, in aggregate, the abstract style will elicit the characteristics shown in Figure 12-14.

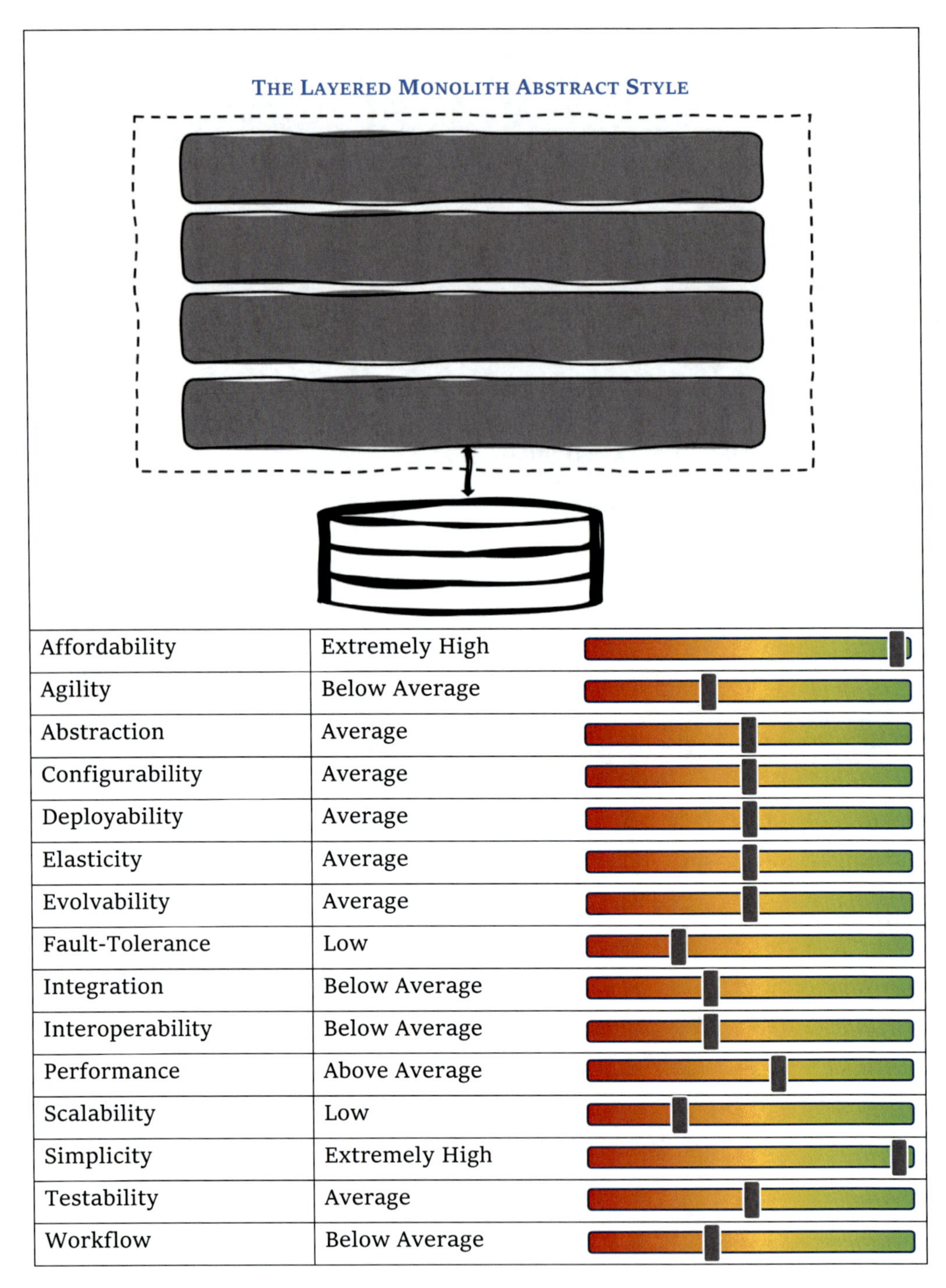

Affordability	Extremely High
Agility	Below Average
Abstraction	Average
Configurability	Average
Deployability	Average
Elasticity	Average
Evolvability	Average
Fault-Tolerance	Low
Integration	Below Average
Interoperability	Below Average
Performance	Above Average
Scalability	Low
Simplicity	Extremely High
Testability	Average
Workflow	Below Average

Figure 12-14. *Architectural Capabilities of the Layered Monolith Abstract Style*

CHAPTER 13

The Distributed N-Tier Architecture Abstract Style

> *Layered system constraints allow intermediaries—proxies, gateways, and firewalls—to be introduced at various points in the communication without changing the interfaces between components, thus allowing them to assist in communication translation or improve performance via large-scale, shared caching.*
>
> —Roy Fielding

In the last 15 years or so, there has been a great deal of effort undertaken to decompose layered monoliths into microservices which is, as has already been noted in this section, incredibly difficult. In truth, the microservices architecture is not the only path to decomposing a layered monolith into standalone services. Prior to the introduction of that pattern (along with the various, enabling X factors), the next logical step in a growing system was the Distributed N-Tier Architecture. Let us explore this evolutionary path by continuing along the architecture continuum to our first distributed abstract style.

Imagine you are responsible for the architecture of a successful, growing software system. The MVP was built using a tailored version of the Layered Monolith Abstract Style; however, a consequence of the success of the system means it has outgrown its architecture.

M. Carducci, *Mastering Software Architecture*, https://doi.org/10.1007/979-8-8688-0410-6_13

Following a detailed requirements analysis effort (based on the process described in Chapter 4), you determine the current architecture is underperforming in key areas. First, performance and scale are becoming problematic. The current architecture offers **Low** scalability, but current needs are closer to **Above Average** or **High** scalability. Likewise, the current system exhibits **Above Average** performance, but the business now requires **High** performance. Occasional downtime is also causing complaints; the system must evolve from **Low** fault tolerance to **Above Average** or **High** fault tolerance. Success has led to increased competition, and the business would like to remain competitive by getting new features to market faster. Agility must shift from **Below Average** to **High**. You have determined the improvement in agility will require enhanced testability and deployability. Ideally, both testability and deployability must go from **Average** to **Above Average**. Finally, although the current system is **Extremely** simple with high **affordability** with respect to the cost to maintain and run; both the business and implementation teams do not mind sacrificing cost and simplicity to achieve these new goals. In short, the architectural capabilities necessary for success have changed; consequently, the system's architecture must change accordingly.

Conventional wisdom insists this will require either a complete rewrite or a very lengthy monolith-to-microservices refactor. In a competitive market, both options are risky, perhaps to the point of becoming an existential threat. If all resources are directed to reaching feature parity in a new architecture rather than keeping up with market demand, more agile competitors might seize the opportunity to overtake your system. That is not to say there is *never* a time for a rewrite or a monolith-to-microservices migration, but, for the sake of argument, assume this is not one of those times.

In contrast to conventional wisdom, we know that the system's architecture simply needs ongoing tailoring to add additional room in the places we have outgrown. This tailoring is accomplished by adding or changing constraints. Let us look at one possible path available to us by evolving our Layered Monolith into a Distributed N-Tier system. Assume the existing system architecture is defined by the core constraints of the Layered Monolith Abstract style, namely:

- Monolithic Component Granularity
- Monolithic Deployment Granularity
- Separation of Concerns
- Shared Database

- Layered System
- Technical Partitioning

Adding Constraints

The Client/Server Constraint

We can modestly improve evolvability, agility, deployability, elasticity, scalability, simplicity, and testability by adopting the **Client/Server constraint**. There are notable trade-offs to this approach. First, it may require a complete frontend rewrite to operate as a standalone client (which introduces time and cost overhead). Second, we are already entering the territory of distributed systems. Distributed systems introduce new complexity that, if not carefully considered and accounted for, can come back and bite you. In other words, team skills may constrain your options.

The Fallacies of Distributed Computing

In Everett Rogers' landmark book, *Diffusion of Innovations*, he notes that "*Individuals cannot deal with an innovation except on the basis of the familiar.*"[1] This often manifests in applying an old mindset to a new situation, one where the old mindset may no longer apply. This phenomenon has been so pervasive in the realm of distributed computing that Peter Deutsch enumerated a list of false assumptions that virtually every developer makes when they first build a distributed application. The original list was compiled in 1994, when Deutsch was a Fellow at Sun Microsystems, and they are

1. The network is reliable.
2. Latency is zero.
3. Bandwidth is infinite.
4. The network is secure.

[1] Rogers, E. (2003). *Diffusion of Innovations, 5th Edition,* Free Press

5. Topology doesn't change.

6. There is one administrator.

7. Transport cost is zero.

In 1997, James Gosling, inventor of Java and another Sun Fellow, added an eighth:

8. The network is homogeneous.

What are the consequences of these fallacies?

Assuming the network is reliable will result in overlooking the numerous failure conditions that can occur during an operational request. During a network outage, an application may stall or enter an infinite retry loop or fail to restart when the network becomes reliable again.

Network latency and bandwidth limitations are another fact of life, both between client and server as well as within a cloud environment. Failure to account for this will result in unanticipated bottlenecks and performance potentially falling short of expectations.

Complacency regarding network security can have massive consequences. Notable incidents include authentication cookies sniffed and stolen on public Wi-Fi networks. Even within "private" networks, this is not a safe assumption. Should a threat actor gain entry to a private VLAN in your cloud environment, this assumption often enables unrestricted lateral movement within the network.

Network topology can—and often will—change. Ignoring this reality can have negative effects on both bandwidth and latency, causing similar problems.

Multiple administrators may implement conflicting traffic policies. Ignorance of these will often result in complications.

Transport costs will, almost universally, be nonzero. These can be quite significant, and failure to consider this reality will often result in budget overruns and revenue shortfalls.

Finally, if the network is erroneously believed to be homogeneous, the system can experience the same problems that manifest from the first three fallacies.

Some would argue that High-Availability (HA) clusters have addressed this among the subcomponents of your architecture. Two aspects that have not been addressed are connectivity between the HA cluster and the client, and the clusters become a restriction on your architecture's ability to scale.

Distributed systems incur what architects occasionally refer to as the *distributed system tax*—additional latency, overhead, complexity, additional failure conditions, and cost that are not present in nonnetwork-based architectures. In our hypothetical scenario, however, these costs are justified.

Given our system will soon be comprised of at least two discrete, networked components, they should have some mechanism to communicate. We must prescribe an API Constraint.

API Constraints

At first glance, the specifics of an API strategy may seem like an implementation detail. After all, API strategies all appear functionally identical, but architecture *transcends functionality*. Architecture defines the essence of the software, everything it can do beyond providing the features and functions. Different API approaches bring consequences that significantly impact architectural capabilities and their measure.

When creating APIs, Kent Beck offers a philosophy defined by three rules for API design in his *JUnit Pocket Guide*:[2]

- "Frameworks should be intersections not unions"
- "Do your best"
- "Evolve slowly"

An explanation for the first rule is that it makes the API simple while maximizing the utility for the API's target user base. The second recognizes that your API will have wide-reaching positive or negative impact. The third recognizes the frustration that the user community experiences when APIs frequently introduce breaking changes. Providing

---

[2] Beck, K. (2004). *JUnit Pocket Guide.* O'Reilly

an API with good cohesion and low coupling will make it a pleasure to use your API. Notably, some API strategies address this philosophy better or worse than others. For completeness, we will compare and contrast different potential API constraints.

Formally Defining REST—Again

REST was first formally defined in Fielding's 2000 doctoral dissertation, *Architectural Styles and the Design of Network-Based Architectures.*[3] While the paper was largely about the design-by-constraint approach to software architecture, the REST Architectural Style was defined in Chapter 5 as an example of how the approach was used to design the architecture of the World Wide Web. Fielding gave us the tools to define our own architectural styles, but our industry collectively dismissed this and instead corrupted REST. Once the idea was out in the wild, REST became yet another victim of semantic diffusion. Like architecture patterns, so many different APIs have been described as "REST" that the word has lost all meaning and we revert to a lowest common denominator definition.

The common definition of REST is little more than HTTP+JSON, while, in reality, REST is an architectural style defined by six constraints. Virtually no REST APIs in production today adhere to all the defining constraints. Although we know that a different set of constraints begets a different architectural style with a different name, the broader industry historically did not, and the name stuck. In 2008, Leonard Richardson, in an effort to disambiguate all the competing definitions, introduced a maturity model[4] for evaluating how close a "REST" API is to the formal definition.

Level Zero was originally defined as "One URI, one HTTP method" (think SOAP, XML-RPC, and graphQL where one endpoint serves all requests via HTTP POST operations) and has since come to encompass most RPC-over-HTTP APIs since they do not meet the criteria of a level one system.

---

[3] Fielding, R. (2000). *Architectural Styles and the Design of Network-based Software Architectures.* Doctoral dissertation, University of California, Irvine

[4] Richardson, L. (2008). *Justice Will Take Us Millions of Intricate Moves – Act Three: The Maturity Heuristic,* `https://www.crummy.com/writing/speaking/2008-QCon/act3.html`

Level One is where we begin to decouple client and server. Rather than applying the old mental model of invoking methods and functions, the system defines information (or non-information) resources as a means of abstracting the implementation. URIs become stable (i.e., they do not change) identifiers for resources rather than function endpoints. A level one system does not properly utilize HTTP's uniform interface.

Level Two requires use of the resource abstraction, stable URIs as identifiers, and correct use of the HTTP uniform interface.

Level Three is the only maturity level that fully adopts all REST's defining constraints which includes Hypermedia As the Engine of Application State (HATEOAS), a key component of the REST Architectural Style's Uniform Interface constraint. Each of REST's constraints positively and/or negatively impact architectural capabilities; hence, API strategy is architecturally significant.

GraphQL API Constraint

GraphQL is a popular API approach that does not require a client to invoke certain functions or prescribe any particular resource representation. Instead, graphQL exposes a query endpoint with which a client may invoke any arbitrary query to retrieve or modify data. It is exceedingly flexible and efficient from a client perspective as over-fetching/under-fetching (a common criticism of RESTful APIs) becomes a thing of the past. This consumer-driven approach significantly influences client agility and client portability. Initial implementation is also relatively fast.

There are significant trade-offs, however, chief among these being security. Without great care, exposing an out-of-the-box graphQL endpoint to a web client will expose far more data than business rules might permit. Securing a public-facing graphQL endpoint often requires evaluating permissions for every entity and field returned which can introduce significant performance overhead. Allowing a client to issue any arbitrary query can result in simple denial-of-service attack vectors by exploiting cycles in entity relationships. Rate limiting and metering are also challenging as there is no common unit of per-query cost.

Level 1 REST API

Abstracting identity and representation from implementation results in a significantly more evolvable system. The generality of even a level 1 REST interface improves client portability, reusability, and composability. This often improves overall agility. Securing a REST API does not typically need the kind of fine-grained controls and verification required by graphQL, allowing security to be managed at the resource or collection level. Request metering and throttling are also significantly easier. Finally, as REST is the architecture of the World Wide Web, it may be the *only* truly web-scale architecture out there.

Once again, the trade-offs are significant. It takes a great deal of effort to design a good API; the cost of longevity and evolvability must be paid up front. The generality of the REST interface also comes at a cost of network efficiency, with over-fetching/over-posting common. Client-side resource composition might require several network requests vs. one graphQL query or a client-optimized remote-procedure call.

Backend-for-Frontend (BFF) Constraint

It can be difficult to design an API that satisfies multiple clients, particularly when different clients have vastly dissimilar needs. As an alternative to designing an API that seeks to satisfy all clients, this approach prescribes client-specific APIs for the various supported frontends (e.g., SPA, mobile app, CLI, etc.). Each API is optimized for a specific client, improving speed to market, network efficiency, and design simplicity.

The trade-offs here include maintaining multiple APIs and tight coupling (although less significant since an organization typically controls the release cycles of both client and server).

RPC API Constraint

Remote Procedure Call (RPC) is a style of API that exposes methods and functions to the network. RPC APIs are very quick and easy to build, relatively easy to understand, and can be useful when decomposing monolithic systems into distributed systems. Stack method invocation is replaced with network invocation (ideally while also accounting for the fallacies of distributed computing). They can also perform reasonably well given request and response payloads can both be optimized around the specific operation.

On the other hand, exposing code in this way leads to tight coupling between API and implementation. This results in APIs that can be difficult to change and evolve and may not be suitable for a wide variety of clients.

Given the ubiquity and overall simplicity of RPC-style APIs, we will select this constraint for our abstract client-server style despite the numerous trade-offs. Remember, however, that you have options.

Changing Constraints

So far, we have a **Layered-Client Server RPC Monolith** architectural style, derived by extending our layered monolith with the Client/Server constraint and an RPC API constraint. Although the addition of these constraints will improve the system's architectural capabilities in the desired direction (with acceptable trade-offs), more work is required.

To continue to improve scalability, elasticity, deployability, and agility, we need to begin to decompose the system. Breaking apart the monolith will provide the system with smaller, standalone components that may be scaled independently both on demand and over time. The reduced binary sizes will also positively impact start time. Further, smaller components exposing well-defined API interfaces will provide improved deployability by reducing overall change risk surface area.

Coarse-Grained Component Granularity Constraint

In the same manner that the Client/Server constraint sliced off the UI into a standalone component, we can carve out standalone services by extracting additional layers (Figure 13-1). This is accomplished by replacing the Monolithic Component Granularity Constraint with the Coarse-Grained Component Granularity Constraint which results in a new style, the **Distributed Layered Client/Server RPC Style**.

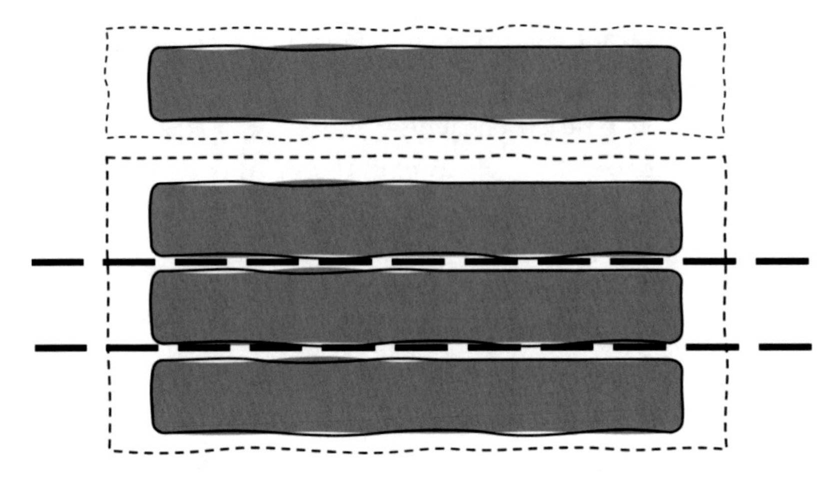

Figure 13-1. *Slicing a Monolith Along the Seams*

The key to the success of this approach for decomposing a layered monolith lies in the fact that we are not changing the module boundary constraint; this is still a technically partitioned architecture. As a natural consequence, **we are decomposing the system along existing module boundaries, rather than redefining them across the codebase**.

Although decomposing a system by following existing seams and boundaries is straightforward and will induce improvements in scalability, fault tolerance, and elasticity, this constraint brings trade-offs. Notably operational cost and complexity increases, as well as reduced performance due to the introduction of multiple network hops to satisfy requests.

Any change to the Component Granularity Constraint will require additional environmental constraints. For a monolith, a simple Platform as a Service (PaaS) is fine. However, when the monolith is decomposed, we must begin to think about how to put Humpty Dumpty together again.

Running a distributed system requires more than APIs to connect our components together; we must be able to monitor each service, aggregate logs, and trace requests across multiple distributed components or services. To properly orchestrate such a system, our environment needs a mechanism to add hosting resources to the environment as the system grows or changes, ideally through Infrastructure as Code (IaC) which implies the **Simple Environment Automation Environmental Constraint**. Additionally, request routing, service discovery, and authentication must be baked into the entire environment—a **Distributed System Environmental Constraint**.

That being said, to achieve an improvement in overall agility, one more constraint is necessary, **Independent Deployability**.

Independent Deployability

If we have decomposed our monolith into multiple standalone services but we continue to deploy it like a monolith, what have we really accomplished? Without changing the Monolithic Deployment Granularity Constraint, we simply end up with a different kind of monolith, a *distributed monolith*. In many ways, a distributed monolith offers the worst of both worlds—all the complexity and overhead of a distributed system with the constrained agility and deployability of a monolith. Deployments require high coordination costs, huge testing scopes, and increased risk. Consequently, releases become less frequent while productivity-diminishing code freezes become more frequent. For this reason, we must replace the Monolithic Deployability Granularity Constraint with the Independent Deployability Constraint. In essence, this constraint dictates that each component of the system must have independent development and release cycles. This constraint requires more than a simple *dictate from on high*; **the teams, organization, and environment must evolve to enable this constraint.**

Team, Organizational, and Environmental Constraints

Virtually, all distributed systems will contain some amount of interservice dependency. Accordingly, achieving independent deployability requires significant changes to how teams have historically worked in monolithic environments, beginning with how APIs and public interfaces are defined.

The overwhelmingly common approach to API development today centers around *emergent design*; as code is written, the API emerges (in direct violation of Beck's second rule—"Do your best"). As changes are made to the codebase, a new API emerges. Other teams who rely on this API can make little progress until a final API is published. A high-churn API results in a high-churn client, which will incur additional integration testing overhead (thus violating Beck's third rule—"Evolve slowly"). Often, this integration testing happens in a shared development environment (which may reside in the cloud or locally using desktop container orchestration tools like Docker Compose). When the client is tested and validated in the shared environment, it might appear to be ready to deploy, but, with independent release cycles, there is no guarantee the version of the server in dev—and its API—will match what exists in production (which suggests the need for a **Development Environment Isolation Environmental Constraint**). Ultimately, the development and release cycles of both the client and server are coupled, meaning releases must be coordinated. Scale this to multiple teams and services and the Independent Deployability Constraint goes out the window.

Alternatively, teams depending on an emerging API simply wait for the definitive version of the API to emerge and be released. The agility promised by the Independent Deployability Constraint evaporates as independent development and deployment cycles become *sequential* development and deployment cycles. In either case, as additional breaking changes emerge, additional coordinated releases must take place. Contrast this with an **API-first** or **design-first** approach to API development. In this scenario, the API is fully designed before writing a single line of code, and this design becomes a standalone artifact in the form of a well-defined interface that can be mocked or faked by implementation teams who depend on the API. Design first is also a path toward more stable APIs as the design phase requires deeper and more deliberate thought. This design must act as a contract which includes an implicit promise not to break it. Although defining abstractions is not always easy, and rarely a skill that comes naturally to developers, effort in this area will almost always yield benefits in terms of agility and loose coupling within the environment. In short, an **API-first** team constraint trades simplicity for long-term agility and deployability.

API first is generally easier with REST APIs than, say, RPC APIs as the resource abstraction naturally decouples the API from implementation. In contrast, RPC API styles depend, in part, on the code. To achieve independent deployability, the up-front design effort is equally important.

More frequent independent deployments also require the investment of effort into pipelines and automation. The production environment is not the ideal place to first discover integration failures; the feedback must be "shifted left" which requires additional testing, additional quality gates, and more sophisticated automation. To achieve the desired agility, teams can no longer delegate deployment to an operations team but instead must practice DevOps either on their own or in collaboration with operations.

The organization must also adjust how they organize backlogs. Features or stories that require changes to multiple services must be decomposed and sequenced. This is significantly more challenging in a technically partitioned system when compared with a domain-partitioned system (as you will see in subsequent chapters).

In short, we cannot simply *prescribe* independent deployability or a distributed granularity as these constraints depend on team, organizational, and environmental constraints that must be in place, addressed, or you must select a different set of constraints with fewer dependent constraints. **For an architecture to "fit," your designs must be in reach of the teams and organizations.**

The Distributed N-Tier Abstract Style

Through composition of constraints, we have derived a new abstract style (Figure 13-2).

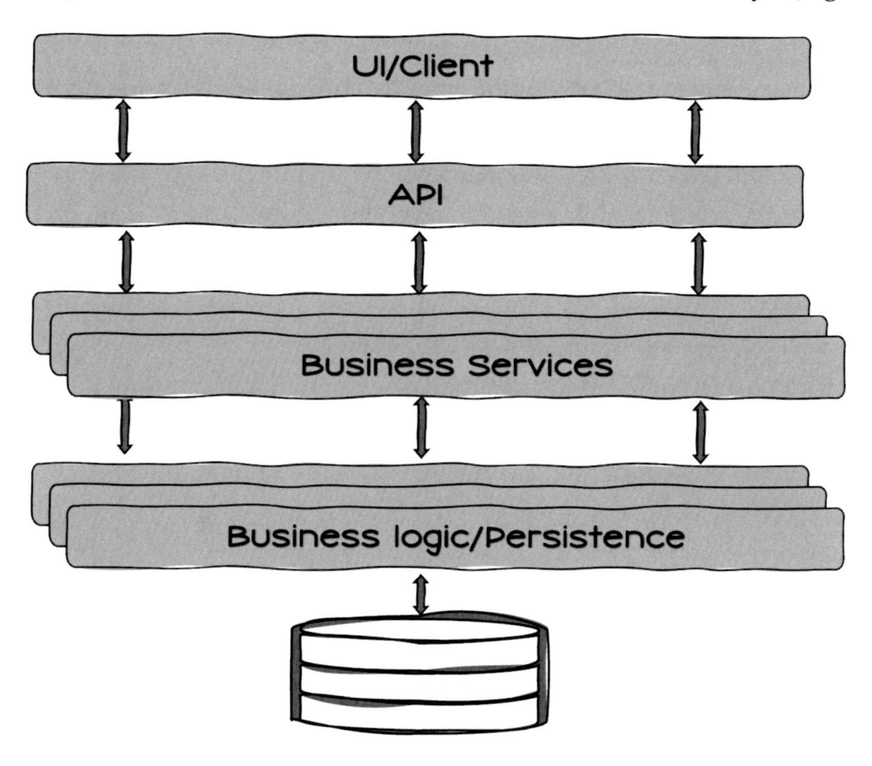

Figure 13-2. *The Distributed N-Tier Abstract Style*

When adopting this style, many concepts from the Layered Monolith style are carried over since this style is an evolved variation of the foundational pattern. It should be noted that this style is not necessarily a layer-for-layer decomposition. Perhaps business logic and persistence make sense to be grouped, or API and business services. This layered architecture also opens opportunities to not only abstract the database but also legacy and external systems, as well as shared caches. The possibility for broader reuse of business logic components is also now present.

A detailed breakdown of the capability ratings for this abstract style will appear in the summary at the end of this chapter, but, before we get there, we will explore additional potential concrete styles that bring us closer to the architectural requirements stated at the beginning of this chapter.

Tailoring This Abstract Style

By decomposing the system into standalone services, the overall amount of available resources has increased. Each component may also be independently scaled, which further improves scalability, elasticity, and offers better overall resource utilization. Scale will influence overall performance, but gains will be slightly offset by network latency. This is why thinking carefully about service granularity is important, particularly for distributed technically partitioned styles where most requests will require coordination of multiple services.

As the system grows, the bottleneck will inevitably move to the database. As we explored in Chapter 12, NoSQL databases will often *scale out* easier than relational databases, although that is not to say that relational databases cannot scale. One approach is to apply the Command Query Responsibility Segregation (**CQRS) Constraint**.

The CQRS Constraint

CQRS, at a high level, describes a strategy to route reads and writes to different servers which can have significant effects on the overall architectural capabilities. Many applications perform significantly more reads than writes, and, in such cases, it can be valuable to distribute read queries across multiple database replicas, routing only writes to the primary database (Figure 13-3). In essence, we are *segregating* the *responsibility* of *commands* and *queries*. Because of this constraint, scalability and performance will increase. Additionally, this approach retains the simplified integration and logic that is inherent to a monolithic database.

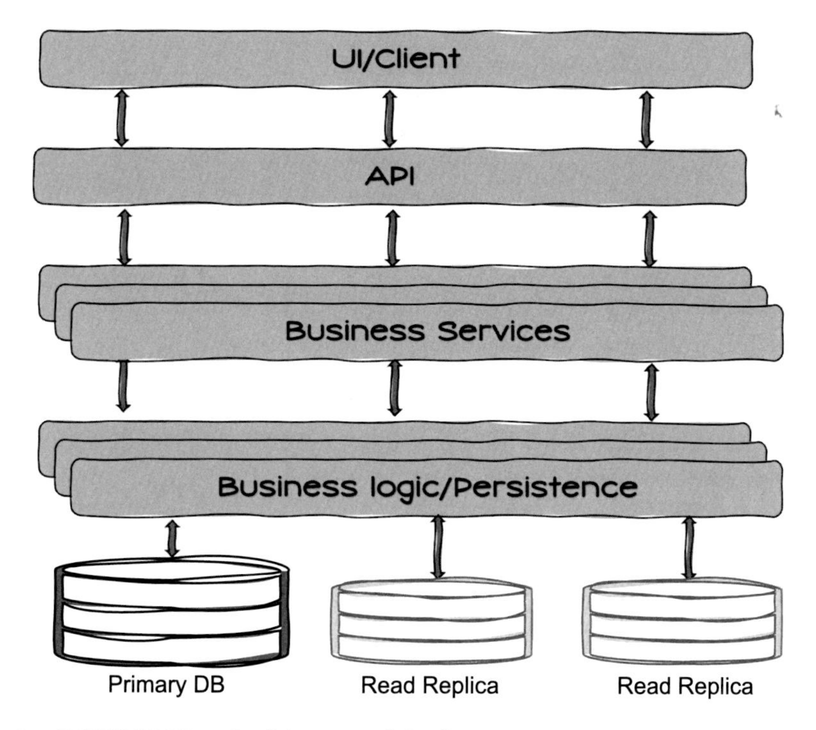

Figure 13-3. *CQRS N-Tier Architectural Style*

Like all constraints, the CQRS constraint will bring trade-offs. First, with more moving parts comes more complexity. Rolling out schema changes as part of a release can be challenging. Finally, CQRS introduces edge cases that teams and architecture must account for.

A single relational database offers ACID (Atomic, Consistent, Isolated, and Durable) properties; however, when writes are routed to the primary instance and reads to replicas, there will be cases where a read returns stale or missing data due to replication latency. Acceptance of this fact or more sophisticated routing logic is necessary in such cases.

CQRS and Flexibility: Overcoming Write Saturation

Approximately 15 years ago, I was working as the chief architect at a social media startup. Prior to being recruited, the MVP was designed and built using a MySQL database. Over time, this database was beginning to struggle due to increased load. After building multiple read replicas, we implemented CQRS by way of MaxScale, a DB Proxy which acted as an intermediary, routing writes and certain read requests to the primary while load balancing read queries to the replicas. This approach opened up tremendous growth, but we did eventually reach a point of write-saturation on the primary. The long-term solution, of course, was to decompose the system but the economics of startups sometime require creative short-term solutions.

Ultimately, we discovered a handful of write "hotspots." The worst offender was integrated telemetry and logging that was tightly coupled to both the database and the broader codebase. Knowing this would be difficult to untangle from the codebase given time and budget constraints, we turned to an axis of flexibility that CQRS offered by reconfiguring the primary DB along with most of the read replicas.

MySQL supports pluggable storage engines, with options well beyond the common InnoDB and MyISAM. To alleviate write pressure, we replaced the default storage engine with the very niche "blackhole" storage engine. Blackhole performs no I/O at all; writes are acknowledged, then discarded. These writes are, however, *replicated*. Most read replicas also utilized the blackhole storage engine, so the heavy write load only occurred on the one or two instances actually persisting the writes (and were not included in the load balancing rotation).

The flexibility offered by CQRS combined with the creativity of the team enabled rapid remediation of the performance problems, buying time for implementing longer-term solutions.

Mixed Component Granularity Constraint

In the abstract, the Distributed N-Tier Style prescribes coarse-grained components; however, there may be components that benefit from further decomposition (Figure 13-4). Business services are often a good candidate for this decomposition, particularly if they become shared across multiple applications. Doing so will generally improve agility, scalability, elasticity, and MTTR.

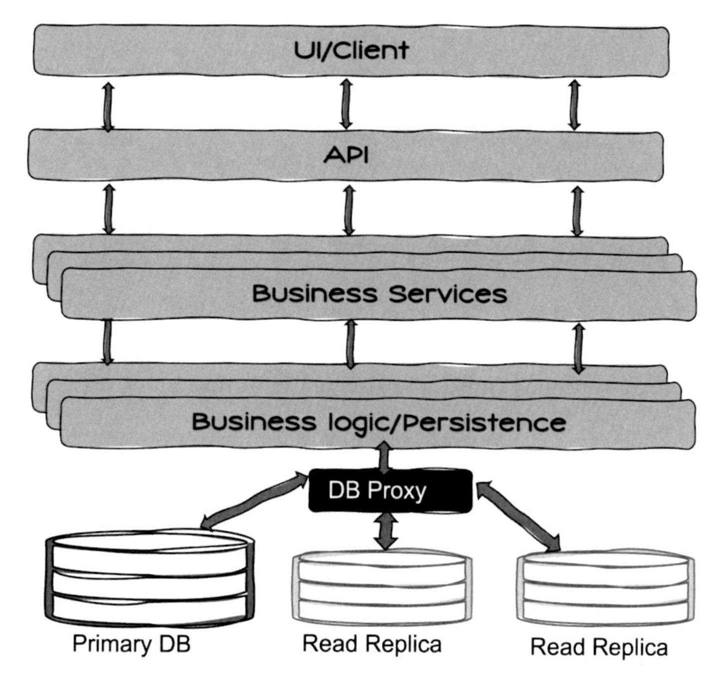

***Figure 13-4.** Multigrain Proxy CQRS N-Tier Style*

Precision Tailoring for a Precision Fit

Based on the business requirement received at the beginning of this chapter, we decomposed our monolith and tailored the architecture in a straightforward manner that is largely compatible with the existing architecture, the teams, the environment, and the organization. The design-time feedback of the Tailor-Made model shows a near perfect alignment of architectural capabilities for this example derived style with the new requirement targets. This can be visualized and explored using the Tailor-Made Workbook (introduced in Section 1) which incorporates the model's capability trade-off weighting for rapid evaluation of candidate styles.

Summary

Although we have looked at some concrete variations of this abstract style, let us close this chapter by summarizing this abstract style's defining constraints:

- Coarse Component Granularity
- Layered System
- Technical Partitioning
- Client/Server
- Independent Deployability
- Separation of Concerns
- Shared Database
- RPC API

This collection of constraints requires the following team, organization, and environmental constraints:

- ENV: Development environment isolation
- ENV: Simple environment automation
- ENV: Distributed system environment support
- ORG: Optimized backlog for independent development
- TEAM: API-first development
- TEAM: Pipeline development skills
- TEAM: Automation skills

The non-architectural constraints are necessary for the successful adoption of non-monolithic granularity and independent deployability. The base capabilities of this abstract style are shown in Figure 13-5.

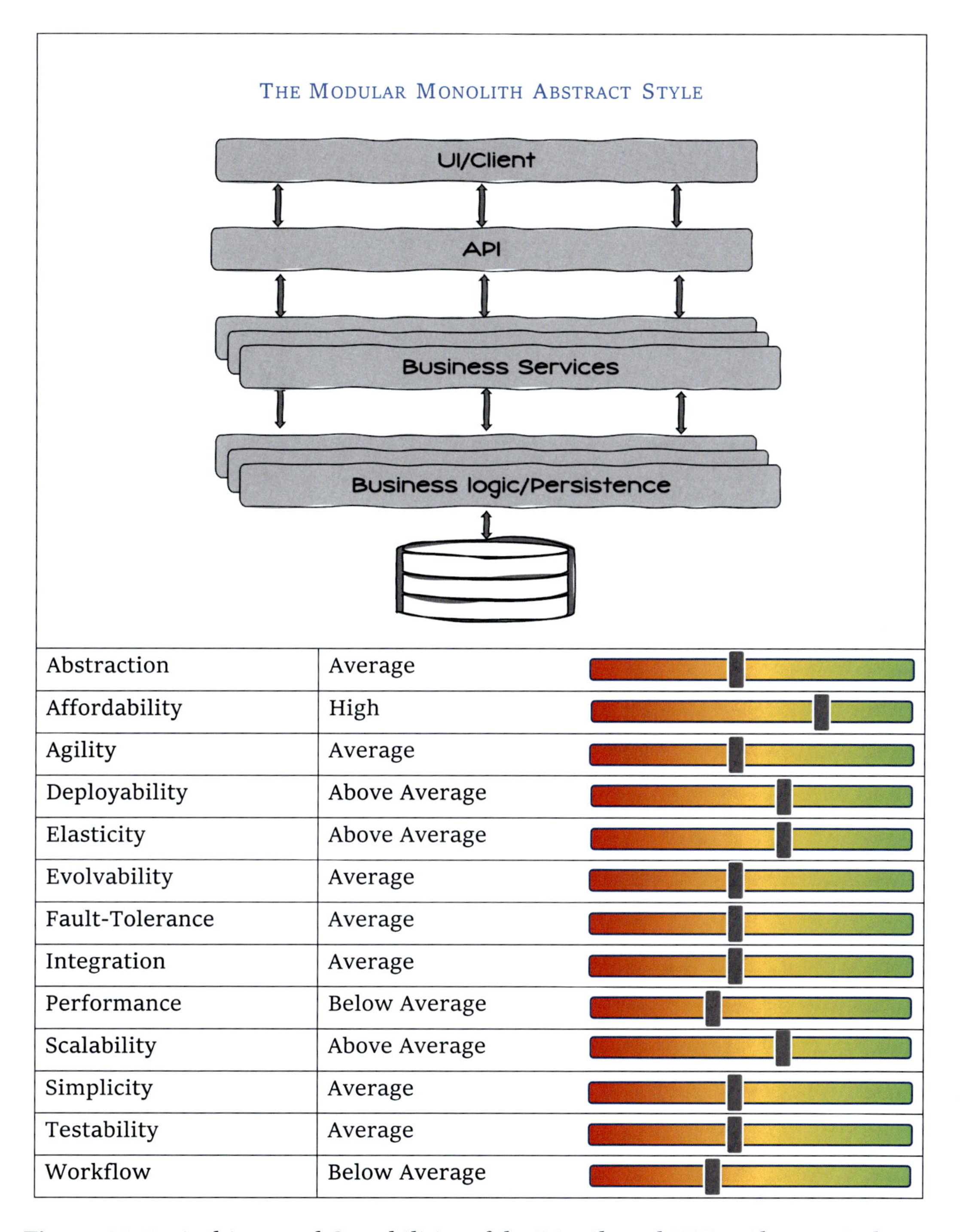

Abstraction	Average	
Affordability	High	
Agility	Average	
Deployability	Above Average	
Elasticity	Above Average	
Evolvability	Average	
Fault-Tolerance	Average	
Integration	Average	
Performance	Below Average	
Scalability	Above Average	
Simplicity	Average	
Testability	Average	
Workflow	Below Average	

Figure 13-5. *Architectural Capabilities of the Distributed N-Tier Abstract Style*

CHAPTER 14

The Modular Monolith Abstract Style

> *Enter the 'Goldilocks' architecture: the Modular Monolith. This architecture promises to strike a balance that is 'just right' for many applications, offering the simplicity of a monolith with the flexibility of microservices.*
>
> —Steve Smith

In Chapter 13, we explored one path to evolve the Layered Monolith style into a new, distributed style. Agility improved, but only modestly. Why? Because the challenge with technically partitioned layered architectures is that routine development often involves changes to most or all layers. These multilayer changes require a full regression test of the entire system, and, when these changes introduce breaking changes, releases require coordination. A large component of the agility the microservices architecture promises derives from defining module boundaries not by technical area, but by bounded context. This approach to granularity enables the overwhelming majority of changes to be confined to a single microservice. The trade-offs inherent to microservices, as you will see in the chapter on this style, are vast. Can a system exhibit comparable agility to microservices without the cost and complexity? The Tailor-Made model says "yes." We start with just a subset of the constraints that define the microservices architecture to derive an abstract style that offers a compelling balance of flexibility and simplicity. Consequently, this style achieves a comparable level of decoupling seen in a microservices architecture within a monolith. This architectural style just might make architects love the monolith again.

Since architecture is a multifaceted continuum—and the tailoring process is how we move along said continuum—we will derive this abstract style by tailoring our Layered Monolith. As with the previous chapter, we will start with a hypothetical existing system

M. Carducci, *Mastering Software Architecture*, https://doi.org/10.1007/979-8-8688-0410-6_14

that is ready to move beyond the limitations of the layered architecture. As we continue this process through additional architectural styles in subsequent chapters, you will further see the power of this model and how an agile, evolvable architecture can remain reliably within reach.

Imagine our hypothetical system is an MVP that launched in the form of a layered monolith six months ago. The positive reception of the release has validated product fit and resolved any market uncertainty. On the strength of the MVP, the business has been able to raise significant capital and has now set a course for long-term growth and evolution.

Consequently, agility, deployability, and evolvability are high priorities with the requirements analysis process determining the needs for these capabilities are **Above Average**, **Above Average**, and **High**, respectively. The system has a good base of users, but not so many that scale and elasticity are becoming problematic yet; **Average** is fine for both. The business would prioritize a lower defect escape rate over scale and elasticity. You have quantified this as a requirement for **Above Average** testability. Integration plays a significant role in the future vision of the system, so integration and abstraction need to be **Average** to **Above Average**. That said, it is still a smallish organization so it would like to maintain a **High** level of simplicity but can certainly be flexible on affordability.

It is important to note that the abstract style described in this chapter will not perfectly align with these quantified needs. For example, integration and abstraction will score **Below Average**; however, this can be overcome either through the prescription of additional architectural constraints or additional human capital investment. Scale and elasticity also fall short of targets; however, this style will prove to be a useful intermediary style which enables further decomposition and architectural evolution over time. Sometimes, the best course of action for us is incremental improvement and evolvability rather than over fixating on the "perfect" architecture.

Changing Constraints: Domain Partitioning Constraint

So far, we have only looked at module boundaries defined by technical concern, as defined by the Technical Partitioning Constraint. If we replace this constraint with the Domain Partitioning Constraint, it requires us to identify vertical slices of functionality (Figure 14-1). Each vertical slice captures a bounded context or subdomain. The result of this approach to modularity is significantly improved agility as most changes will only touch a single slice. Typically, changes within a single slice will involve only a single team, and the testing scope and blast radius of the change will be well constrained.

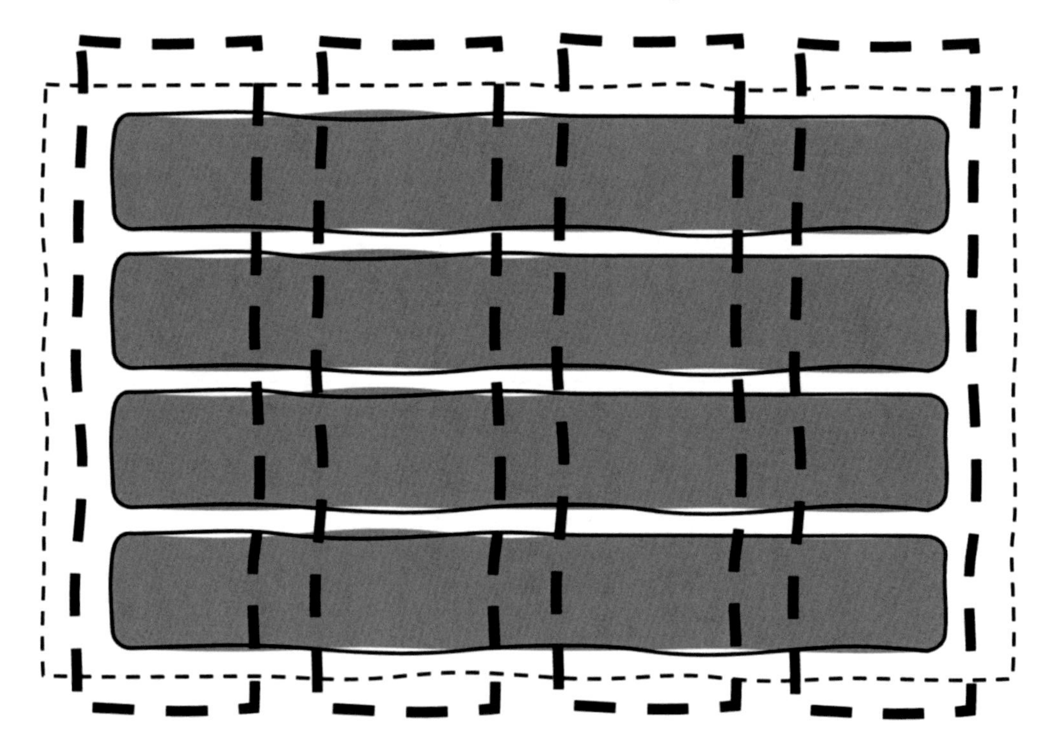

Figure 14-1. *Taking Vertical Slices from a Layered Monolith*

By applying the Domain Partitioning Constraint, we have a new style, the **Domain Partitioned Monolith Style** (Figure 14-2). In this style, each domain module is built as a separate, precompiled, package or assembly that is imported by the host application at startup by virtue of dynamic linking. To enforce modularity, everything in these packages is scoped as `internal` with the host application configured to be able to see and expose controllers or other relevant public interfaces. This enforced modularity approach is a form of architectural governance, making it difficult for a team to decide to take a shortcut and bypass another module's API and directly access code methods. This can—and should—be part of a broader strategy of architectural governance (which will be discussed more in Chapter 25).

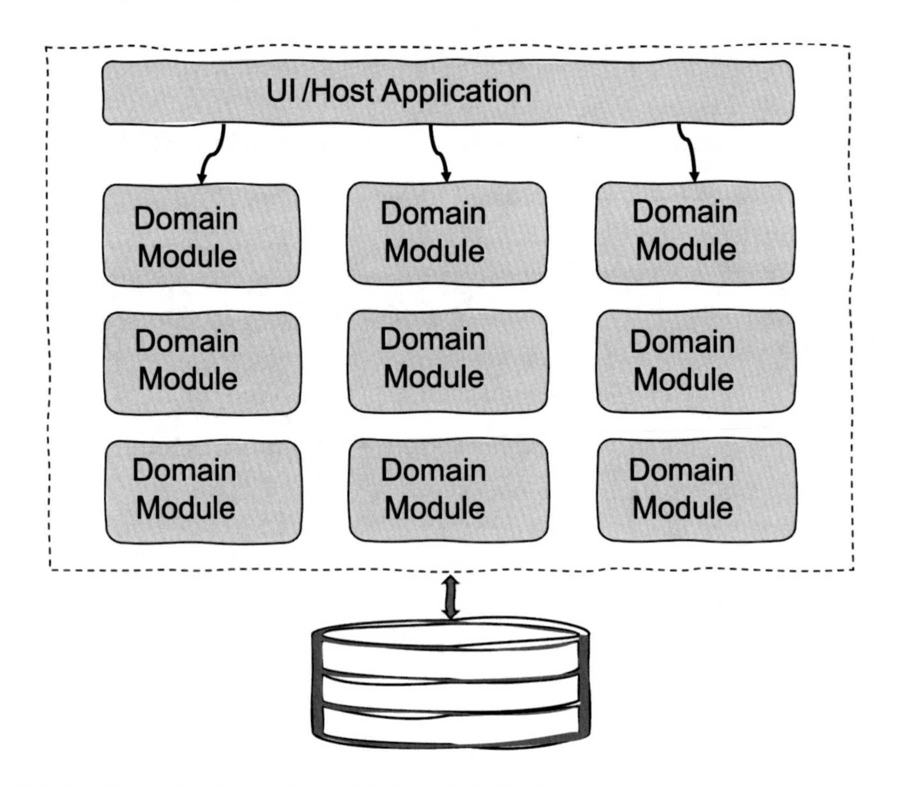

Figure 14-2. *Domain Partitioned Monolith Style*

When building a Domain Partitioned Monolith from scratch, typically development will begin with a host application that contains the bare minimum to bootstrap the application (API or MVC framework code, authentication, logging, and any other cross-cutting concerns). Likewise, when migrating from a layered monolith, the process is to extract individual domain modules into the separate packages/assemblies over time. Whether your long-term goal is a more agile and maintainable monolith or succeeding with microservices, this style offers a safe and pragmatic path for modular decomposition with a great deal of architectural flexibility and long-term agility.

The important question here is: *"How do we determine module scope and module boundaries?"* A common mistake is to simply design modules around entities; however, this approach is not only simplistic, but it will also undermine the goals of this level of modularity. Instead, this is where Domain-Driven Design (DDD) comes in.

A Little More on DDD

Domain-Driven Design is a strategic approach to software development that emphasizes the importance of understanding the business domain and using that knowledge to inform the design and architecture of a system. At its core, DDD is about creating a shared understanding of the domain among all stakeholders, which is facilitated through a set of collaborative practices and ceremonies.

The key ceremonies in DDD include[1]

Domain Modeling: Collaborative sessions where developers and domain experts create models that reflect the business processes and rules. These models help ensure everyone has a collective understanding of the domain.

Event Storming:[2] A workshop-style technique used to explore complex domains by mapping out domain events. It helps identify key events, commands, and aggregates, fostering a deeper understanding of how the system should behave.

Ubiquitous Language: The practice of using a consistent vocabulary shared by both domain experts and developers. This language permeates the code, documentation, and discussions, reducing misunderstandings and ensuring alignment.

By engaging in these practices, teams can identify and define bounded contexts—the specific boundaries within which a particular domain model is valid. Each bounded context is effectively a module, with clear boundaries and responsibilities, allowing teams to determine module boundaries in a system naturally. This alignment of module boundaries with business domains ensures that the system's architecture reflects the real-world processes it aims to support, leading to more maintainable and adaptable software.

[1] Vernon, V. (2013). *Implementing Domain-Driven Design*. Addison-Wesley Professional

[2] Brandolini, A. (2015–2021). *Introducing EventStorming: An Act of Deliberate Collective Learning*. LeanPub, `https://www.eventstorming.com/book/`

Adopting the Domain Partitioning Constraint requires architecture to champion the idea and either arrange or facilitate one or more DDD ceremonies. These usually involve getting numerous business stakeholders and domain experts in the same room and working over a period of hours or days until the domains are well defined. The **Well-Defined Domains Constraint** is a necessary enabling organizational constraint and thus a prerequisite for adopting the Domain Partitioning Constraint.

In accordance with Conway's Law, communication structures within the organization will dictate the ultimate module topology that emerges through the development process. For a clean, decoupled, standalone module to go from design to implementation, team/communication structures must be similarly modularized and decoupled. To achieve this, typically, teams will own either one or a small number of modules, and that team is responsible for the full stack within the module. This reality dictates that the **Domain-Aligned Teams Constraint** is a second necessary, enabling organizational constraint. As Conway's Law has shown repeatedly, without these two organizational constraints, you are unlikely to succeed with the Domain Partitioning Constraint.

Ultimately, to succeed with the Domain Partitioning Constraint, the architecture and the org chart must align. When architecture precedes team formation, we have much more latitude to influence team topologies. When the inverse is true—the teams are already in place—we must either constrain our architecture decisions to reflect this reality or restructure the teams to align with architecture. The latter is known as "the inverse Conway maneuver" and requires considerable political capital.

Although the Domain Partitioning Constraint, in partnership with the necessary DDD work, will illuminate natural boundaries in the system needed to carve out modules, this effort will rarely inform module granularity.

Module Granularity

With a technically partitioned architecture, the layer boundaries are usually quite clear. In contrast, domains are comprised of multiple subdomains, which typically contain multiple bounded contexts. The modules derived from domain analysis can range from coarse to extremely fine. Naturally, both "coarse" and "fine" are subjective and depend on the environment and context. How do we get granularity correct for a given project?

First, consider purpose. Each domain module should be functionally cohesive, contributing one significant domain behavior on behalf of the overall system. Beyond domain modeling, event storming can be useful to model various business workflows or processes. Armed with this information, we can draw a candidate architecture and model various business processes to see how modules interact or depend on each other. Pay attention to how entities interact. Entities that consistently need to cooperate or form part of a common atomic database transaction are good indicators of shared module boundaries. Be aware that this can lead to tight coupling within modules if one is not careful. Coupling within a module is not always bad; however, coupling that spans multiple modules can prove to be problematic. During this modeling process, if you notice that a workflow involves orchestrating multiple modules, the odds are that those modules are too fine and may require consolidation prior to finalizing the architecture and design.

Use caution during this process as it is easy to overengineer modularity. Ultimately, determining optimal module boundaries is an iterative process. Performing as much iteration as possible at design time is optimal, but post-implementation revisions are often common. For this reason, it is important to favor an iterative process that begins with more coarse-grained modules (likely more coarse-grained than you might otherwise be comfortable with) and subsequently introducing further decomposition, as necessary. Splitting one module into two is typically easier as the domain behavior being extracted in the decomposition process has already been shown to stand alone. When module boundaries are very fine, the code required to manage these modules increases, leading to more work and higher risk when combining them at runtime.

Notably, this process is much easier within a Domain Partitioned Monolith. Consequently, the abstract style emerging in this chapter is a powerful starting point for microservices architectures as the modules can easily be extracted into standalone services as needed in the future. Beginning with coarse-grained modules decreases infrastructure requirements, provides a practical space for iterating on granularity, and reduces overall architectural risk.

Organizing Code Within a Domain Module

Each domain module is, in essence, a micro-application (micro as in *scope*, not necessarily lines of code). The limited scope means that, if the behavior is correct and the interface stable, the contents do not particularly matter, and an individual module could be quickly rewritten if necessary. That said, generally some structure is desirable. It is extremely common for the contents of a domain module to be organized in layers (Figure 14-3); this is particularly common when migrating from a layered monolith. Alternatively, a domain module may be a more coarse-grained module representing a portion of a subdomain and containing some number of more fine-grained mini-domain modules (Figure 14-4).

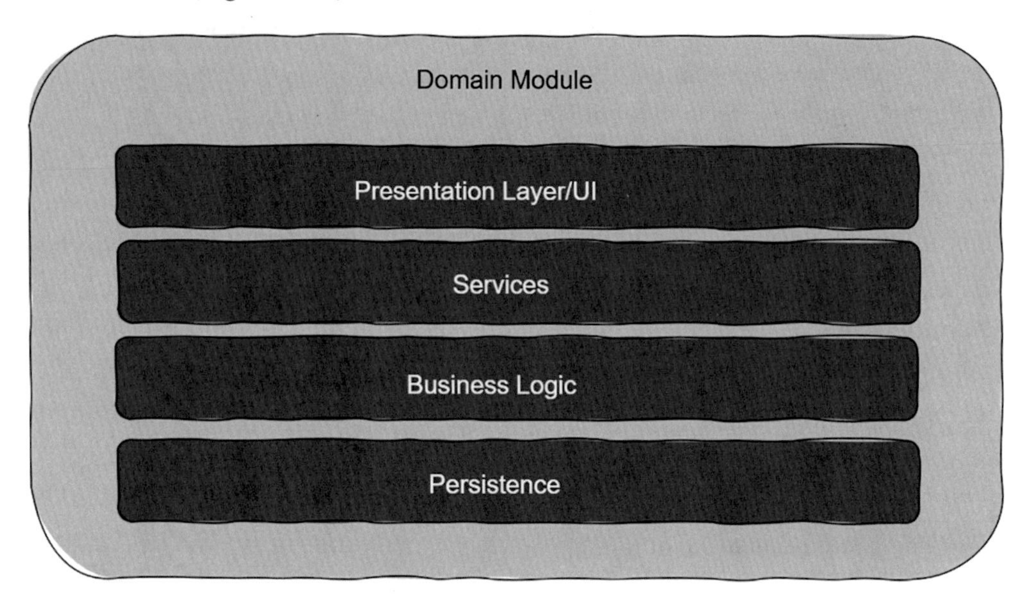

Figure 14-3. *A Layered Domain Module*

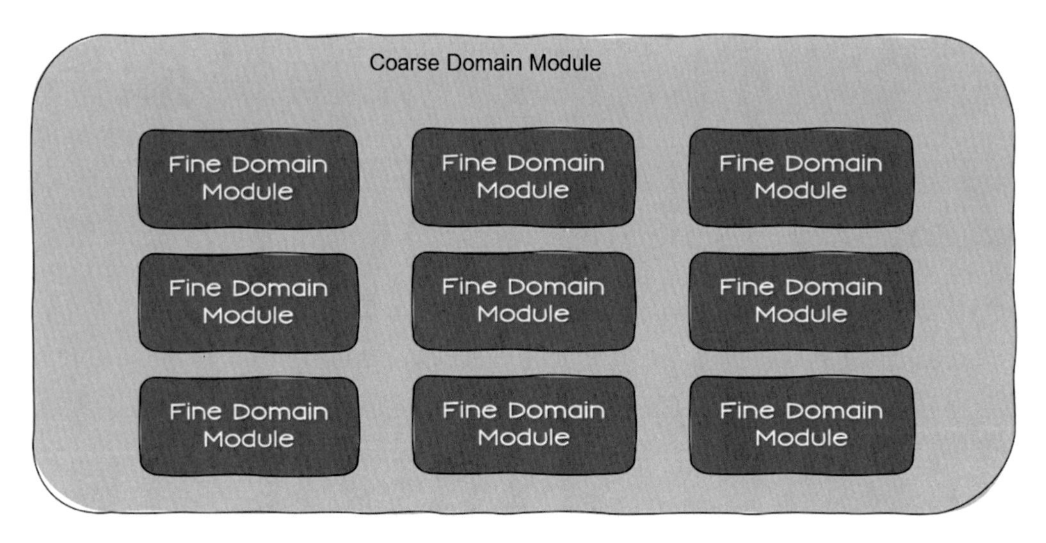

Figure 14-4. *A Coarse-Grained Domain Module Containing Smaller Modules That Represent Individual Bounded Contexts*

If you have experience with the microservices architecture, you will note that individual domain modules look remarkably like individual microservices, albeit without the complexity of a fine-grained distributed system. This is how we achieve, as Steve Smith describes it in this chapter's introductory quote, "*...the simplicity of a monolith with the flexibility of microservices...*" In fact, this modular approach achieves much of the same decoupling and improved cohesion found in microservices architectures.

Like microservices, we must now consider how to handle shared or common code. Because this style prescribes a monolithic deployment granularity and a monolithic build artifact, we will receive build-time integration feedback, so a single "shared" module may be used to make shared utilities and interfaces available to the individual modules. That said, multiple strategies have been pioneered to address cross-cutting concerns, including Aspect-Oriented Programming (AOP), Object-Oriented Programming (OOP), dynamic module loading, and static module compilation. As the architect, you must determine both the boundaries of the shared code modules and which mechanism(s) should be deployed for a given project. This will ensure good encapsulation and independence of individual modules, keeping code changes tightly scoped and increasing agility while reducing risk.

In this style, code changes are almost always scoped to a single module, but what about code changes that require database schema changes? Microservices architectures tend to follow a principle which prescribes that each microservice owns its own data, but, in the absence of any additional constraints, coupling still exists in the database. A domain module might opt to join directly to a table that rightfully belongs to another module for the sake of expediency which will cause problems if/when that schema changes. To truly achieve the desired agility and change safety, we must not only decouple the code but also decouple the database.

Partitioned Shared Database Constraint

A database-per-domain module is excessive at this point, given that much of the simplicity of this style is a function of the monolithic application and database. Remember, this style aims to achieve a comparable level of decoupling seen in a microservices architecture within a monolith. A simplified database decoupling can be accomplished by defining a distinct schema or catalog for each top-level domain module. The same way this style prescribes scoping all classes within a domain module as internal to prevent code boundaries from "leaking," this constraint applies additional enforcement of module boundaries within the database. It provides yet another feedback loop for determining optimal module granularity. If a single atomic business transaction requires crossing module boundaries to commit, it is an indicator that the modules may be too fine.

Breaking apart databases is often challenging. If you have ever looked at an entity relationship diagram (ERD), you have undoubtedly seen wide-reaching entities serve as the nexus for countless dependency relationship lines. Consequently, in any nontrivial system, there will be edge cases—scenarios where queries or transactions must span multiple data boundaries. The earlier we can address these in the design, the better. Module-crossing transactions might be painless now, but, as the system evolves, you may be baking complex, distributed transactions into the future architecture which can impede evolution or introduce other long-term challenges.

In both the **Partitioned Shared Database Constraint** that we have just introduced and its distributed sibling, the **Isolated/Independent Database Constraint** that we will discuss in later chapters, our primary options for each edge case are as follows:

- **Accepting the boundary-crossing edge cases as is**
- **Consolidating the modules**
- **Replicating the data**
- **Using coarser "data domains"**

Each of these options brings trade-offs that you must consider.

Accepting boundary-crossing edge cases as is will introduce additional complexity both short term and long term. For boundary-crossing write transactions (whether applied to a partitioned shared or discrete database), a single atomic commit is no longer available. New transactional failure conditions are introduced that must be accounted for. Partial failures require rollback or remediate/retry logic which introduces additional complexity that is only compounded when services and databases are distributed, and the Fallacies of Distributed Computing must be overcome. Boundary-crossing read transactions are inherently less complex but can be extremely expensive. Read queries that span two or more domain boundaries cannot perform traditional joins inside the database; instead, the join logic must take place on the application side. A database join can take advantage of indexes, reducing I/O by performing the join operation on a subset of the data, but an application-side join requires reading most or all the table, sending everything across the network, loading the full dataset in memory, then joining the datasets in code. Only if the edge cases are rare, and the risk/complexity can be adequately mitigated long term, does this become an acceptable option.

Consolidating the modules can often be a useful strategy if the edge cases are less "edgy" and more frequent than expected. In such a case, we may opt to simply consolidate the modules and their respective data partitions (or databases), effectively refactoring the domain model mapping within the architecture. This approach correlates positively with cohesion but negatively with agility. Changes that are small in scope and have a highly constrained blast radius are low risk and lend themselves to frequent releases. As domain modules become larger, the blast radius of each change increases along with testing/validation scope. Frequent and repeated consolidation of modules can become a slippery slope that leads back to the layered monolith.

Replicating the data is common in the microservices world for otherwise module-spanning read operations.

This approach is often the most expedient and effective solution. In a shared database, triggers, periodic batch jobs, or even views imbued with specific permissions to cross domain boundaries all function as simple mechanisms for replication. A shared database can also be denormalized. In a distributed system, strategies for replication include using event sourcing, linked tables, or periodic batch jobs.

In contrast with the inflated cost and overhead of application-side joins, replicated data takes advantage of database-level optimizations, but this frequently raises the issue of eventual consistency. Whether an event-sourcing approach is taken (where one service broadcasts state changes in the form of events that other services can consume as a source of truth), or some sort of ETL/batch job that is periodically invoked, there will be some delay before the replicated data is consistent across the system. Some domains can tolerate eventual consistency; others cannot. Within a partitioned shared database, this latency might be zero if triggers or views are used, but we have reintroduced coupling to the database layer. Which team should own the triggers or views? How will schema changes be coordinated to avoid difficult-to-detect regression outside the scope of the module boundaries? You must answer these questions, either at design time or in an incident postmortem. When the strategy of denormalization is deployed, there must be a mechanism in place to cascade updates to maintain logical consistency, which adds complexity and reintroduces challenges around eventual consistency.

Finally, you must consider the long-term expectations of the system. If evolution into a distributed system is anticipated, it would be valuable to consider both short-term and long-term replication strategies when selecting this option.

Using coarser data domains is one more tool in our toolbox. There is no rule that states there must be a 1:1 relationship between code module boundaries and data boundaries. From a pure domain logic standpoint, we may end up with one model for the code and a separate model for the data. A data domain is a distinct set of logical boundaries within the database that might span multiple domain modules or microservices.

Note that this approach can quickly become a blunt instrument when not wielded carefully. A sufficiently large data domain will inevitably span multiple teams which reintroduces increased coordination cost that the modularity of this style aims to avoid. The value of the Partitioned Shared Database Constraint diminishes as the database becomes increasingly monolithic.

On paper, this constraint seems simple and logical. However, in practice you will uncover many such edge cases and learn that there is no best practice or one-size-fits-all solution. Consequently, you may find yourself applying any or all these options on a case-by-case basis.

The Modular Monolith Abstract Style

As a result of changing the module partitioning constraint and the shared database constraint, we arrive at the next common pattern and another abstract style, the Modular Monolith Abstract Style (Figure 14-5).

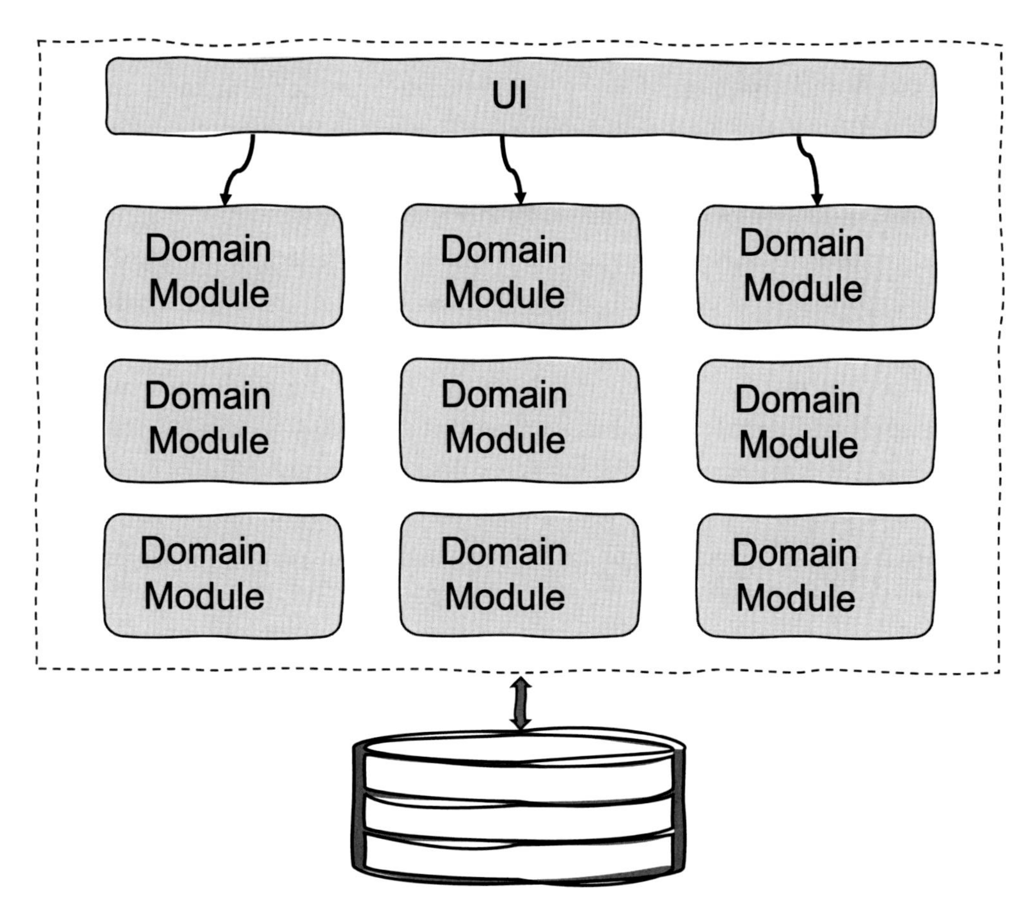

Figure 14-5. *The Modular Monolith Abstract Style*

Monolithic applications have existed for as long as software has existed. The layered approach to organizing larger, monolithic codebases has remained largely unchanged for a period spanning decades; however, this style reimagines the structure of a monolith by applying the new techniques and lessons learned in the 21st century ranging from the problems identified in the Agile Manifesto and the software craftsmanship movement[3] to the techniques pioneered by Eric Evans[4] and the early DDD community, as well as the success of microservices. This style embodies the Tailor-Made philosophy of borrowing just enough architecturally significant decisions from styles like microservices to induce necessary capabilities in a monolith. The Tailor-Made model's emphasis on constraints makes this process explicit and better informs future evolution.

[3] McBreen, P. (2001). *Software Craftsmanship: The New Imperative.* Addison-Wesley

[4] Evans, E. (2003). *Domain-Driven Design: Tackling complexity at the heart of software.* Addison-Wesley

The modular monolith is often a suitable place to start a greenfield project. Typically, proving your MVP and capturing market share are more immediate business concerns over massive scalability and elasticity at the project inception. With the foundation of a modular monolith, the initial time to value for the code is short, but architectural flexibility and long-term evolution is baked into its foundations.

The architectural flexibility of this style is an antidote to the trend of up-front overengineering and premature optimization. Rather than *guess* what the architectural requirements will be in 3–5 years, we can take a more agile approach. As metrics, KPIs, and telemetry begin to show that scale requirements have changed, we can scale the monolith or apply additional constraints such as the CQRS constraint or the Client/Server constraint. If the nature of the domain requires any orchestration of multiple modules, it can be useful to consider prescribing the team constraint of **API-first development** to further reduce coordination costs, increase team independence, and drive more stable and well-thought-out public interfaces. Finally, if the data shows a need for decomposition into a distributed system, you will see in the next chapter that extracting a standalone service or microservice is trivial compared to decomposing a traditional monolith since the hard part—redefining module boundaries vertically—is already complete. A modular monolith is also already partway toward microservices. In fact, the modular monolith style is also a popular, pragmatic, and low-risk step in the process of decomposing an existing monolith into "miniservices" or microservices without requiring the recombination of components necessary when migrating from a distributed n-tier style.

Summary

The modular monolith is a powerful way to balance cost and simplicity against architectural agility and long-term evolvability. If a monolith provides *enough* capabilities for the short term (whether it be an MVP or a system that is still ramping up users and market share), and the organizational constraints are within reach and can be applied, this style should be given thoughtful consideration.

This abstract style is defined by the following architectural constraints:

- Monolithic Component Granularity
- Monolithic Deployment Granularity
- Domain Partitioning
- Partitioned Shared Database

This collection of architectural constraints requires the following organizational constraints:

- ORG: Well-Defined Domains
- ORG: Domain-Aligned Teams

By adopting the same constraints that drive modularity and encapsulation in the microservices architecture, this style offers significant advantages over its layered counterpart. The notable improvements over the **Layered Monolith Abstract Style** are shown in Figure 14-6.

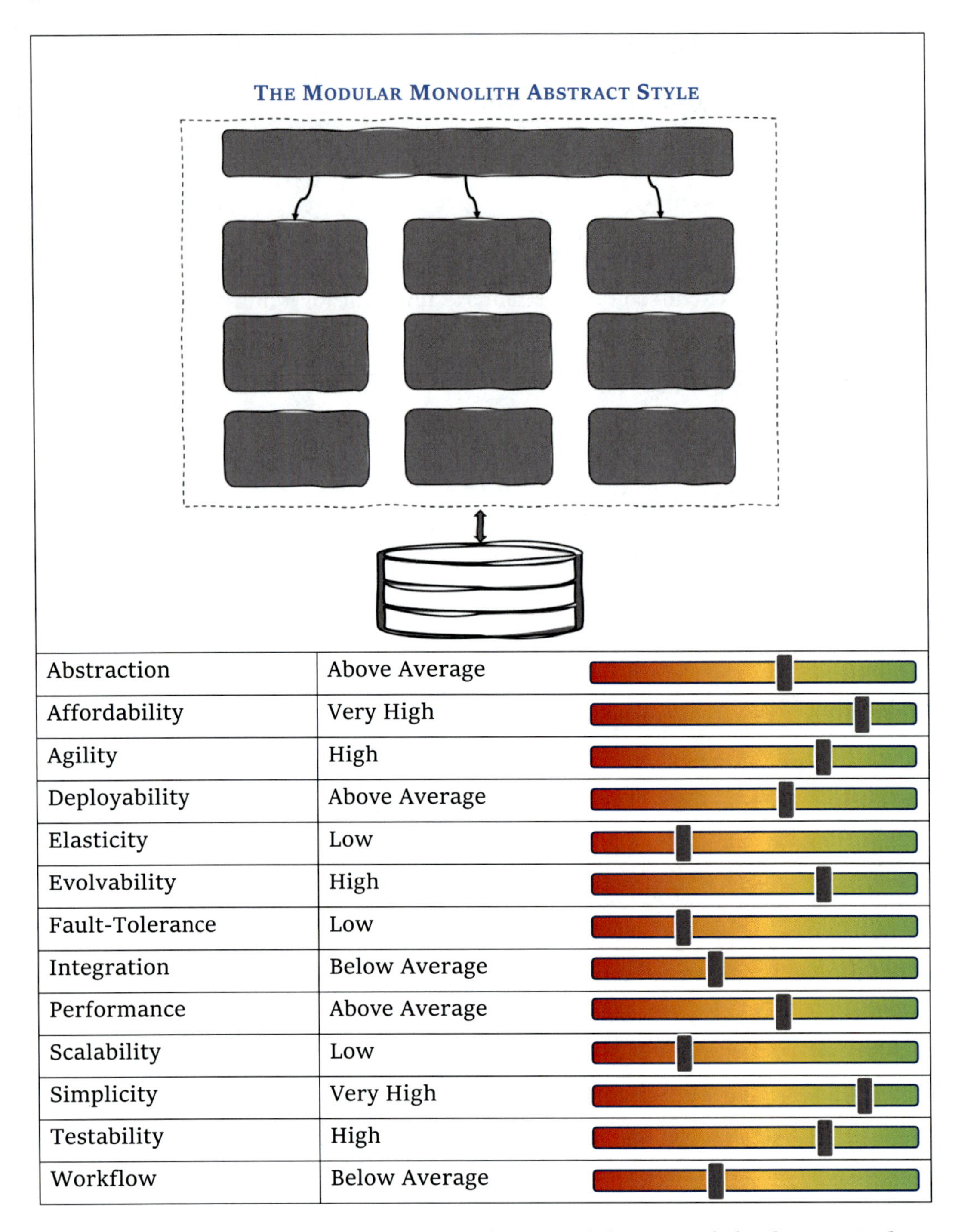

Abstraction	Above Average
Affordability	Very High
Agility	High
Deployability	Above Average
Elasticity	Low
Evolvability	High
Fault-Tolerance	Low
Integration	Below Average
Performance	Above Average
Scalability	Low
Simplicity	Very High
Testability	High
Workflow	Below Average

Figure 14-6. *Architectural Capabilities of the Modular Monolith Abstract Style*

CHAPTER 15

The Service-Based Abstract Style

> *It's exciting to see modular thinking—along with loose coupling and high cohesion—to reenter our software design. Microservices is an extreme that is a fit for a few. The lessons from it are a fit for many.*
>
> —James Higginbotham

In Chapter 14, we evolved a layered monolith into a modular monolith in response to changing architectural needs and a directive from the business to invest in long-term agility and evolvability. While many of the qualified and quantified requirements from that scenario have been satisfied by the Modular Monolith Abstract Style, elasticity, integration, and scalability are still falling below target. Additional tailoring, in the form of adding or changing constraints, will lead us further along the continuum toward an optimal fit. To achieve increased scale, we will decompose our monolith by changing the component granularity constraint and adding the Client/Server constraint (Chapter 13). To improve integration and interoperability, we will prescribe an API strategy.

Changing Constraints: Medium Component Granularity

Improving scalability in line with the stated business requirements requires decomposing our monolith into smaller, standalone services. When we previously decomposed a monolith in Chapter 13, we took the simple approach of decomposing the system along the existing, horizontal module boundaries. Since each module was a broad, horizontal slice, our only practical option (barring significant refactoring and

M. Carducci, *Mastering Software Architecture*, https://doi.org/10.1007/979-8-8688-0410-6_15

rewrites) was Coarse Component Granularity. Following the effort to redefine module boundaries using domain-derived boundaries in Chapter 14, we have more options available to us.

Recall that the domain components inside the modular monolith are closely analogous to embedded microservices. At this point, there may be a temptation to jump directly to fine-grained microservices, extracting each domain module as a separate service. In this context, however, such a leap would be both premature and unwise. For our project, High scalability is sufficient, thus making the Extremely High scalability of microservices styles—along with the added expense and complexity—excessive.

The pragmatic solution in this case is to choose Medium Component Granularity. The goal is to design a topology that offers *enough* scalability, *enough* elasticity, and *enough* agility while keeping cost and complexity manageable. As we saw with our efforts to define new module boundaries in the previous chapter, we must take care when defining component/service boundaries. In fact, getting module granularity right matters more in a distributed topology, and the network introduces new complexity and operational challenges. Defining granularity as "monolithic" leaves little room for interpretation; everything is inside the monolith. However, "coarse," "medium," and "fine" granularities all leave room for interpretation with "medium" potentially being the vaguest of the three. For the purposes of this book, these terms are used in the relative sense. To continue our couture metaphor, they are analogous to small, medium, and large; none of which are likely to fit you perfectly without tailoring. Likewise, in architecture, *optimal* granularity within any such constraint will vary from system to system. Instead of grasping for absolutes, while we wait for someone to invent mechanism(s) or metric(s) to absolutely measure and define component granularities, we simply consider our goals within the scope of this book and the Tailor-Made model. Medium Component Granularity seeks to balance performance, cost, complexity, and scale.

One of the benefits of the Medium Component Granularity Constraint of this style over the Fine Component Granularity of microservices is increased cohesion and lower complexity. This cohesion manifests as reduced or eliminated cross-service coordination. Complexity is lower as this granularity prescribes fewer services to manage and fewer distributed transactions. Ford and Richards suggest that services of this granularity tend to range from four to twelve.

> *Because the services typically share a single monolithic database, the number of services within an application context generally range between 4 and 12 services, with the average being about 7 services.*[1]

This granularity also improves performance because, beyond communication between client and server, or component and database, there is little to no network I/O and associated latency.

Determining optimal granularity can seem arbitrary or driven by a judgment call; however, more mindful approaches are available to us. Defining services by domain or subdomain is usually a good starting point for a first draft design. Use this design to model domain behaviors and workflows. When two services must frequently cooperate, there is a good case for consolidation. When this process identifies groups of models within a single service that do not interact, they may benefit from being extracted into a separate service.

Beyond domain boundaries, data-driven approaches may also inform your topology. Telemetry data, for example, might highlight specific domain behaviors or workflows that have higher-than-average or bursty loads. In such a case, this may warrant further decomposition in support of improved elasticity and scalability.

In all cases, pay particular attention to distributed transactions. These are another signal that the granularity of a particular service is too fine. Getting granularity right is an iterative process. The more we iterate on service granularity at design time, the less disruptive rework will be necessary by the implementation teams.

Interservice Communication

Although a single service designed according to this constraint will be able to single-handedly satisfy the domain behaviors and workflows within its scope, some amount of cross-service coordination may be unavoidable. When such cases emerge, we must consider how these services will communicate in different scenarios.

If services already expose an API, communication can take place in the form of synchronous API calls. *The Fallacies of Distributed Computing* caution us, however, against making assumptions about network performance and reliability. Response times *will* vary, and requests *will* occasionally time out. Consider the following scenarios that

[1] Richards, M., Ford, N. (2020). *Fundamentals of Software Architecture: An Engineering Approach* O'Reilly

take place within a simple topology of a user, Service A and Service B, where the user is making a request to Service A, and Service A needs to call Service B to satisfy this request.

The most direct failure occurs when the request from Service A to Service B simply times out (Figure 15-1). Service A will have no visibility into why the request failed and where it failed. Did Service B receive the request? Did it process the request? Without a response, Service A simply cannot know the answer. Should Service A retry the request? It depends on the request.

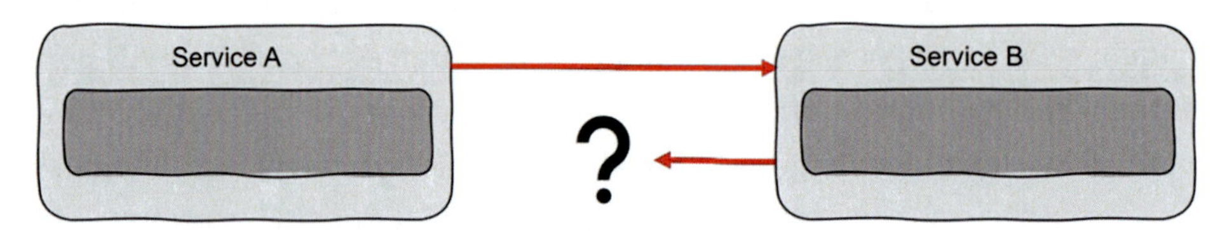

Figure 15-1. *Failed Call to Service B from Service A*

If the operation is *safe* (meaning the operation does not have side effects) or *idempotent* (meaning the operation will produce the same result regardless of the number of times it is performed), the retry option is available to us. If the operation is *unsafe* and not *idempotent* (e.g., Service B is a payment service attempting to charge the user's credit card), the interaction may need to be refactored to allow retries without double-billing the user. A more robust design for such an interaction would require Service A to include a session ID, request token, or *nonce* (a single-use random or unique value) in the request to allow Service B to evaluate if it has already completed the work in a previous request.

A defensively designed or otherwise idempotent request enables Service A to retry the request; however, what if Service B is overloaded and unhealthy? Rapid, repeated retries will only compound the problem. The request from the user's client to Service A is also a network interaction, with little visibility into failures. If the client's request to Service A times out while it waits for a response from Service B, the client may also retry the request. Furthermore, if Service A is actively processing multiple similar requests that are all suffering the same failures in Service B, parallel retry loops may snowball into an accidental denial-of-service (DOS) attack on Service B. Service A might also start to experience issues, such as timeouts or slow responses. This can lead to a cascading failure, where the problem within one service spreads to others, potentially bringing down the entire system.

Circuit breakers are a pattern that developers and architects put in place to prevent cascading failures. Put simply, the circuit breaker is normally in a "closed" state, meaning it allows requests from Service A to Service B to flow. When a circuit breaker detects the problem, however, it moves to an "open" state, which causes Service A to immediately fail any request to Service B, without even attempting it. This prevents further load in Service B and allows it time to recover. Service A must either defer to a fallback code path or a fallback response (e.g., "Please try again later") instead of failing entirely.

A Cautionary Tale of Cascading Failures

On Monday, May 6, 2024, a SaaS-powered email client experienced an issue where its backend services were unable to communicate with their database. Clients depend on this service for synchronization and sending/receiving messages. When the client's sync requests failed, the client would simply retry. With all running clients repeatedly retrying sync requests, the backend services went from unhealthy to completely offline.

According to public updates from the software vendor, developers had to update database client libraries in multiple places across the codebase. The remediation work was challenging as there was little abstraction in place. Developers had to implement fixes all over the codebase. In total, the fixes took four days, yet the downtime persisted.

For undisclosed reasons, the backend fix required client updates. Consequently, outdated clients were still DDOSing backend services. Additional effort was needed to mitigate the traffic and roll updates out to the software's installation base. Even after hot fixing backend services and updating clients, the app was still nonfunctional, leaving users either frustrated or abandoning the product in droves as downtime rolled into a fifth day.

It turns out a backend agent responsible for synchronizing email between providers and their platform had been operating in an infinite retry loop for the duration of the downtime. These agents were responsible for a DOS attack on third-party email servers. This traffic pattern forced email providers to rate-limit or block traffic from this app. Both the company and their customers had no choice but continue to wait while access was restored.

In total, this email app was unusable for seven days. There were clearly multiple contributing factors in this failure; among them is an illustration of the importance of planning for failure conditions. An *exponential backoff* (where retry attempts are increasingly delayed) on the synchronization agent could have avoided email providers rate-limiting or blocking their traffic. Additionally, circuit breakers elsewhere in the system would have arrested cascading failures. Finally, better abstraction of the database could have reduced the time to repair.

An alternative to synchronous communication is asynchronous communication. Does Service A *truly need* a synchronous acknowledgment or success confirmation from Service B? Or is a response from Service A that indicates the work performed by Service B is *pending* acceptable?

Consider again the case where Service B is the payment service. Service A could simply enqueue a request to process the payment, then immediately return a response to the user. User-perceived performance is significantly higher in this scenario. The system also becomes more fault tolerant as Service A can enqueue requests whether Service B is overloaded or idle, online or offline. A queued request will simply be processed as resources allow, and a separate asynchronous request can communicate state changes back to Service A. Service B is also better positioned to handle retries; however, architecture or development must define a strategy and a plan to handle persistent failures. This may be a "dead letter" queue, writing to a log, or simply an update to the caller indicating that the request failed.

The downside of the asynchronous approach is that queues and services can still fail which can result in dropped messages. More robust asynchronous communication mechanisms might promise *at least once delivery* instead of *exactly once delivery* which might result in the queue or topic consumer service double-processing a message if appropriate safeguards are not in place.

The third option is to bypass external services and perform coordination directly in the database. If Service A relies on Service B for additional data, and the two services share a single database, Service A can simply bypass the API altogether and reach directly into Service B's tables. This approach is simple, fast, and cheap; however, these benefits come at a cost. Cross-service coordination via the database introduces additional coupling which will undermine agility and evolvability. Teams must coordinate database changes across teams and services, resulting in more frequent coordinated releases. It is also important to note that this coupling is not always immediately visible, causing additional deployment risk.

Shared Code Across Services

In a modular monolith (Chapter 14), many cross-cutting concerns are handled by the *host* application, breaking apart that monolith requires distributing those responsibilities. These typically include logging, authentication, and—if the Shared Database Constraint is present—the data model and persistence layer.

The conventional solution for sharing code is extracting that functionality into a series of versioned, shared libraries. This can be a good option if the shared libraries either exhibit low code volatility or can be versioned in such a way that each service can manage its own upgrade cycles. Be cautious, however, as external libraries introduce a new potential point of coupling. When a medium-to-high volatility library frequently introduces breaking changes, the system will inevitably violate the Independent Deployability Constraint. Designing a distributed system that lacks independent deployability will result in a distributed monolith, which is an anti-pattern which we must strive to avoid.

Another possibility is the creation of a shared service. Like the shared library approach, this creates a single source of truth with the added benefit of an independent release cycle that will not impact running services unless a breaking change is introduced. The downside, of course, is that calls to this service incur network overhead and latency. Either architects or development teams must determine a plan for request timeouts, retry logic, circuit breakers, and fallbacks for each service or prescribe some alternative approach.

The extreme and counterintuitive solution is to duplicate code in each service. This might appear to violate the best practice of "Don't Repeat Yourself" (DRY); however, in architecture, there are no best practices, only trade-offs. There are advantages and disadvantages both to DRY and "Please Repeat Yourself" (PRY). The chief advantage of the latter approach is that it aggressively eliminates coupling and reduces coordination costs to achieve consensus on changes to the code. That said, such an approach introduces trade-offs and new challenges that might better be avoided, particularly in a medium-grained topology where the trade-offs might not make sense. This approach is often necessary in larger environments with many services that require extreme agility and extreme deployment velocity. We will undertake a detailed exploration of the trade-offs for this approach in the next chapter where it is more applicable.

Team, Environment, and Organizational Constraints

Like the Coarse-Grained Component Granularity Constraint introduced in Chapter 13, this constraint brings dependencies to induce the desired capabilities in the system. For reference, these are

- ARCH: Independent Deployability
- ORG: DevOps Commitment
- ENV: Loose Coupling Between Components
- ENV: Development Environment Isolation
- TEAM: API First
- TEAM: Automation Skills
- TEAM: Pipeline Development Skills

Independent Deployability

Our (now) distributed system will be a distributed monolith unless we replace the Monolithic Deployment Granularity Constraint with the Independent Deployability Constraint and its enabling team, organizational, and environmental constraints (described in Chapter 13).

Implementation Guidance

Independent deployability always introduces risk. Even with good modularity and component isolation, it can be difficult to predict when a change might have knock-on effects that will require coordinated deployments. In general, an investment into DevOps, automation, a fairly representative test bed with similar hardware and configuration to the production environment, along with a decent worst-case scenario automated test data generator will help to identify issues before shipping/deploying the product. In other words, our build pipelines and quality gates must do more than build and test a single component; pipelines must also run integration tests against other services and, ideally, run all component integration tests prior to release (and continually after release). The goal is to detect integration failures with external dependencies before releasing to production as well as early detection of integration failures when other services are updated.

Adding Constraints

As we decompose this system, we must also prescribe the Client/Server constraint (described in Chapter 13). Both improving integration and interoperability and enabling the Client/Server constraint will require, at a minimum, prescribing an API Constraint. Chapter 13 noted that API strategy is architecturally significant and explored the trade-offs between the available options. The emphasis in the requirements on integration and evolvability suggests a Level 1 or Level 2 REST API; however, for the sake of simplicity when defining this abstract style, we will select the RPC API Constraint.

The Mature, Medium-Grained, Domain Partitioned RPC Client/Server Style

Through the composition of constraints, we have arrived at a concrete architectural style (Figure 15-2) that satisfies the business requirements outlined in the previous chapter while balancing cost and complexity.

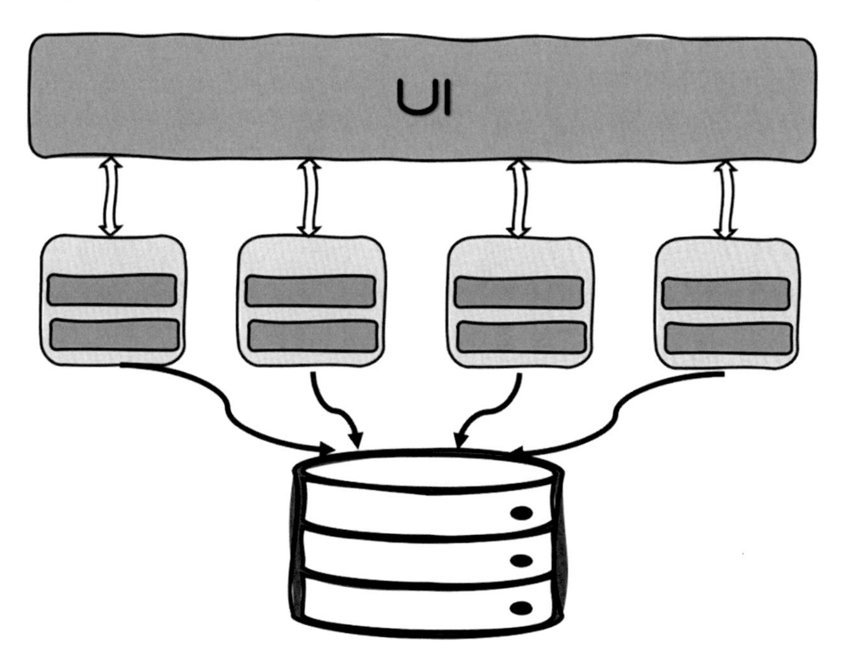

Figure 15-2. *The Mature Medium-Grained, Domain Partitioned, RPC Client/ Server Style*

The following constraints define this style:

- Medium Component Granularity
- Independent Deployability
- Domain Partitioning
- Client/Server
- RPC API
- Partitioned Shared Database

This collection of constraints requires the following team, organization, and environmental constraints:

- ORG: Well-Defined Domains
- ORG: Domain-Aligned Teams
- ORG: DevOps Commitment
- ENV: Loose Coupling Between Components
- ENV: Development Environment Isolation
- TEAM: API First
- TEAM: Automation Skills
- TEAM: Pipeline Development Skills

Although we have arrived at this style through a process of evolution, this style is a slight variation on the Service-Based Abstract Style. The only difference between the set of constraints in this concrete style and the defining constraints of the Service-Based Abstract Style is the *Partitioned Shared Database Constraint.* The abstract style does not prescribe this constraint (but it can be added through the tailoring process—see the section "Tailoring This Abstract Style").

The Service-Based Abstract Style

This abstract style offers a highly pragmatic approach to building distributed systems. Components exhibit manageable granularity, ACID transactions remain the norm, it requires limited cross-service coordination, and the enabling practices are within reach of most teams.

Because of the Domain Partitioning Constraint, the evolutionary path, both to and from this style, is low friction, low risk, and straightforward. Migration to this style involves breaking a modular monolith into multiple mini-modular monoliths (Figure 15-3). For projects that do not yet require the scale and complexity of a distributed system, the agile architecture approach is to begin with a modular monolith and let the business and metrics determine the decomposition decision. The modular nature of this style offers significant flexibility for tailoring or further decomposition, again, as metrics and business needs dictate. *Microservice styles are always overkill, except when they are not.* Up-front overengineering and premature optimization are not necessary when incremental, data-driven evolution is baked into the system's design.

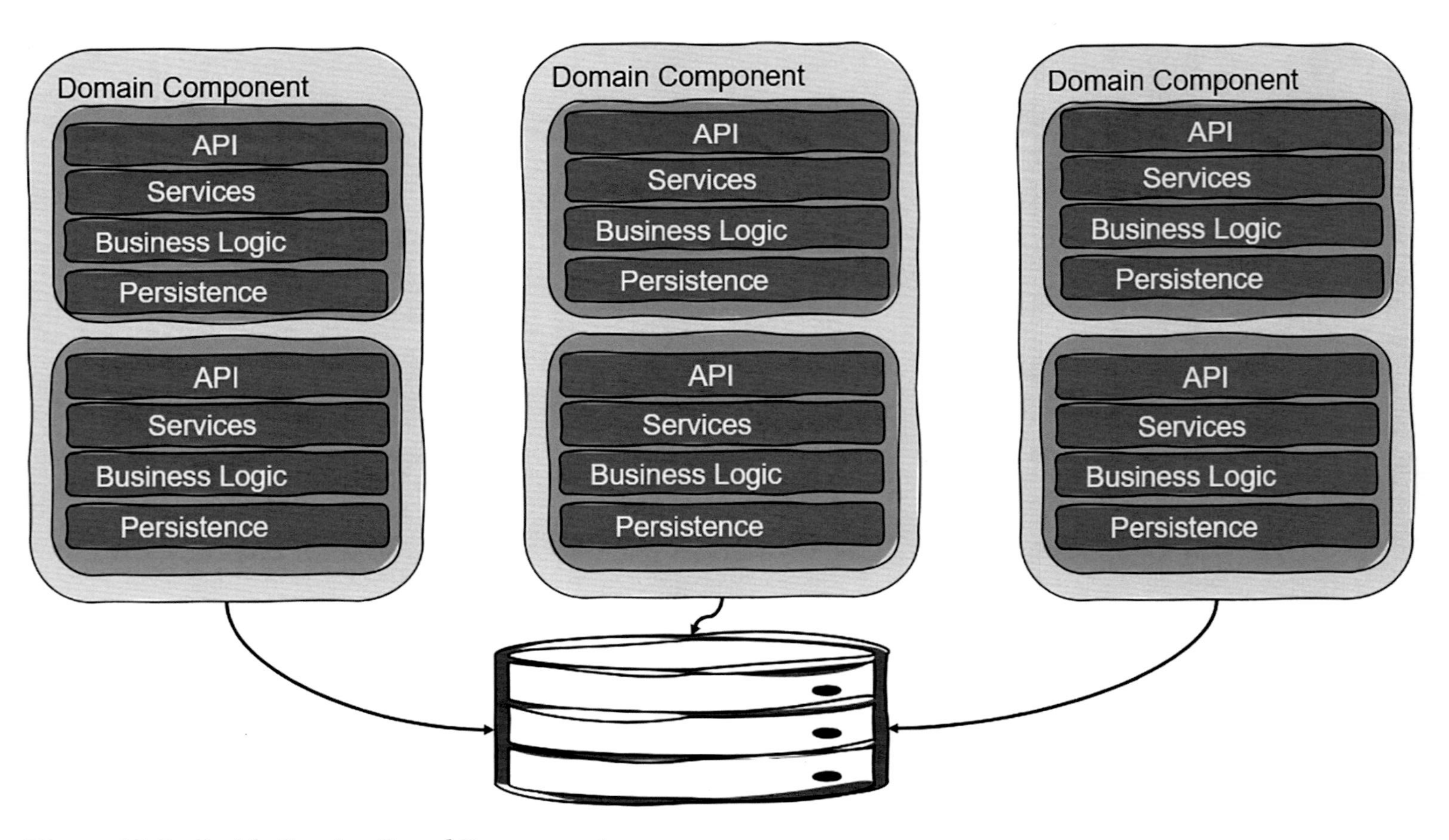

***Figure 15-3.** Inside Service-Based Components*

Tailoring This Abstract Style

Variations of this style replace the Domain Partitioning Constraint with the Technical Partitioning Constraint. This is often due to organizational incompatibility that cannot be easily or immediately overcome. Replacing this constraint brings additional simplicity, but that comes at a cost. The Domain Partitioning Constraint is the engine of both High evolvability and Very High agility. A Technically Partitioned Service-Based Style does not require the organizational constraints but will inherit the trade-offs inherent in all technically partitioned systems, and further decomposition will require significant work to carve out vertical slices.

Although this variation is not the goal or focus of this chapter, styles can be tailored to meet different needs and align with different organizational realities. In short, keep in mind that Layered Monolith and Distributed N-Tier styles are not the only options for technically partitioned systems.

Partitioned Shared Database Constraint

This is another optional constraint that will improve both agility and evolvability. In essence, this constraint will move the style along the continuum toward microservices and the capabilities they bring without inheriting their complexity. Additionally, should future needs dictate further evolution toward microservices, the migration will be simplified as less effort will be necessary to break apart the database.

CQRS Constraint

As described in Chapter 13, distributed systems are inherently more scalable; however, a single, shared, monolithic database will still introduce a bottleneck. This constraint allows reads to be load balanced across multiple database server instances.

Coarse Federated Databases

If you already have a partitioned shared database, an option to achieve higher scale is to begin to split apart the database (Figure 15-4). If a logical data domain is already isolated in the form of a distinct schema or catalog with a unique connection string, it is trivial to simply move that schema to its own server. Agility and scale go up, but complexity does as well.

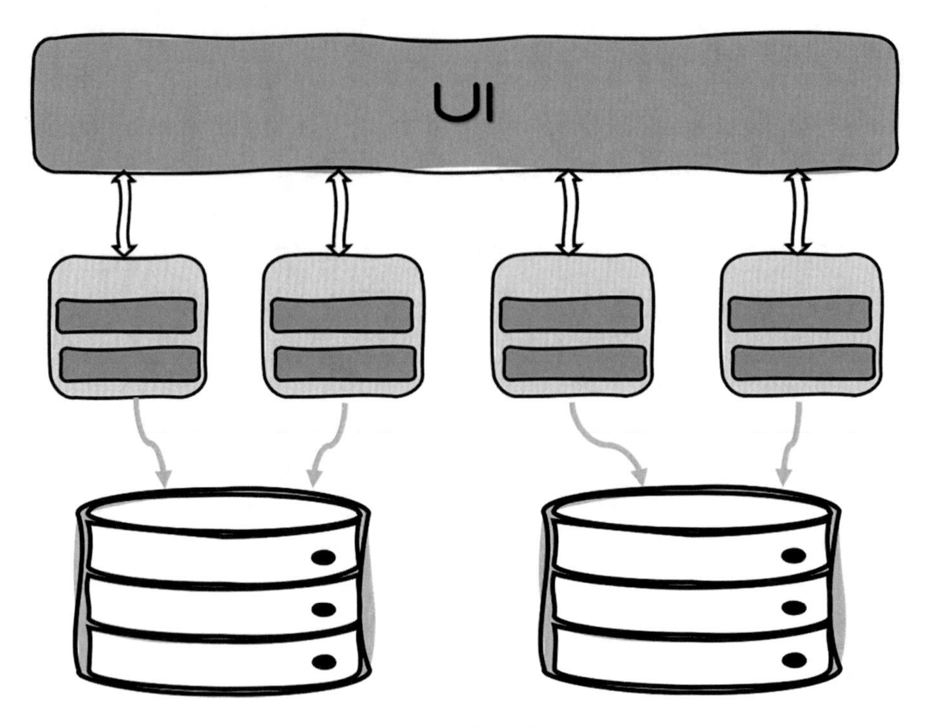

Figure 15-4. *Federated DB Service-Based Style*

Summary

In Chapter 9, we referenced Gartner's prediction that 90% of organizations who try microservices will find the paradigm too disruptive. In contrast, the Service-Based Abstract Style is a balanced and deeply pragmatic approach to distributed system design that will satisfy all but the most extreme requirements for agility and scale. However, like the modular monolith, this style leaves doors open for further architectural evolution.

The superficial topological similarity between this style and microservices leads many developers and architects to conflate this style with microservices; however, there are key differences in the underlying constraints as you will see in the next chapter.

The following architectural constraints define this abstract style:

- Medium Component Granularity
- Independent Deployability
- Domain Partitioning

- Client/Server
- RPC API
- Shared Database

This collection of constraints requires the following team, organization, and environmental constraints:

- ORG: Well-Defined Domains
- ORG: Domain-Aligned Teams
- ORG: DevOps Commitment
- ENV: Loose Coupling Between Components
- ENV: Development Environment Isolation
- TEAM: API First
- TEAM: Automation Skills
- TEAM: Pipeline Development Skills

A concrete style derived from this abstract style may require additional architectural constraints or implementation guidance around interservice communication. Additional environmental constraints may also be necessary to support things like circuit breakers and self-healing services.

This style is a waypoint on the architectural continuum between the modular monolith and microservices offering numerous advantages over the former with what are often manageable trade-offs. The notable improvements over the **Modular Monolith Abstract Style** are shown in Figure 15-5.

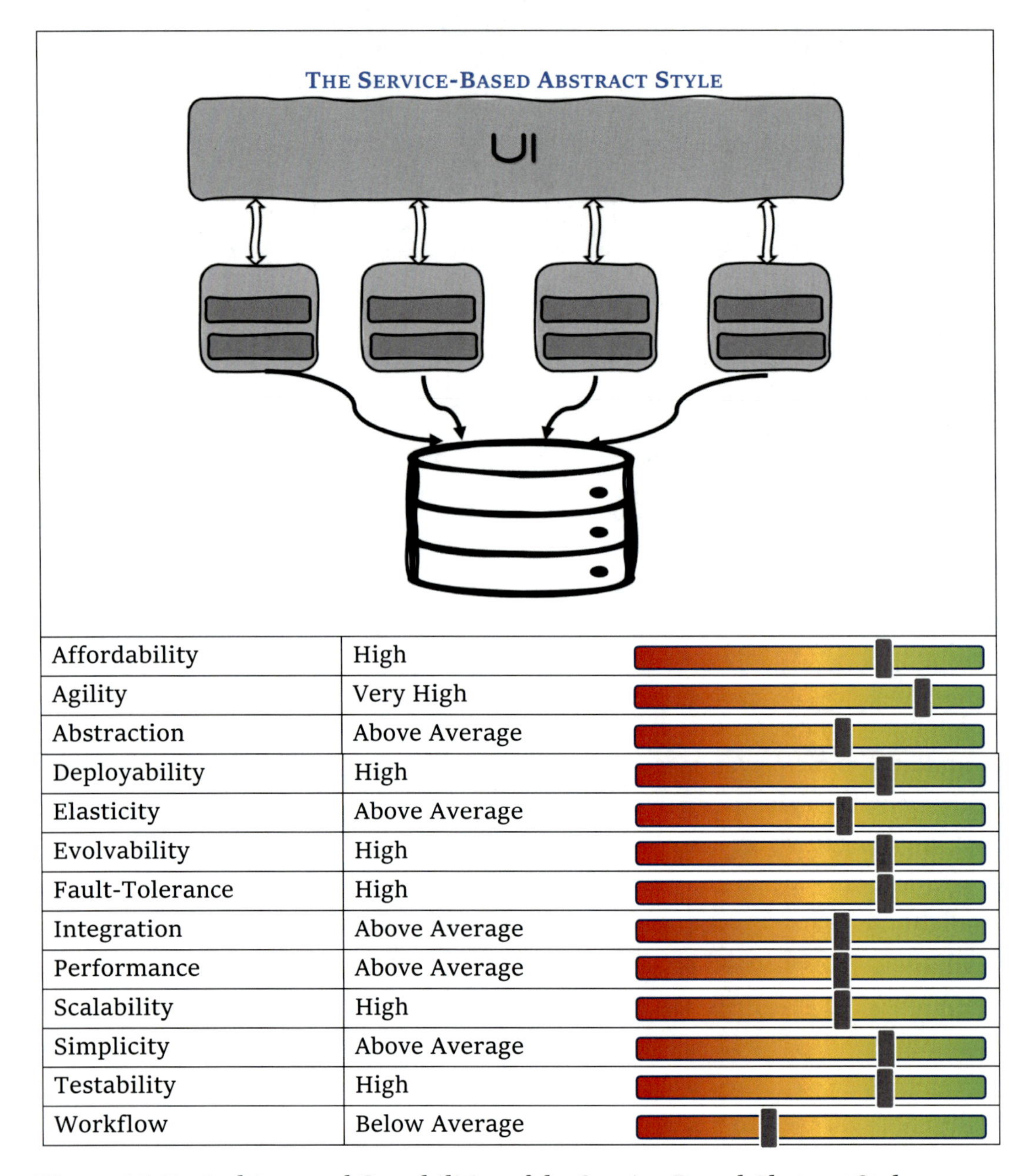

Affordability	High	
Agility	Very High	
Abstraction	Above Average	
Deployability	High	
Elasticity	Above Average	
Evolvability	High	
Fault-Tolerance	High	
Integration	Above Average	
Performance	Above Average	
Scalability	High	
Simplicity	Above Average	
Testability	High	
Workflow	Below Average	

Figure 15-5. *Architectural Capabilities of the Service-Based Abstract Style*

CHAPTER 16

The Microservices Abstract Style

> *A microservice is a single purpose, independently deployable unit of software that does one thing well.*
>
> —Mark Richards

The Service-Based Abstract Style, introduced in the previous chapter, offers many Above Average and High capabilities balanced against manageable cost and complexity. The capabilities afforded by the defining constraints of that style will satisfy all but the most extreme demands. However, there do exist systems where anything less than extreme agility, extreme scalability, and extreme fault tolerance poses an existential threat. Achieving such extremes is not easy and requires a similarly demanding set of architectural constraints to maximize the capabilities of the system.

We will progress along the continuum by introducing and modifying constraints. Throughout this process, we will significantly enhance many of the capabilities provided by the Service-Based Abstract Style, elevating them to an extremely high level.

Changing Constraints

Fine Component Granularity

In the pursuit of the extremes the Microservices Abstract Style promises, the first change we must prescribe is a further reduction of individual component granularity. Microservices takes the approach of decomposing a software system into its smallest *practical, irreducible* components. Ideally, each medium-grained service component in the Service-Based style is already a mini-Modular Monolith, with standalone domain

M. Carducci, *Mastering Software Architecture*, https://doi.org/10.1007/979-8-8688-0410-6_16

components that are ready to be extracted into discrete microservices. In this case, changing granularity is, once again, straightforward. However, regardless of the level of difficulty you or your development teams will face during decomposition, the challenges this constraint introduces are only beginning.

First, this constraint offers little in the form of guidance on what this level of granularity looks like in practice. Good answers rarely materialize until we begin to ask the right questions. In accordance with the First Law of Software Architecture,[1] "*Why is more important than how*," let us first explore the "why."

Fine component granularity drives the characteristic "micro" scope of the microservices architecture. In many ways, this constraint is analogous to the Single-Responsibility Principle (SRP) of object-oriented design. SRP states that only the necessary cohesive functionality needed for a single responsibility be present in each OO class. As developers introduce additional responsibilities into a single class, coupling increases and additional code paths emerge that developers and architects must identify and test. The code becomes harder to change as, often, the changes result in unexpected side effects. Adherence to the SRP favors composition of multiple single-purpose classes to achieve a single domain behavior, rather than inheritance to fully encapsulate the domain behavior in a single, concrete class. By way of the Fine Component Granularity Constraint, the microservices style advances this concept from code-level to architecture-level. A fine-grained microservice serves as a single-responsibility component that, through composition with other microservices, delivers more coarse-grained domain behaviors (with trade-offs, of course).

The parallels between SRP in OO and its microservices cousin are not exact.[2] Does single responsibility imply microservices scope should be as "micro" as a single function? Perhaps, but not necessarily. Generally, the distinction between the two SRP guidelines is that, in microservices, a single service should encapsulate a single *domain* responsibility (vs. a single code responsibility in OO). There are also times where separation of a single domain may be done because of constraints like cyber security (e.g., read being absolutely separated from create, update, and delete), data persistence (e.g., writes may be pushed through a different interface than reads for certain high-volume circumstances or in situations where a query interface may be available but

[1] Ford, N., & Richards, M. (2020). *Fundamentals of software architecture: An engineering approach*. O'Reilly Media

[2] Merson, P. (2020). *Principles for Microservice Design: Think IDEALS, Rather than SOLID*. InfoQ. Retrieved from https://www.infoq.com/articles/microservices-design-ideals/

a data stream is also available), or in situations where a domain service with certain options is provided to one group of consumers but a different set is made available to other users (paying vs. free service users). In such cases, you will need to decide whether these sorts of isolation occur at the service component level or whether a service will encapsulate these alternatives. Precision in domain modeling is especially important in getting granularity right at design time.

A well-designed, single-purpose, fine-grained service offers the possibility of significant gains in evolvability, enabling increased product or organizational agility. When interfaces are stable, and the service's behavior well designed and scoped, development or implementation teams can implement, test, and deploy changes with great velocity. Not only does this constraint enable implementation teams to release individual changes as soon as they are ready, but a frequent release cadence of small changes will significantly reduce risk. In fact, should a team discover that the most recent change is somehow faulty, rolling back that deployment will only affect that single service, while other, successful changes continue to roll forward, leaving overall product and organizational agility extremely high. Good service boundaries form important bulkheads that both limit the testing surface while also isolating the impact of any individual change. However, when services have unstable interfaces and abstractions that multiple other microservices depend on, the resulting coupling can complicate this process, introducing unexpected side effects which are difficult to anticipate.

The bulkheads afforded by this constraint also offer the potential for massively improved fault tolerance. When a monolithic application is offline, all functionality is unavailable. Distributed architectures have the capability to remove single points of failure within a system, and a fine-grained distributed architecture further reduces the impact of a failure down to, potentially, a single domain behavior. You must exercise care when designing these fine-grained architectures to avoid the scenario where a whole group of interdependent services introduces a *many single points of failure* scenario. As a simple example of a *many single points of failure scenario*, consider cheap Christmas lights where every bulb forms an integral part of a single circuit. A single bulb coming lose or burning out will black out the entire string of lights and, perhaps, all subsequent daisy-chained strings. Finding the failed component is so difficult and time-consuming that many will simply opt to purchase an entirely new string of lights. We rarely have such luxuries in software (but customers often do—see "A Cautionary Tale of Cascading Failures" in Chapter 15).

As we explored in the last chapter, cascading failures emerge as a new scenario that we must identify and mitigate. However, so long as architecture mitigates this risk through application of the required environmental constraint of bulkheads and circuit breakers to enable dependent services to gracefully indicate that a portion of their functionality is unavailable, overall fault tolerance will increase.

The single responsibility "micro" scope of microservices this constraint prescribes will correlate strongly with similarly "micro" binary artifact sizes. These artifacts will boast a significantly reduced cold start time. Consequently, a burst in demand can be met with additional capacity by dynamically scaling a single service horizontally (or vertically). As demand for that service subsides, the system can similarly react by reducing the number of available individual instances.

In addition to offering elastic response to demand, this granularity enables individual atomic domain behaviors to adapt to persistent load and demand. Overall compute and storage capacity can be applied where needed with extreme precision through horizontal and vertical scaling. This enables efficient resource allocation which offers levels of scale well beyond what coarse-grained architectures are capable of.

This constraint is clearly a crucial ingredient to achieving the highest possible levels of evolvability, agility, fault tolerance, scalability, and elasticity. These gains, however, come at a significant cost.

First, this architecture will test the mettle of any architect during the design stage. Getting granularity right requires detailed and sophisticated domain modeling and a deep alignment between the organizational structure and the domain model. Unlike other granularity constraints, the Fine Component Granularity Constraint *requires* domain partitioning which, consequently, requires *well-defined domains* and *domain-aligned teams*. One litmus test for microservice granularity is to attempt to specifically describe the service's domain behavior. A typical microservice can be described in a single sentence, without the use of conjunctive words like *and/or*. This is not to say that service descriptions will never deploy a conjunctive word indicating multiple domain behaviors, but such cases will suggest additional scrutiny in the design. This is sometimes referred to as a "design smell."

On paper, service boundaries may initially appear obvious, but lurking just beneath the surface are countless edge cases waiting to be discovered. Each edge case must be identified and compensated for. Sometimes, architecture can address an edge case through service consolidation, or a data replication strategy, or the creation of a shared service, a data domain, or through some other mechanism. You must evaluate and address each edge case on a case-by-case basis; there are currently no broad best practices or objective test for optimal granularity that can be applied here.

Beyond boundary edge cases, you must also meter the amount of performance that this style exchanges for the other architectural capabilities. At this level of granularity, many domain workflows that rely on in-process function invocation in coarse-grained architectures become out-of-process network calls—network calls that necessarily incur bandwidth and latency overhead. Optimal granularity necessitates that performance does not fall below a threshold defined by the business or product.

Beyond reduced performance, a new challenge arises in the form of observability. When a process fails in a monolithic component, the application will dump the entire state and stack trace into a single log. Contrast this with a failure that spans several microservices. The logs from any single service only offer a piece of the puzzle which rarely tells the whole story. This constraint requires the *Distributed Tracing and Logging Environmental Constraint.*

Tracing is a technique to track and log the flow of requests across service boundaries to monitor, debug, and optimize distributed systems. Tracing enables the production of a distributed stack trace for analyzing and resolving problems and failures. For total visibility, an engineer investigating an issue will require more than the trace; they must also piece together the rest of the story from the logs of multiple services.[3] To achieve this, we require some mechanism to collate related log entries (some common options are enumerated in Chapter 3 under "Observability"). Often a request will be assigned a unique request ID or correlation ID that is common across all service hops for the life of that single request. Through this unique identifier, multiple interservice requests can be tracked to form a single, end-to-end trace and the mechanism by which otherwise disparate logs can be combined to surface a complete picture of what happened. There are many tools and cloud services that will collate log entries and make them visible on a dashboard or through proactive notifications. The practices that enable this constraint—along with the prescribed tooling—must form part of the development process' standard operating procedure.

Fine Component Granularity requires an environment that supports a high degree of operational automation. Beyond build, test, and deployment automation, development teams must define each service's infrastructure requirements and conditions for scaling up and down. This will necessitate some knowledge of Kubernetes or another cloud orchestration system as well as Infrastructure as Code (IaC) skills.

---

[3] Fowler, S. (2016). *Production-Ready Microservices.* O'Reilly

In such an automated environment, where service instances are spinning up or down based on demand and where unhealthy instances are terminated and restarted, request routing must become dynamic. There must be a mechanism for each service instance to broadcast its availability, status, health, and location. Architecture must prescribe an environmental constraint of *Service Discovery and Routing.*

Finally, as with other non-monolithic granularity constraints, this constraint depends on *Independent Development Cycles, Independent Deployability,* and *API-first* development.

Getting granularity right under this constraint is more difficult than in medium or coarse-grained styles. The disadvantages and trade-offs of this constraint will provide feedback on when a service is "too micro." Remember the advice in Chapter 14 on evaluating granularity and iterating where possible in the direction of coarser to finer. Use the presence of distributed transactions (discussed in the next constraint) as another "design smell" that granularity might be too fine-grained. Likewise, use the business metrics introduced in Chapter 5 as a signal for when further decomposition by architecture is required.

Scenario Granularity

To illustrate the nuanced challenges inherent to this constraint, below is a hypothetical scenario where architecture must make a judgment call. In this (and subsequent) scenario, there is no objective "right answer." These exercises are, instead, focused on providing practice for you to think through the options and their trade-offs.

Scenario Each call to a microservice requires an authorization step (either from a client or between services). Your choices are to create a shared authorization service, a shared library, an authorization sidecar, or a shared/coupled API layer. Describe your choice and trade-off analysis.

Other Info:
110 Microservices
Low volatility
100ms latency between services
30 Requests/second
350ms AVG response time

In total, this constraint depends on the following non-architectural constraints:

- ORG: Well-Defined Domains
- ORG: Domain-Aligned Teams
- ORG: DevOps Commitment
- ENV: High Operational Automation
- ENV: Distributed Tracing and Logging
- ENV: Bulkheads and Circuit Breakers
- ENV: Service Discovery and Routing
- ENV: Development Environment Isolation
- TEAM: API First
- TEAM: Automation Skills
- TEAM: Pipeline Development Skills
- TEAM: Cloud/Orchestration Skills
- TEAM: IaC Skills

Isolated Databases

An additional ingredient to this style's extreme agility, scalability, and fault tolerance is prescribing that each microservice owns its own database. As with the Partitioned Shared Database Constraint described in Chapter 14, this constraint precludes database coupling across components. When one microservice completely controls one database, the code and database changes can be released atomically and confidently. All changes are safely scoped, so long as the API contract of the service remains stable.

Unlike the case with the Partitioned Shared Database Constraint, this constraint eliminates the single monolithic database from the architecture. This removes both a scaling bottleneck and a single point of failure.

As previous chapters in this section (Chapters 14 and 15) have already noted, breaking apart data along clean boundaries is extremely difficult. The need for distributed transactions increases in proportion with service granularity; finer granularity results in more individual microservices that must communicate and coordinate. Consistent with what this and previous chapters have stated, we should avoid distributed transactions; they are often a symptom of granularity problems. However, with more fine-grained styles, we cannot always avoid them. Where distributed transactions are inevitable, we must make a choice on how we will navigate the CAP theorem (Figure 16-1).

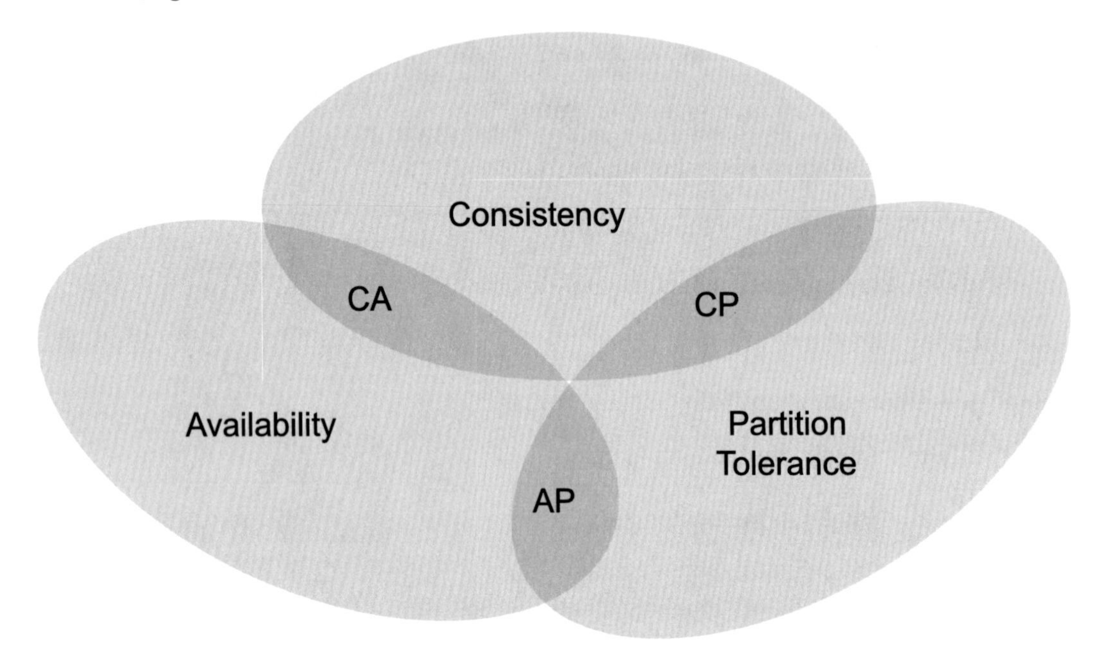

Figure 16-1. *CAP Theorem Diagram*

CAP Theorem The CAP theorem, or Brewer's theorem,[4] is a fundamental concept in distributed systems that highlights the inherent trade-offs when designing such systems. It states that in the context of a distributed data store, you can only achieve up to two out of the following three guarantees at any given time: consistency, availability, and partition tolerance.

- **Consistency** means that every read request will receive the most recent write (or an error), ensuring all nodes see the same data simultaneously.

[4] Gilbert, S., Lynch, N. (2002). "Brewer's conjecture and the feasibility of consistent, available, partition-tolerant web services." *ACM SIGACT News*. **33**. Association for Computing Machinery (ACM): 51–59

- **Availability** ensures that every request receives a response—success or failure—without waiting indefinitely (although it may not reflect the latest state).
- **Partition Tolerance** is the ability of the system to continue operating despite an arbitrary number of messages being dropped (or delayed) between nodes or other network failures that divide the system into isolated segments.

The theorem forces us to make choices. For instance, if you prioritize consistency and availability, you might have to sacrifice partition tolerance, meaning the system could fail if network issues occur. On the other hand, if you opt for availability and partition tolerance, you might have to relax consistency rules, leading to scenarios where different nodes could see different data. Finally, choosing consistency and partition tolerance might mean the system is not always available, especially during network partitions.

The CAP theorem is a reminder that in distributed systems, perfection is not achievable. It is about understanding which trade-offs align with your system's requirements and making informed decisions accordingly.

With the Isolated Database Constraint in effect, the traditional ACID guarantees offered by monolithic relational databases—Atomicity, Consistency, Isolation, and Durability—are no longer feasible across multiple services. This limitation poses a significant challenge in ensuring data consistency and reliability in complex, distributed architectures. However, we can address this challenge by adopting the Saga Pattern, a powerful mechanism for managing transactions in a distributed system. The Saga Pattern provides a way to maintain consistency by orchestrating a series of local transactions, each confined to a single service.

The Saga Pattern

In the Saga Pattern, a transaction is broken down into a sequence of smaller, discrete steps, each of which can be handled independently by different services. If a step fails, the system attempts to undo the changes made by previous steps using *compensating transactions*, ensuring that the system remains consistent. Notably, the approach of compensating transactions is not always possible, which further informs our approach to distributed transactions.

Key Concepts in the Saga Pattern

Compensable Transactions: These are transactions that can be reversed by executing another transaction with the opposite effect. For instance, if a service successfully debits an account, but a subsequent service fails to complete the corresponding credit, a compensable transaction will credit the account to undo the debit. This compensating mechanism is crucial for maintaining consistency when parts of a distributed transaction fail.

Pivot Transaction: The pivot transaction is the critical decision point in a saga. It determines whether the saga will continue to completion or abort. Once the pivot transaction commits, the saga is committed to running to the end. Pivot transactions are typically non-compensable and non-retriable, thus serving as the go/no-go point in the saga. You can look at these transactions as the final checkpoint before the system fully commits to the transaction.

Retriable Transactions: After the pivot transaction, retriable transactions follow. These transactions are guaranteed to succeed eventually, even if temporary failures occur. They provide resilience to the saga, ensuring that once the system passes the pivot point, it can handle intermittent issues and still complete the process.

Coordination in the Saga Pattern

Distributed transactions require coordination across multiple services, and the Saga Pattern offers two primary approaches for this: choreography and orchestration.

Choreography

Choreography involves a decentralized approach to coordination. Each service involved in the saga listens for events from upstream services and reacts accordingly, executing its transaction and publishing events to signal the next step. This approach is akin to a dance where each participant knows its steps and responds to others.

Advantages

- Ideal for simple workflows with few participants, where the logic is straightforward.
- There is no need for additional coordination services, reducing overhead and maintenance.
- Avoids creating a single point of failure, as responsibilities are distributed across the participants.

Drawbacks

- As a transaction workflow grows in complexity, choreography can become difficult to manage, with services becoming entangled in a web of dependencies.
- Adding new steps can be confusing, as it is hard to track which services are listening for which events.
- There is a risk of cyclic dependencies between services, complicating the system further.
- Integration testing is challenging, requiring all services to be operational to simulate a full transaction.

Orchestration

Alternatively, orchestration centralizes the control of the saga in a single orchestrator service. The analogy here is that of an orchestra with many players who all take their respective queues from a central conductor. Each player knows their respective notes, but the conductor brings the whole symphony together.

In an orchestrated saga, the orchestrator issues commands to each participant service, dictating the global sequence of actions. This method provides more control over the flow and makes it easier to manage complex transactions involving many services.

Advantages

- Well suited for complex workflows with many participants or scenarios where new services or behaviors may be added over time.
- Centralized control over the process flow and participants, reducing the risk of cyclic dependencies.
- Participants are isolated from each other's commands, leading to a clear separation of concerns and simpler business logic.

Drawbacks

- Introduces additional design complexity, as the orchestrator needs to manage the entire workflow.
- The orchestrator becomes a potential point of failure, requiring robust failover strategies to ensure resilience.

Challenges and Considerations in Implementing the Saga Pattern

Implementing the Saga Pattern requires a shift in mindset, especially when transitioning from monolithic systems to microservices. Some challenges to consider include

- **Debugging Complexity**: The distributed nature of sagas makes them hard to debug, particularly as the number of participants grows. Careful monitoring and logging are essential to trace issues effectively.
- **Data Rollback Limitations**: Unlike traditional transactions, data in a saga cannot be easily rolled back. Once a service commits its local transaction, that change is permanent unless explicitly reversed by a compensating transaction.
- **Handling Transient Failures and Ensuring Idempotence**: Services must be designed to handle transient failures gracefully. This often involves ensuring that operations are idempotent, meaning they can be repeated without causing unintended side effects. For instance, when processing messages, the system should be able to retry operations without altering the outcome, maintaining consistency even in the face of failures.

- **Observability**: Given the complexity of sagas, it is crucial to implement observability tools to monitor and track the progress of transactions. This visibility is key to managing and debugging sagas effectively.
- **Durability Challenges**: The lack of isolation between participants poses durability challenges. Each participant commits changes to its local database at different stages, which can lead to inconsistencies if not properly managed. Implementing measures to minimize anomalies and ensure data durability is critical.

Saga Forces

In *Software Architecture: The Hard Parts*,[5] the authors identify three fundamental forces that influence the design and implementation of sagas:

- **Communication**: Whether to use synchronous or asynchronous communication between services. This choice affects the responsiveness and reliability of the saga.
- **Consistency**: The decision between requiring strict atomic consistency and allowing eventual consistency across the system.
- **Coordination**: The choice between orchestration and choreography, each with its trade-offs in terms of control, complexity, and resilience.

How these forces interact will determine other properties of the saga, such as coupling.

The Saga Pattern is a powerful tool for managing distributed transactions, but it comes with its own set of challenges and considerations. Understanding the trade-offs between choreography and orchestration, ensuring idempotence, and implementing robust observability are crucial for success. As with any architectural strategy, the key is to align the Saga Pattern with your system's specific needs and constraints, using it to achieve the desired balance between consistency, availability, and partition tolerance in your distributed microservices style architecture.

[5] Ford, N., Richards, M., Sadalage, P., Dehghani, Z. (2021). *Software Architecture: The Hard Parts: Modern Trade-Off Analyses for Distributed Architectures*. O'Reilly Media

Sharing Data

In addition to coordinating database writes, we must also often coordinate reads. Unfortunately, tables and columns do not always file neatly into isolated data domains; there is inevitably some amount of overlap. For a concrete example, let us look at a hypothetical ecommerce system that has been decomposed according to the constraints prescribed in the Microservices Abstract Style.

Among various components, we find three that are germane to our data sharing scenario, the Product Catalog service, the Inventory service, and the Cart service.

The Product Catalog's database contains entries for each product, including Stock Keeping Unit (SKU), images, name, description, and other properties. The Inventory service tracks the quantity and locations of each SKU in the warehouse, and the Cart service knows which SKUs are currently in the customer's cart along with the desired quantity. Of course, a customer does not care about the SKU or other database keys; they care about the product's name. Product also wants the cart UI to display a thumbnail image of the product. Finally, business rules dictate that out-of-stock items cannot remain in the cart. The Cart service, therefore, depends on data that is owned and controlled by at least two other services (Figure 16-2).

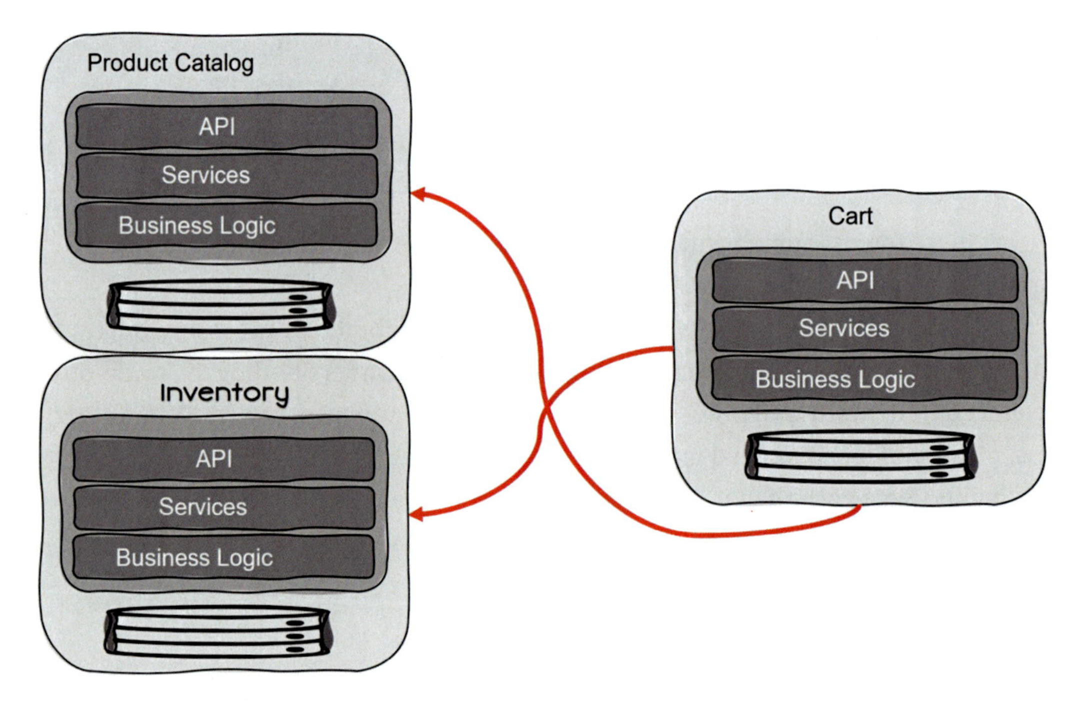

Figure 16-2. *Service Data Dependencies*

What are our options? One of the first approaches that will come to mind for developers is to simply perform one or more calls to the other service(s) API. This is commonly known as the *aggregator pattern*, where the service request will gather and aggregate all the necessary data to return the response. This is a useful pattern to have at your disposal. However, beware of chaining together too many microservices as interservice calls incur latency and bandwidth overhead. Additionally, these branching and chaining aggregates can quickly begin to involve ad hoc orchestration of several microservices. This undermines performance and fault tolerance while increasing coupling (thus lowering agility). There are other trade-offs as well. Let us look at different ways to implement the aggregation requests and close with a brief look at an asynchronous, event sourcing approach.

Simple REST API

The simplest option is for the client to make a request to the Cart service which, in turn, makes synchronous REST requests to the dependent services.

```
GET /product/id/1234
Accept: application/json

200 OK
Content-Length: 247469
...
...
```

While this approach will certainly work, there are trade-offs. First, this decision has reduced user-perceived performance as a synchronous request to load the cart requires a chain of requests behind the scenes that must complete before a response is returned to the customer. If one or both requests fail, the Cart service must also implement fallback logic to gracefully degrade behavior and arrest cascading failures. Another issue is a REST API will typically return a full representation of the resource. Among other problems, we have now introduced bandwidth overhead.

Even if our service only needs the product name (~200 bytes), a REST API that serves a complete representation of the product will often be orders of magnitude larger. A 250kb response or larger is well within the realm of possibility. The unnecessary bandwidth overhead can really add up. At just 2000 requests/sec, our service is already consuming half a gigabyte of bandwidth.

Our REST approach also introduces *stamp coupling* to our component. Stamp coupling, also known as data-structured coupling, occurs in software architecture when components or modules share a composite data structure, but only use a portion of it. This type of coupling is a form of interdependence where the modules rely on the structure of the data rather than just the specific data elements they need. Stamp coupling introduces a higher level of dependency between components, making the system more brittle and harder to modify or extend.

Optimized REST API

REST does not dictate that representations are always one-size-fits-all. In fact, we can suggest or prescribe that the Catalog Service support *content negotiation*, where a client can request a custom representation of the resource that is optimized for this use case by supplying more precise `Accept:` headers in the request.

```
GET /product/id/1234
Accept: application/cart+json

200 OK
Content-Length: 548
...
...
```

This more refined approach will reduce bandwidth overhead but does not necessarily solve stamp coupling unless a custom representation is available for every common use case.

Alternatively, the REST API might offer some kind of custom field selector.

```
GET /product/id/1234?fields=name
Accept: application/json

200 OK
Content-Length: 281
...
...
```

The optimized REST approaches also offer the benefit of the cacheability of GET requests. As a trade-off, the optimal implementation of the customized approaches will require further API standardization and likely some form of architectural governance to ensure conformance.

GraphQL

GraphQL offers an out-of-the-box solution for consumer-driven contracts which introduces flexibility and optimization, but such requests are not cacheable and still potentially introduce data model coupling.

Synchronous approaches will guarantee consistency, but availability of the dependent services will impact the availability of the Cart service.

Asynchronous Replication and Event Sourcing

As an alternative to synchronous approaches to response composition, asynchronous options are also available to us (Figure 16-3).

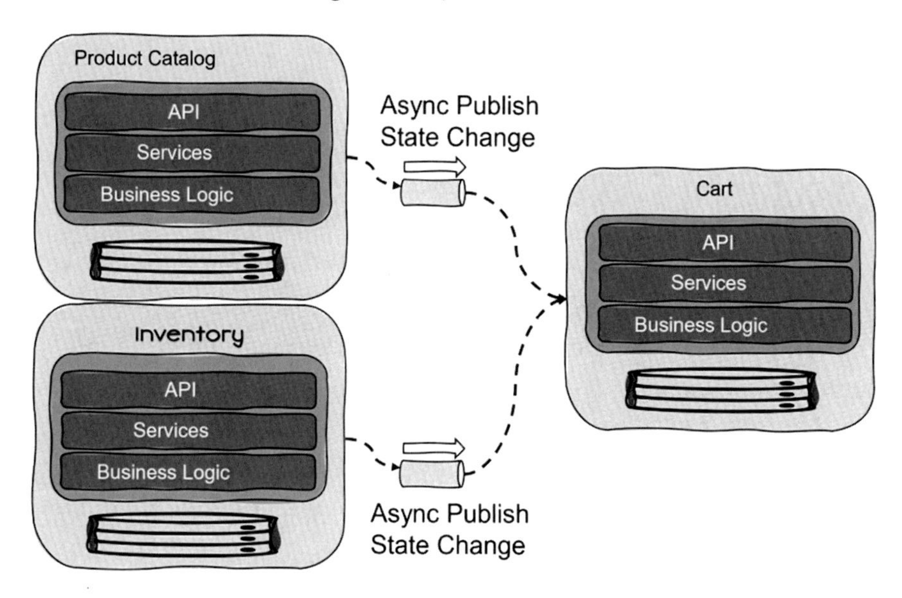

Figure 16-3. *Asynchronous Data Replication*

In this arrangement, upstream services will asynchronously broadcast state changes as they happen. These might be in the form of a dedicated, point-to-point queue or as part of a fan-out, PubSub approach. Here, the Cart service (or a standalone agent that shares the database with the main microservice) will subscribe to updates via the queue or PubSub topic and update a local copy of state as changes are consumed. *Event Sourcing* is an example of this approach, which we will explore in more detail in the next chapter when describing the *PubSub Messaging Constraint.*

The asynchronous solution to this problem eliminates stamp coupling, eliminates the interservice requests, caching necessary state locally and thus improving performance while making more efficient use of bandwidth. With a queue or a PubSub in between the services, we achieve a topology that provides independent availability of the Cart service, and asynchronous communication is inherently partition tolerant; however, this approach can only guarantee *eventual consistency.*

Once again, we must consider and handle these scenarios on a case-by-case basis. A concrete style derived from the Microservices Abstract Style must prescribe these additional constraints and specify their scope.

Adding Constraints

In addition to changing the granularity and database constraints (with their dependent team, organizational, and environmental constraints), this abstract style requires the addition of the following architectural constraints.

Highly Decoupled Components

The Microservices Abstract Style achieves agility and fault tolerance by, among other constraints, prescribing a shared-nothing approach to system design. Fine Component Granularity and Isolated Databases Constraint will eliminate much—but not all—coupling (specifically *afferent coupling,* which measures how many different classes call upon a particular class, and *data coupling,* respectively). This additional constraint continues to aggressively remove coupling (specifically *efferent coupling,* which measures the number of different classes a particular class calls upon) between components wherever practical.

One of the most common sources of *efferent coupling* is shared code. In the frictionless plane of theoretical architecture, each microservice will stand entirely on its own. However, in the real world, there inevitably exist many cross-cutting concerns and overlapping code implementations that span many or all services. How we handle this reality will depend on additional constraints prescribed in a concrete style.

Handling Shared Code

Versioned Libraries

Sharing common code across multiple codebases is not a new requirement. Dedicated repositories and package managers exist to support this model for external dependencies. We can extend this model to manage our internal dependencies by publishing shared libraries to a private repository and managing these semantically versioned dependencies using the same tooling and process as our external dependencies.

The Open/Closed Principle (Chapter 7) offers a path to extend and customize these libraries; however, once again, we need to consider granularity. Large common libraries will exhibit increased code volatility and increase coupling across, potentially, hundreds of microservices. When a shared library has the potential to require an update and redeployment of any number of microservices, it is time to consider other strategies.

Advantages

- A simple and well-understood approach to code sharing.
- Offers the ability for library developers to make versioned changes.
- Shared libraries are easy to extend and expand.
- Provides a "single source of truth" for the implementation of common/shared behavior.
- Ideal for well-scoped, low-code volatility libraries.

Drawbacks

- Introduces an axis for coupling that this style aims to avoid
- Introduces complexity around version adoption and depreciation
- Poorly suited for polyglot and heterogenous code environments

Shared Services

Another "single source of truth" approach to addressing the need for shared code is to encapsulate the code into a *shared service.* A shared service is a microservice that exposes the shared code via some kind of API. Using this approach, services that require the behavior or functionality exposed by one of these shared services perform a network call when needed.

Extracting common functionality into a shared service completely decouples individual microservices from the common code. The shared service has its own independent lifecycle, and a single update to that service will immediately cascade the change to all dependent services without requiring a coordinated redeployment of running services, thus honoring the independent deployability constraint. We must, however, consider the performance and fault tolerance trade-offs inherent to this option. Network calls incur overhead and reduce performance. The unavailability of the shared service may also result in cascading failures across the system.

Advantages

- Maintains a "single source of truth" for implementation
- Particularly well suited to polyglot environments
- A useful option for shared code with high volatility

Drawbacks

- Versioning is more difficult. Breaking changes may still require coordinated redeployments.
- Network requests introduce a performance penalty.
- A shared service is a potential single point of failure and may introduce further availability or fault tolerance issues.
- A shared service may introduce a bottleneck that introduces scalability and throughput issues.
- There is a higher probability of releasing a breaking change that has broad impact within the system.

Service Consolidation

Depending on the scope of the shared dependency, we may simply opt for *service consolidation*. For example, if a common code dependency spans only two or three microservices within the same subdomain, we can make the case that the most expedient and pragmatic solution is to merge these two or three services into a new, single service.

Advantages

- No code sharing
- No network performance or bandwidth penalty
- No need for version management

Drawbacks

- Larger services bring a larger testing scope (reducing evolvability, deployability, and agility).
- Larger services are slower to start, reducing elasticity.
- Increased service scope correlates to increased deployment risk.
- This approach only works for some code-sharing scenarios.
- Coarser services reduce overall agility.

The Sidecar Pattern

For some cross-cutting concerns, we can colocate the shared code with a service without directly coupling the two through the adoption of the *sidecar pattern*.

The sidecar pattern is a microservices design pattern that addresses the challenges of managing cross-cutting concerns in a distributed system. In this pattern, a sidecar is a companion service that runs alongside the primary service, typically in the same execution environment, such as a pod in Kubernetes. Incoming and outgoing requests for a microservice will typically flow *through* the sidecar, rather than the microservice directly invoking behavior in the sidecar. The sidecar handles auxiliary tasks that are not part of the core domain logic but are essential for the service's operation, such as tracing, logging, monitoring, configuration management, or network security.

By offloading these responsibilities to a sidecar, the primary service can remain focused on its core functionality, leading to a more modular and maintainable system. The sidecar pattern promotes separation of concerns, as the primary service does not need to be aware of the sidecar's existence or operations. This decoupling makes it easier to evolve and scale individual components without affecting the rest of the system. Additionally, because the sidecar and the primary service share the same lifecycle, they can communicate directly and efficiently, often over a loopback interface, minimizing latency and overhead. The sidecar pattern is especially useful in environments like service meshes, where it can enforce consistent policies and behaviors across a fleet of microservices, ensuring that cross-cutting concerns are handled uniformly across the system.

Advantages

- Decouples cross-cutting concerns from the primary service, leading to cleaner and more maintainable codebases
- Enhances the modularity of the system, allowing the primary service to focus on its core logic without being burdened by auxiliary tasks
- Simplifies the evolution and scaling of individual components since the sidecar can be updated or replaced independently of the primary service
- Minimizes latency and overhead through direct communication between the sidecar and the primary service, often via a loopback interface
- Ensures uniform handling of cross-cutting concerns across multiple services, particularly in service mesh environments
- Reduces the blast radius of faults, as issues within the sidecar do not directly impact the primary service's core functionality
- Supports polyglot environments, as the sidecar operates independently of the service's implementation language

Drawbacks

- Introduces additional components that must be managed, monitored, and maintained, which can increase overall system complexity.
- Adds to the resource footprint, as each service must now allocate resources for both the primary service and its sidecar.
- While the sidecar and primary service are decoupled in functionality, they share the same lifecycle, which may complicate deployments and restarts.

- The introduction of a sidecar can make debugging more complex, as issues may arise from the interaction between the primary service and the sidecar.
- A sidecar and a service mesh may take competing approaches to retry failed transactions which may cause conflicts or performance issues.
- Requires robust deployment and lifecycle orchestration as well as monitoring tools to manage the sidecar and ensure that it is correctly deployed and functioning as expected.

Please Repeat Yourself

In addition to the options listed above, we may simply opt to *duplicate the code* in each microservice that is dependent on the code. Although this approach appears to violate an entire career's worth of best practice, in an environment where we must apply extreme decoupling to achieve extreme scale, fault tolerance, and agility, this practice often makes sense. In contrast with environments and codebases where "Don't Repeat Yourself" (DRY) is the law of the land, microservices environments are more apt to declare "reuse is abuse" and "please repeat yourself."

The copy/paste approach to code sharing is yet another trade-off to evaluate. Prescribing this constraint in relevant scenarios requires teams that are *mature with respect to trade-offs*. Also, it can be valuable for teams to maintain a registry of where code is duplicated. This way, if a bug is found that affects one thing, the other places can be scrutinized. It mitigates some of the consequences of not using shared code while also allowing the similar code to diverge and specialize over time.

Advantages

- Simple approach to code sharing.
- Ideal for code with low volatility
- Offers maximum decoupling across services

Drawbacks

- It can be exceedingly difficult to coordinate the deployment of changes due to bugs or evolution in the shared code.
- Polyglot environments will require multiple implementations of the same code, which adds even more bug fix/evolution challenges.

- Replicated code can be difficult to expand.
- When a development team tweaks their copy of the code to tailor behavior for a single microservice, coordinating updates becomes even more difficult.
- Teams new to this approach may reject this constraint.

Scenario Code Sharing

Each call to a microservice requires an authorization step (either from a client or between services). Your choices are to create a shared authorization service, a shared library, an authorization sidecar, or a shared/coupled API layer. Describe your choice and trade-off analysis.

Other Info:
110 Microservices
Low volatility
100ms latency between services
30 Requests/second
350ms AVG response time

The Microservices Abstract Style

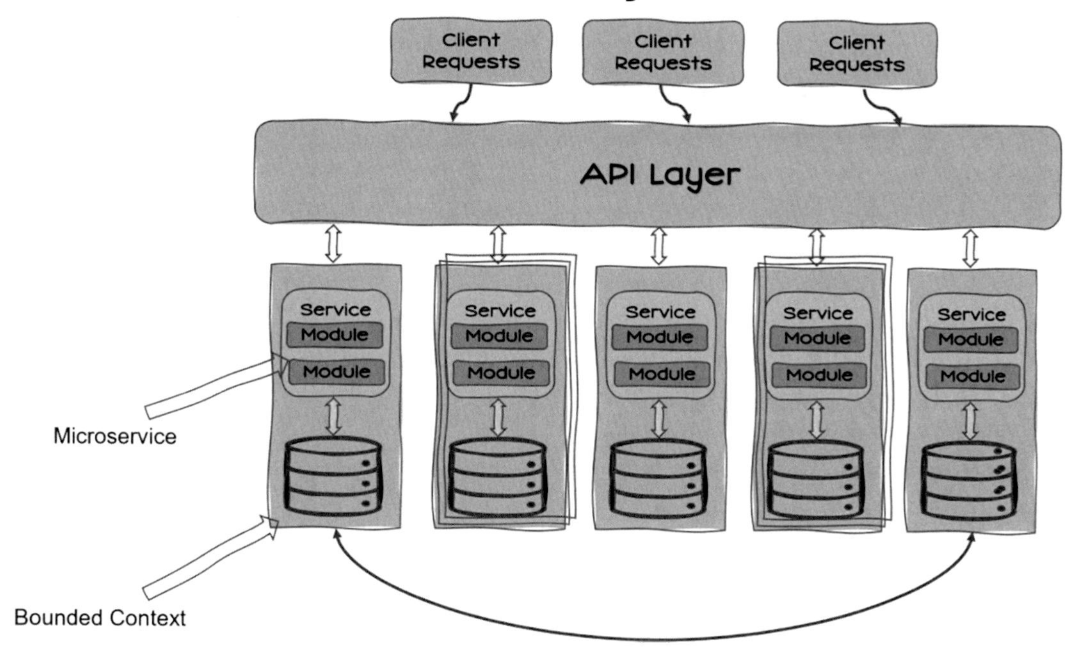

Figure 16-4. *The Microservices Abstract Style*

> *Rice is great when you're really hungry and want to eat 2,000 of something*
>
> —Mitch Hedberg

A visualization of the microservices abstract style can be seen in Figure 16-4. Forward-leaning software engineer, thinker, speaker, and author Brian Sletten uses the above quote to illustrate the absurdity of quantity for quantity's sake. We should not design a system composed of hundreds of microservices simply because we can; we should instead only prescribe such extreme constraints when they translate to tangible business value. The more I have learned about microservices over the past 15+ years, the more convinced I am that anyone who truly understands microservices would never adopt this style unless it was absolutely necessary, and no other option will suffice. Scenarios where this is the case are unusual yet ever-present in our industry.

The landscape of software has evolved considerably since the late 1980s and early 1990s, when software architecture began to arise as a formal discipline. The emergence—and subsequent popularity—of the Web has created new, global markets with vastly different dynamics and economics. The reach of software today is vast and no longer constrained by requiring a particular operating system or processor architecture. Physical location, time zone, device hardware, or operating system are increasingly irrelevant. We are in an era where businesses can measure the total addressable market of a piece of software in the hundreds of millions—and occasionally billions—of users. Regardless of the depth and quality of a system's functionality, if it cannot scale to meet genuine demand, the system will consistently fall short of its potential.

Beyond simply scaling to meet demands, global-scale software introduces a new challenge; when the entire world is a potential customer, the entire world is also a potential competitor. Disruption is rife, and a business running a system that cannot evolve quickly in response to changing market conditions will frequently be disrupted by one that can. Agility, in such markets, becomes yet another first-class concern.

Finally, at this scale, the potential impact of outages and failures grows alarmingly fast. In 2023, Amazon.com saw a total of $12.90 billion in revenue over their highest-grossing 48-hour period[6] or $74,700 per second. With an average spend of $58.67 per customer, we can calculate a minimum of 1274 checkouts/second (if we generously assume each customer made all their purchases in a single transaction). A 99.9% availability SLA that might be more than adequate for a different system could potentially cost more than $15.7 *million* in lost revenue *without violating the SLA*. A major outage could cost billions in lost retail sales. In short, this style is extreme, but there is a time for extremes in software architecture.

Summary

The Microservices Abstract Style is a successful and proven approach to achieve extremely high agility, deployability, elasticity, evolvability, scalability, and testability, but the trade-offs are legion. This is one of the most difficult architectures to execute well, and you should only adopt this after empirically proving that only extremely high quantification of key capabilities will suffice.

The following architectural constraints define this abstract style:

- Fine Component Granularity
- Highly Decoupled Components

[6] Capital One Shopping Team (2024). "Global Impact of Amazon Prime Day 2023." The Capital One Shopping website, `https://capitaloneshopping.com/research/amazon-prime-day-statistics/`

- Independent Deployability
- Domain Partitioning
- Client/Server
- RPC API
- Isolated Databases

This collection of constraints requires significant team, organization, and environmental constraints:

- ORG: Well-Defined Domains
- ORG: Domain-Aligned Teams
- ORG: DevOps Commitment
- ENV: Development Environment Isolation
- ENV: High Operational Automation
- ENV: Service Discovery and Routing
- ENV: Bulkheads and Circuit Breakers
- ENV: Distributed Tracing and Logging
- TEAM: API First
- TEAM: Automation Skills
- TEAM: Pipeline Development Skills
- TEAM: Maturity with Respect to Trade-Offs
- TEAM: IaC Skills
- TEAM: Independent Development Cycles

The composition of these constraints offers capability improvements over those offered by the Service-Based Abstract Style (see Figure 16-5).

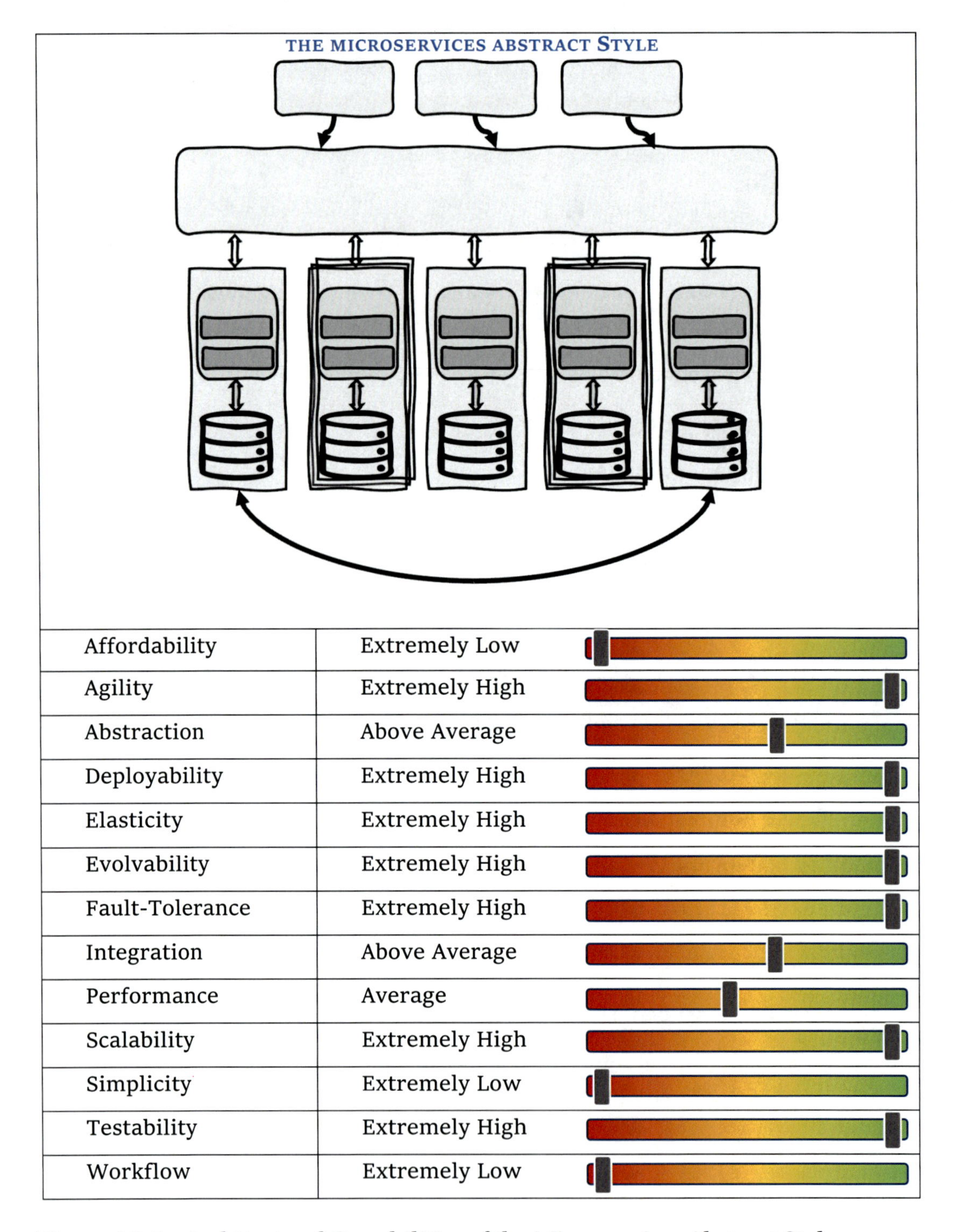

Affordability	Extremely Low
Agility	Extremely High
Abstraction	Above Average
Deployability	Extremely High
Elasticity	Extremely High
Evolvability	Extremely High
Fault-Tolerance	Extremely High
Integration	Above Average
Performance	Average
Scalability	Extremely High
Simplicity	Extremely Low
Testability	Extremely High
Workflow	Extremely Low

Figure 16-5. *Architectural Capabilities of the Microservices Abstract Style*

CHAPTER 17

Choreographed Event-Driven Abstract Style

It's really become clear to me in the last couple of years that we need a new building block and that is the domain events.

—Roy Schulte (2003)

In the last chapter, we explored the constraints that describe the Microservices Abstract Style. The conclusion of that chapter introduced the concept of "Domain to Architecture Isomorphism" and how microservices styles are generally not well suited to workflow-driven workloads. The root of this weakness lies in the architectural topology of the microservices style, which first emerged in *request-driven* systems. In such systems, the overwhelming majority of functionality is designed to be invoked through some kind of *request* that initiates a defined behavior and then returns a response. For example, if we return to our ecommerce microservices example, clicking "add to cart" will initiate a request to the Cart service to perform that action. The Cart service will, in turn, update the state of the customer's cart in the database before returning a response. In a microservices style, each service will handle a narrow set of requests.

Complications arise when we introduce workflows that require orchestrating requests across multiple microservices according to a set sequence of operations. This is particularly true when the workflow demands conditional logic to determine the next step based on information gained in the current step. This is not intended to imply that microservices styles cannot support such workloads—in fact, as we learned in the section on sagas (Chapter 16), workflows can be supported in those styles—however, tying together request-driven microservices undermines the significant effort to decompose the system into isolated, standalone microservices and, consequently, degrades the overall architectural capabilities of the system.

M. Carducci, *Mastering Software Architecture*, https://doi.org/10.1007/979-8-8688-0410-6_17

Contrast this with *event-driven* systems, where each component in the architecture does not listen for requests; instead, it *reacts* to *domain events*. Typically, once a reactive component performs some action in response to a domain event, it broadcasts a new event that another component might react to and further the processing of the workflow. A key distinction is that requests instruct the system to *do something*, while events, on the other hand, announce that *something has happened*.

Designing such a system begins with making a choice between *orchestration* and *choreography*. In this chapter and the next, we will look at two event-driven styles which offer exceptional workflow support beginning with the choreographed event-driven style.

A choreographed event-driven system consists of four main components (Figure 17-1). First, there is the *initiating event* which triggers the entire workflow. This event is published on an event channel on the *event broker* (which is usually federated, and divided into event channels or topics), our second component. An *event processor* asynchronously consumes events from the event channel and performs a specific task before it produces a *processing event* to a new event channel in the *event broker* to be consumed by the next event processor and the workflow continues. The event broker facilitates asynchronous communication and decouples producers and consumers.

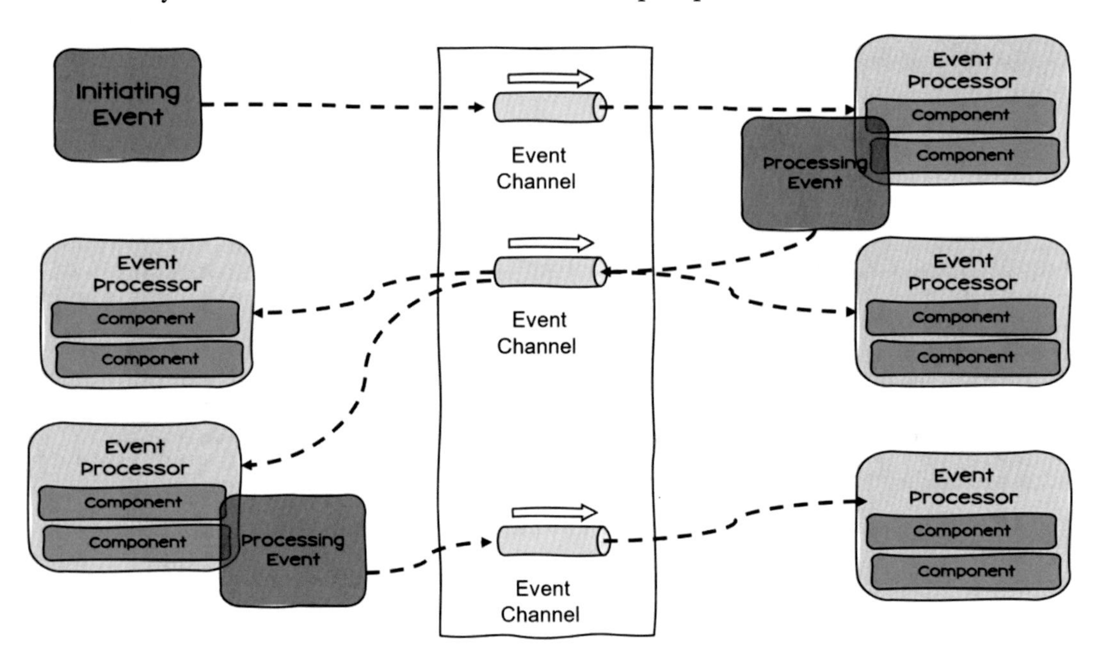

Figure 17-1. *Components in Choreographed Event-Driven Systems*

On the architecture continuum, it is common for concrete implementations of the Microservices Abstract Style to apply constraints from event-driven styles such as asynchronous communication and utilizing the broker topology. Introducing such constraints into a microservices-derived concrete style forms a "reactive" or "hybrid" microservices style. However, consistent with the previous chapters, we will focus on the distinct constraints that define these "pure" event-driven abstract styles, arming you with additional tools to derive a tailored architecture capable of boasting a perfect fit.

Changing Constraints

Technical Partitioning

In its pure form, this style supports—but does not require—domain partitioning; in fact, technical partitioning is the norm and thus forms a defining constraint of this abstract style. This style continues the use of the Fine-Component Granularity Constraint; however, each component is not a domain service but rather an even finer-grained *event processor*. Event processors generally focus on a single technical behavior.

As a concrete example for this chapter, I was once an architect on a system that ingested and processed unstructured data to feed an AI-powered engineering platform (Figure 17-2). Whenever the system received a new file, the workflow published an *initiating event*. An *event processor* would consume the *initiating event* and classify the file type based on metadata in the event payload. Following the file classification step, the classifier component publishes the first *processing event* which various format-specific event processors would subsequently consume to continue the ingestion workflow.

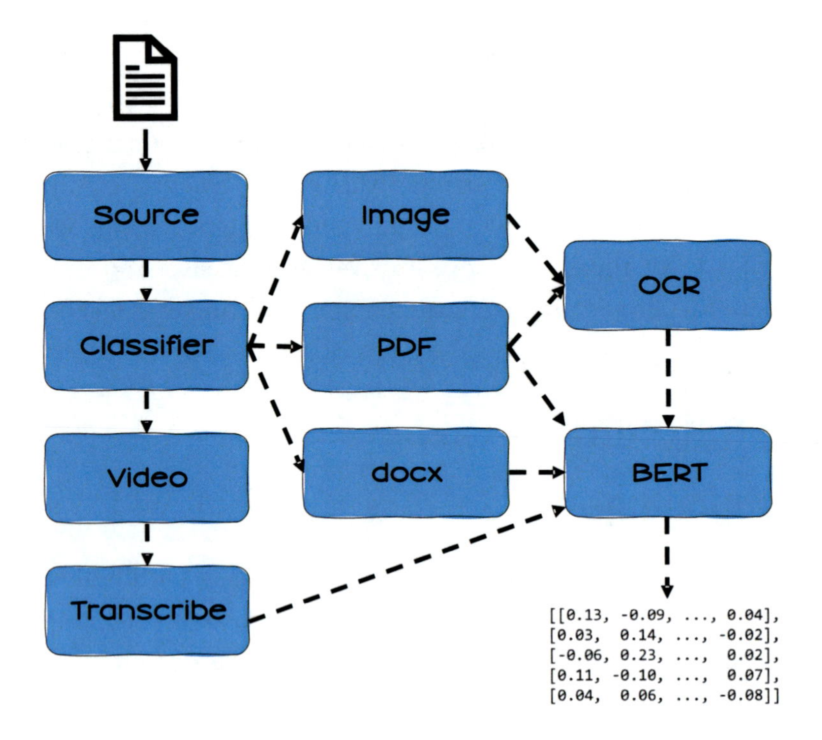

Figure 17-2. *File Processing Workflow*

If the file triggering the event was a PDF, a PDF-specific event processor would attempt to extract the text. If the text extraction process was successful, the processor would publish another *processing event* to trigger text indexing and vectorization. If the PDF only contained images of text, the processor would produce a different event to extract text using Optical Character Recognition (OCR) before publishing another *processing event* to resume the workflow.

In the above example, event processors are defined by technical boundaries rather than by domain boundaries. These processors are either continuously running microservice-style components that poll or subscribe to an event channel or serverless functions invoked by new events.

Choreography-Driven Interactions

The second departure from the constraints that define the Microservices Abstract Style is how components communicate. The microservices style prescribed an RPC API, necessary for a request-based system. This style, however, is *event based.* This style replaces the RPC API Constraint with the Choreography-Driven Interactions Constraint.

Choreography requires only that each component understands its individual role while remaining agnostic of the rest of the workflow. Every event processor will publish a new processing event upon completion of its work, even if there is no component to consume the event. Events, in this context, are just that—*things that have happened* rather than *requests to do something.* Not all asynchronous communication between components in a distributed system necessarily need to operate this way, but **communication via idempotent, post-processing notification events** is central to the Choreography-Driven Interactions Constraint. To model events as requests requires foreknowledge of what component(s) will process the request which introduces coupling and violates a core tenant of choreographed event-driven architectures. **Consumers do not know about producers and producers do not know about consumers**, just where to listen for, and where to publish, relevant events.

Architectural Extensibility

This constraint results in highly decoupled event processors, with the only coupling being the initiating event(s) an individual component listens for and the processing event(s) it produces.

The *listen-process-publish* flow of the Choreography-Driven Interactions affords a surprising amount of architectural flexibility and extensibility. If an event processor publishes a processing event, and there is no component to consume it, the event either remains in queue indefinitely or the event is removed after a defined retention period. At any point, development teams may deploy a new event processor to consume these events, and the processor instantly becomes part of the workflow with no additional coordination effort.

Consider an event-driven ecommerce system. Clicking the "add to cart" button fires an initiating event that the cart processor will consume. Once the cart processor updates the state of the cart, it, in turn, publishes a processing event. Each time an item is added or removed from the cart, the cart processor publishes an additional "cart changed" event. The state of the cart is finalized when an initiating "checkout" event is fired.

In this scenario, of what use are the "cart changed" events? If the state of the cart at checkout is one of Product A, one of Product B, and one of Product C, does it matter how we arrived at that state? Is there a difference between three "added to cart" events or two "added to cart" events, a "removed from cart" event, and two more "added to cart" events? It depends on your perspective. A developer or fulfillment employee might only care about the final state, but a data scientist might be deeply interested in events that led to that final state. If all the "cart changed" events accumulate in the event channel on the broker with an indefinite retention period, at any time a development team can deploy a new event processor to consume the accumulated events to tune recommendation and ranking models.

Beyond serving as an example of architectural extensibility, the ability to replay state changes that have taken place over time is an example of *event sourcing* which the previous chapter briefly introduced in the section on sharing data between microservices. Event sourcing is a powerful pattern within event-driven and hybrid architectures that focuses on capturing all changes to the state of a system as a sequence of immutable events. Rather than simply storing the current state of an entity, event sourcing records every state change as an event in an append-only log. This approach provides a complete audit trail, allowing the system to reconstruct any past state by replaying the events in sequence. It also enables advanced scenarios such as temporal queries, where you can see the state of the system at any point in time, and easy integration with other systems through event streams. By adopting event sourcing, you not only gain a robust method for maintaining eventual consistency in distributed systems but also unlock new possibilities for analytics and system evolution over time, as every decision and action in the system is transparently recorded.

Performance and Scale

The broker does more than decouple components, it also absorbs bursts of events to prevent a processor from becoming overwhelmed. Each processor can also be scaled independently in response to broker backpressure. This constraint also results in workflows that parallelize particularly well, as multiple event processors can consume the same event if the broker supports fan-out communication. Consequently, this constraint results in high-performance systems, both in terms of absolute performance and user-perceived performance (as a client does not have to wait for anything more than an acknowledgment that the initiating event has been published). This constraint can even enable real-time processing in styles such as the Kappa architecture (described below).

The asynchronous nature of communication under this constraint favors availability and partition tolerance over consistency, which will significantly improve overall fault tolerance.

Kappa Architecture

Kappa architecture is a streamlined approach to real-time data processing,[1] often considered a special case of choreographed event-driven architectures. In both paradigms, events are the central unit of work, driving system behavior and enabling highly decoupled, scalable, and responsive systems. The Kappa architecture builds on this foundation by focusing exclusively on processing events as a continuous stream, eliminating the need for separate batch processing layers.

In choreographed event-driven architectures, services or components respond to events without a central orchestrator, leading to a more organic flow of information through the system. Each service reacts to relevant events, triggering other events in turn, creating a chain of reactions that drives the system forward. Kappa architecture can be seen as an application of this idea but with an emphasis on handling large volumes of data in real time. It uses event streams as the backbone of its processing pipeline, where each event triggers transformations, computations, or actions as soon as it arrives, aligning with the principles of event choreography.

By treating all data as part of an event stream, Kappa architecture naturally fits within the broader category of choreographed systems. It leverages the decoupling and reactivity inherent in event-driven designs to achieve high throughput and low-latency processing, making it an excellent choice for modern applications that require real-time insights and actions. The elimination of batch processing not only simplifies the architecture but also ensures that all components are aligned around the same flow of events, reinforcing the core principles of event-driven choreography.

---

[1] Kreps, J. (2014). *Questioning the Lambda Architecture.* O'Reilly. `https://www.oreilly.com/radar/questioning-the-lambda-architecture/`

Failures and Error Handling

When designing a choreographed workflow, we must think about more than the happy path and consider failure cases as well. What should happen if an event processor is unable to perform its task? *Failure* events are often equal in value to *success* events. At a minimum, an event processor should publish failure events to a "dead letter queue" for periodic human review. As these reviews unveil novel failure conditions, development teams can build new event processors that listen to the dead letter queue, resolve the issue, and republish the event to the upstream event channel for reprocessing.

We must also consider failures that *do not* produce a failure event. Consider a scenario where an event processor simply crashes. Choreography-driven systems do not involve an external mediator that is monitoring and controlling steps in the workflow. If a processor consumes an event but does not publish a processing event on the other side, the business process abruptly ends, potentially leaving the system in an inconsistent state. Because choreographed workflows are dynamic and evolving, there is rarely a clear "process completed" state or event which further obscures such failures. Recovering in such scenarios cannot be as simple as restarting the workflow either, as upstream components may have already performed some amount of work. There must also be automated and manual processes to handle silent failure scenarios.

Error handling becomes even more challenging as workflows grow more complex. Consider a "checkout" event on a cart that multiple processors (e.g., payment, inventory, fulfillment) consume. In this topology, a payment failure will not prevent the inventory service from decrementing available stock, nor will it prevent the fulfillment service from directing warehouse employees to pick and pack the order.

Beyond error handling, we must consider scenarios where event processor components process events in a sequence that is different from the order of events we might assume. Most asynchronous communication middleware will follow a first-in-first-out (FIFO) sequence; however, when there are delays or other workflow exceptions, we can no longer rely on any order of message processing. The workflow process must either be designed to be resilient to out-of-order messages or an orchestration-driven approach (Chapter 18) must be chosen.

In short, you must model choreographed systems extremely carefully. Ask as many "what if" questions as possible during the design process and ensure you have a plan to handle every edge case as well as for detecting unanticipated failures. Also, consider that any change to the event flow will require extensive regression and exploratory testing to uncover any surprise outcomes from the new changes.

Modeling Choreographed Systems

Modeling choreographed event-driven systems can be complex due to the decentralized nature of the architecture. However, there are several tools, techniques, and processes that can help architects, business actors, and developers to design, visualize, and implement these systems effectively.

Tools

EventStorming

EventStorming is a Domain-Driven Design technique created by Alberto Brandolini[2] in 2015 offering a lightweight way to explore and identify what is happening within the domain of a software program. Although we are introducing this constraint in the context of a technically partitioned system, domain modeling still holds immense value in building a shared understanding of the domain, its full behavior, and complexity that can be valuable in designing any system's architecture. It is particularly germane to this constraint as EventStorming tackles domain modeling through business process modeling. Think of EventStorming as a form of event-first design that focuses first on the flow of information, rather than the *Cart Before the Horse* approach of service-first design.

EventStorming involves architecture or development teams bringing key product stakeholders and domain experts together in the same room to visualize the domain by representing various domain concepts as sticky notes, laid out sequentially on a wall or large roll of paper, with different colored sticky notes denoting different classes of concepts. The basic process is as follows:

1. Identify various *domain events*, events that occur in the business or domain process. By convention, orange sticky notes are used for *domain events* and always written in the past tense.
2. Identify the *command* that caused each domain event. *Commands* may be user-initiated or process-initiated. By convention, *commands* are written on blue sticky notes and placed directly before each event.

[2] Brandolini, A. (2015–2021). *Introducing EventStorming: An Act of Deliberate Collective Learning.* LeanPub, `https://www.eventstorming.com/book/`

3. Where appropriate, identify the *actor* responsible for initiating a command. In the case of event-driven architectures, the *actor* is usually responsible for the command that generates the *initiating event*. By convention, *actors* are written on small, yellow sticky notes and are connected to the lower-left corner of the *command* sticky.

4. Where appropriate, identify *aggregates*. Aggregates are clusters of domain objects that can be conceptually treated as a single unit. By convention, these are larger yellow sticky notes placed above *command* and *domain event* pairs.

5. Identify *business processes*, the elements which process a command according to business rules or logic and create one or more *domain events*. Subsequent iterations in the EventStorming process should expand these processes out to visualize the sequence and rules. By convention, these are written on purple sticky notes.

6. Identify *external systems* on which a command or aggregate depends. By convention, *external systems* are represented with pink sticky notes.

7. Identify *views*, the interfaces through which users interact to carry out a task in the system. By convention, *views* are written on green sticky notes.

EventStorming produces a unified and shared understanding of the domain, processes, and domain events, as well as their relationships within the system. The resulting picture (Figure 17-3) will not only inform the design of an event-driven system but is also useful for identifying domain boundaries and aligning communication within domains and subdomains by surfacing each domain's ubiquitous language.

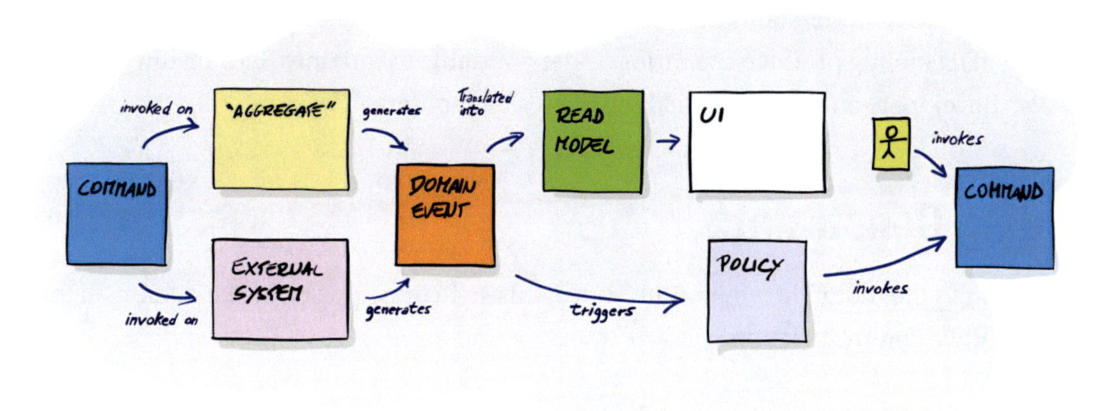

***Figure 17-3.** An Example EventStorming Visualization*[3]

Activity Diagrams, State Machines, and Statecharts

Often, workflows can be modeled as state machines that aim to reach a desired end state. In this case, a chart of possible states and potential changes provides another mechanism for visualizing and understanding the workflow. Thinking about the process in this way can be useful to determine how each state change impacts the workflow, and services should respond to events. Statecharts, which extend state machines with hierarchical states and parallelism, can be particularly useful for complex event-driven workflows.

A comprehensive *event-centric* visualization of a domain is also a useful tool for exploring the various "what if" scenarios described in the "Failures and Error Handling" section above, guarding against errors of omission.

Behavior-Driven Development (BDD)

Using BDD with a focus on event flows can help in defining and testing the expected behavior of the system in response to different events. BDD tool syntax can be extended to describe event interactions and outcomes, guiding both development and test. BDD scenarios are typically defined using a natural domain-specific language (DSL) to

[3] Chapuy, J. (2021). *The Elements of Event Storming and Their Interactions*. Retrieved from: `https://jordanchapuy.com/posts/2021/11/les-ingredients-d-un-event-storming-et-leurs-interactions/` Image Licensed CC-BY 4.0

formalize a shared understanding of how the system should behave. The DSLs typical to modern BDD tooling produce scenarios understandable to not only BDD testing tools but also developers and nontechnical business stakeholders.

Adding Constraints

In addition to the modified constraints above, this style must prescribe a mechanism for asynchronous communication.

PubSub Messaging

In their pure form, distributed event-driven systems do not communicate directly; instead, communication takes place via asynchronous messages passed between components which requires some form of message-oriented middleware (broker) to facilitate such communication. The dominant options in this category are queues and the Publish/Subscribe (PubSub) model. Although both offer asynchronous communication, offering an additional axis of elasticity by smoothing out workload spikes, each of these options will influence architecture capabilities in different ways. Consequently, the asynchronous communication paradigm is an *architecturally significant decision.*

In a PubSub model,[4] we conceptually divide components into publishers and subscribers. Publishers emit events to a centralized broker, which then distributes these events to all interested subscribers. In a choreographed event-driven system, most subscribers are also publishers as each *event processor* will broadcast events following the completion of a task.

The superficial similarity of PubSub and queues will sometimes cause developers or architects to conflate the two (this is compounded by the fact that many commercial and open source queues can be configured to behave like a PubSub and vice versa); however, there are differences that you must understand.

Queues generally follow a push/pop flow, where producers *push* a message into a queue and consumers subsequently *pop* messages from the queue as they are read, resulting in *exactly once delivery.*

[4] Berglund, T. (2020). *Kafka as a Distributed System.* InfoQ. `https://www.infoq.com/presentations/kafka-controller-zookeeper`

In contrast, PubSub producers place messages in a *topic* that is defined within a *broker*. Topics form an append-only log of activity, meaning that there are no direct side effects when consumers read messages from a topic to which they subscribe. The broker retains the messages (either indefinitely or for a defined period known as the *retention period*). Of course, this introduces a new wrinkle in event-driven system design; PubSub topics promise *at least once delivery*, meaning an event processor might react to the same event more than once. Processing the same message multiple times increases in likelihood as the number of running instances of an individual *event processor* increases. Each consumer of a PubSub topic must maintain some kind of state. Typically, each message in a topic is assigned an ever-increasing identifier known as an offset. Services must maintain some state with respect to the topic(s) to which it subscribes. This "last offset" state is typically shared across instances, allowing each service to receive and process only messages with an offset greater than what has been seen last. Even sharing this state, however, will not prevent every possible race condition or double read. We must keep this reality top of mind and design idempotence into each domain event or component.

Although the persistence of messages within PubSub topics introduces challenges in preventing duplication of work, the append-only nature of a topic also brings benefits. *At least once delivery* enables multiple distinct consumers to subscribe to the same topic in parallel, which is useful for more complex workflow scenarios. Additionally, this fact improves fault tolerance. If an *event processor* crashes while processing a message, once the processor restarts it can resume processing starting at the first unprocessed message. Let us look at how PubSub works under the hood.

Inside a PubSub Broker

In its simplest form, a PubSub consists of a *broker* which hosts one or more *topics*. To support both high throughput and fault tolerance, *brokers* are often federated and *topics* partitioned (Figure 17-4). Each federated *broker* hosts distinct *topic* partitions as well as replicas of other *topic* partitions. Both reads and writes can be distributed across multiple *broker* instances, with writes distributed across *topic* partitions based on a defined *partition key*. When a message is sent to a *broker*, it will hash the *partition key* and use that hash to determine which partition the message should be appended to.

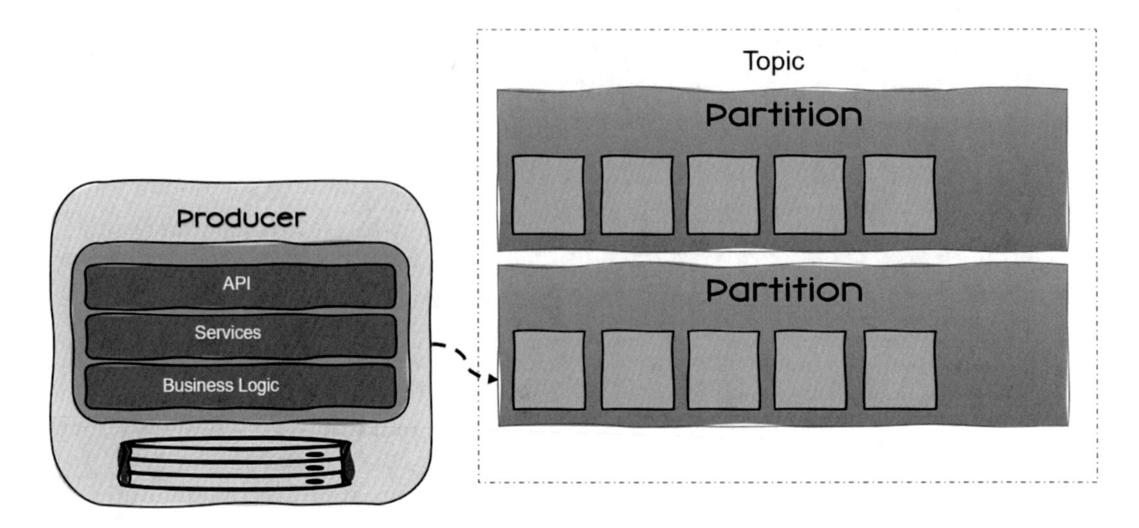

Figure 17-4. *Partitioned Topics in a PubSub*

Partition key selection can be important for two reasons. First, the *partition key* should be a property or value with a uniform distribution to prevent overutilizing a small number of partitions. Second, although writes to a *topic* follow a FIFO sequence, a precise order of message consumption can only be guaranteed within a single partition. Consider the following example of a stock trading platform.

Within a high-performance trading platform that handles highly variable volume, a choreographed event-driven architecture offers a reasonable architectural foundation. However, in our modern era of high-frequency trading, order of processing not only matters, but it is also *essential* to the success of this system.

Suppose a trader initiates a BUY order of 100 shares of AAPL, a second BUY order of 50 shares of MSFT, then a SELL order of 50 shares of AAPL: all in rapid succession. We can guarantee FIFO order if we limit our topic to a single partition. However, a single topic partition will introduce a bottleneck that will unacceptably constrain throughput. If those trade events are distributed arbitrarily across multiple topic partitions, we eliminate a bottleneck and solve our throughput issues, but we have introduced the possibility that the AAPL SELL order is processed before the AAPL BUY order.

Partitioning is still an option, but we need to be mindful in our *partition key* selection. Of the three example trades, only the BUY and SELL orders on AAPL must happen in FIFO order. The MSFT trade, however, can happen in any sequence relative to trades on other securities. If we define the partition key by the ticker symbol on the trade order topic, all trades on a single ticker will always be written to the same topic partition in FIFO order. Through careful selection of the partition key, we have eliminated bottlenecks in the broker while still guaranteeing processing order only where it matters.

Another consideration is topic retention. Storing every message indefinitely can grow costly over time, particularly when using commercial, managed PubSub offerings. You should consider what retention periods make sense for each subdomain, then fine-tune on a topic-by-topic basis. If there is not a clear answer, or you find that a small number of edge cases seem to be pushing you in the direction of indefinite retention, pick a retention period that will satisfy 90% of cases and build a small consumer that serializes aging messages and store them in a lower-cost blob storage service or a data lake. These archived messages can always be replayed through a topic, if necessary.

A widely used PubSub is Apache Kafka (`https://kafka.apache.org/`). Although Kafka began as a PubSub, it has grown into a framework with a vast ecosystem of tools to solve common problems.

A notable utility in the Kafka ecosystem is the *schema registry*, which is part of Kafka's commercial offering, Confluent Cloud. The *schema registry* offers an additional layer of decoupling components. Because *producers do not know about consumers and consumers do not know about producers*, it can be difficult to determine the potential impact to consumers when evolving or changing a message schema. The *schema registry* further decouples producers and consumers by simultaneously supporting multiple versions of a message schema, similar in concept to content negotiation in REST. A V2 schema, for example, would include mapping information from the V1 schema. Consequently, the producer could switch to the new V2 schema without risk. Existing consumers simply specify the V1 schema as part of their `consume` operation, and Kafka automatically transforms the message.

The Choreographed Event-Driven Abstract Style

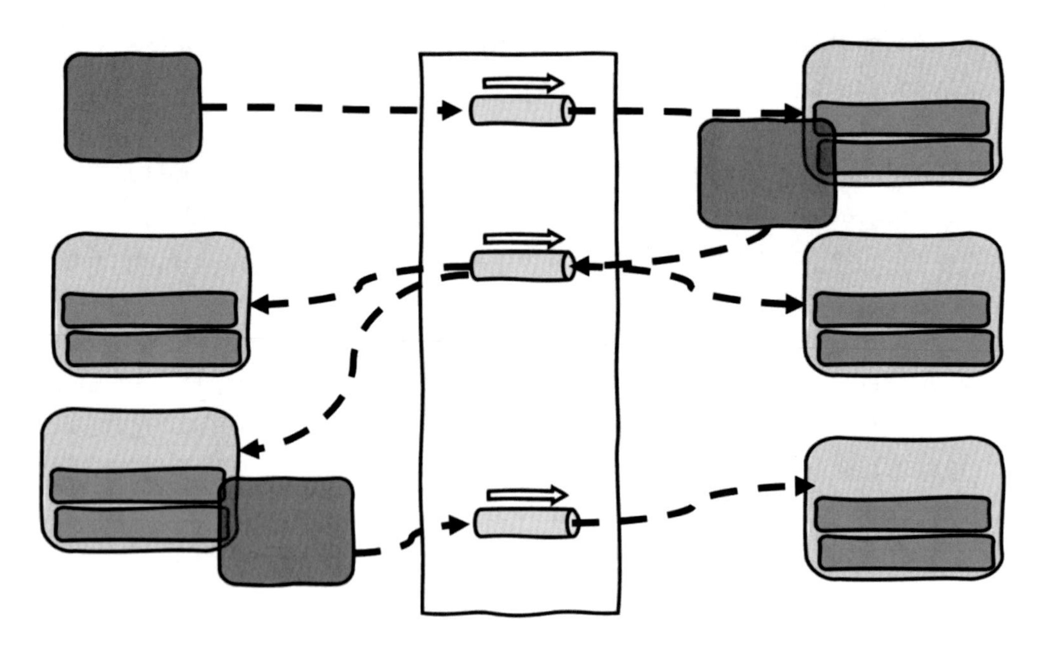

Figure 17-5. *Choreographed Event-Driven Abstract Style*

A visualization of the choreographed event-driven abstract style can be seen in Figure 17-5. Although we changed only two constraints that define the Microservices Abstract Style, and added one, we arrive at a style that looks topologically similar but offers notably different capabilities. When workloads are naturally event driven, and the workflow is not too complex, variations of this style are worth exploring.

Often, event processors are exceedingly small with blazingly fast start times. Since their sole purpose is to react to events, rather than wait for requests, they only need to be running when an event occurs. This style is a good fit for serverless architecture.

Serverless Architecture

Serverless architecture is a cloud computing model where the cloud provider automatically manages the infrastructure, scaling, and provisioning of resources needed to run applications.[5] In a serverless setup, developers write and deploy functions—small, stateless units of code—that are executed in response

[5] Sbarski, P., Cui, Y., Nair, A. (2020). *Serverless Architecture on AWS*. Manning

to specific events or triggers. The serverless platform handles all aspects of infrastructure management, including scaling the application up or down based on demand and charging only for the compute time consumed. This model allows developers to focus on writing code rather than worrying about the underlying infrastructure, reducing the complexity of the High Operational Automation Constraint.

In the context of choreographed event-driven systems, serverless architecture offers a compelling approach to managing the execution of event-driven workflows with high efficiency, minimal operational overhead, and simplicity in deployment and maintenance. This aligns well with the principles of event-driven systems, where the logic is naturally broken down into discrete, independent components that react to events as they occur.

One of the key advantages of using serverless architecture in a choreographed event-driven system is its ability to automatically scale in response to varying workloads without additional development team effort. As events are published, serverless functions can be triggered in parallel, with the underlying platform handling the scaling to meet demand. This ensures that the system remains responsive even under heavy loads, without the need for pre-provisioning or managing servers. Additionally, because serverless platforms typically charge based on the actual execution time and resources consumed, this approach can be cost-effective, especially in systems with unpredictable or spiky traffic patterns.

However, it is important to be mindful of the limitations and challenges of serverless architecture. Cold start latency, for example, can introduce delays when functions are invoked after being idle, which might impact performance in time-sensitive applications. Additionally, the stateless nature of serverless functions requires careful management of state and context between invocations, often necessitating the use of external storage or state management services.

Serverless architecture offers a highly compatible and scalable option for implementing choreographed event-driven systems, allowing for rapid development and deployment while aligning with the key principles of decoupling and flexibility inherent in such systems.

One of the most notable downsides of this style is complexity in debugging, performance analysis, and monitoring. Since components do not directly interact, tracing the flow of an event through the system can be difficult, especially in complex architectures with multiple publishers and subscribers. This can lead to challenges in identifying the root cause of issues, as there is no direct linkage between the origin of an event and its consumers without the use of SIEM tools like LogRhythm or Splunk.

As workflows grow more complex, the suitability of this style falls. The *understandability* of implementations of this style falls exponentially over time, while the "what if" modeling of edge cases grows exponentially. Imperfect understanding of the system can cause issues such as cycles emerging in the workflow.

Finally, observability can be extremely challenging which makes it hard to know when many workflows are "done." It requires careful consideration and management to mitigate complexities and potential pitfalls inherent to this style.

All that said, architecture is not an *all or nothing* proposition. Rarely will you see a "pure" event-driven system. Software often needs users, and users need interfaces, and interfaces need to make requests. Choreographed event-driven architectural styles may not be suitable for the entire system, but a subdomain may exist where this family of styles is a perfect fit. Architectural styles may be prescribed at the enterprise level, the system level, the subdomain level, or even the component level. It just depends.

Also, remember *architectures are not chosen, they are designed.* As you have seen in the preceding chapters, the capabilities are the product of the constraints. The defining constraint of this architectural style shows up in many hybrid applications.

Hybrid microservices and service-based architectures are increasingly common. Tailoring a distributed style by introducing the PubSub constraint will result in a style that offers both a *request-based* API and an *event-based data backplane*. When the Choreography-Driven Interactions Constraint is introduced to microservices, the workflow deficiencies quickly evaporate. Even in a monolithic system, there can be instances where it makes sense to extract a few services to handle higher-volume, simple workflows.

Finally, choreography is not our only option for event-driven styles. In the next chapter, we will explore the constraints that make up the Orchestrated Event-Driven Abstract Style.

Summary

The Choreographed Event-Driven Abstract Style is a powerful tool. Its defining constraints offer much in terms of scalability, elasticity, and fault tolerance. The broadcast nature of PubSub offers an extremely high degree of decoupling. Being asynchronous, the entire system is incredibly responsive. The PubSub broker will also buffer activity spikes without necessarily needing to scale compute resources. Workflows can evolve organically with little to no coordination cost, and the features in various PubSub ecosystems provide many useful tools and implementation options.

This style does bring challenges and trade-offs. Complex workflows are not well suited to this style as we must grapple with increased error handling complexity, silent failures, the potential for cycles, out-of-order processing, debugging, understandability, and observability/monitoring.

The following architectural constraints define this abstract style:

- Fine Component Granularity
- Technical Partitioning
- Highly Decoupled Components
- Independent Deployability
- Choreography-Driven Interactions
- PubSub Messaging

This collection of constraints requires the following team, organization, and environmental constraints:

- ORG: DevOps Commitment
- ENV: Development Environment Isolation
- ENV: High Operational Automation
- ENV: Distributed Tracing and Logging
- TEAM: Automation Skills
- TEAM: Pipeline Development Skills
- TEAM: Maturity with Respect to Trade-Offs
- TEAM: IaC Skills
- TEAM: Independent Development Cycles

The composition of these constraints offers capability improvements over those offered by the Microservices Abstract Style (see Figure 17-6).

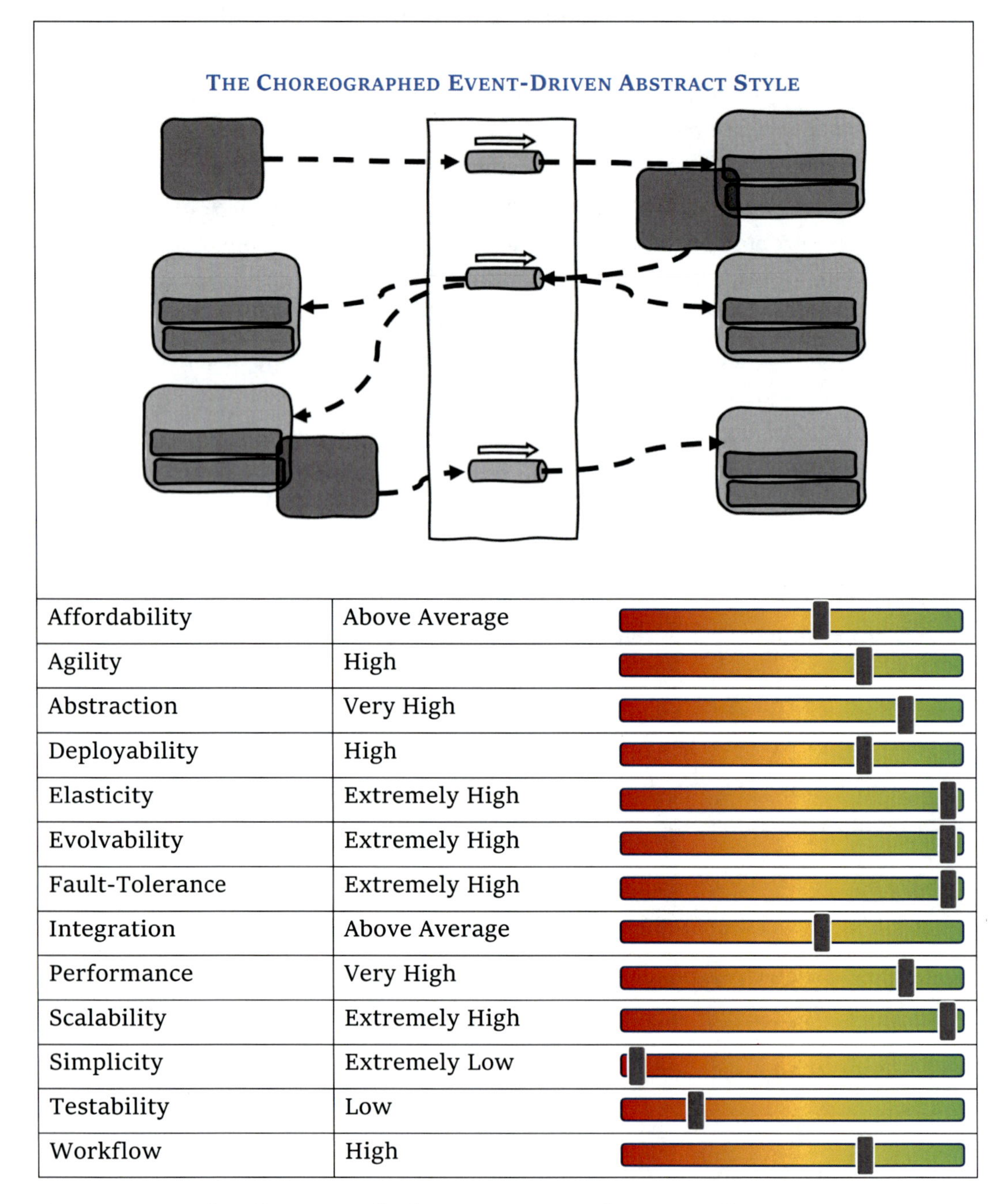

Affordability	Above Average
Agility	High
Abstraction	Very High
Deployability	High
Elasticity	Extremely High
Evolvability	Extremely High
Fault-Tolerance	Extremely High
Integration	Above Average
Performance	Very High
Scalability	Extremely High
Simplicity	Extremely Low
Testability	Low
Workflow	High

Figure 17-6. *The Choreographed Event-Driven Abstract Style*

CHAPTER 18

Orchestrated Event-Driven Abstract Style

Four years from now, 'mere mortals' will begin to adopt an event-driven architecture (EDA) for the sort of complex event process that has been attempted only by software gurus...

—Roy Schulte (2003)

Event-driven styles are, undoubtedly, well suited for workflow-driven workloads, but the nature and complexity of the processing will influence your choice of underlying constraints. The Choreographed Event-Driven Abstract Style introduced in the last chapter offers a very high degree of agility and architectural extensibility, but this approach brings certain limitations. In this chapter, we will look at another event-driven abstract style that changes two defining constraints to address some of those limitations. Every architectural style introduces a different set of trade-offs. It is up to you to determine which set of trade-offs make the most sense in the context of a project or to derive a tailored style that provides the right capabilities where they are needed most.

Changing Constraints

Orchestration-Driven Interactions

The first constraint we change is how components interact. In contrast with the Choreography-Driven Interactions Constraint, where each component only knows its individual role, orchestration introduces a central *mediator* (or *orchestrator*) which controls the workflow from start to finish through direct interaction with each of the required *processing components* in sequence (Figure 18-1).

M. Carducci, *Mastering Software Architecture*, https://doi.org/10.1007/979-8-8688-0410-6_18

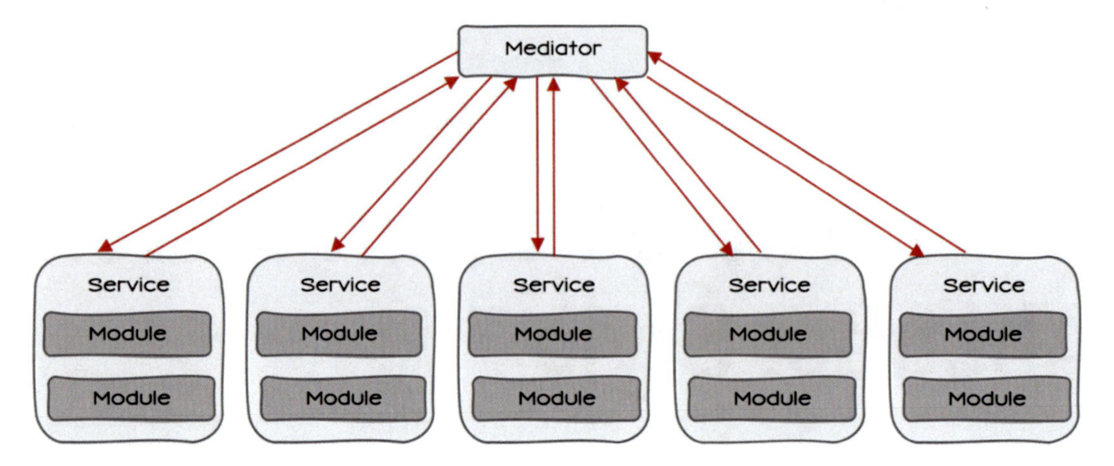

Figure 18-1. *Depiction of a Mediator-Orchestrated Workflow*

With a central *mediator* orchestrating the workflow, we eliminate the need for detailed choreography of every exception and edge case. The *mediator* has visibility into errors and can manage these to either roll back or restart/recover. This makes it much more difficult to lose messages or get into an inconsistent state. The Orchestration-Driven Interactions Constraint also guards against accidental cycles in the workflow process and other potential negative emergent behaviors.

This constraint enables the modeling and implementation of both simple and complex workflows with less complication and risk. The *mediator* is inherently coupled with the workflow and the *processing components* as this style requires that the *mediator* has knowledge of each component with which it must interact as well as how to interact with them. The *mediator* must also know each step of the workflow and how to handle exception conditions.

The coupling of *mediator* and *processing components* results in a workflow that is more difficult to evolve. Coordinated deployments are often inevitable, meaning our testing scope increases and our deployability decreases. Agility is also constrained.

Mediator Topology

This abstract style is a variation of choreographed style described in the previous chapter. As such, this style describes a technically partitioned, distributed system. Consequently, in many cases, we do not want a single, monolithic *mediator*. Often multiple *mediators* will be associated with each domain, and a single *mediator* will exist for each domain workflow or for each subcomponent of a domain workflow where a *mediator* is warranted. This opens some useful topological possibilities in our design. In an orchestrated event-driven style, a single *mediator* will listen for an *initiating event* on the relevant event channel; however, this does not imply that a single *mediator* must orchestrate every step or every possible permutation of a single domain workflow.

When designing a system to support an orchestrated workflow, begin by categorizing the overall workflow as simple, hard, or complex. Simple workflows can easily be handled by a single simple, lightweight *mediator* (like the example in Figure 18-1). In the case of hard or complex workflows, we have a choice to either expand the scope and complexity of a single *mediator* or utilize multiple *mediators* in a hierarchical topology to isolate and contain the overall complexity.

To determine whether to expand the *mediator* or expand the topology, first take a critical look at the problem to ensure you are dealing with *essential complexity* and not compounding *accidental complexity*.[1] In the latter case, I would recommend taking a step back to the drawing board and evaluating the architectural requirements. It is always important to check our assumptions and, in this case, ensure such a topology is truly necessary.

Assuming the complexity is *essential*, next break down the business process to determine if the entire workflow is complex or if there merely exist pockets of complexity in the overall flow. Even in complex workflows, there is often a mix of simple and complex stages (hence, pockets of complexity). Often these pockets of complexity take two distinct forms that each will inform the overall workflow topology:

1. An inherently complex *subset* of steps in the overall workflow
2. An inherently complex *edge case*

In the case of the first form, it can be useful to bundle the subset of individual, atomic steps into a single, molecular delivery. In such a topology, all requests flow through a common, lightweight *mediator* that will orchestrate both the *processing components* responsible for performing simple tasks as well as child or delegate *mediators* which control the more complex sequences.

In the case of the second form, where complexity emerges from certain edge cases, once again all requests flow through a common, lightweight *mediator* acting as the entry point for the workflow, and this mediator will make the determination of whether a given instance of the workflow triggered by the initiating event can follow the comparatively

[1] Brooks, F. (1986). *No Silver Bullet—Essence and Accident in Software Engineering*. Proceedings of the IFIP Tenth World Computing Conference

simple "happy path" or if the workflow instance will require a more powerful *mediator*. In the latter case, the simple *mediator* will hand off the work to a more specialized and complex *delegate mediator*.

In both scenarios, you are decomposing the problem to isolate complexity and limit testing scope, which will marginally improve testability, deployability, and overall agility.

Building/Implementing Mediators

Orchestration is a common need in many distributed environments. Consequently, we have many implementation options available to us, with each option capable of supporting different levels of complexity. Depending on the system's environment, existing tools may already be in place and ready to utilize. When considering various possibilities, consider the following features which are useful in an event-driven architecture:

- **Routing**: Determine how messages are passed from one component to another.
- **Transformation**: Convert message formats as they move between services.
- **Mediation**: Act upon the message content or headers to make decisions about business logic.
- **Adapters/Connectors**: Connect to various systems and protocols.

There is no one-size-fits-all solution, and you will need to consider ecosystem and language compatibility, complexity, performance, community, and support. Let us look at a few common options along with their advantages and trade-offs.

Custom Component

The first option is building a custom orchestration service component that listens to events and triggers other services via APIs or events. For simple workflows, this may be more than adequate.

This option allows developers to utilize existing software development skillsets to develop a *mediator* component. Teams have full control over the domain-specific orchestration logic, allowing them to implement complex workflows, customize error handling, and adjust the behavior as their needs evolve. With a custom solution, teams can implement detailed logging, monitoring, and tracing specifically designed for their workflows, making it easier to identify and resolve issues.

Developing and maintaining a custom orchestration service can be complex, especially as workflows evolve. This approach often requires a significant investment of time and resources, both during development and ongoing maintenance. Over time, the service may become difficult to manage, requiring significant effort to maintain and extend. As workflows change, the custom service might accumulate technical debt, particularly if not carefully managed. This can lead to increased maintenance burdens and potentially limit agility in adapting to new requirements. There is also a risk of overengineering the solution, adding unnecessary complexity that might not be needed immediately or at all. This can make the service harder to understand and maintain.

Additionally, custom solutions may rely heavily on the knowledge of the developers who built it. If those developers leave the organization, it could be challenging to maintain or extend the service. Consequently, maintaining good documentation in such cases is a necessary countermeasure that trades incremental cost for improved maintainability.

Finally, in many cases, we are reinventing the wheel. As you will see below, there are many existing orchestration frameworks, platforms, and tools that provide robust workflow orchestration capabilities. Building a custom solution might mean duplicating functionality that already exists, diverting resources from differentiating efforts that provide concrete user value.

Cloud Services

AWS Step Functions, Azure Logic Apps, and Google Cloud Workflows are all tools to build powerful integration solutions and orchestrate data and services. When considering cloud-based orchestration solutions such as these, the inherent advantages include rapid deployment and scalability, allowing you to leverage the vast infrastructure and reliability of these platforms. These services are designed to integrate seamlessly with other cloud services, providing out-of-the-box connectors and simplifying the orchestration of complex workflows without the need to manage underlying infrastructure. However, the trade-offs include additional cost and potential vendor lock-in, which might limit your flexibility if you need to switch platforms later. Additionally, while these services reduce the need for custom code, they might also impose constraints on your workflows, limiting customization to what the platform supports, which could be a significant drawback for highly specialized or complex processes.

Service Mesh

If available, using a service mesh like Istio or Linkerd combined with custom controllers offers a powerful and flexible approach to managing microservices communication and orchestration. The inherent advantages of this solution include fine-grained control over service-to-service interactions, enhanced security with features like mutual transport layer security (TLS), and advanced observability through metrics, logging, and tracing. By integrating custom controllers, you can automate and extend the orchestration capabilities to fit your specific needs, providing a tailored solution that leverages the robust features of the service mesh. However, the trade-offs include increased complexity in managing the service mesh itself, which can be resource-intensive and require a steep learning curve. Additionally, the overhead of maintaining both the mesh and custom controllers can lead to higher operational costs and potential performance implications, especially as your system grows in complexity.

RabbitMQ with Workflow Plug-ins

Leveraging RabbitMQ in conjunction with workflow plug-ins provides a message-driven approach to orchestrating workflows, offering robust, asynchronous communication between services. The inherent advantages of this option include high reliability and fault tolerance, as RabbitMQ ensures messages are delivered even in the face of service failures. Workflow plug-ins can add orchestrated control flows, making it easier to manage complex sequences of tasks across distributed systems. However, the trade-offs include potential latency due to message queuing, the added complexity of managing message brokers, and the challenge of ensuring the system remains performant as the number of messages and services scales. Additionally, while RabbitMQ provides strong guarantees for message delivery, the orchestration logic might become more challenging to maintain and debug as workflows grow more intricate.

Apache Camel

Apache Camel offers a highly flexible and lightweight approach to integrating and orchestrating workflows across diverse systems. As an integration framework, it allows you to route and transform data between various protocols and technologies using a wide array of predefined enterprise integration patterns (EIPs). The inherent advantages of Apache Camel include its ease of integration, extensive library of connectors, and the ability to create complex routing and mediation rules with minimal overhead.

This makes it particularly well suited for environments where agility and lightweight integration are key. However, the trade-offs include its focus on integration rather than full-featured process management, which may limit its utility for comprehensive workflow orchestration, and the potential complexity in managing and debugging intricate routing logic as your system scales.

Business Process Management (BPM) Tools

Commercial and open source BPM tools offer powerful orchestration capabilities in distributed systems. A few examples that are relevant at the time of this writing are as follows.

Camunda BPM is a highly flexible BPM tool designed to model, automate, and monitor business processes. It integrates seamlessly with Java applications and provides a comprehensive suite of tools for defining workflows using business process model and notation (BPMN), case management model and notation (CMMN), and decision model and notation (DMN) standards. The main advantages of Camunda BPM are its rich feature set, strong community support, and ease of integration into existing enterprise systems. However, it can introduce complexity in terms of setup and maintenance, particularly in large-scale distributed systems, and may require considerable resources to manage effectively.

Zeebe is a cloud-native workflow engine designed by Camunda specifically for orchestrating microservices in distributed systems. It offers scalable workflow orchestration using BPMN 2.0, making it ideal for high-throughput environments where traditional BPM solutions might struggle. Zeebe's strengths lie in its scalability, fault tolerance, and seamless integration with distributed architectures. However, as a relatively newer solution, it may not have as extensive a feature set or community support as more established BPM tools, and its focus on cloud-native environments may limit its applicability in certain on-premise scenarios.

Cadence and **Temporal** are open source workflow orchestration engines that provide strong guarantees for the execution of complex, long-running business processes. Developed by Uber (Cadence) and later forked into Temporal, these tools offer rich features like fault tolerance, state management, and seamless integration with microservices. The primary advantage is their ability to handle workflows that require consistency, retries, and time-based triggers, making them highly reliable. However, these tools come with a steep learning curve and can introduce significant operational overhead due to the complexity of their infrastructure.

The main advantages of BPM tools include the ability to model, automate, and monitor complex workflows with strong guarantees for reliability and scalability. These tools excel at managing long-running processes and integrating diverse systems. However, the trade-offs often involve increased complexity, both in terms of learning curve and operational overhead, and, in some cases, limitations in feature sets or community support. BPM-driven engines are overkill for simple flows, but powerful for complex flows. Choosing the right BPM tool—or a non-BPM alternative—depends on the specific requirements of your distributed system and the balance you seek between flexibility, scalability, and ease of management.

Mediator Communication

In contrast to choreographed styles, *mediators* communicate with processing services or components in a direct, point-to-point manner and rely on a request/response pattern of interaction. Consequently, processors do not typically broadcast results. Although this constraint is presented in the context of an event-driven style, *mediators* may communicate synchronously or asynchronously with processing services.

When an individual workflow step can take place within a reasonable timeout period, the *mediator* can adopt synchronous communication (Figure 18-2) utilizing existing APIs to perform workflow steps. This approach has the advantage of simplicity and the ability to reuse existing APIs. Synchronous communication also makes it easier to manage dependencies between tasks since the orchestrator can wait for a response before moving on to the next step, ensuring that tasks are completed in a specific sequence. However, synchronous calls can limit the scalability of the system. If the orchestrator must wait for each task to complete, it can become a bottleneck, particularly under high load or if there are multiple long-running tasks. Synchronous communication will also lead to tighter coupling between the orchestrator and processing components, making the system less flexible and harder to evolve over time. A final downside of this approach is the inherent stateful nature of the mediator. Additional design and effort must be put in place to handle long-running workflows and restart logic should the mediator crash.

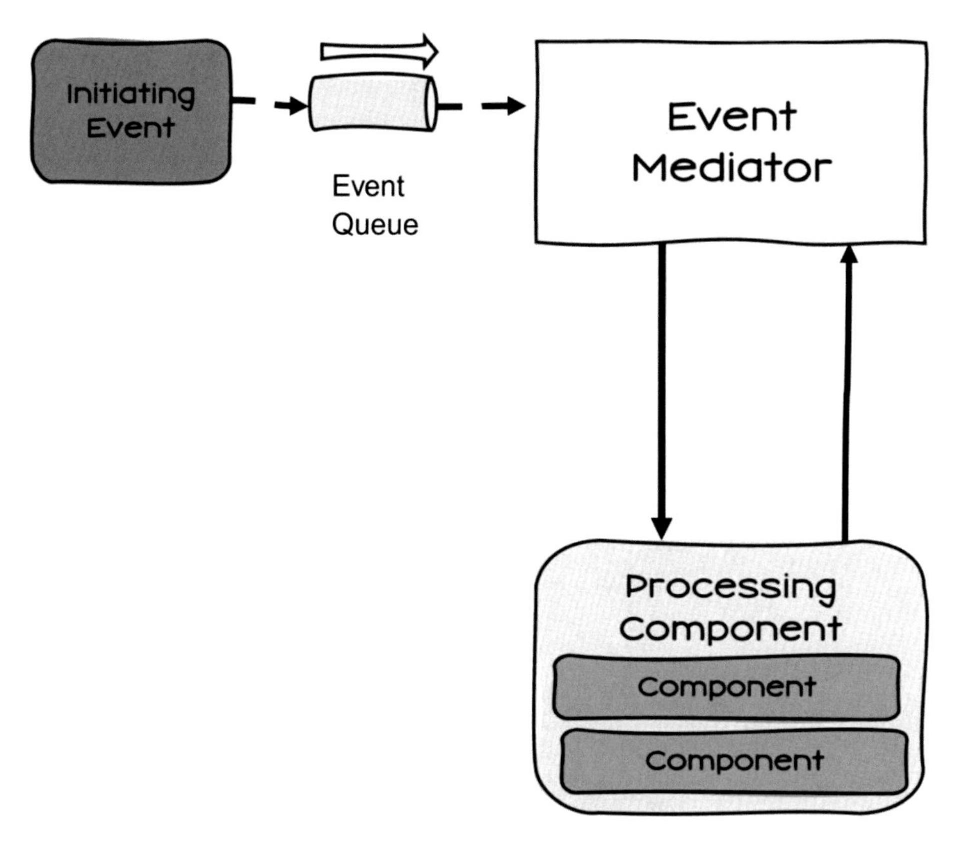

Figure 18-2. *Synchronous Communication Between Mediator and Processor*

Alternatively, communication can take place asynchronously. In this configuration, two mediator/component-specific point-to-point *messaging channels* are utilized. The first channel is reserved for requests; the second is reserved for responses. Since the request and response will always occur in separate execution contexts, a correlation ID is used to connect initial requests to their asynchronous responses (Figure 18-3). Unlike choreography, where messages represent events that *have happened* and are modeled in the past tense, asynchronous requests in this style are typically *request driven*, meaning messages are *requests* for the processor to perform some action.

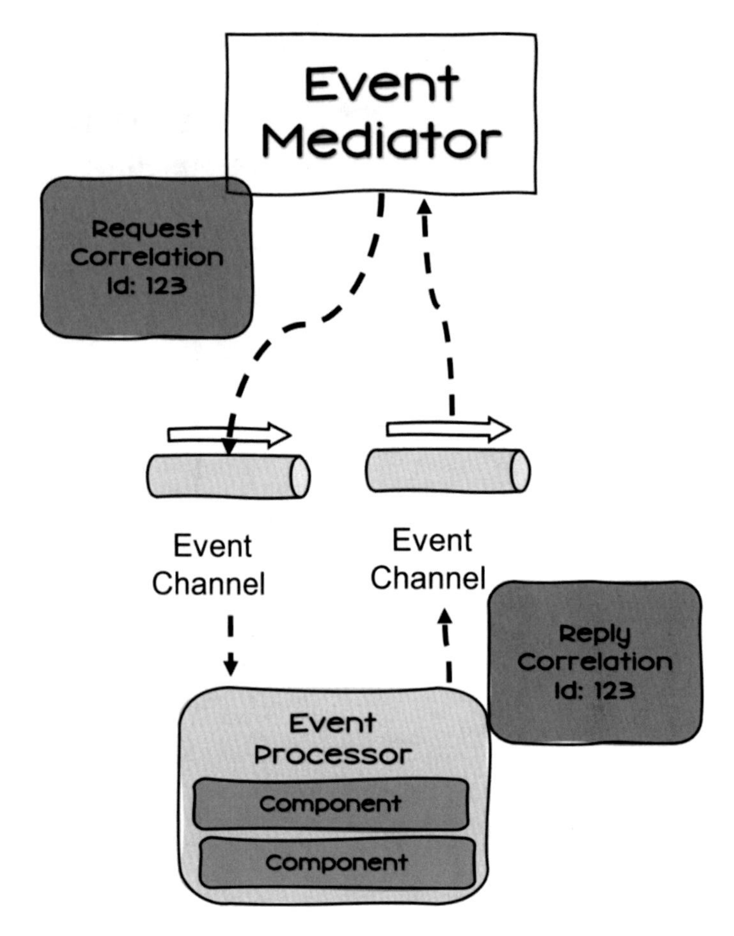

Figure 18-3. *Asynchronous Event/Workflow Request Orchestration*

Asynchronous communication allows the orchestrator to send a task to a processing component and immediately move on to other tasks. This decouples the orchestrator from the processing speed of individual components, enabling better scalability and throughput, especially in distributed systems. The orchestrator also does not need to wait for a response, reducing latency in the workflow, particularly when tasks can be processed in parallel or when the orchestrator can continue with other independent tasks.

As we learned in the previous chapter, asynchronous systems are typically more resilient to failures. If a processing component is temporarily unavailable, the message remains in the queue to be consumed when the service is available, ensuring that tasks are eventually processed without blocking the entire workflow. Asynchronous communication encourages loose coupling between components, making the system more modular and easier to maintain and extend. It also allows for greater flexibility in replacing or scaling individual components.

Unlike the fire-and-forget asynchronous communication approach common in choreographed styles, the *mediator* will require some notification mechanism when the processing step has completed. The biggest challenge can be determining how long to wait for a response. Synchronous communication enables the *mediator* to catch and handle errors in real time, simplifying the process of managing exceptions and ensuring that the workflow can respond to failures as they occur. When communication is asynchronous, the *mediator* must wait an unspecified amount of time for a response. Consequently, errors are not immediately apparent to the orchestrator, which may only learn about failures after a significant delay. This can complicate error handling and recovery, particularly in workflows where timely responses are critical.

The choice between synchronous and asynchronous communication in an orchestrated event-driven architecture hinges on the specific needs of your workflow. Synchronous communication offers simplicity and immediate feedback, but can introduce latency, scalability issues, and tighter coupling. Asynchronous communication, on the other hand, provides greater scalability, resilience, and flexibility but at the cost of increased complexity in managing workflows and handling delayed error responses.

As this is an abstract style to be tailored, we will prescribe the common case of asynchronous communication.

Persistent Queue Messaging

The Choreographed Event-Driven Abstract Style utilizes PubSub semantics for communication. The inherent broadcast capabilities and at least once delivery behavior are very useful in a choreographed context. Orchestrated event-driven architectures typically use queue semantics rather than PubSub for several key reasons:

1. **Message Ordering and Delivery Guarantees**
   Queues are designed to ensure that messages are delivered in a specific order (typically FIFO—first in, first out) and are processed exactly once by a single consumer. This is crucial in orchestrated workflows where the sequence of events and tasks must be strictly controlled to maintain the integrity of the process.

PubSub, on the other hand, typically delivers messages to multiple subscribers, and the order of message processing may vary depending on the subscriber's processing capabilities and the underlying infrastructure. This can lead to inconsistencies in workflow execution if strict ordering is required.

2. **Task Coordination and State Management**

   In an orchestrated architecture, the *mediator* needs to coordinate tasks across various services. Queues allow the orchestrator to assign tasks to specific services, ensuring that each task is processed once and in the correct sequence. This is critical for managing the state and ensuring that each step in the workflow is completed before moving to the next.

   PubSub systems broadcast messages to all subscribers, which is ideal for services and multiple consumers to react to the same event independently. However, in orchestrated workflows, this can lead to challenges in managing state and coordinating tasks, as the orchestrator needs to have tight control over the execution flow, particularly as workflows grow more complex.

3. **Scalability and Load Management**

   Queues allow for effective load balancing by distributing messages to consumers based on their availability and capacity. This ensures that tasks are processed efficiently without overwhelming any single service. The orchestrator or environment can scale consumers up or down as needed, which is vital in maintaining performance in large-scale systems.

   While PubSub also supports scalability, it is more suited to scenarios where multiple independent services need to be notified of the same event rather than coordinating the execution of a series of dependent tasks.

4. **Reliability and Fault Tolerance**

   Queues typically offer stronger reliability guarantees, such as ensuring that messages are persisted until they are successfully processed by a consumer. This is crucial in orchestrated workflows where failure to process a message could disrupt the entire workflow. Queues often support features like message retries and dead-letter queues, which help in handling failures gracefully. PubSub systems can also offer reliability, but the focus is more on delivering messages to multiple subscribers rather than ensuring that each message is processed exactly once in a controlled manner.

Preventing Data Loss

In the past, queues have struggled with issues surrounding data loss as the contents of the queue is frequently held in volatile memory; however, this constraint prescribes the use of a *persistent queue*, namely, one that offers data retention, even if the queue crashes and requires a restart. When avoiding data loss is important, it is necessary to wait for a full write acknowledgment when pushing a message into a queue and potentially configuring a queue to hold a pending message until the consumer fully acknowledges the read. These guarantees might be off by default in pursuit of favorable throughput benchmarks, but we must ensure these guarantees are in place when needed.

Orchestration-Driven Event-Driven Abstract Style

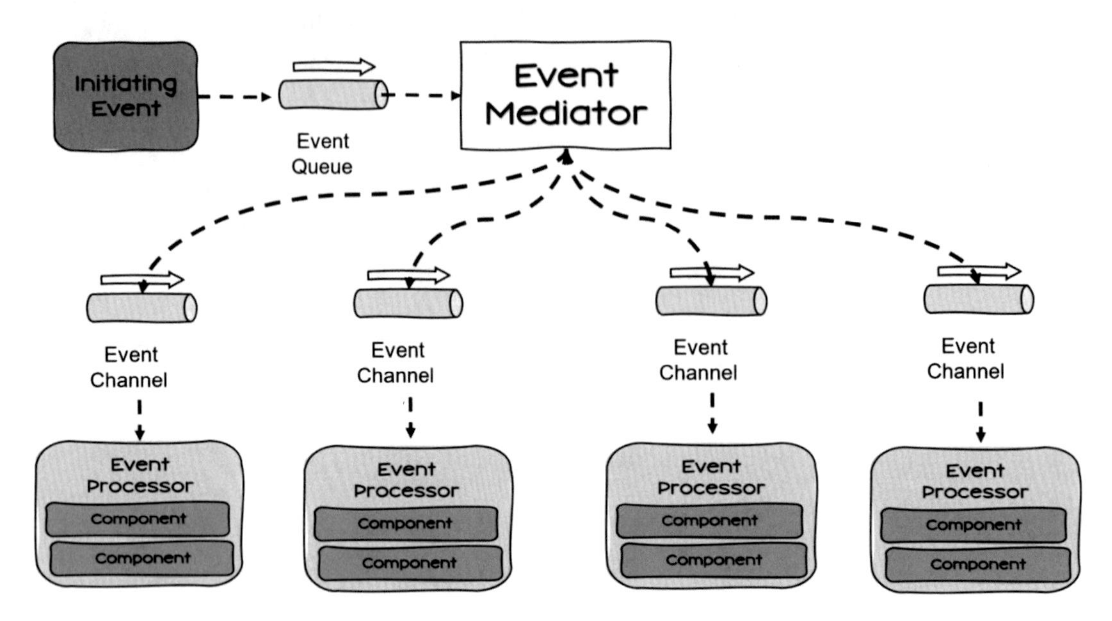

Figure 18-4. *Orchestrated Event-Driven Abstract Style*

Orchestrated event-driven architecture (Figure 18-4) is all about managing complex workflows by coordinating the interactions between various services, or *processing components*, through central *orchestrators*. These orchestrators act as *mediators*, directing the flow of tasks, ensuring that each step in the process is executed in the correct order, and handling any errors or exceptions that arise. The beauty of this architecture lies in its ability to decouple services, allowing each component to focus on its specific task while the orchestrator manages the overall process.

Orchestration-Driven Service-Oriented Architecture

One of the earliest distributed architectures to leverage orchestration was Service-Oriented Architecture (SOA), which emerged in the 1990s. By then, many organizations had already made significant strides in their digital transformation efforts, implementing numerous business systems. However, the cost of developing these systems was steep, and computing resources were both scarce and expensive. This context pushed architects toward distributed architectures that prioritized reuse as a fundamental principle, thereby reducing costs and improving efficiency. This strategy led to the creation of a service taxonomy, with distinct layers of business, enterprise, application, and infrastructure services, all coordinated by a central orchestration engine (Figure 18-5).

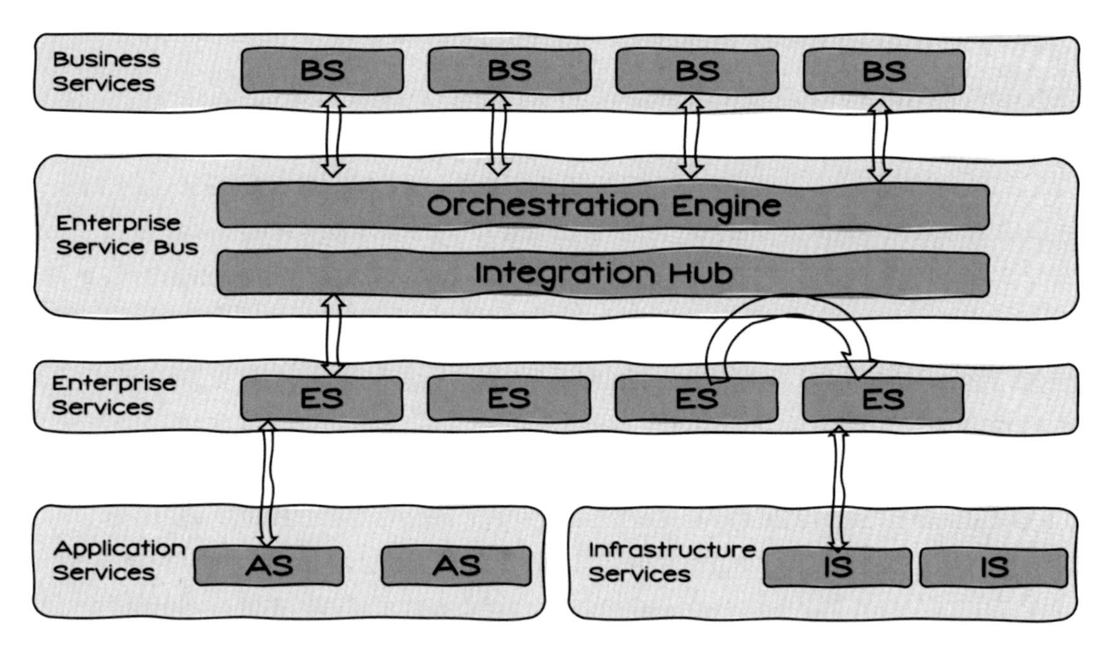

***Figure 18-5.** Orchestration-Driven Service-Oriented Architecture*

In this architecture, Business Services often served as the entry point for defined behaviors. These were not typically code modules but rather definitions of inputs, outputs, and sometimes schema, usually shaped by business users. Below this, Enterprise Services were fine-grained, shared implementations—think of operations like `calculateTax` or `createCustomer`—that served as the building blocks for the more coarse-grained business services, all tied together by the orchestration engine. Application Services, on the other hand, were typically one-off utilities, such as geolocation services, designed for specific needs without the intention of broad reuse. Infrastructure Services handled cross-cutting concerns like logging, monitoring, and authentication, providing the necessary operational backbone.

At the heart of this architecture was the orchestration engine, typically in the form of an Enterprise Service Bus (ESB), which connected and coordinated everything. The orchestration engine played a crucial role in integrating business services and managing transactional behavior across the system. However, while SOA aimed to provide flexibility and promote reuse, it quickly became evident that this approach introduced significant challenges. The heavy emphasis on reuse led to substantial coupling between services, making incremental changes risky and complex. The necessity for coordinated deployments and extensive testing further complicated the development process, often stalling progress and leading to inefficiencies.

Moreover, the architecture's focus on technical partitioning turned out to be a practical nightmare. Domain concepts became so fragmented across the architecture that even simple tasks required changes to multiple services and database schemas, undermining the original goals of reuse and efficiency. This fragmentation also resulted in significant coupling within the architecture, particularly around the orchestration engine, which became a bottleneck and a single point of failure.

While this architectural style did achieve some success in areas like scalability and elasticity, its poor performance, deployability, and testability, coupled with high complexity and cost, ultimately led to its downfall. The lessons learned from this era underscored the value of standardized service interfaces, the challenges of managing distributed transactions, and the practical limits of technical partitioning, paving the way for more modern, adaptable architectural styles that could better meet the evolving needs of the industry.

The Orchestrated Event-Driven Abstract Style is comprised of a unique set of constraints that offer very strong workflow capabilities. Like this style's choreographed counterpart, defining constraints of this style often show up in other tailored and hybrid styles. For example, orchestration is common when implementing the Saga Pattern in microservices styles.

Summary

Orchestrated event-driven architecture offers several key architectural capabilities. It provides centralized control, where the orchestrator manages and coordinates the execution of workflows, ensuring tasks are completed in the correct sequence and handling exceptions gracefully. This architecture supports decoupled processing services, allowing each service to focus on its specific tasks while the orchestrator manages the overall process flow, improving maintainability and enabling services to evolve independently. Additionally, it excels in scalability, especially with asynchronous communication, allowing the orchestrator to handle multiple tasks concurrently and distribute workloads without the need for immediate responses. This architecture also offers flexibility in process management, enabling the modeling and management of complex workflows with branching logic, conditional tasks, and long-running processes to suit a wide range of business scenarios.

However, these strengths come with trade-offs. This architecture introduces additional complexity, particularly in managing workflow states, handling asynchronous communication, and ensuring message ordering and delivery, which can make development, debugging, and maintenance more challenging. Synchronous communication, while offering immediate feedback, can reduce system performance due to tight coupling between services, while asynchronous communication, despite improving scalability, increases the complexity of task coordination. There is also an operational overhead in managing the orchestrator and the supporting infrastructure, as ensuring the high availability and reliability of the orchestrator is crucial due to its central role. Finally, the orchestrator can become a potential bottleneck or single point of failure, which, if not properly designed for scalability and fault tolerance, can disrupt the entire workflow execution and impact the overall system.

The following architectural constraints define this abstract style:

- Fine Component Granularity
- Technical Partitioning
- Independent Deployability
- Orchestration-Driven Interactions
- Persistent Queue Messaging

This collection of constraints requires the following team, organization, and environmental constraints:

- ORG: DevOps Commitment
- ENV: Development Environment Isolation
- ENV: High Operational Automation
- ENV: Distributed Tracing and Logging
- TEAM: Automation Skills
- TEAM: Pipeline Development Skills
- TEAM: IaC Skills
- TEAM: Independent Development Cycles

When compared with the Choreographed Event-Driven Abstract Style, the following capabilities are improved by the two changed defining constraints (Orchestration-Driven Interactions and Persistent Queue Messaging). See Figure 18-6.

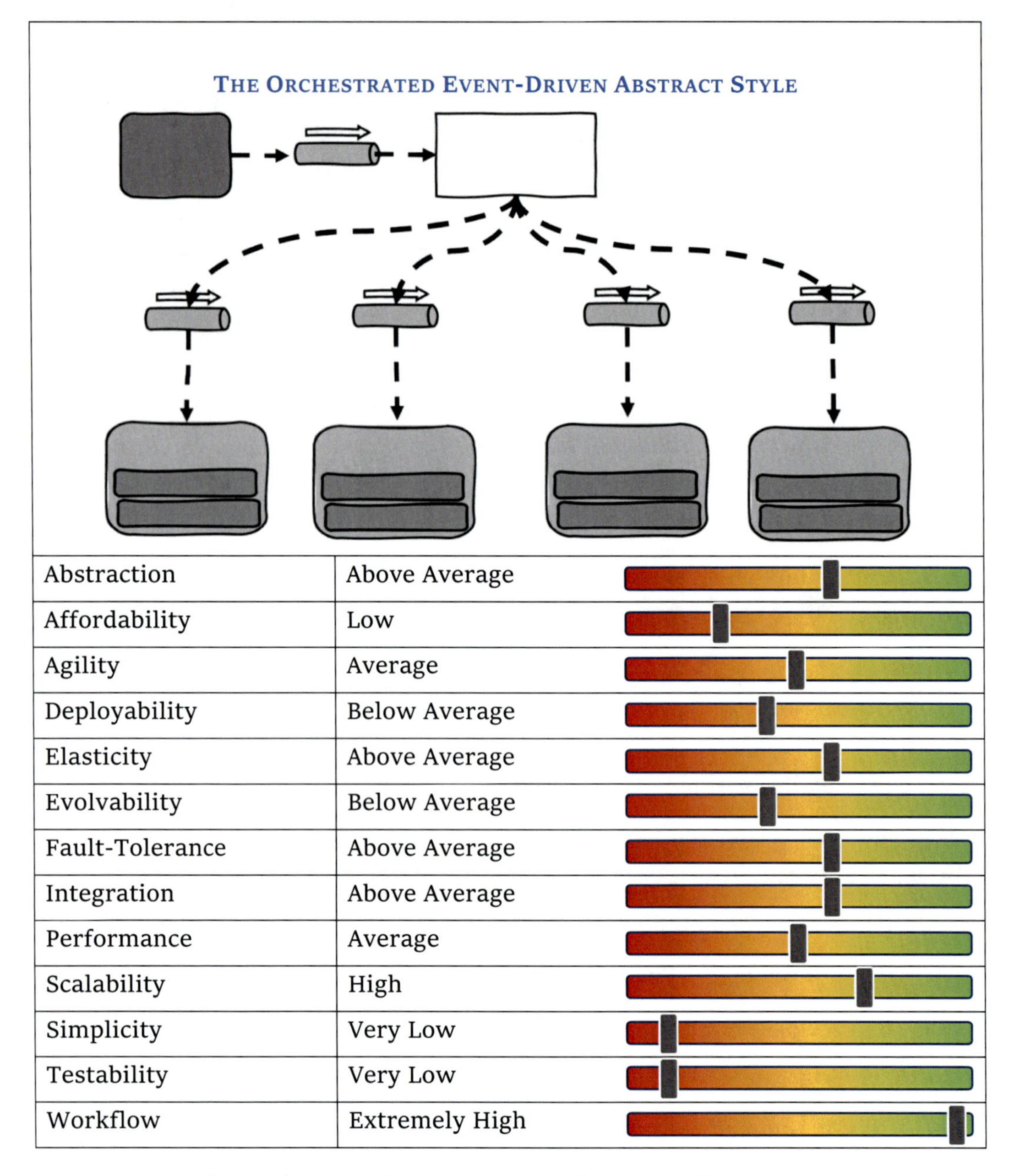

Abstraction	Above Average
Affordability	Low
Agility	Average
Deployability	Below Average
Elasticity	Above Average
Evolvability	Below Average
Fault-Tolerance	Above Average
Integration	Above Average
Performance	Average
Scalability	High
Simplicity	Very Low
Testability	Very Low
Workflow	Extremely High

Figure 18-6. *The Orchestrated Event-Driven Abstract Style*

CHAPTER 19

The Space-Based Abstract Style

Any optimization that is not about the bottleneck is an illusion of improvement.

—Federico Toledo

Despite the advantages of architecture design by constraint and the Tailor-Made Software Architecture Model, achieving holistic fit in software architecture is not easy. As you know, every architectural constraint will strengthen some capabilities while weakening others. Moreover, the benefits of different capabilities do not always materialize immediately, providing uneven visibility of architectural value which can undermine your efforts.

Take, for example, the capability of *evolvability*. Many factors influence the overall evolvability of a system; however, while those factors are often measurable, true visibility into a system's overall evolvability only emerges as the system repeatedly demonstrates an ability to gracefully adopt and absorb both business and technical change. Notably, it is also significantly easier to notice the presence of a problem than to notice the absence of a problem. Without careful communication with development teams, architectural constraints that induce long-term benefits might be rejected or abandoned by development teams in favor of more directly visible capabilities.

One such directly visible capability is that of *performance*. When some aspect of the system's runtime-based behavior is optimized, in contrast with evolvability, the performance improvement is immediately visible. Software engineers often desire to produce elegant and efficient code, with performance as a key measure. This fact often puts architecture and engineering teams in tension.

M. Carducci, *Mastering Software Architecture*, https://doi.org/10.1007/979-8-8688-0410-6_19

Many architectural styles strive to balance performance with other capabilities based on relative business value. As such, we have not yet seen an architectural style that offers extremely high performance. That changes in this chapter as we introduce an abstract style that is laser focused on delivering the highest possible performance, the Space-Based Abstract Style.

When compared with the other abstract styles introduced in this section, this style's closest sibling is the Service-Based Abstract Style. Both styles utilize a distributed topology with medium-grained domain components, both styles utilize a shared database, and both prescribe an API (RPC style, in the abstract). In addition to the common constraints, this style prescribes three additional constraints to massively boost performance (at the expense of reduced agility, affordability, deployability, simplicity, and testability.

Adding Constraints

Transactional Data Stored In-Memory

Systems responsible for online transaction processing (OLTP) typically make heavy use of databases in every request, potentially introducing a bottleneck that places a ceiling on the maximum performance at scale. The simple act of retrieving state requires a network call to the database server, which must parse and compile each query it receives before execution. Execution may require physical I/O if the necessary data is not already in memory on the database. Finally, the response is transmitted back over the network to the calling service. In extremely performance-sensitive environments, these factors all add up to potentially unacceptable latency.

Developers and architects have long known that an in-memory cache can outperform even the most powerful databases. Conventionally, these caches are standalone services although it is common for some services to cache certain data locally for simplicity or to avoid the network overhead of an external cache.

This constraint takes the idea of a local cache to its logical extreme by dictating that *all* necessary data is preloaded in memory, eliminating all physical and network I/O when handling requests. When a service receives a request to get state, the service simply fetches the data from RAM, and when the service receives a request to modify state, it makes the modification in memory before returning a response. Depending on the nature and the structure of the data, the in-memory dataset may exist in the service's heap memory, may utilize an embedded in-memory database, or it may be handled by a private, colocated in-memory DBMS.

Such an extreme constraint will naturally raise questions like

- What happens if the service crashes?
- What happens if we dynamically add new processing nodes?
- How do we handle data drift between service instances?
- What if the full dataset does not fit in memory?

The next two constraints will address the first three questions; however, the final question must still be addressed in the context of this constraint.

Granularity and Near Cache

The service modeling process for this style is similar to that of the Service-Based Abstract Style. Individual modules need to be highly cohesive and able to stand alone when handling requests. Through this process, we once again must identify data domains that can be isolated from other components; however, unlike microservices styles, this style prescribes a shared database, meaning the data domains represented in the various space-based domain service components can easily overlap. Under this constraint, a new variable of dataset size is introduced and must be considered. Ideally, we aim to achieve a highly cohesive, standalone service with the smallest practical dataset.

Today, cloud services offer options for high-memory instances within their compute platforms. These instances are often purpose-built for the task of running large, in-memory databases, and an individual instance can currently scale to tens of terabytes of memory per instance.[1] With these high-memory instances, cost can quickly become a limiting factor especially since processor core count typically increases proportionally with memory allocation.

It can be tempting to adopt a distributed caching strategy known as *near cache*. A near cache is a hybrid caching model that combines in-memory data grids (the front cache) with a distributed cache (the full backing cache). The front cache holds a smaller subset of data from the full backing cache, using an eviction policy—such as Most

[1] AWS (2024). *Amazon EC2 High Memory (U-1) Instances.* `https://aws.amazon.com/ec2/instance-types/high-memory`

Recently Used (MRU),[2] Most Frequently Used (MFU),[3] Least Frequently Used (LFU),[4] or Random Replacement (RR)[5]—to manage space. While front caches are synchronized with the full backing cache, they are not synchronized across different service instances, leading to potential inconsistencies in performance and responsiveness. This lack of synchronization makes the near-cache model unsuitable for space-based style.

Replicated Shared Data Grid

The previous constraint asked two important questions, namely:

- What happens if we dynamically add new processing nodes?
- How do we handle data drift between service instances?

This constraint prescribes that styles lean on a replicated cache model, where each processing unit maintains its own in-memory data grid. These grids are synchronized across all units sharing the same cache, ensuring that updates in one unit are quickly propagated to the others. This approach offers exceptional speed and fault tolerance, with no single point of failure since there is no central cache server. However, replicated caches can face challenges with large data volumes or high update rates. When the internal cache grows beyond certain limits or the update frequency becomes too intense, the synchronization process might lag, impacting performance and scalability. In these scenarios, a tailored style might prescribe a distributed cache—centralized and accessed by processing services via a common protocol—that might be more appropriate, though it sacrifices some performance and fault tolerance for improved consistency. The choice between replicated and distributed caching hinges on the specific needs of the system, such as the type of data being cached, the required consistency, and the balance between performance and fault tolerance.

[2] GeeksForGeeks (2022). *Program for K Most Recently Used (MRU) Apps.* `https://www.geeksforgeeks.org/program-for-k-most-recently-used-mru-apps/`

[3] GeeksForGeeks (2023). *Most Frequently Used (MFU) Algorithm in Operating System.* `https://www.geeksforgeeks.org/most-frequently-used-mfu-algorithm-in-operating-system/`

[4] GeeksForGeeks (2024). *LRU Cache – Complete Tutorial.* `https://www.geeksforgeeks.org/lru-cache-implementation/`

[5] Luu, D. (2014). *Caches: LRU v. random.* `https://danluu.com/2choices-eviction/`

Decoupled Database

The final challenge we must address is data volatility. Although, under normal circumstances, data in this style is held in-memory and replicated to other instances, a complete failure of all instances or a global restart of all instances of a given service (perhaps due to deployment of a new version) will lose data not backed on disk somewhere. Direct communication with the database introduces a bottleneck this style seeks to eliminate; consequently, this constraint prescribes the database is entirely decoupled from the services. In other words, a service will never perform direct database I/O. Instead, the asynchronous replication of data between service instances will also asynchronously write data to the database. In the case of a cold start, the entire dataset needed by a service will be asynchronously published to one or more service instances or directly introduced into the data replication fabric. Specialized components referred to as *data pumps* handle asynchronous database I/O. We will describe *data pumps* in the next section.

The Space-Based Abstract Style

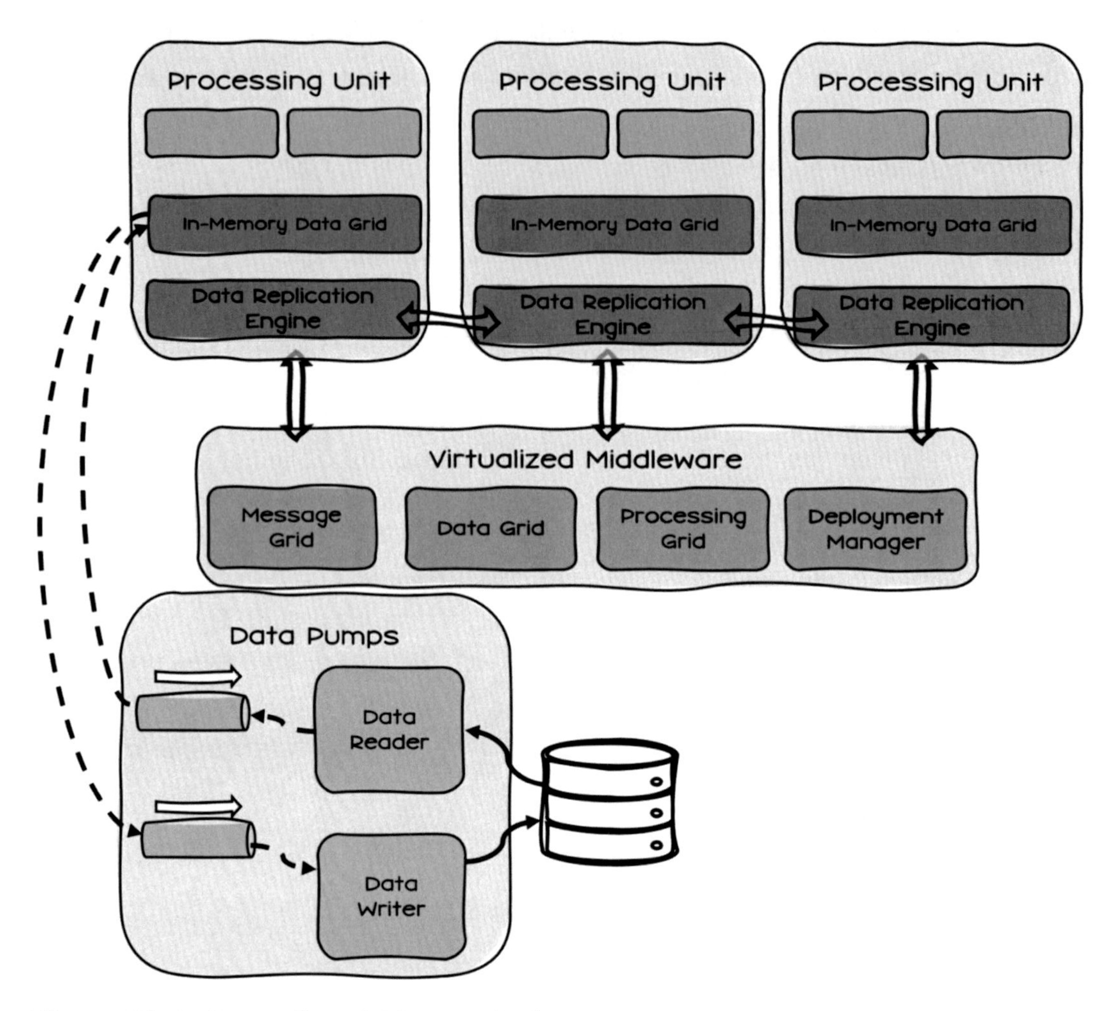

Figure 19-1. *Space-Based Abstract Style*

The composition of constraints yields a very high-performance style known as the Space-Based Abstract Style. This style takes its name from the concept of tuple space, an implementation of a shared memory space for parallel/distributed computing. It provides a repository of tuples that can be addressed and manipulated concurrently.

In this style, the defining constraints aggressively eliminate potential performance bottlenecks which results in a high performance and massively scalable architecture. The database is decoupled from the application by choosing to have each processing unit store the entire dataset in memory in the form of replicated data grids and eliminating all direct database reads and writes. Writes to the in-memory dataset are synchronized between worker nodes through some form of middleware which also asynchronously reads and writes to the underlying database. A separate component monitors overall load and scales the number of available workers up or down based on demand.

Although not easy (nor cheap), this abstract style forms the foundation of a highly performant, highly scalable, and highly elastic system architecture which offers a meaningful alternative to attempting to scale a database or adding in caching technologies to a less scalable architecture. Let us explore what this model looks like in practice.

The Processing Unit

The *processing unit* is the component of the system that contains the application logic and performs the business functions (whatever they may be). For practical reasons, the processing unit is generally a medium-grained component with carefully scoped data and optimal cold start times. In other words, there may be multiple tuple spaces depending on the size and scope of the overall system. Tuple space boundaries are often most easily identified through domain modeling and system modeling. In addition to the application logic, the *processing unit* contains the in-memory data grid and replication engine.

The Data Grid

The *data grid*[6, 7, 8] is the replicated in-memory state of the processing units and is a central concern of this architecture. It is essential that each processing unit always contains an identical state. The data grid may reside entirely within the processing unit with replication happening asynchronously between processing units, but, in some implementations, an external controller is necessary in which case the controller element of the data grid would form part of the virtualized middleware layer.

[6] Apache Ignite, `https://ignite.apache.org/use-cases/in-memory-data-grid.html`
[7] GridGain, `https://www.gridgain.com/`
[8] Hazelcast, `https://hazelcast.com/`

The Virtualized Middleware Layer

This layer contains components that handle infrastructure concerns that might control some aspects of the data synchronization and request handling and might take the form of off-the-shelf products or custom code.

The Message Grid

The *messaging grid* is a load balancer in this style. The messaging grid manages requests and session state and will determine which processing units are available and distribute requests appropriately.

The Processing Grid

This is an optional component that handles request orchestration, should multiple processing units be required to satisfy a given request.

The Deployment Manager

The *deployment manager* acts as the supervisor in this style, observing load and capacity and either adding or removing processing units to/from the pool as required.

Data Pumps

Although, in theory, this architecture could indefinitely hold all critical data in volatile memory, we must plan for inevitable cold start/cold restart scenarios. Data pumps provide eventual consistency between the in-memory datasets and the persistent storage with the database.

Data pumps come in two forms, the *data reader* and the *data writer*. Data readers subscribe to the state changes asynchronously broadcast by processing units and then synchronously write state changes to disk. A *data reader* is a separate pump responsible for providing initializing state to the processing units in the event of a cold start scenario. With both this component and the *data grid*, remember the CAP theorem and the challenges inherent to eventual consistency introduced in Chapter 16.

I feel the need—the need for *speed!*

Years ago, I was the chief architect on a project to build a highly extensible knowledge platform. At the heart of this platform was an enterprise knowledge graph built from data gathered from dozens or hundreds of systems of record. Although the knowledge graph offered a comprehensive and highly connected view of the entirety of the organization's knowledge, access to—and visibility of—any individual node in the graph was dependent on the end user's access privileges within the source system. As new source systems became integrated and existing systems were updated, our policy graph was also frequently changing.

In addition to the core knowledge graph, many microservices hosted aggregates and subgraphs, optimized for particular domain functions. Consequently, every user interaction within this system required both early and late authorization to take place. The former would verify the user was authorized to request a specific resource, and the latter would filter the response to ensure that it only contains graph nodes the user has explicit permission to access. A single user request could potentially require hundreds or even thousands of authorizations to take place in real time. Access control introduced a significant bottleneck into normal operations of this system.

The architecture team made the decision to implement the policy system as a space-based style since extremely high performance and throughput were *business-critical* capabilities.

In our implementation, we utilized our existing Kafka infrastructure to handle replication across the shared data grid. This enabled individual processing units to broadcast state changes to other instances as well as the data writer. The data reader initially populated this topic, and because our topology used a variation of event sourcing, once this initial load took place the reader was largely idle/unnecessary. Should a cold start become necessary, a processing unit could read the entire state from the Kafka topic.

The result was an extremely high-performance policy system that met our high service–level objectives and did not degrade as load and scale increased.

Although this abstract style is nominally a domain-partitioned architecture, there are also elements of technical partitioning to be found in the *data pumps* and *virtualized middleware*.

Summary

Typical OLTP systems involve requests that flow from a user's client to a server, then to a database server. This setup works fine with a small user base but quickly encounters bottlenecks as user load increases, particularly at the database layer, which can be the hardest and most expensive to scale. This style addresses these scalability challenges by eliminating the database as a real-time constraint and instead using replicated in-memory data grids, removing the bottleneck associated with database scaling, allowing the system to handle high user loads and variable concurrency with near-infinite scalability. As load increases, additional processing units can be dynamically deployed, and when the load decreases, they can be shut down, ensuring efficient resource usage. This architecture style is particularly suited for applications with unpredictable and extreme spikes in demand, such as online ticketing or auction systems, where rapid scalability and elasticity are critical. While space-based architecture offers significant performance and scalability benefits, it introduces complexity in terms of data consistency and testing, requiring careful management to avoid data loss and ensure reliability.

The following architectural constraints define this abstract style:

- Medium Component Granularity
- Technical Partitioning
- Domain Partitioning
- Decoupled Database
- Transactional Data Stored In-Memory

- Replicated Shared Data Grid
- Shared Database
- RPC API

This collection of constraints requires the following team, organization, and environmental constraints:

- ORG: Well-Defined Domains
- ORG: Domain-Aligned Teams
- ORG: DevOps Commitment
- ENV: Loose Coupling Between Components
- ENV: Development Environment Isolation
- ENV: High Operational Automation
- ENV: Service Discovery and Routing
- TEAM: API First
- TEAM: Automation Skills
- TEAM: Pipeline Development Skills

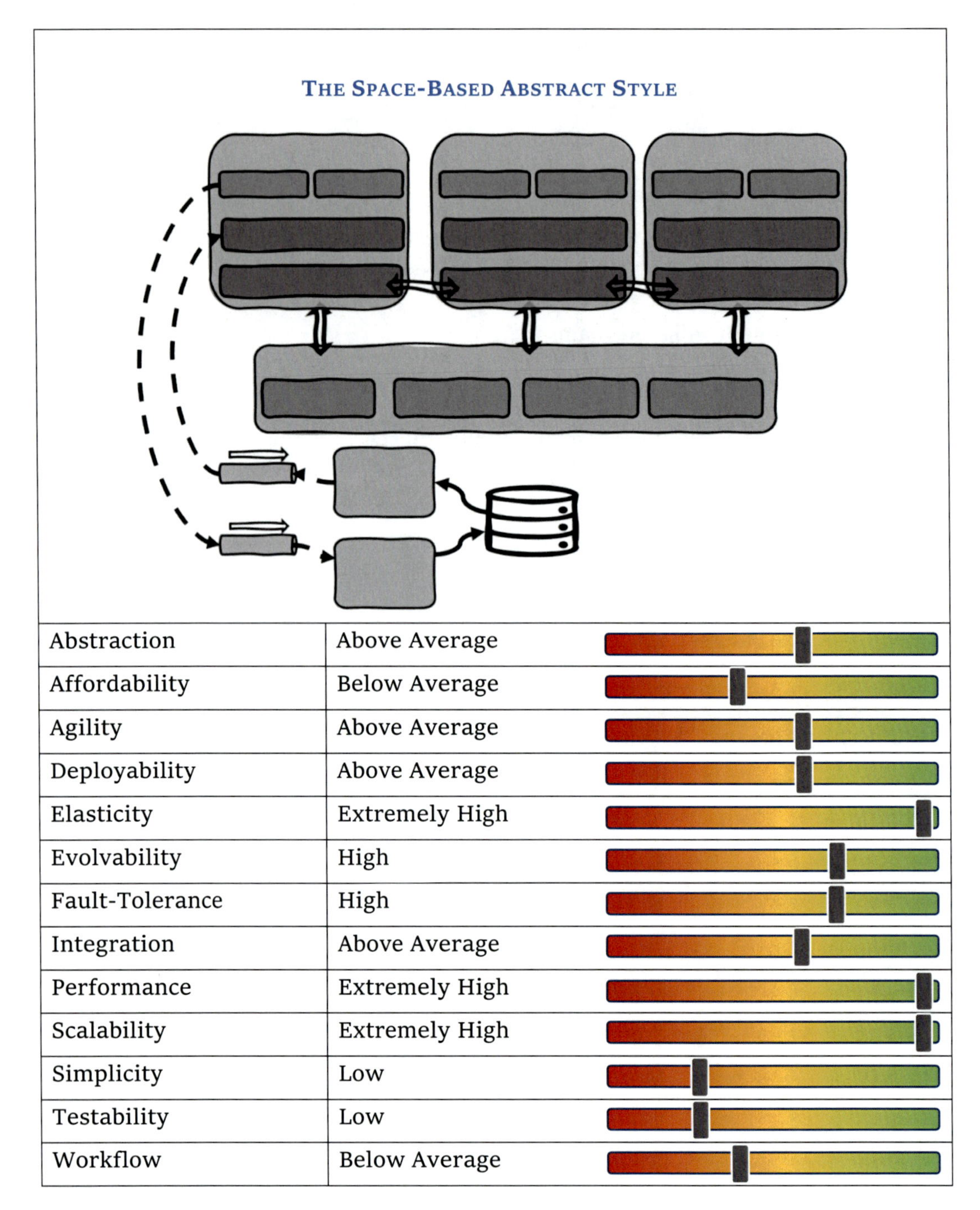

Abstraction	Above Average
Affordability	Below Average
Agility	Above Average
Deployability	Above Average
Elasticity	Extremely High
Evolvability	High
Fault-Tolerance	High
Integration	Above Average
Performance	Extremely High
Scalability	Extremely High
Simplicity	Low
Testability	Low
Workflow	Below Average

Figure 19-2. *The Space-Based Abstract Style*

CHAPTER 20

The Microkernel Abstract Style

A system is never the sum of its parts; it is the product of their interaction.

—Russell Ackoff

Some time ago, I was in a meeting with a development team at a client site when the vice president of IT made an unscheduled visit to say hello and meet new team members. Apropos of nothing, he announced, *"I like modularity! Software that can be assembled like Lego bricks."* Composable software is, indeed, an attractive vision—a vision shared by Brad Cox, an early and influential exponent of the Object-Oriented Programming (OOP) movement. OOP offered Cox a glimpse at the future potential for composable software architectures that would usher in *"A software industrial revolution based on reusable and interchangeable parts…"* that would, he promised, *"…alter the software universe.*[1]*"*

Composition has always been at the heart of engineering, and everything in our modern world exists as a composite of basic elements. The architectural styles we have examined in this section are no different; every architectural style is simply a composite of different architecturally significant decisions. In both architecture and engineering, as we create various composites new properties frequently emerge. For example, the basic elements of iron and carbon have known properties. When we create a composite of the two, we get something new; we get steel. Steel has unique properties that neither iron nor carbon possess. When we create a composite of calcium carbonate, silica and alumina, iron ore, and calcium sulfate, we get cement (which, again, yields useful new properties). A composite of cement, water, sand, and gravel, we get concrete, and when we combine concrete and steel, we get reinforced concrete. Nearly every new composite

[1] Cox B. *There is a Silver Bullet.* Byte 1990; Vol. 15, No. 10:209–218

M. Carducci, *Mastering Software Architecture*, https://doi.org/10.1007/979-8-8688-0410-6_20

opens the door to possibilities that were previously out of reach. The prospect of creating arbitrary software composites on demand continues to tease our industry with powerful potential.

Since 1990, when Cox penned his influential essay, software development has gradually shifted in this direction. Most modern software involves both creation and composition with reusable and interchangeable parts taking the form of libraries hosted in various package repositories. Design-time composition has dramatically increased developer productivity; however, the full flexibility of this vision often remains elusive. In this chapter, we will explore an architectural style that offers unique, runtime composability.

This style can be seen as an extension of the Modular Monolith Abstract Style (Chapter 14), so we will derive this abstract style by first beginning with that style's defining constraints and adding additional architectural constraints to create a new composite with novel properties.

Changing Constraints

This style does not prescribe a partitioning model, as the composition of a microkernel architecture might include domain modules, technical modules, or both. Consequently, the domain partitioning constraint is not prescribed and is removed from this style in the abstract. Additionally, the abstract style this chapter describes assumes a shared database (Chapter 12) but does not prescribe a partitioned shared database (Chapter 14).

Adding Constraints

Uniform Interface

Contrary to that VP's assertion, modularity alone does not beget truly composable systems. As an analogy, modularity produces simple bricks, and simple bricks require cement to assemble. Once the cement dries, however, those bricks are no longer interchangeable and rearrangeable. What makes Lego bricks distinct from other types of bricks is the presence of *studs* and *anti-studs* which enable the bricks to be easily connected, disconnected, and rearranged without cement or mortar. *Studs* in Lego are the distinctive cylindrical bumps or knobs on the surface of the brick that universally measure 1.6mm in height and 4.8mm in diameter. *Anti-studs* are the 4.8mm wide indentations in the bottom of Lego bricks and plates that serve as a *stud* receptacle.[2] It is the standardization and uniformity of the *stud/anti-stud* interface that gives Lego bricks their unique property of composability and interchangeability. In other words, every Lego brick ever created conforms to a common *uniform interface.*

Although Cox's idea of interchangeable, composable software modules was novel when it was first published, the idea was not entirely new. In fact, we first saw this approach to software take shape in the 1960s, and it strongly influenced the design and philosophy of UNIX.

> *We should have some ways of [connecting] programs like garden hose - screw in another segment when it becomes necessary to massage data in another way.*
>
> —Doug McIlroy, Internal Bell Labs Memo 1964[3]

The key to adopting this constraint lies in creating our own system of *studs* and *anti-studs*, a common interface with which all modules must conform. The most successful uniform interfaces are usually quite simple. Designing such an interface, however, is not easy.

> *I think most people just make the mistake that it should be simple to design simple things. In reality, the effort required to design something is inversely proportional to the simplicity of the result.*
>
> —Roy Fielding

Interface Constraints

> *In order to obtain a uniform interface, multiple architectural constraints are needed to guide the behavior of components.*
>
> —Roy Fielding

[2] Bartneck, C. (2019). LEGO Brick Dimensions and Measurements. `https://www.bartneck.de/2019/04/21/lego-brick-dimensions-and-measurements/`

[3] Kernighan, B. (2020). *UNIX: A History and a Memoir.* Kindle Direct Publishing

A uniform interface must be defined by *interface constraints*, the rules that all components must follow. The first notable example of these *interface constraints* appeared a decade after Doug McIlroy's ideas were circulated around Bell Labs, when Ken Thompson found a practical solution and implemented it into the third edition of UNIX. The core interface constraints are as follows:

- Every program shall interact with text streams: `stdin`, `stdout`, and `stderror`.
- *"Expect the output of every program to become the input to another, as yet unknown, program. Don't clutter output with extraneous information. Avoid stringently columnal or binary input formats. Don't insist on interactive input."*[4]

By adopting these interface constraints, the output of one program could become the input of another using the vertical bar character | which is now commonly referred to as the "pipe" character. When Thompson first tried this technique, he called the result "mind blowing," and this set of *interface constraints* remains relevant and valuable 50+ years later.

> *The addition of pipes led to a frenzy of invention that I remember vividly...Everyone in the Unix room had a bright idea for combining programs to do some task with existing programs rather than by writing a new program.*
>
> —Brian Kernighan, *UNIX: A History and a Memoir*

Another notable example is the REST architectural style. A uniform interface is one of the six constraints that define the style; however, the description of this constraint includes the following *interface constraints*:[5]

- Identification of resources (URIs)
- Manipulation of resources through representations of state
- Self-descriptive messages
- Hypermedia as the engine of application state

---

[4] McIlroy, D. *The Bell Labs Technical Journal on UNIX*. July 1978

[5] Fielding, R. *Architectural Styles and the Design of Network-based Software Architectures*. Doctoral dissertation, University of California, Irvine, 2000

Once again, although remarkably simple, the value and utility of this uniform interface continues to power the evolution of the Web more than three decades later.

The longevity of both *uniform interfaces* is a function of their generality. Both REST and UNIX pipes take a very generalized approach to component interaction and do not presume to know how any individual component will interact with another in the future. The trade-off, however, is a degradation of efficiency as information must be transferred in a standardized form rather than one that is specifically designed for an application or use case's needs.

Adopting the uniform interface constraint will typically require additional *interface constraints*.

Designing an Interface

Interfaces must be general and stable. Therefore, designing a *uniform interface* requires abstracting as much component implementation detail as possible. Two common approaches to expose a uniform interface are *APIs* and *hooks*.

REST adopts an API approach. The common case of REST is HTTP interactions. The request methods of HTTP (GET, PUT, POST, DELETE, PATCH, etc.) form one half of the "self-descriptive messages," and the standardized response codes, headers, and semantics embedded in hypermedia form the other. You may notice that these additional interface details are absent from the *interface constraints* enumerated above. This is because REST does not explicitly prescribe HTTP. Instead, the first *interface constraint* "Identification of Resources" explicitly prescribes URIs as identifiers. A URI is composed of multiple components, including

- A *scheme*—for example, `https://,` or `urn://`
- An *authority* (host name + port for http, or a namespace for URNs)—for example, `example.com`
- An optional *path*—for example, `/books/mastering-software-architecture`

Depending on the *scheme*, a client will use the appropriate communication protocol and context-specific data elements to interact with the *authority* and request the resource by its *path*.

When designing a uniform API interface, consider a wide variety of use cases. Look for ways to generalize interactions such that new use cases do not continuously need the addition of new API endpoints.

Hooks offer a different mechanism for implementing a uniform interface. *Hooks* are publicly exposed functions or mechanisms that allow a component to "hook into" a system or framework to extend its functionality or modify its behavior without changing its original code. They provide a way to interact with the system in a consistent and standardized manner. *Hooks* form the *anti-studs*, and tapping into a hook from another component will form the *studs*. This allows for a modular and flexible design where developers can add or override certain functionalities as needed while still adhering to a consistent interface provided by the framework or system.

Beyond *hooks*, *APIs*, and *streams* (UNIX pipes and filters), asynchronous events (Chapter 17) can form the basis of a *uniform interface* when the self-descriptive messages interface constraint is added. Whether you intend to use hooks, streams, messages, APIs, or some other approach, the ultimate implementation of your uniform interface will likely depend on how your architecture implements the next constraint.

Plug-In Architecture

The uniform interface constraint prescribes standardized, interchangeable components. Our system also needs the ability to perform dynamic, runtime composition of these uniform components. UNIX and its derivatives adopt a *Pipeline Architecture*, a style where components are connected in series, and the output of one component is the input of the next one. In the case of this style, we aim to build a cohesive set of functionalities available through a single interface that is customized and configured by adding discrete plug-in components. We induce this capability by adopting the *Plug-In Architecture Constraint*.

This constraint prescribes some mechanism for plug-ins to be introduced into the system, and there are many options. Adopting a plug-in architecture is a common requirement for creating extensible and modular applications.[6] In most technology ecosystems, a variety of options are available, ranging from open source libraries to commercial products and custom-built solutions.

[6] Acher, M., Cleve, A., Collet, P. et al. (2013). *Extraction and evolution of architectural variability models in plugin-based systems.* `https://doi.org/10.1007/s10270-013-0364-2`

Roll-Your-Own

When implementing this approach, a bespoke option may be suitable for simple use cases. An example of a simple approach can be found in OhMyZsh, a framework for managing Zsh that enables users to customize their shell through the addition of hundreds of available plug-ins. Plug-ins are installed in a directory (`~/.oh-my-zsh/plugins/`) and enabled by enumerating desired plug-ins in the `~/.zshrc` configuration file. The configuration file is loaded and processed implicitly when the shell session begins, dynamically modifying the features of the shell at runtime. The configuration file can also be reloaded after a shell session begins and a `.zshrc` file has been modified by using the `source` command.

Depending on the system and the profile of the end user (who might not be a Linux power user comfortable editing configuration files), you may want to provide a user interface for managing plug-ins. When rolling your own implementation of this constraint, you may need to dynamically load compiled code modules. Most common languages, frameworks, and runtimes support dynamic loading of modules.

In the .NET ecosystem, you can manually load assemblies using `Assembly.Load` and dynamically discover types using reflection.[7] This approach provides maximum flexibility but requires significant effort to manage dependencies, versioning, and security. It is ideal for scenarios where existing frameworks are too restrictive or when custom features are needed.

In the Java ecosystem, you can create custom ClassLoader implementations to load plug-ins dynamically at runtime.[8] Like .NET's custom assembly loading, this approach offers flexibility but at the cost of increased complexity. In both cases, you need to handle classpath management, potential compatibility issues, and isolation of plug-ins. Additionally, you must consider and mitigate both runtime performance penalties as well as potential security issues.

---

[7] Pine, D., Wagner, B., Dykstra, T., Schonning, Nick., Sherer, T., Peterson, T. (2021). *How to: Load and unload assemblies.* `https://learn.microsoft.com/en-us/dotnet/standard/assembly/load-unload`

[8] Baeldung (2024). *Class Loaders in Java.* `https://www.baeldung.com/java-classloaders`

Open Source Options

In the .NET ecosystem, one popular option is the Managed Extensibility Framework (MEF).[9] MEF is a built-in library in .NET that facilitates the creation of extensible applications by allowing the discovery and composition of parts (plug-ins) at runtime. Although MEF is mature and integrates seamlessly with .NET applications, it can become complex when dealing with nontrivial dependencies between plug-ins or when plug-ins need to be loaded/unloaded dynamically. Unfortunately, at the time of writing, MEF targets the older .NET Framework and may not be compatible with the latest, cross-platform .NET versions.

In the Java/JVM ecosystem, Open Service Gateway Initiative (OSGi) is a popular and robust framework for building modular Java applications.[10] It supports dynamic discovery, installation, and updating of components (bundles) at runtime. OSGi is powerful but comes with a steep learning curve. The complexity of managing OSGi's lifecycle and dependencies can be overwhelming for smaller projects.

Another option is the Plug-in Framework for Java (PF4J). PF4J is a simple and extensible plug-in framework for Java, focusing on ease of use. It supports dynamic loading of plug-ins and integrates well with existing Java applications. PF4J is less complex than OSGi but also less feature rich. It is an excellent choice for applications where ease of use is a priority over advanced features.

Commercial Options

In the Java/JVM ecosystem, Eclipse Rich Client Platform (RCP) might be worth exploring. Eclipse RCP is a commercial framework based on OSGi that provides tools for building rich client applications with a plug-in architecture. While powerful and backed by the Eclipse Foundation, it is complex and can be overkill for smaller projects. It is best suited for large-scale enterprise applications.

Choosing the right approach depends on your project's specific requirements:

- Use open source frameworks (MEF, OSGi, PF4J) if you need a balance of features and community support without licensing costs.

---

[9] Mak (2024). C# – *How to load assemblies at runtime using Microsoft Extensibility Framework (MEF)*. `https://makolyte.com/csharp-how-to-load-assemblies-at-runtime-using-microsoft-extensibility-framework-mef/`

[10] Baeldung (2024). *Introduction to OSGi*. `https://www.baeldung.com/osgi`

- Consider commercial options if your project requires enterprise-level features, support, and you have the budget for licensing.
- Roll your own if you need maximum flexibility or if existing frameworks do not fit your unique requirements, but be prepared to handle the additional complexity.

Each option has its trade-offs, so the choice should align with your project's scale, complexity, and long-term maintenance needs. In other words, you are looking for a holistic fit.

Fine Component Granularity

This style is unique in that the core system is a monolith; however, the plug-in components are typically fine-grained. Because granularity is mixed, some of the benefits of Fine Component Granularity (e.g., agility, deployability, testability, etc.) are present but without introducing the complexity and demanding team, organizational, and environmental constraints of a fine-grained distributed system.

The Microkernel Abstract Style

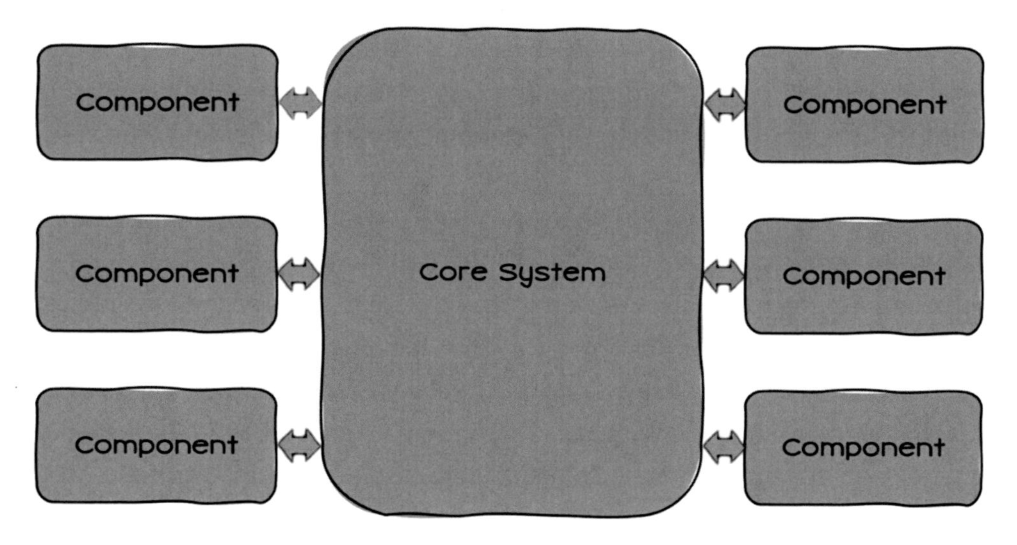

Figure 20-1. *The Microkernel Abstract Style*

The microkernel abstract style (shown in Figure 20-1), sometimes referred to as the "plug-in" architecture, applies constraints affecting the overall modularity of the application and builds on the concept of a microkernel from computer science. At the center of the pattern is the core system. In both computer science and in this pattern, the core system microkernel is the near-minimum amount of code necessary to implement the system. External plug-ins provide additional functionality. This approach isolates a codebase with low code volatility from *plug-in* modules that typically have much higher volatility. Users can add, remove, and swap plug-ins at runtime without requiring a redeployment of the core system, and the nature of this architecture dramatically reduces impact from changes in plug-in modules. Therefore, plug-in modules can be quickly developed that extend the core system, and, at runtime, plug-in modules can be added in various combinations and configurations to build arbitrary collections of functionalities.

To see this pattern in action, one need only look as far as the popular editor, Visual Studio Code. The core system provides basic functionality (primarily a text editor), and the functionality is extended by installing plug-ins. As an authoring tool, the core system is not especially powerful. With the addition of plug-ins that introduce spell-checking capabilities, markdown support, git support, and terminal support (among others), VS Code quickly becomes a powerful authoring environment with all necessary tools and capabilities. Likewise, when performing software development, data modeling, and even personal knowledge management[11] using this tool, additional plug-ins will enable all these features. Syntax support for a new language is as simple as another plug-in. As you see, the Microkernel Architecture Pattern is highly configurable. Any instance of the core system is free to select the set of plug-ins optimal for the given use case. The instance also typically controls its update frequency improving overall configurability.

If a given concrete implementation of this style utilizes storage, plug-ins often share access to a single shared data store. A good practice to consider when plug-in components have access to a shared database is to enforce some mechanism to namespace tables to avoid object naming collisions. VS Code utilizes the file system for persistence, but another example of this style is WordPress which allows plug-ins to not only create database objects (tables, indexes, views, etc.) in a single shared database, but the shared nature of that resource also means a plug-in has access to other tables in the system. If there are potential security or privacy considerations, a concrete implementation of this style should prescribe the Partitioned Shared Database Constraint.

[11] Eväkallio, J. "Foam PKM Project." `https://foambubble.github.io/foam/`

Although the Abstract Microkernel Style prescribes a Monolithic Deployment Granularity, the fine granularity of plug-ins overcomes the traditional limitations of this component granularity. Users of the system can easily extend it in unforeseen ways, improving agility, adaptability, extensibility, and evolvability. To achieve this, the core system exposes a uniform interface that defines both plug-in entry points and an API or other mechanisms for plug-ins to interact with the core system (and, potentially, each other). Given the uniform interface constraint will constrain the interaction of plug-ins with the core system, the system becomes slightly more fault tolerant. A malfunctioning plug-in rarely takes down the entire system (often the core system will simply disable a problematic plug-in).

On the surface, it may appear that this style is best suited for software products that are stored and run locally (e.g., VS Code); however, the broader applications of this style should not be overlooked. Many web-based and SaaS applications use this approach to make their platform configurable and extensible (both by the vendor and third parties). The abstract style is monolithic; however, it is possible to scale the ideas to allow dynamic runtime composition of external services in a distributed system.

NetKernel: A Distributed Microkernel Architecture

NetKernel is an innovative software system that extends the microkernel architecture to distributed computing, applying the principles of Resource-Oriented Computing (ROC) and the REST architectural style representing a significant evolution in how we think about and design distributed systems.

In traditional microkernel architectures, a minimal core (the microkernel) provides basic services, such as low-level hardware communication, while higher-level services run in user space, independent of each other. This separation promotes modularity, fault isolation, and ease of extension. NetKernel takes these principles and applies them to a distributed system, effectively creating a microkernel for the Web.

NetKernel abstracts all system resources—data, services, or even code—as addressable resources that adopt a uniform interface, much like the REST approach to web services. This generalization of the microkernel idea to a distributed environment allows components to communicate over a network with the same simplicity and consistency as they would within a single system. The abstractions provided by NetKernel result in a system whose design does not care if it is monolithic or distributed; those details are completely transparent to the system.

One of NetKernel's most brilliant innovations is its application of the REST architectural style, originally designed for the Web, to distributed computing. NetKernel treats everything as a resource, accessible via uniform resource identifiers (URIs). Resources can be dynamically composed, cached, or transformed, allowing for an incredibly flexible system where the boundaries between local and remote, static and dynamic, data and services blur. This extended approach to REST is the enabler for ROC.

ROC, the paradigm on which NetKernel is built, treats all software components—whether data, processes, or services—as resources that can be composed and interacted with dynamically. ROC provides a high degree of abstraction, where resources are not merely passive entities but can represent complex computations or data transformations.

This approach enables loose coupling between components, which is essential for building scalable and resilient distributed systems. Since resources are addressable through URIs and interact via standard protocols, the system can scale horizontally, distribute workloads efficiently, and maintain considerable flexibility in how components are assembled and reused.

NetKernel represents a significant advancement in distributed computing by extending the microkernel architecture into the realm of distributed systems. It provides a powerful, scalable, and flexible platform that simplifies the development and maintenance of complex distributed systems. This approach not only leverages the strengths of the microkernel design but also opens new possibilities in how distributed systems can be architected, operated, and even rearchitected dynamically at runtime.

NetKernel is a significant shift to how we currently design, build, and run distributed systems, and the mental model is foreign to many but has shown far-reaching benefits in many cases. We may well see this idea come into the mainstream in the future.

Summary

The Microkernel Abstract Style is a minimalist approach to software design, where the core system only handles essential functions and most functionality is extended through the addition of plug-ins. This separation enhances modularity and fault isolation, as plug-in failures do not typically crash the entire system, making it easier to update or replace individual components without affecting others. Although not suitable for every system, this style comes close to delivering the vision of "*Software that can be assembled like Lego bricks.*"

When adopting this style, care and forethought must go into the design and specification of the uniform interface. The interface must be stable (or backward compatible) as combinations of plug-ins and versions cannot be known at design time. Testability can be challenging as any number of plug-ins and configurations may exist at runtime. There typically must also be some kind of discoverability of available plug-ins. Consequently, in addition to developing the core system, development teams may need to invest time and effort into the creation of a plug-in registry.

The following architectural constraints define this abstract style:

- Monolithic Component Granularity
- Separation of Concerns
- Shared Database
- Plug-In Architecture
- Uniform Interface
- Fine Component Granularity

This collection of constraints requires only few additional team and environmental constraints:

- TEAM: Interface First
- ENV: Plug-in Registry (optional)

When compared with the Modular Monolith (Chapter 14) upon which this abstract style has been derived, the capability improvements provided in Figure 20-2 are seen.

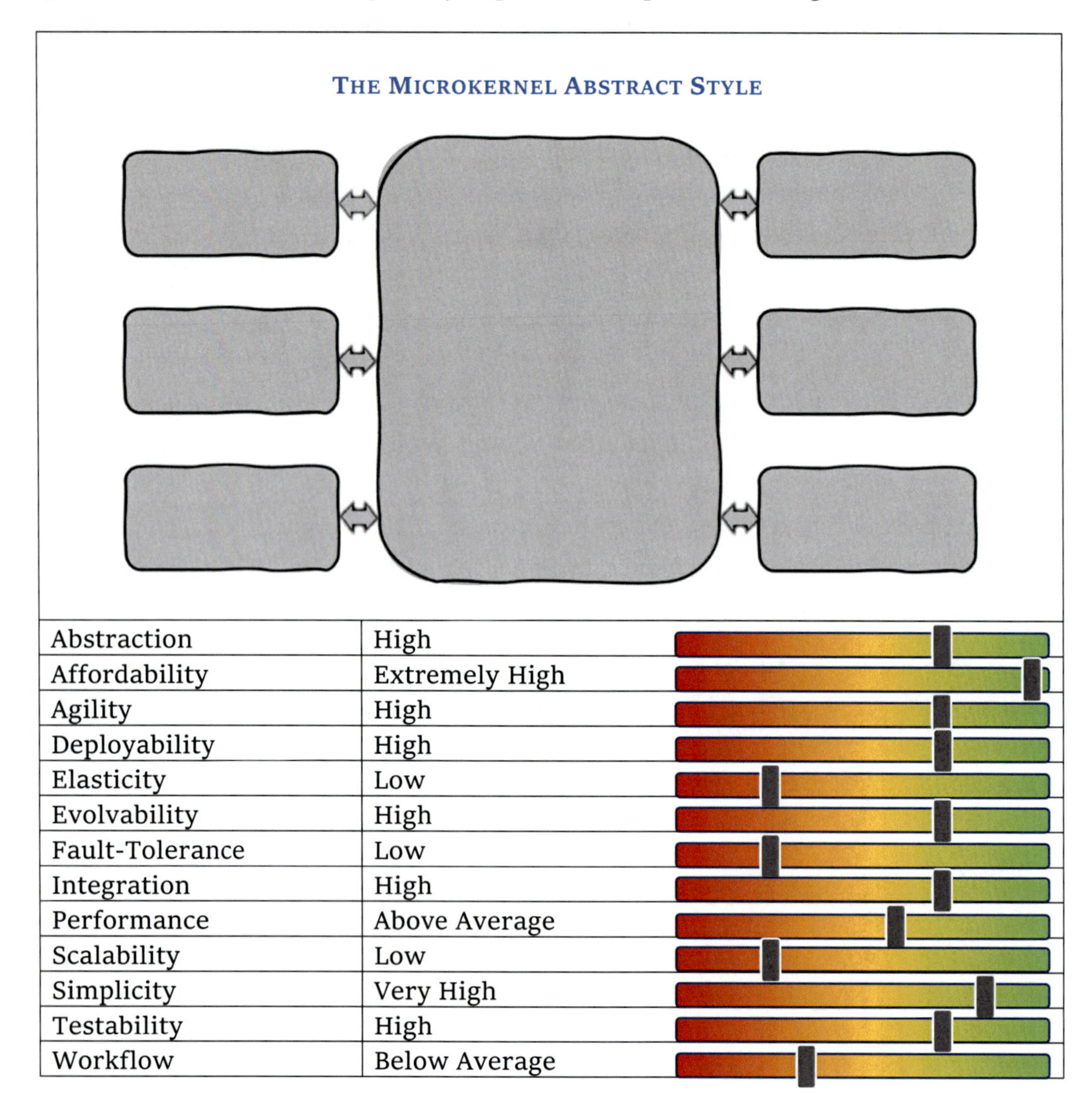

Abstraction	High
Affordability	Extremely High
Agility	High
Deployability	High
Elasticity	Low
Evolvability	High
Fault-Tolerance	Low
Integration	High
Performance	Above Average
Scalability	Low
Simplicity	Very High
Testability	High
Workflow	Below Average

Figure 20-2. *The Microkernel Abstract Style*

CHAPTER 21

Summary of Constraints and Abstract Styles

> *Software architecture is the set of design decisions which, if made incorrectly, may cause your project to be cancelled.*
>
> —Eoin Woods

Throughout this section, we have seen the power of architectural design by constraint. Beginning with the Big Ball of Mud style in Chapter 12, we navigated the architectural continuum by adding and changing constraints until we have derived the nine abstract styles that align with their corresponding established mainstream architecture patterns. This underexplored approach to software architecture yields many novel insights.

Let us visualize these insights in the form of a new taxonomy of architectural styles.

A Taxonomy of Architectural Styles

Historically, most software architecture literature has focused on monolithic and distributed styles; however, this mental model obscures many nuances of architectural evolution. Take, for example, the relative ease with which we may decompose a monolithic system into discrete services or components. In both Chapters 13 and 15, we accomplished this by changing the granularity constraint. In both cases, the necessary effort was straightforward, and we can typically measure the overall effort in weeks, rather than a period of *years* that conventional thinking would suggest. The disconnect between expectations and reality is a product of *pattern-based* thinking and a historical overemphasis on the transition between layered monolithic styles and microservices styles. You now know the true complexity lies in changing the module partitioning

M. Carducci, *Mastering Software Architecture*, https://doi.org/10.1007/979-8-8688-0410-6_21

constraint. In fact, many popular approaches to this migration involve first carving out vertical slices of functionality—evolving the layered style into a modular monolith style—before beginning the decomposition process. As we build a new taxonomy of architectural styles, we must recognize that the effort of changing constraints is not uniform. The hierarchy of our taxonomy, therefore, will reflect the relative difficulty of changing a given constraint. As this is, potentially, the most difficult constraint to change, we will define this as the top level of our taxonomy of styles.

Level 1: Module Partitioning

Moving beyond the Big Ball of Mud style, we must introduce some kind of separation of concerns and model for modularity which requires constraining the degrees of freedom surrounding the definition of module boundaries. The determination of module boundaries is one of the most foundational architectural constraints and thus form the first level of our architectural styles taxonomy tree as shown in Figure 21-1.

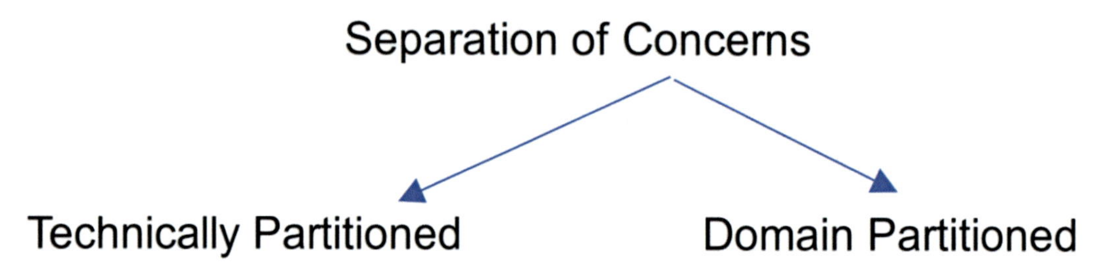

Figure 21-1. *Taxonomy Level 1*

The ubiquity of the Layered Monolith style is a consequence of Conway's Law[1] which states "*Organizations, who design systems, are constrained to produce designs which are copies of the communication structures of these organizations.*" The natural and default organizational structure will delineate responsibilities across teams by their technical focus, skillset, and clear responsibility models. Often, organizational will have *frontend* teams (or subteams) and *backend* teams. Depending on the scale and complexity of the system, the organizational structure will define backend teams focused on a subset of functionality such as API development, database development, business logic development, etc. Under this organizational structure, it does not matter what type of architecture we design; the structure of the system will mirror the organizational

[1] Conway, M. E. (1968). "How do Committees Invent?" *Datamation*, 14(5), 28–31

structure. Our options, as architects, are to either ignore the realities of Conway's Law (to our peril), accept the realities of Conway's Law (constrain our architecture designs to match the existing structure of the organization), or first change the communication structure of the organization (known as the Inverse-Conway Maneuver[2]).

Adopting the **Domain Partitioning Constraint** (described in Chapter 14) first requires we champion the effort to satisfy the **Well-Defined Domains** organizational constraint. This means either leading the effort to perform a detailed domain analysis with business stakeholders and domain experts or bringing in an expert to lead this effort. As architects, leading such an effort requires sufficient knowledge of Domain-Driven Design (DDD). The definitive work on this subject remains Eric Evans' 2003 book *Domain-Driven Design.*[3] If you choose to read that book (which dwarfs the book you are currently holding), follow the advice your author wishes he had when he first read it; read section 1, then section 4, followed by section 3, and finally section 2. Alternatively, there have been several books that followed Evans' seminal work on the subject. Vaughn Vernon's *Implementing Domain-Driven Design*[4] is a practical and accessible resource written to prepare developers and architects to apply the important concepts of DDD. For a more lightweight introduction, I recommend Vernon's comparatively light volume, *DDD Distilled.*[5] One other valuable resource is Alberto Brandolini's important work on event storming.[6]

Understanding the nuances of the domain is the first step. We can design a domain-partitioned system based on the structure and boundaries within a domain; however, we remain constrained by the organizational structure. Our design will require **Domain-Aligned Teams** which may require deploying the Inverse-Conway Maneuver to restructure the organization. This process is both expensive and difficult, but many organizations have successfully made the transition. By building on the wisdom and experience of the authors listed above—as well as the advice on effecting meaningful change in the next section—you will be better positioned to make this change.

[2] Leroy, J. (2010). "Dealing with Creaky Legacy Platforms." *Cutter IT Journal*

[3] Evans, E. (2003). *Domain-Driven Design: Tackling Complexity in the Heart of Software.* Addison-Wesley Professional

[4] Vernon, V. (2013). *Implementing Domain-Driven Design.* Addison-Wesley Professional

[5] Vernon, V. (2016). *Domain-Driven Design Distilled.* Addison-Wesley Professional

[6] Brandolini, A. (2015–2021). *Introducing EventStorming: An Act of Deliberate Collective Learning.* LeanPub, `https://www.eventstorming.com/book/`

Level 2: Persistence Options

In Chapter 14, we got our first glimpse of the effort needed to break relational databases along domain lines as well as how those lines begin to blur as we find multiple bounded contexts that need to share some amount of data. You will notice that it is the *domain-partitioned* parent constraint that enables the Partitioned Shared Database and Isolated Database Constraint (Chapter 16). The addition of this level to our taxonomy tree is shown in Figure 21-2.

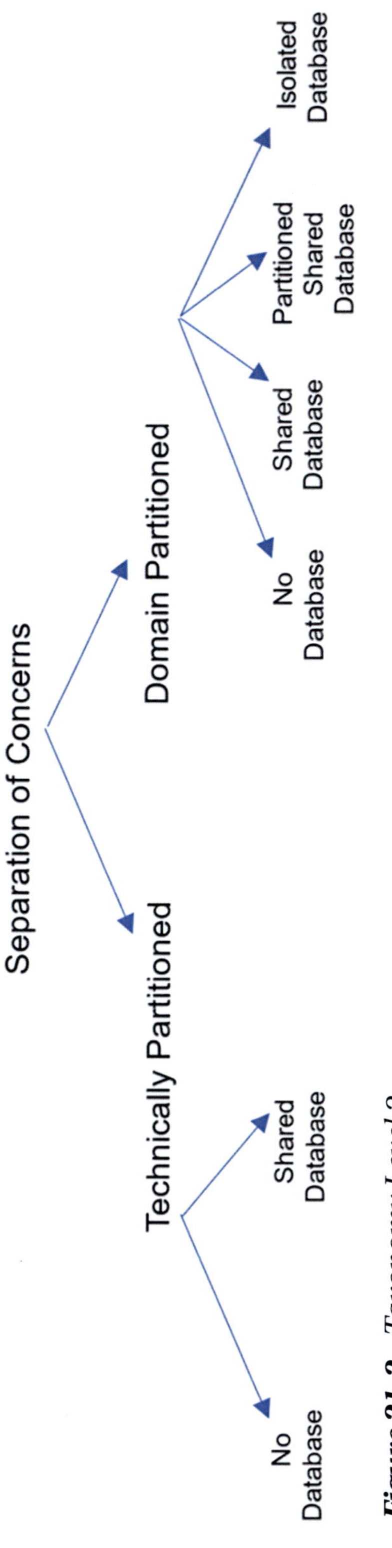

Figure 21-2. *Taxonomy Level 2*

The taxonomy tree focuses on architectural constraints and styles introduced in this section but is not exhaustive. Additional persistence constraints, such as a *multitenant shared database*, or *database-per-tenant* constraints, for example, can be applied to evolve/extend a style but are not represented in this conceptual taxonomic tree. Moving forward, where the branches from a node in the tree are substantially similar to its neighbors, a dotted arrow will be used as an abbreviation.

Level 3: Granularity

Component granularity is a straightforward change when decomposing along existing module boundaries and comparatively easier than changing any of the parent constraints. Our updated taxonomy tree is shown in Figure 21-3.

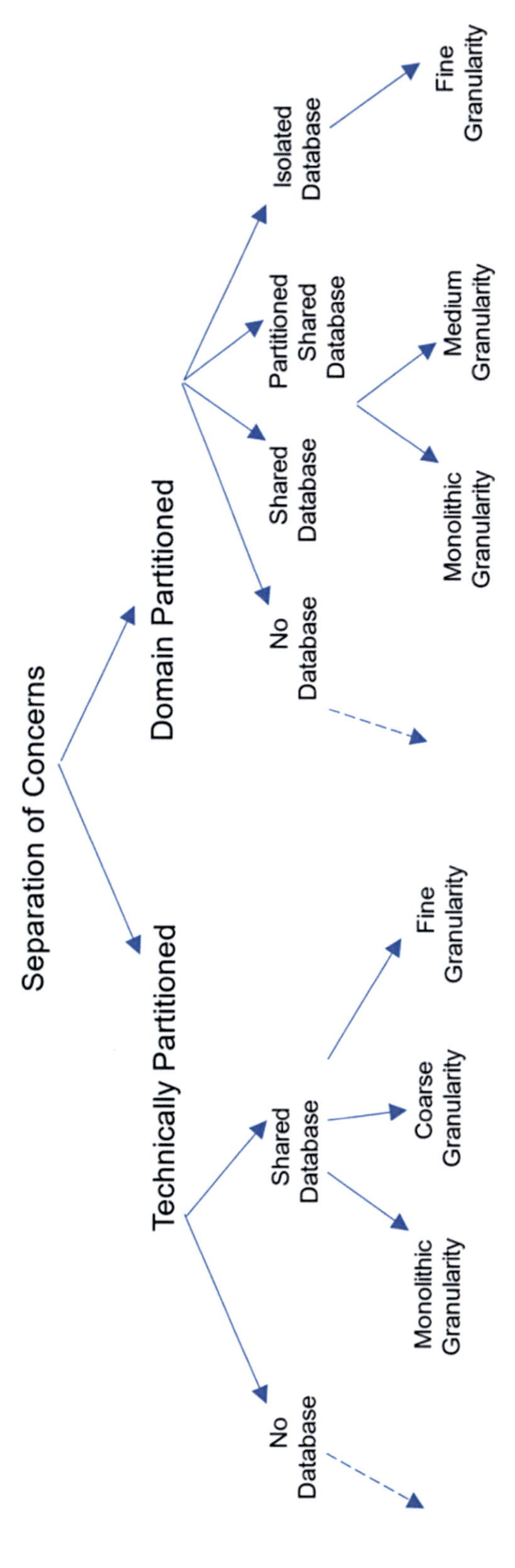

Figure 21-3. *Taxonomy Level 3*

When an architectural style crosses into the realm of distributed systems, you must prescribe additional constraints. The most important of these is the *Independent Deployability Constraint* (Chapter 13). Without this constraint, the promised benefits surrounding agility, testability, deployability, and evolvability all suffer. In short, a distributed style without this constraint will produce a *distributed monolith* which is an anti-pattern (or anti-style).

Independent deployability is enabled by the following non-architectural constraints, namely:

- TEAM: Pipeline Development Skills (Chapter 13)
- TEAM: IaC Skills (Chapter 13)
- TEAM: Automation Skills (Chapter 13)
- TEAM: API-First Development (Chapter 13)
- TEAM: Independent Development Cycles (Chapter 13)
- ENV: Development Environment Isolation (Chapter 13)
- ORG: DevOps Commitment (Chapter 13)

Fine Component Granularity requires additional non-architectural constraints, namely:

- ENV: High Operational Automation (Chapter 16)
- ENV: Service Discovery and Routing (Chapter 16)
- ENV: Bulkheads and Circuit Breakers (Chapter 16)
- ENV: Distributed Tracing and Logging (Chapter 16)
- TEAM: Maturity with Respect to Trade-Offs (Chapter 16)
- TEAM: IaC Skills (Chapter 16)

Level 4: Component Communication

When we add this final level to our basic taxonomy, you begin to see how the abstract styles defined in this section find their way into this model. Of course, Figure 21-4 shows only a subset of the abstract styles and offers only a partial representation of all possible architectural styles.

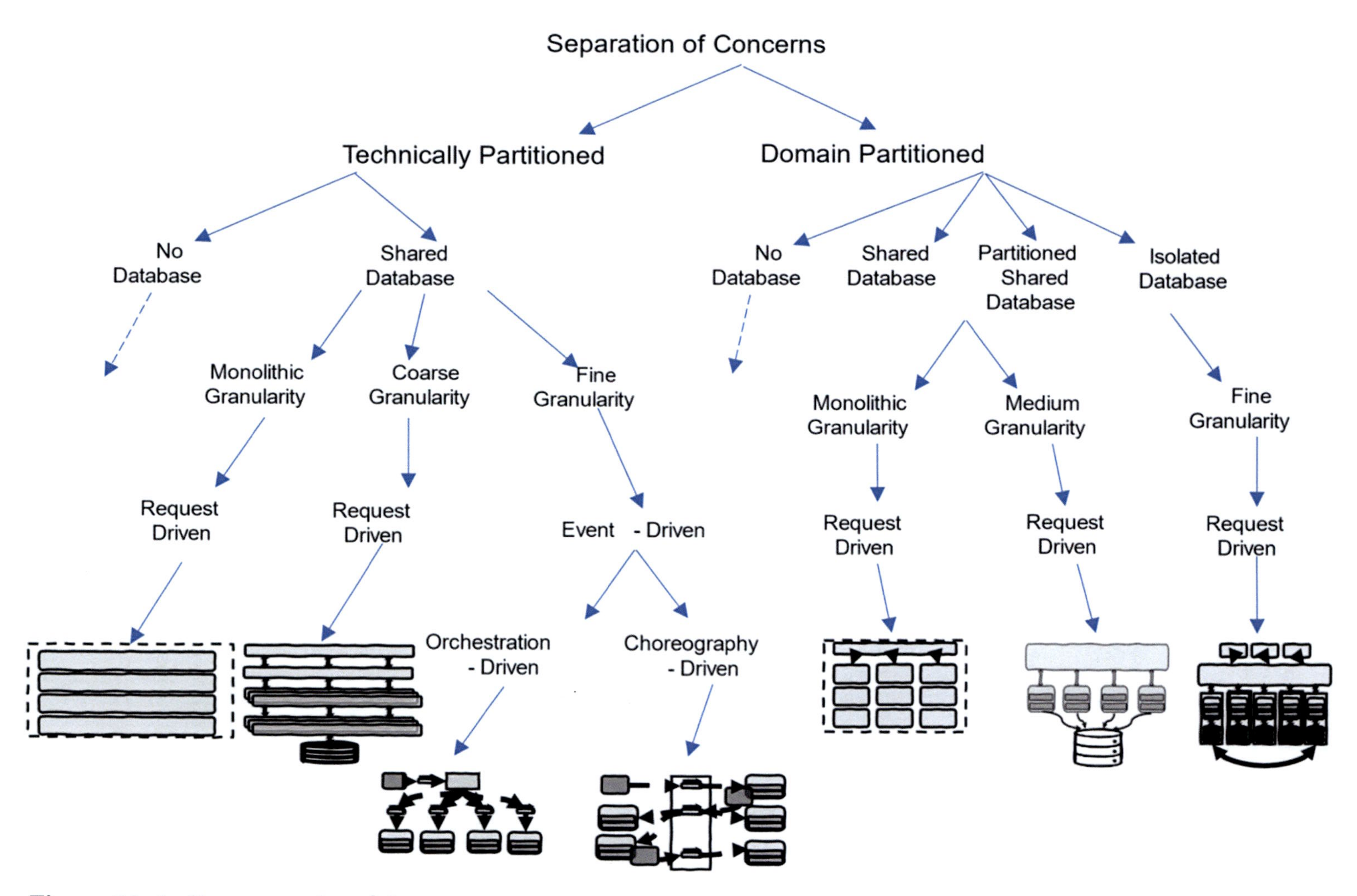

Figure 21-4. *Taxonomy Level 4*

The Modular Monolith Abstract Style and Space-Based Abstract Style either do not prescribe module partitioning or span both module partitioning schemes. These are also not absolutes, and the diagram excludes hybrid styles and derived variations.

The intent of Figure 21-4 is to demonstrate the directions we have thus far derived abstract styles. This taxonomy also demonstrates the relative effort to evolve one style into another (as well as potential intermediary waypoints on the continuum for incremental evolution). Notably, the Layered Monolith Abstract Style and the Microservices Abstract Style are on extreme ends of the tree, indicating a considerable amount of effort to make the necessary architectural modifications to realize the final style. In contrast, the Service-Based Abstract Style and Microservices Abstract Style are adjacent to each other, indicating a lower amount of effort to evolve the system between those two styles.

When considering multiple potential architectural styles for a given problem, creating a similar diagram can be useful to visualize the available paths for architectural evolution over time. This will allow you to provide an architectural style that meets immediate needs with confidence that the long-term evolution in an anticipated future direction remains possible and practical.

Summary of Abstract Styles

This section has derived and described nine abstract styles, as well as several intermediary and tailored styles. Each chapter introduced new architectural constraints, which are combined in different ways to derive a diverse set of abstract styles. Because constraints are reusable and composable architecture primitives, each chapter provides details and implementation guidance as it introduces each new constraint, rather than giving implementation guidance at the style level. Below is a summary of the defining constraints of each abstract style, along with a reference to the chapter that first introduces and describes the constraint. Finally, we break down the dependent non-architectural constraints necessary to achieve the architectural capabilities induced by each constraint. This review will provide you with a quick reference for each abstract style along with a visualization of the body of architectural knowledge you have developed after reading this section.

Layered Monolith Abstract Style (Chapter 12)

Abstract Style	Defining Constraints	Constraint Dependencies
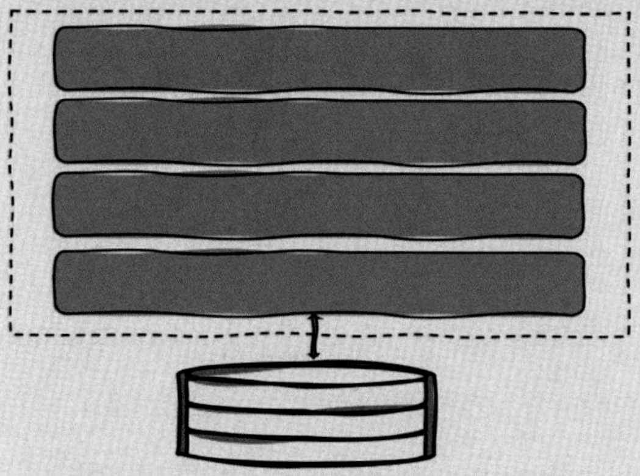 The Layered Monolith Abstract Style	Monolithic Component Granularity (Chapter 12)	N/A
	Technical Partitioning (Chapter 12)	N/A
	Monolithic Deployment Granularity (Chapter 12)	N/A
	Separation of Concerns (Chapter 12)	N/A
	Shared Database (Chapter 12)	N/A
	Layered System (Chapter 12)	N/A

Figure 21-5. *Summary of the Layered Monolith Abstract Style*

Distributed N-Tier Abstract Style (Chapter 13)

Abstract Style	Defining Constraints	Constraint Dependencies
The Distributed N-Tier Abstract Style	Coarse Component Granularity (Chapter 13)	ENV: Simple environment automation ENV: Distributed system environment support
	Technical Partitioning (Chapter 12)	N/A
	Independent Deployability (Chapter 13)	ENV: Development environment isolation (Chapter 13) ORG: DevOps Commitment (Chapter 13) TEAM: Pipeline development skills (Chapter 13) TEAM: Automation skills (Chapter 13) TEAM: API first Development (Chapter 13)
	Separation of Concerns (Chapter 12)	N/A
	Layered System (Chapter 12)	N/A
	Client/Server (Chapter 13)	N/A
	Shared Database (Chapter 12)	N/A

Figure 21-6. Summary of the Distributed N-Tier Abstract Style

Modular Monolith Abstract Style (Chapter 14)

Abstract Style	Defining Constraints	Constraint Dependencies
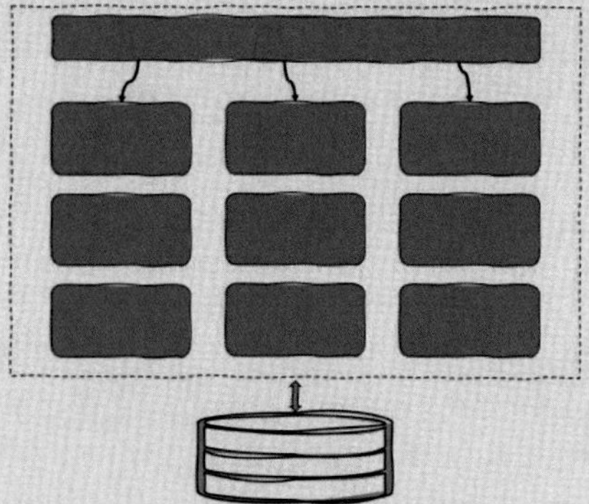 The Modular Monolith Abstract Style	Monolithic Component Granularity (Chapter 12)	N/A
	Monolithic Deployment Granularity (Chapter 12)	N/A
	Domain Partitioning (Chapter 14)	ORG: Well-Defined Domains (Chapter 14) ORG: Domain-Aligned Teams (Chapter 14)
	Partitioned Shared Database (Chapter 14)	Domain Partitioning (Chapter 14) Data-Domain Definition (Chapter 14) Data-Sharing Strategy (Chapter 14)

Figure 21-7. *Summary of the Modular Monolith Abstract Style*

Service-Based Abstract Style (Chapter 15)

Abstract Style	Defining Constraints	Constraint Dependencies
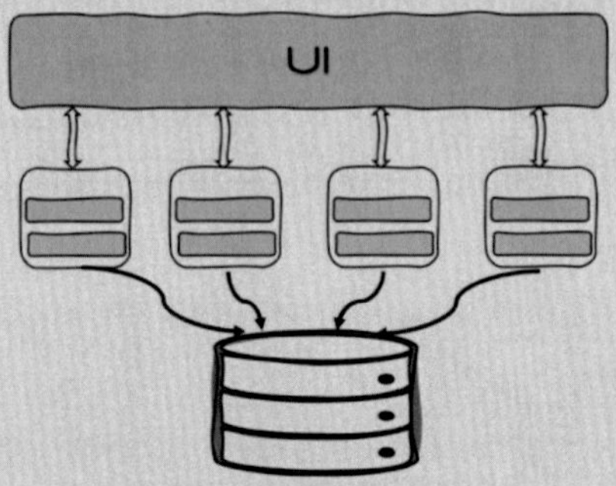 The Service-Based Abstract Style	Medium Component Granularity (Chapter 15)	ENV: Simple environment automation (Chapter 13) ENV: Distributed system environment support (Chapter 13)
	Independent Deployability (Chapter 13)	ENV: Development environment isolation (Chapter 13) ORG: DevOps Commitment (Chapter 13) TEAM: Pipeline development skills (Chapter 13) TEAM: Automation skills (Chapter 13) TEAM: API first Development (Chapter 13)
	Domain Partitioning (Chapter 14)	ORG: Well-Defined Domains (Chapter 14) ORG: Domain-Aligned Teams (Chapter 14)
	Separation of Concerns (Chapter 12)	N/A
	Shared Database (Chapter 12)	N/A
	RPC API (Chapter 13)	N/A

Figure 21-8. *Summary of the Service-Based Abstract Style*

Microservices Abstract Style (Chapter 16)

Abstract Style	Defining Constraints	Constraint Dependencies
The Microservices Abstract Style	Fine Component Granularity (Chapter 16)	ENV: High Operational Automation (Chapter 16) ENV: Service Discovery & Routing (Chapter 16) ENV: Bulkheads & Circuit Breakers (Chapter 16) ENV: Distributed Tracing & Logging (Chapter 16) TEAM: IaC skills (Chapter 16)
	Independent Deployability (Chapter 13)	ENV: Development environment isolation (Chapter 13) ORG: DevOps Commitment (Chapter 13) TEAM: Pipeline development skills (Chapter 13) TEAM: Automation skills (Chapter 13) TEAM: API first Development (Chapter 13)
	Domain Partitioning (Chapter 14)	ORG: Well-Defined Domains (Chapter 14) ORG: Domain-Aligned Teams (Chapter 14)
	Highly Decoupled Components (Chapter 16)	TEAM: Maturity w/r/t Trade-offs (Chapter 16)
	Isolated Databases (Chapter 16)	Domain Partitioning (Chapter 14) Data-Domain Definition (Chapter 14) Data-Sharing Strategy (Chapter 14)
	RPC API (Chapter 13)	N/A

Figure 21-9. *Summary of the Microservices Abstract Style*

Choreographed Event-Driven Abstract Style (Chapter 17)

Abstract Style	Defining Constraints	Constraint Dependencies
The Choreographed Event-Driven Abstract Style	Fine Component Granularity (Chapter 16)	ENV: High Operational Automation (Chapter 16) ENV: Distributed Tracing & Logging (Chapter 16) TEAM: IaC skills (Chapter 16)
	Independent Deployability (Chapter 13)	ENV: Development environment isolation (Chapter 13) ORG: DevOps Commitment (Chapter 13) TEAM: Pipeline development skills (Chapter 13) TEAM: Automation skills (Chapter 13) TEAM: API first Development (Chapter 13)
	Technical Partitioning (Chapter 12)	N/A
	Highly Decoupled Components (Chapter 16)	TEAM: Maturity w/r/t Trade-offs (Chapter 16)
	Choreography-Driven Interactions (Chapter 17)	Workflow Modeling (Chapter 17)
	PubSub Messaging (Chapter 17)	ENV: PubSub Broker (Chapter 17)

Figure 21-10. *Summary of the Choreographed Event-Driven Abstract Style*

Orchestrated Event-Driven Abstract Style (Chapter 18)

Abstract Style	Defining Constraints	Constraint Dependencies
The Orchestrated Event-Driven Abstract Style	Fine Component Granularity (Chapter 16)	ENV: High Operational Automation (Chapter 16) ENV: Distributed Tracing & Logging (Chapter 16) TEAM: IaC skills (Chapter 16)
	Independent Deployability (Chapter 13)	ENV: Development environment isolation (Chapter 13) ORG: DevOps Commitment (Chapter 13) TEAM: Pipeline development skills (Chapter 13) TEAM: Automation skills (Chapter 13) TEAM: API first Development (Chapter 13)
	Technical Partitioning (Chapter 12)	N/A
	Orchestration-Driven Interactions (Chapter 18)	Domain Partitioning (Chapter 14) Data-Domain Definition (Chapter 14) Data-Sharing Strategy (Chapter 14)
	Persistent Queue Messaging (Chapter 18)	ENV: Queue (Chapter 18)

Figure 21-11. *Summary of the Orchestrated Event-Driven Abstract Style*

Space-Based Abstract Style (Chapter 19)

Abstract Style	Defining Constraints	Constraint Dependencies
The Space-Based Abstract Style	Medium Component Granularity (Chapter 15)	ENV: Simple environment automation (Chapter 13) ENV: Distributed system environment support (Chapter 13)
	Domain Partitioning & Technical Partitioning (Chapter 14 & 12)	ORG: Well-Defined Domains (Chapter 14) ORG: Domain-Aligned Teams (Chapter 14)
	Shared Database (Chapter 12)	N/A
	Decoupled Database (Chapter 19)	ENV: Data Reader (Chapter 19) ENV: Data Writer (Chapter 19)
	Transactional Data Stored In-Memory (Chapter 19)	ENV: High-Memory Compute Instances (Chapter 19)
	Replicated Shared Data Grid (Chapter 19)	N/A
	RPC API (Chapter 13)	N/A

Figure 21-12. *Summary of the Space-Based Abstract Style*

Microkernel Abstract Style (Chapter 20)

Abstract Style	Defining Constraints	Constraint Dependencies
The Microkernel Abstract Style	Monolithic + Fine Component Granularity (Chapter 12 + Chapter 16)	N/A
	Independent Deployability (Chapter 12)	N/A
	Separation of Concerns (Chapter 12)	N/A
	Shared Database (Chapter 12)	N/A
	Uniform Interface (Chapter 20)	ARCH: Interface Constraints (Chapter 20) Team: Interface First (Chapter 20)
	Plug-in Architecture (Chapter 20)	ENV: Plug-in Framework (Chapter 20) ENV: Plug-in Registry (Chapter 20)

Figure 21-13. *Summary of the Microkernel Abstract Style*

Summary of Constraints

We will close this chapter and this section with an overview of all the architectural constraints introduced. This list is not exhaustive, as you may identify various additional architectural constraints as you progress through your career, designing and evolving the architecture of various systems. Figure 21-14 will, however, be instructive when introducing new architectural constraints into this model. Each constraint introduces a relative influence on the overall capabilities of a style, which we will indicate as follows.

A minus (–) symbol indicates the constraint will negatively impact a particular architectural capability, a (+) indicates a positive influence on a capability, and the plus-minus (±) indicates a mixed influence that may depend on additional constraints or domain details to resolve. Although the Tailor-Made model aims to be more precise by including weighted values for each of the trade-offs, this generalization will provide a rough overview appropriate for this book. The weights and calculation model will be available in the tools introduced in the next section.

	Architectural Constraint	Abstraction	Affordability	Agility	Deployability	Elasticity	Evolvability	Fault-Tolerance	Integration	Performance	Scalability	Simplicity	Testability	Workflow
Async Communication	Persistent-Queue Messaging	+		±		+		+	+	+	+		-	+
	Pub-Sub Messaging	+	±	±		+	+	+	+	+	+	-		+
	Queue Messaging	+		±		+		±	+	+	+		-	+
	Replicated Shared Data Grid		-	-	±	+		±				-	-	
Component Constraint	All Data stored in-memory		-		-			-		+	±	-		
	Highly Decoupled Components		-	+	+	+		+			+	-	+	-
	Separation of Concerns		+	+			+					+	+	
Deployment Constraint	Independent Deployability		+	+	+		+				+	±		
	Monolithic Deployment Granularity		-	-	-			-				+		
Environment	High Operational Automation				+	+		+		+	+			
Granularity	Coarse Component Granularity		-	+	+	+	+	+		+	+	-	+	+
	Fine Component Granularity		-	+	+	+	+	+	-	±	+	-	+	-
	Medium Component Granularity			+	+	+	+	+	-	+	+	±	±	-
	Monolithic Component Granularity	-	+	-	-	-	-	-		+	-	+	-	

Figure 21-14. *Summary of Constraints*

Integration	graphQL API	+		+	+			±	+	±		+	±	-
	gRPC API	±	+	-	-		-	+	+	+				-
	Level 1 REST API	+	-	+	+	+	+		+	-	+	±	+	-
	Level 2 REST API		±	+	+	+	+	+	+	-	+	±	+	-
	RPC API	+			-	+	-	-	+	±	+	±		-
Int era	Choreography Interactions	+	+	±	±		+	-	+	+			-	+
	Orchestration-Driven Interactions		-	±	-	±	-	±	+	±		-	-	+
Interface	Plug-in Architecture	+	+	+	+		+	+	+	+		-	+	
	Uniform Interface	+		+			+		+	-	±		+	
Module Partitioning	Domain Partitioning	+	±	+	+		+	+				±	+	
	Technical Partitioning	-	+	±	-		-					+	±	
Persistence	Decoupled Database				+	+	±	±		+	+	-		
	Isolated Databases		-	+	+		+	+	-	+	+	-	+	-
	Partitioned Shared Database		+	+	+	-				±	-	-		
	Shared Database	-	+	-	-	-	-			±	-	+		

Figure 21-14. *(continued)*

Synchronization	CQRS		-	-			+	+	+	+	+		-	
	Event-sourcing		-					+	+	+	+	-	+	±
Topology	Client-Server													
	Layered System	+	±		+	±	+			-		+	-	

Figure 21-14. *(continued)*

SECTION 3

Executing Architecture Effectively

CHAPTER 22

Deriving a Tailor-Made Architecture

> *Software and cathedrals are much the same; first we build them, then we pray.*
>
> —Samuel T. Redwine Jr.

The aim of the Tailor-Made Software Architecture model is achieving holistic fit. Your reading to this point will prepare you to execute on this mission in a manner that exceeds many established practitioners in this space. The first and most obvious dimension of fit is aligning the capabilities of the system with the business needs. The requirements analysis process introduced in Chapter 4 produces a prioritized set of capabilities along with target scores that range from –5 (Extremely Low) to +5 (Extremely High) with several steps in between.

In your conversations with business stakeholders, it is rare that the business will assert that architecture should score "extremely low" or even negatively on any given capability. This is why the effort associated with ranking and prioritizing capabilities is so important. Styles that offer high scores in one capability often display the inherent trade-offs in other capabilities which score either average or in the negative range. The ranking of each individual capability is instructive of the direction that trade-offs must take place. An important or business-critical capability can come at the cost of degrading a lower priority capability, but not a higher priority capability. Negative scores (–1/below average or lower) do not reflect a business requirement but rather an *organizational tolerance*. For example, affordability and simplicity of microservices styles typically score Extremely Low; when the relative business value of the system's agility, fault tolerance, scalability, and elasticity is sufficiently high, this factor will influence the business's

M. Carducci, *Mastering Software Architecture*, https://doi.org/10.1007/979-8-8688-0410-6_22

overall tolerance for extremely low simplicity and affordability qualities. In short, balancing the highs and lows of any candidate style requires careful calculus on the part of the architect.

The Mad Potter on the Value of Enough

Many years ago, I was driving across the state of Wyoming on a long and desolate highway. I eventually passed through a small town that was entirely devoid of life save for a former automotive service station with the hand-painted words "Monk King Bird Pottery" emblazoned across the exterior. It was the studio of independent potter, Byron Seeley, established in a ghost town that had been abandoned decades ago. Curiosity got the better of me, and I pulled over to view his wares.

Byron greeted me and gave me a tour of his live-in studio and retail space. I was impressed with his creations but baffled by the choice of location. At one point, I asked him "Do you get a lot of business?" which seemed a fair question given the lack of traffic or local population.

He looked at me and asked, "What's 'a lot?'"

It was a question I was unprepared for, so I blurted out "I don't know." And his response has stuck with me to this day.

"Neither do I," he replied. "But I know what *enough* is. I get *enough* business."

Since then, I tend to favor the quantifiable concept of *enough* over the vague notion of *a lot*. Our architectures should do the same, offering *enough* of important capabilities as *a lot* can easily turn into *too much* and come at unexpected cost.

Tailoring Existing Architectures

When approaching an existing system that requires enhancement or evolution, first strive to understand the current set of constraints. This may require examining the codebase, reviewing current and target metrics and KPIs, and several conversations with developers and stakeholders. During this process, you are both documenting the existing architecture and performing a modified version of the requirements analysis process described in Chapter 4.

Once you understand where the system is, you must tailor this architecture to arrive at where the business needs the system to be. From here, you can begin the *made-to-measure* design process with one small modification. Rather than starting with an abstract style or style(s), you will be starting with the current architectural style as you have now defined it.

Made-to-Measure Architecture

When approaching a greenfield project, the most pragmatic approach is often to follow the Made-to-Measure approach (Chapter 10).

Phase I: Identifying Abstract Styles

We begin this process by looking at the qualified and quantified capabilities you enumerated during the requirements analysis process (Chapter 4) and evaluating them against the capability scores of the abstract styles in Section 2. Although you may have identified several valuable capabilities for the prospective system, it is exceedingly unlikely that any abstract style will align perfectly with the business's requirements. You should be focusing primarily on alignment with only the *business-critical* capabilities at this stage as other capabilities can later be modified through addition and modification of architectural constraints.

The Tailor-Made Architecture Model introduces a tool to support this process,[1] where you can define target capabilities and visualize these target scores against the base scores of each abstract style.

It is possible you will identify multiple abstract styles that are potential candidates. This is a good thing and highlights the fact that there is more than one path to a solution in software architecture. For each abstract style, add or modify the constraints inside the worksheet with the goal of approximating alignment with the various target scores you defined in the analysis process. Figure 21-14 in Chapter 21 is a helpful reference for this

[1] https://masteringsoftwarearchitecture.com

process, as it highlights the capabilities each constraint influences. In the worksheet, the constraints introduced in this book are present and pre-weighted to provide design-time feedback on the relative influence of each constraint.

It is important to note that your goal is not simply to find a collection of constraints that will make the targets line up as this will generally result in a nonsensical architectural style that looks good in the worksheet but offers little value in practice. Instead, this process must be guided first by your architectural intuition and understanding of how constraints operate and interact with your design and, secondarily, on how those constraints influence the scores of your candidate derived architecture. The worksheet is a tool, and, like any tool, its utility is a function of the skill of the person who wields it. The worksheet is useful for rapid design efforts and early feedback but cannot replace the unique skill of a thoughtful architect.

At the conclusion of this process, you will have one or more candidate architectural styles for consideration and evaluation.

Phase II: Evaluating for Temporal Fit

Often, the business documents that will influence your efforts will communicate a grand vision of the future, painting a picture of what long-term success looks like. While this is useful, it will often lead to overengineering. Let us look at a concrete example.

Ted Neward, a software architect, has adapted Dave Thomas' concept of "Code Katas" for software architects.[2] One such architectural kata that Ted has made available to the community is called "Going Green." A description of this hypothetical project is below:

Going Green

A large electronics store wants to get into the electronics recycling business and needs a new system to support it. Customers can send in their small personal electronic equipment (or use local kiosks at the mall) and possibly get money for their used equipment if it is in working condition.

***Users**: Hundreds, hopefully thousands to millions*

[2] Neward, T. (2012). *Architecture Katas: Practicing Architecture.* `https://www.architecturekatas.com`

Requirements

Customers can get a quote for used personal electronic equipment (phones, cameras, etc.) either through the Web or a kiosk at a mall. Customers will receive a box in the mail, send in their electronic, and if it is in good working order receive a check. Once the equipment is received, it is assessed (inspected) to determine if it can be either recycled (destroyed safely) or sold (eBay, etc.). The company anticipates adding five to ten new types of electronic that they will accept each month. Each type of electronic has its own set of rules for quoting and assessment.

Additional Context

This is a highly competitive business and is a new line of business for us. If we haven't received a type of electronic equipment in a year, we will remove it from our system. We need to maintain a list of electronic equipment we are willing to accept as it changes often.

Each piece of equipment has its own assessment (inspection) rules. We have the right to change the original quote to the customer if the product isn't in the condition they said it was.

When approaching this system, the forward-looking nature of this project brief might lead one to designing a complex and high-scale architecture with advanced workflow capabilities. However, by reading between the lines, it becomes clear that the most immediate value is releasing a Minimum Viable Product (MVP) and quickly iterating on it.

Optimally, you would design the anticipated end-state architecture (what the system will look like if/when the system is rolled out nationwide) and then determine what constitutes *enough* of the architectural capabilities for the initial MVP. Chapter 21 introduced a taxonomy of constraints that define our abstract styles in a structure that indicates their relative evolvability. If you believe a tailored version of the Service-Based Abstract Style is the ideal end state, a tailored Modular Monolith might form an ideal style for the MVP. In this case, you will have a concrete style that is practical for temporal fit, with an idea of how the architecture can evolve over time.

Phase III: Evaluating for Team, Organizational, and Environmental Fit

When evaluating an abstract style, you must consider the *feasibility* of a given style. As you learned in the previous section, many architectural constraints carry dependencies that must be satisfied for the capabilities they promise to materialize. One or more constraints that make significant demands will require either driving significant change in the organization or compromising the architecture to better fit the teams, environment, and organization. Both options carry risk, and there is no clear answer to which option is better in any given scenario. You will need to rely on your judgment, objectivity, and candid conversations with business stakeholders.

In the case of our architectural kata, this is a new business line, so it may be possible to influence the communication structure of this new division, thus opening the possibility of domain-partitioned styles. In other cases, it may not be cut and dried.

Phase IV: Reviewing Candidate Styles

Before you are ready to receive feedback on one or more candidate styles, you must first step back to take a critical look at the constraints the styles prescribe. It is important to take a balanced approach when prescribing architecture. When you are *too prescriptive*, you risk micromanaging the architecture. Likewise, when you *under-support* constraints, you risk becoming an ivory tower architect, leaving teams to fend for themselves when challenges arrive. In both cases, teams may ultimately reject parts or all of the prescribed architecture.

Review each constraint that defines the proposed style(s). You should be able to succinctly articulate the *why* behind each constraint. Next, objectively assess if the constraint is truly *architecturally significant*. Could the project be sufficiently successful if this constraint were omitted? Is this a decision that can be left to implementation teams? Architecture necessarily constrains the degrees of freedom available to developers, but, when we constrain freedom too much, we end up micromanaging teams in a way that robs them of the joy of software engineering. Follow the philosophy of the judiciary and *"do not decide that which need not be decided."*

When examining each constraint, determine the extent to which each constraint deviates from established practices and norms within development teams. Some constraints will simply formalize the requirement to continue standard operating procedures, while others will represent a significant shift. In the latter case, you must begin to think about how you will support such a change. Will the teams accept such a change? Must the change happen all at once, or is there a path toward incremental maturity? In either case, we must also ask if the shift in behavior the constraint requires is well described by any existing source. Are there books, training, tutorials, examples, reference implementations, or tools available? If such resources exist, begin to enumerate these in your notes. If not, you need a plan to create these resources.

Every constraint requires team and organizational buy-in which may be challenging when it represents a significant change. That said, resist the temptation to prematurely optimize a style for organizational compatibility. Too often, when making any kind of request, we censor ourselves. We assume "*they will never go for that*" and present the diluted option without ever giving them an opportunity to say "yes" to the original/ideal option. Instead, we should keep our simplified or phased approach to constraint adoption in our metaphorical back pocket. When you present the proposed architecture (as described in the next section in this chapter), begin by presenting your full vision of the new architecture and the process to get there. Only when a constraint is rejected outright by the teams should you retreat to the compromise option—and be prepared to do this right away, in the current conversational context. It is not what we typically do, but it is the optimal approach. In a study cited by Dr. Robert Cialdini, he found this approach can triple the number of "yes" responses to the exact same question.[3]

Keep in mind that an architectural style *is not your system's architecture*. The *architecture* is the blueprints for the system. The *style* represents the constraints governing decisions within the blueprint.

Phase V: Presenting Candidate Architectures for Review

It is at this point that the candidate style(s) should be presented to representatives of the various development teams. Your goal is to show one or more *architectural blueprints* for each candidate style and get feedback on the feasibility. These can be fairly high level at this stage but provide sufficient detail to show what the concrete implementation of the system will look like when following the various architectural styles. You will also communicate what it will take for the organization to get there.

[3] Cialdini, R. (1993). *Influence: The Psychology of Persuasion*. Quill

Invite team leads and the executive stakeholders that the team lead(s) report to. First, articulate the business context and your understanding of the immediate and long-term requirements. This represents the *why* of the architecture you are about to present. Answer any questions as they arise. Once you have reached consensus on the problem, present the candidate architecture(s).

Your goals in this meeting are as follows:

- Achieve alignment on the problem context and the desired outcomes
- Identify potential implementation challenges that must be addressed to move forward
- Foster a sense of cooperation and collaboration between the business, development teams, and architecture

The teams may have other ideas about how this system should be designed. Although you should be prepared to articulate why you are prescribing an alternative direction, the goal is not to railroad the teams but rather to *collaborate*. Rather than simply shutting down an idea, take time to understand the drivers behind these counterproposals. Strive to understand why the team representative feels their suggestion has merit. If you have already evaluated this option and rejected it for cause, communicate your evaluation and how you arrived at this conclusion. Ask if you have overlooked any key aspects and be open to the possibility that you have. Being honest and open-minded is crucial to building a collaborative relationship between architecture and teams and mirrors an approach championed in Dale Carnegie's timeless book, *How to Win Friends and Influence People,* where he advises that "*If you want to gather honey, don't kick over the beehive.*" Consider borrowing this turn of phrase from this work to diffuse potential conflict:

> *I may be wrong, I frequently am, let's examine the facts*
>
> —Dale Carnegie[4]

As in the process detailed in Chapter 4, listen carefully to the various viewpoints expressed in this meeting and take detailed notes. Remember, this may be your final opportunity to course correct in the event of an error or omission. As such, approach these conversations with an open mind. Ultimately, what matters most is what is right, rather than who is right.

[4] Carnegie, D. (1936). *How to Win Friends and Influence People.* Simon & Schuster

Another, asynchronous approach to getting feedback on a candidate architecture, constraint, or project standard is to publish a Request for Comments (RFC) document.

An RFC is a formal document used in the technical community, most commonly seen in use by the Internet Engineering Task Force (IETF), to propose new standards, protocols, procedures, or revise on existing ones. These documents serve as the primary means by which protocols and standards are developed and disseminated across a community or organization.

Key Points About RFCs

1. **Purpose**: RFCs are used to propose and discuss new ideas or modifications to existing protocols and standards. They document the technical details and provide a basis for consensus building among experts.

2. **Process**: The process starts with the creation of an RFC draft, which is then reviewed and commented on by the community. After sufficient discussion and revision, it may be published as an official standard.

3. **Numbering**: RFCs are sequentially numbered, and once published, they are never revised or updated beyond notating errata or referencing superseding RFC. If changes are needed, a new RFC is created to supersede the old one.

4. **Categories**: RFCs can be informational, experimental, best current practice (BCP), or standards track documents. Standards track RFCs, in particular, can eventually become standards after going through a rigorous review process.

5. **Historical Significance**: The first RFC was published in 1969, and since then, they have become the cornerstone of Internet standards development, including foundational protocols like TCP/IP.

In essence, an RFC is a collaborative way for a technology community to develop and agree on the protocols and standards that underpin their work while providing transparency about decisions as well as the process leading up to them.

If the RFC approach is new to an organization, you may face challenges with engagement as reviewing and commenting on RFC is not yet standard operating procedure. In such cases, a combination of publishing RFCs for asynchronous review, then hosting the real-time meeting described above will offer a suitable level of engagement for these discussions.

Each constraint that defines your architectural style will carry risk. Following the meeting or RFC process (or both), you will be poised to evaluate the risk associated with each candidate style and mitigate it. One useful tool for this approach is the constraint risk matrix (Figure 22-1).

Constraint	Adoption Risk	Implementation Risk	Consequence	Mitigation
Domain Partitioning	Feature-Teams	Reorg failure	High coupling, low agility	Get organizational support for DDD and Reorg
...				

Figure 22-1. *Constraint Risk Matrix*

The risk associated with a constraint may be mitigated through offering various support resources to implementation teams. These might take the form of training, reference implementations, developer tooling, or some other mechanism depending on the unique situation of the teams and the constraints.

Although many of these support resources will land in the backlog of the architecture team to prepare, it is worth asking the lead of the team or teams who raised a concern if there are members of that team who may be interested in exploring the solution. Ideal candidates for such collaboration are developers who are naturally curious, enjoy exploring new ideas, and perhaps those interested in a future career in software architecture. Your collaborators in the various development teams will also be useful as reference points and champions of the architecture during implementation. Finally, this approach furthers a collaborative relationship between development and architecture.

Phase VI: Design and Document the Architecture

Once you have arrived at one or more styles that align with the current needs of the business (with a path to future evolution), a final architecture style must be selected and formally documented. Chapter 24 provides tools to document your architectural style as well as subsequent *architecturally significant decisions*.

Your work as an architect is not complete with the derivation or selection of an architectural style. From here, you will begin to describe the specific implementation of the systems. What are the components, where are their boundaries, how do they communicate? Which teams are responsible for which components? What does the runtime environment look like?

It is here your architecture goes from high-level architectural style to concrete and actionable blueprints. Again, Chapter 24 provides detailed guidance for documenting and diagramming architecture. Describing what your system will look like after adopting your chosen architectural style(s) forms the final, crucial steps that must take place before your initial design work is completed.

Summary

The Tailor-Made Software Architecture Model is your tool for achieving a holistic fit between business needs and system capabilities. This chapter has guided you through the nuanced process of aligning architectural decisions with business priorities, emphasizing the importance of balancing trade-offs to achieve *enough* rather than an excess of certain capabilities. Whether you are tailoring an existing architecture or designing a new system, the key lies in thoughtful, measured adjustments that respect both the current organizational context and future evolution. By meticulously evaluating and adjusting architectural styles, considering temporal fit, organizational readiness, and fostering collaboration through tools like RFCs, you are positioned to design architectures that are not only technically sound but also pragmatically aligned with business goals and organizational reality. Your success as an architect hinges on this delicate balance—where every decision is justified, every constraint purposeful, and every system fit for its unique environment and future evolution.

CHAPTER 23

Paved Roads and Variances

> *How can organizations streamline their development processes and ensure that their teams are productive and aligned? The solution lies in adopting the 'paved road' approach.*
>
> —Joshua Morris

To be effective as a software architect, there are many core truths we must accept. Among these

- There are no one-size-fits-all solutions in software architecture.
- There are multiple paths to achieve an end.
- Architectural constraints are only part of the answer.

The precision of fit offered by an architectural style is inversely proportional to the scope of the architecture. A large and complex system that is comprised of many subdomains with different architectural requirements cannot be effectively served by a single style.

> *Some architectural styles are often portrayed as 'silver bullet' solutions for all forms of software. However, a good designer should select a style that matches the needs of the particular problem being solved.*
>
> —Roy Fielding

M. Carducci, *Mastering Software Architecture*, https://doi.org/10.1007/979-8-8688-0410-6_23

Fielding's words ring true a quarter century after they were written[1] and will continue to resonate for the foreseeable future. Does this mean we should treat each subdomain as discrete and disjoint entities, requiring a distinct architectural style for each? Not necessarily. This approach will often result in a fragmented ecosystem of tools, practices, conflicting architectural constraints, increased cognitive load, and an inconsistent level of knowledge and expertise. Instead, seek to define a top-level architectural style from which other styles in the system are derived. Remember, an architectural style is simply a named, coordinated set of architectural constraints. Styles may be composed of individual, atomic constraints, or they may be comprised of a combination of other styles and individual constraints.

A top-level style specifies the core, guiding principles that govern all development within the system. You, or architects closer to the various problem domains, will then define new styles, derived from the top-level style that will apply to individual subdomains or subsets of the system's components.

If, over the course of your career, you find yourself in an *Enterprise Architect* role, you may adopt this same approach to define a shared foundation for architecture within the enterprise or technical ecosystem. In this role, your primary responsibility is to ensure that the IT infrastructure and software systems are not only effective and efficient but also flexible enough to adapt to the organization's evolving needs. By defining high-level, enterprise-wide governing principles, you can ensure the enterprise's entire hierarchy of architects is aligned in both mission and approach. As the architecture roles get closer to implementation teams, the precision of the styles increases while adhering to common constraints and tooling. An example of such a hierarchy is depicted in Figure 23-1.

[1] Fielding, R. *Architectural Styles and the Design of Network-based Software Architectures.* Doctoral dissertation, University of California, Irvine, 2000

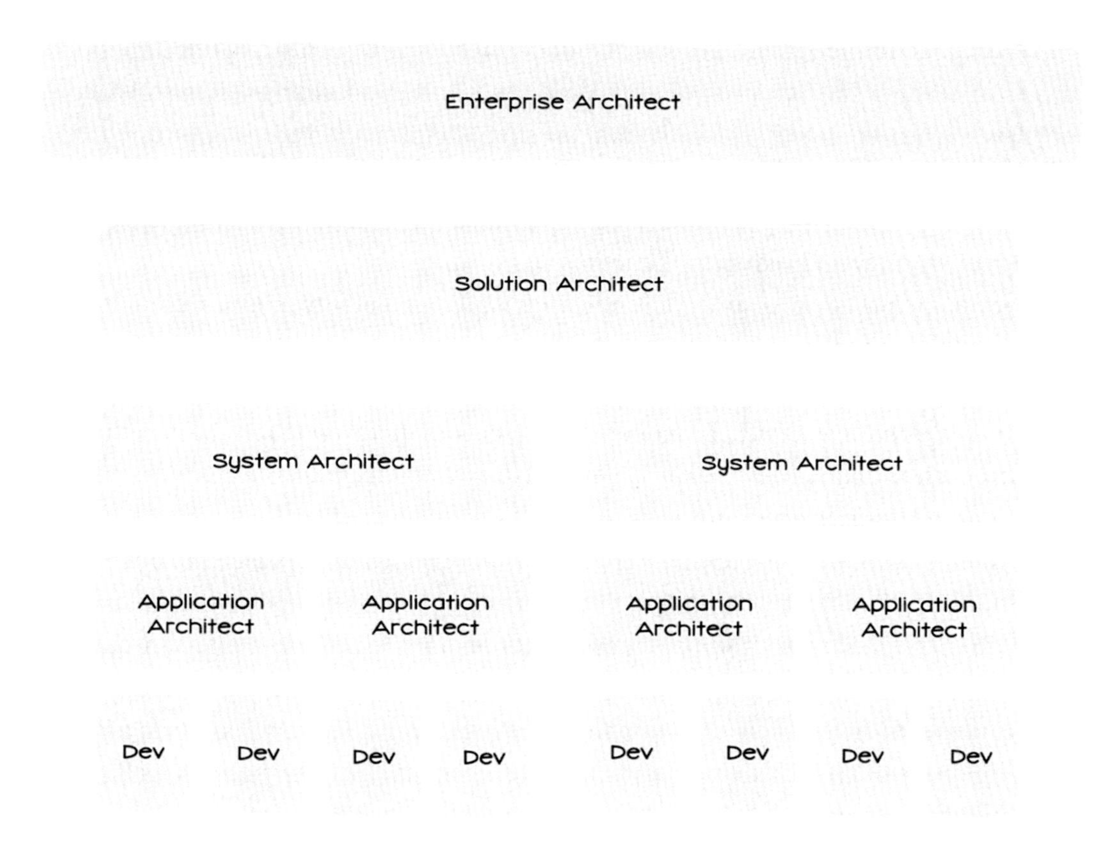

***Figure 23-1.** Hierarchy of Architecture Roles*

The top-level architectural style that cascades down throughout the organization is an example of a *paved road.*

Paved Roads

In software development and architecture, the concept of *paved roads* refers to a set of common architectural constraints, preferred practices, tools, languages, and frameworks that are officially endorsed, supported, or prescribed within an organization. These are the paths that have been tested, optimized, evaluated for holistic fit, and deemed the most efficient and reliable for developers to follow. Think of it as a well-maintained highway, where everything is smooth, predictable, and designed to get you to your destination with minimal friction.

The idea is to reduce cognitive load and decision fatigue by providing developers with a clear, standardized way of building, deploying, and maintaining software. When you follow the "paved road," you are leveraging prebuilt infrastructure, battle-tested libraries, and standardized processes that have been refined over time. This does not just make individual development tasks easier—it also aligns the entire team's efforts, ensuring consistency and reducing the risk of costly mistakes.

However, the paved road concept is not about stifling creativity or innovation. It is about providing a reliable, well-lit path that allows teams to move quickly and efficiently while reserving the off-roading for when it is truly necessary. When a team chooses to deviate from this path, it should be a deliberate decision, made collaboratively with architecture while maintaining full awareness of the trade-offs and potential challenges.

Some paved roads are highly prescriptive. For example, the Choreographed Event-Driven Abstract Style (Chapter 17) includes a constraint that prescribes PubSub messaging but does not explicitly name a particular PubSub. The cohesiveness of the system will quickly fall apart if some teams adopt Kafka while others adopt a fan-out configuration of RabbitMQ, while others adopt yet another approach. A paved road, in this case, would define a single common messaging platform. This also points to a key distinction between an *architectural style* and any particular *implementation*. As Fielding points out, both architectures and architectural styles are abstractions that allow us to design and reason about concrete *systems*.

> *Architecture is therefore an abstraction of implementation, and styles are the named patterns by which we can understand architectures and architectural design.*
>
> —Roy Fielding[2]

Other paved roads offer implementation teams limited degrees of freedom. For example, based on the skills and expertise within the organization, you may define three options for the choice of a database (e.g., *"you can use PostgreSQL, DynamoDB, or Redis"*). You may also leave the choice of architectural style for a given subdomain or component to development teams (e.g., *"you can follow architectural style A, B, or C"*); however, as an exercise in architectural thinking, the team should provide a justification, perhaps in the form of an Architectural Decision Record (introduced in the next

[2] Fielding, R. (2008). *On Software Architecture*. Untangled. `https://roy.gbiv.com/untangled/2008/on-software-architecture`

chapter). This gives some autonomy back to implementation teams without completely compromising the architecture of the system. It also frees teams from *the paradox of choice*[3] where an overabundance of options induces anxiety in individuals and leads to general unhappiness with any chosen outcome.

As you continue through your career as an architect, you will inevitably find unique scenarios where none of the paved roads are suitable for a particular system component or edge case. In this case, you must determine if any of the supported options will be *good enough* or if architecture must issue a *variance*.

Variances

A *variance* refers to an approved deviation from the established architectural standards or guidelines within an organization. It is akin to offering a different route than the one mapped out by your *paved roads*. Variances are intentional choices to diverge from the norm, often driven by specific project needs, environmental limitations, or innovative approaches that do not quite fit within the predefined framework.

In an ideal world, every project would neatly follow the architectural blueprint laid out by the architect. However, neither of us lives in "ideal worlds," and real-world scenarios often require flexibility. A variance might be necessary when a particular technology, pattern, or approach offers significant advantages for a specific use case that the standard architecture does not fully accommodate. For example, a team might opt to use a different database technology because it better supports the performance requirements of a new application, even if it is not the standard choice for the organization.

The Role of Variances in Software Architecture

Variances serve as a safety valve in the rigid structure of architectural governance. They allow for innovation and adaptability while ensuring that these deviations are carefully considered and managed. When a variance is requested, it typically goes through a

[3] Schwartz, B. (2004). *The Paradox of Choice: Why More Is Less.* Harper Perennial

review process where its merits, risks, and long-term implications are evaluated. This helps balance the need for consistency across the organization with the flexibility to meet unique project demands.

Variances are a necessary part of navigating the complex landscape of technology decisions. They provide the flexibility to address unique challenges while ensuring that these decisions are made with full awareness of their implications. When managed correctly, variances can contribute to innovation and agility without compromising the cohesion and reliability of the organization's architectural framework.

Managing Variances

Effective management of variances is crucial. Each variance should be documented as a formal architectural decision with a corresponding architecture decision record (Chapter 24). This documentation must communicate a clear rationale for why the deviation is necessary and how it aligns with the project's goals as well as defining a specific and narrow scope for this variance. It is also essential to assess the potential impact on the broader architecture, such as integration challenges, increased maintenance costs, or potential technical debt. By keeping a close eye on variances, an organization can ensure that these deviations remain the exception rather than the rule, preserving the integrity of the overall architecture.

Summary

In the evolving landscape of software architecture, balancing standardization with flexibility is paramount. The concepts of *paved roads* and *variances* offer a framework for achieving this balance. Paved roads provide a solid, reliable foundation for development, ensuring consistency and efficiency across the organization. They reduce cognitive load, minimize risks, and streamline the development process, allowing teams to focus on delivering value.

At the same time, variances acknowledge the reality that one size does not fit all. They offer the flexibility to innovate and adapt to unique challenges when the paved road is not sufficient. However, these deviations must be carefully managed to prevent fragmentation and maintain the integrity of the overall architecture.

As an architect, your role is to guide the organization through these decisions, ensuring that paved roads are followed where possible and that variances are well justified and thoughtfully implemented. This balance of consistency and adaptability is what allows an organization to build robust, resilient systems that can evolve with its needs, driving long-term success.

CHAPTER 24

Documenting Architecture

> *An architecture that is not documented, and not communicated, may still be a good architecture, but the risks surrounding it are enormous.*
>
> —Len Bass

As you have seen throughout this book, the architectural capabilities of a system are the product of *architecturally significant decisions*. Unfortunately, it is not always clear to all involved which decisions are architecturally significant, the broader scope of these decisions, the "why" behind them, and how they interact to form a cohesive system.

For an architecture to be successful, it must be understood. For example, when the importance of a given decision is not widely understood, the development teams may overlook these decisions when they are not clearly communicated or simply ignore them if the teams lack consensus on the decision drivers. Likewise, both the parts and the whole must be understood. *Effective architects are effective communicators*, and this chapter focuses on several documentation and diagramming tools to support your efforts. The artifacts you create can then be document controlled, versioned, cross-linked, and searchable. Publication in this manner will scale your communication across the organization.

To begin, we will look at an essential artifact for architects everywhere, the Architectural Decision Record.

Architectural Decision Records (ADRs)

An ADR is simply a document that captures *when*, *why*, and *how* every architecturally significant decision was made. Documentation is, undoubtedly, one of the least exciting or popular aspects of software engineering and architecture. I have a uniquely strong aversion to writing documentation. However, I have learned through bitter experience to never "pencil whip" an ADR; instead, I approach every ADR with focus, precision, and attention to detail. Why are ADRs so important?

M. Carducci, *Mastering Software Architecture*, https://doi.org/10.1007/979-8-8688-0410-6_24

ADRs Serve You

First, ADRs offer an environment to ruthlessly evaluate a decision. Neither you nor I am immune to biases and blind spots. In other words, we might naturally gravitate to a familiar or favorite approach or technology even when it is not the optimum solution to a given problem. We may also easily overlook an option that is not top of mind when we are making an architectural decision. The ADR is the first environment where we *prove* the merit of our ideas. The ADR serves as a fast feedback loop on the validity of our decisions.

An ADR with a clear problem context and decision drivers, which weighs the pros and cons of *all* relevant options, will sometimes surprise us by illuminating an overlooked blind spot that leads us to pivot to a different decision.

ADRs Serve *Future* You

As a project grows and evolves over time, it becomes increasingly difficult to keep the entire architectural design and context in your head. At many points in your career, you—or a new architect on the team—will find certain decisions mystifying. The question in this moment will be *"why are we doing this thing that way?"* The ADR that captured that decision would provide a detailed answer to that question.

An ADR that captures a past decision will necessarily include the context and drivers behind that decision. This is crucial as the decision context might change over time. Capturing both the decision and the underlying drivers that led to that decision will provide tools to reevaluate the decision over time and determine when that decision is no longer relevant. In this case, you will document a new decision based on the present problem and business context. This new ADR will supersede the existing ADR.

You may find yourself in an organization where the creation and publication of ADRs has not, historically, been standard operating procedure. In such cases, both architecture and implementation teams will typically continue to follow established conventions without understanding their original purpose and motivation. Retroactively creating ADRs will aid in understanding the historical decisions and enable change and innovation where appropriate.

Every Architecture Decision Will Be Challenged.

Additionally, well-crafted ADRs potentially free *future you* from relitigating every decision over and over again. The recommended structure for ADRs below not only communicates why a particular option was chosen, but why competing options were not. As such, we can avoid lengthy arguments with implementation teams who may prefer other approaches that are more familiar, productive, or performant. Instead, we simply point to the ADR that captures the *what* and the *why* of the decision.

This assumes that the alternative idea—and its trade-offs—is present in the ADR. If the existing ADR did not evaluate that alternative, it may indicate you have overlooked a viable alternative option. In this case, take this as constructive feedback to increase your diligence in future ADRs. To settle the dispute, either you or the developer(s) should submit a superseding ADR that includes this additional option for review and approval.

ADRs Serve Teams

Teams that are committed to excellence still require a concrete definition of what "good" looks like. ADRs are part of this definition and form the basis of a permanent and ongoing point of reference. Moreover, ADRs offer an efficient communication mechanism that aids in the dissemination of key decisions to teams.

Additionally, ADRs are a tool to foster better relationships with development and implementation teams. Architecture often has a reputation for operating from an "Ivory Tower" that is disconnected from the reality of teams. Architecture decisions can often seem arbitrary or excessive. An ADR that effectively captures the *what*, the *how*, and the *why* will challenge this misconception.

ADRs Serve Future Teams

ADRs offer an asynchronous mechanism for communicating and cascading architectural decisions across the organization to both existing and new team members over time. ADRs enable efficient onboarding for new teams without the need for architecture to "hop on a call" to onboard each new team or teammate on a per-architectural decision basis.

The Anatomy of an ADR

Each ADR captures and documents a single, granular, decision that is germane to the architecture of the project or system. This section describes an ADR's constituent components.

Title and Metadata

The first part of an ADR will include a *title* that captures the solved problem and solution. Each ADR will have a *status* (e.g., proposed, rejected, accepted, deprecated, or superseded) along with the names of the individual(s) responsible for the decision. The metadata will also include the *date* of the decision and optionally link to a work item related to this decision. Figure 24-1 shows an example of this section of an ADR.

```
1   # [short title of problem and solution]
2
3   - Status: [Proposed | rejected | accepted | deprecated | - | superseded
    by [ADR](adr.md)] <!-- optional -->
4   - Deciders: [list everyone involved in the decision] <!-- optional -->
5   - Date: [yyyy-mm-dd when the decision was last updated]
6
7   Technical Story: [description | ticket/issue URL] <!-- optional -->
```

Figure 24-1. *ADR Title and Metadata Template*

Context and Problem Statement

The next section of an ADR communicates the problem context. You will typically articulate this context as either a statement of fact or in the form of a question. Figure 24-2 shows a template for this section of an ADR.

```
9   ## Context and Problem Statement
10
11  - [Describe the context and problem statement, e.g., in free form using
    two or three sentences. You may want to articulate the problem in the
    form of a question.]
```

Figure 24-2. *ADR Context and Problem Statement Template*

Decision Drivers

In this section, you will communicate the internal and external factors that must be satisfied by the final decision. As you may recall, the requirements analysis process detailed in Chapter 4 recommended making notes of key statements from business stakeholders. This is a good place to reference both the statements and the individual(s) who made the statements. In addition to backing up the statements in this section, these references allow you to borrow authority from business stakeholders. Figure 24-3 shows an example of this section in an ADR.

```
13    ## Decision Drivers <!-- optional -->
14
15    * [driver 1, e.g., a force, facing concern, …]
16    * [driver 2, e.g., a force, facing concern, …]
17    * … <!-- numbers of drivers can vary -->
18
```

Figure 24-3. *ADR Decision Drivers*

Considered Options

This is the section of the ADR where your up-front effort will first pay dividends in the communication process. Here, you list all the options you have considered when making the decision. When considering options, you want to look at the options that make sense in the context of architecture as well as attempting to anticipate alternatives that development teams may request or counter with. It is important to understand that the latter options are not simply *straw men* to knock down; instead, you must treat each option with equal rigor; otherwise, you risk undermining the credibility of the architecture team. At this point of the document, you are merely enumerating possibilities. A more detailed analysis will come later. Figure 24-4 shows an example of this section in an ADR.

```
19    ## Considered Options
20
21    * [option 1]
22    * [option 2]
23    * [option 3]
24    * … <!-- numbers of options can vary -->
25
```

Figure 24-4. *Considered Options Section of an ADR*

Decision Outcome

Next, you will communicate the chosen option, the *decision outcome*. This section communicates not only the decision but also a summary that communicates the *why* behind that decision. Figure 24-5 shows an example of this section.

```
25    ## Decision Outcome
26
27    - Chosen option: "[[option 1]]", because [justification e.g., only
      option, which meets k.o. criterion decision driver | which resolves
      force |... | comes out best (see below)].
```

Figure 24-5. *Decision Outcome Section of an ADR*

These four sections provide the minimum necessary information for the reader to understand the decision. This structure essentially offers a tl;dr that shows respect for the reader's time, allowing them to get to the meat of the decision quickly, offering an efficient way for the reader to navigate information effectively, and this removes a common barrier to entry present in most documentation. However, this is not the end of the document.

Positive and Negative Consequences

Here, we communicate both the good and the bad of the decision. Remember the first law of software architecture,[1] every decision is a trade-off. In this section, the author provides full transparency of both the good and the bad outcomes that emerge from this decision. This is also a test of your understanding of the decision. If you have not identified any negative consequences of the decision, the odds are you have simply overlooked the trade-off. The corollary to the first law of software architecture states that, if you believe you have identified an architecture decision that is not a trade-off, it is; you just have not identified the trade-off yet.

This section will also head off many debates with implementation teams. For example, if a developer prefers a different option or approach than the decision outcome, they will likely seize upon a negative consequence of the decision to challenge the ADR. If you have done your due diligence when authoring this document, the ADR will express that negative consequence and will show both how and why the positive consequences outweigh the negatives in this context. Conversely, if you have not performed sufficient due diligence, you have left the architecture decision open to being attacked or ignored. Figure 24-6 shows an example of this section.

```
30  ### Positive Consequences <!-- optional -->
31
32  * [e.g., improvement of quality attribute satisfaction, follow-up decisions required, …]
33  * …
34
35  ### Negative Consequences <!-- optional -->
36
37  * [e.g., compromising quality attribute, follow-up decisions required, …]
38  * …
39
```

Figure 24-6. *Positive and Negative Consequences of the Decision*

[1] Ford, N., & Richards, M. (2020). *Fundamentals of software architecture: An engineering approach.* O'Reilly Media

Pros and Cons of the Options

This section is where you demonstrate that you have done your due diligence and carefully considered each option. This is also the section where you prove to *yourself* that this is the optimum decision in the current problem context. Again, it is important not to leave the decision open to attack by omitting key factors that might have led to a different decision outcome. The more effort you put into this section, the stronger the ADR will be when it faces inevitable scrutiny. Figure 24-7 shows an example of this section in an ADR template.

```
40  ## Pros and Cons of the Options <!-- optional -->
41
42  ### [option 1]
43
44  [example | description | pointer to more information | …] <!-- optional -->
45
46  * Good, because [argument a]
47  * Good, because [argument b]
48  * Bad, because [argument c]
49  * … <!-- numbers of pros and cons can vary -->
50
51  ### [option 2]
52
53  [example | description | pointer to more information | …] <!-- optional -->
54
55  * Good, because [argument a]
56  * Good, because [argument b]
57  * Bad, because [argument c]
58  * … <!-- numbers of pros and cons can vary -->
59
```

Figure 24-7. *Pros and Cons of Each Option*

Links

An ADR is a lightweight document, and its length should not exceed a couple of pages. This closing section is where an interested reader who has made it to the end of the document can go to learn more. This section might include links to implementation guidance, tutorials, further reading, or other related documents that support the ADR or those intending to follow the ADR. Figure 24-8 shows an example of this section of an ADR.

```
69   ## Links <!-- optional -->
70
71   * [Link type] [Link to ADR] <!-- example: Refined by [ADR-0005](0005-example.md) -->
72   * [Link Type] [Link to Implementation Guidance] <!-- example: Implementation Guidance [REST API Standards]
     (/standards/001-API-Standards.md)>
73   * [Link Type] [Link to Further Reading]
74   * … <!-- numbers of links can vary -->
```

Figure 24-8. *Links Section in an ADR*

The Constraint Document

Architectural constraints are a special class of architectural decisions. Although the structure of an ADR will adequately capture any given architectural constraint, I recommend using a slightly different format to capture and communicate architectural constraints.

In this book, we have adopted the established convention of defining architectural constraints; however, you may not wish to frame them this way for communication with non-architectural audiences. Depending on the project and organization, you may want to choose a less restrictive sounding moniker such as "Governing Principles."

Title and Metadata

Like ADRs, a constraint document begins with Title and Metadata (Figure 24-9).

```
1   # [short title of constraint] <!--possibly framed as a governing
    principle-->
2
3   * Status: [proposed | rejected | accepted | deprecated | … | superseded
    by [CDR-0005](/principles/CDR0005-example.md)] <!-- optional -->
4   * Deciders: [list everyone involved in the decision] <!-- optional -->
5   * Date: [YYYY-MM-DD when the decision was last updated] <!-- optional -->
```

Figure 24-9. *Constraint Decision Record Title and Metadata*

Motivation

The second law of software architecture states that "*Why is more important than how.*"[2] This section outlines the why behind the constraint the document describes. This is, again, where you return to your efforts from the requirements analysis process described

[2] Ford, N., Richards, M. (2020). *Fundamentals of Software Architecture: An Engineering Approach.* O'Reilly

in Chapter 4. You want to be clear when constraining implementation teams' degrees of freedom and communicate that this is not an arbitrary decision. Cite or link to authoritative statements, people, and documents. See Figure 24-10 for an example of this section.

```
7   ## Motivation
8
9   [Review your requirements documentation - Discuss system capabilities
    and how they are driven by business requirements. Include supporting
    references (people, documents, etc.)]
```

Figure 24-10. *Constraint Motivation*

Description

It is here you describe the constraint. A good description section communicates not only the constraint but also what it means to implementation teams. Where appropriate, provide diagrams or high-level implementation details (more detailed guidance will be linked later in the document). Figure 24-11 shows this section of the constraint document.

```
11   ## Description
12
13   [Describe the constraint at a high-level. Consider including diagrams.
     What does this mean for implementation teams?]
```

Figure 24-11. *Constraint Description*

Considered Alternatives

The table at the end of Chapter 21 listed various constraints and their influence on the architectural capabilities of key interest discussed in this book. Look at any single column, and you will see numerous constraints that will positively influence that capability. There is almost always more than one option. The effort to enumerate these options will benefit both you and your reader. You will be in a position to release this document and decision with much more confidence as this effort should force you to perform necessary due diligence, and it will benefit your reader by communicating the level of care and consideration that went into the decision. As such, you want to express succinctly in this document why the other options were not selected. Figure 24-12 shows an example of this section.

```
15  ## Considered Alternatives
16
17  [What other options are available to induce the system capabilities]
18
19  * [option 1]
20  * [option 2]
21  * [option 3]
22  * … <!-- numbers of options can vary -->
23
```

Figure 24-12. *Considered Alternative Constraints*

Risks

An architecture only has value if implementation teams adopt and follow its core, guiding principles. Building on Chapter 22, we must be continuously mindful of the various risks associated with a given architecture. Performing this analysis at the constraint level is a useful tool to help ensure you do not overlook potential risks. We must ask ourselves the question *"How might this constraint fail? What would be the outcome?"* and express these risks in this document. Figure 24-13 shows this section of the constraint document.

```
40  ## Risks <!-- optional -->
41
42  * [e.g., Possibility constraint may be ignored or abandoned - Consequences and mitigation]
43  * [e.g., Possibility constraint may be ignored or abandoned - Consequences and mitigation]
44  * …
45
```

Figure 24-13. *Constraint Document Risks Section*

Support

Unfortunately, we cannot be consistently effective if we design an architecture and simply "throw it over the wall" to the implementation teams. We are not operating from the architectural "ivory tower"; instead, we aim to align technology strategy with business strategy. Because architecture necessarily constrains developer's degrees of freedom, every constraint must come with support. Support can come in many forms, including tutorials, training, reference implementations, and tooling. In this section, you will enumerate the support resources available to implementation teams. The more care and detail you put into this section, the more sustainable the constraint's adoption. Figure 24-14 shows an example of this section.

```
46   ## Support <!-- optional -->
47
48   * [Link type] [Link to Reference Implementation]
49   * [Link Type] [Link to Implementation Guidance]
50   * [Link Type] [Link to Training Materials]
51   * [Link Type] [Link to Further Reading]
52   * … <!-- numbers of links can vary -->
53
```

Figure 24-14. *Constraint Document Support Section*

Implementation Guidance

The next section of the constraint document will detail any necessary implementation guidance and often forms part of the "paved roads" referred to in the previous chapter. These are typically additional, external links to keep this document lightweight which might include, but not limited to

- Diagrams
- Reference implementations
- Standards
- Tooling
- Recommended frameworks/infrastructure

When linking to external references, it is often helpful to link to both normative and non-normative documents.

Normative documents formally describe a standard and represent the *"letter of the law"* as it were. Normative documents are written with the rigor of a legal contract and are the definitive source of truth. Non-normative documents are more informal in writing style and are usually friendlier to the reader. However, when a document is non-normative, it means any error or omission in the document cannot be construed as overriding the standard. As an example, a blog post describing how to implement the Internet calendar specification is non-normative, while RFC 2445 provides a more detailed and precise, *normative*, description of the standard. The blog post would be a friendlier read, but RFC 2445 is the authoritative source of truth on the topic (and should probably be linked or referenced in the blog post from this example).

Governance

As part of our due diligence as architects, we must also think about how a given architecture constraint will be enforced. For this chapter, we will briefly mention this section of a constraint document and its role in capturing and communicating the governance and enforcement mechanisms for a given constraint; however, Chapter 25 goes into architectural governance in more detail. Your aim here is to capture and communicate how adherence to a constraint is measured by architecture, by implementation teams, and how compliance is enforced. Figure 24-15 shows an example of this section.

```
60    ## Governance
61
62    [How will this constraint be enforced? How can success be measured?]
63
```

Figure 24-15. *Governance Section of a Constraint Document*

Resources

We close our constraint document with any additional resources that might be valuable for the reader or implementation teams. These resources might include ADRs, other constraint documents, or further reading that does not fit in any other section. Figure 24-16 shows an example of this section.

```
64    ## Other Resources <!-- optional -->
65
66    * [Link type] [Link to ADR] <!-- example: Refined by [ADR-0005](0005-example.md) -->
67    * [Link Type] [Link to Further Reading]
68    * … <!-- numbers of links can vary -->
69
```

Figure 24-16. *Other Resources*

The Architectural Style Document

Although it is the atomic constraints that define the architectures you produce, an architectural style is the molecular delivery that describes the style. One more important document in your arsenal is, therefore, the *architectural style document*. This document is a high-level document that defines the style, links to the style's defining constraints, other relevant ADRs, and justifies this style's existence in the current context. As such, an architectural style document may be general and potentially reusable; however, the production on an architectural style should communicate the motivation of the style in the project's context. The architectural style document consists of the following six sections.

Title and Introduction

This section includes your architectural style's name and a brief introduction of the style. In contrast with ADRs, this document does not include status, date, or author information as an architectural style document simply communicates the style's defining constraints and scope. The decision to adopt or deprecate a style and migrate to a new style will be communicated in an ADR. In other words, the *system* evolves, not the style (since a different set of constraints begets a different style). Figure 24-17 shows an example of this section.

```
1   # [Architectural Style Name]
2
3   [TOC]
4
5   ## Introduction
6
7   The purpose of this document is to describe the architecture of XYZ System at a high
    level, outlining the architectural governing principles, why they were selected, and
    links to dive deeper into each element.
8
```

Figure 24-17. *Architectural Style Title and Introduction*

Motivation

This section briefly summarizes why this style was created and why it matters. Remember, every decision that originates from architecture will be challenged. We must justify our decisions.

This section will be strongly informed by the notes you took in the requirements analysis process in Chapter 4. Your document will carry more weight if you rigorously cite your sources. Figure 24-18 shows an example of this section.

```
15  ## Motivation
16
17  [Why are we adopting this architectural style? What problems does it solve? Why does
    this matter?]
18
19  ### Business-Critical Architectural Capabilities
20
21  [What has been defined as the business-critical capabilities? Says who? Who has
    authority here? Cite your sources. How does this architectural style deliver these?]
22
23  ### Important Architectural Capabilities  <!-- optional -->
24
25  [What has been defined as the important capabilities? Says who? Who has authority here?
    Cite your sources. How does this architectural style deliver these?]
26
27  ### Notable Architectural Capabilities  <!-- optional -->
28
29  [What has been defined as the notable capabilities? Says who? Who has authority here?
    Cite your sources. How does this architectural style deliver these?]
30
31  ### Nice-To-Have Architectural Capabilities <!-- optional -->
32
33  [What has been defined as the "nice-to-have" capabilities? Says who? Who has authority
    here? Cite your sources. How does this architectural style deliver these?]
34
```

Figure 24-18. *Architectural Style Motivations*

Summary of Constraints

This section simply lists the style's defining architectural constraints, with links to each constraint's defining document, the *Constraint Definition Record* (CDR). Figure 24-19 shows an example of this section.

```
9    ## Summary of Governing Principles
10
11   * [Constraint 1 - brief description and link to CDR]
12   * [Constraint 2 - brief description and link to CDR]
13   * … <!-- numbers of drivers can vary -->
14
```

Figure 24-19. *Summary of Constraints Section*

Scope

As we have established throughout this book, architecture is not about one-size-fits-all solutions. In a single, nontrivial system, there may be multiple architectural styles that apply to different subdomains or portions of the system. Some styles may exist as a tightly scoped variance or apply to a subset of system components. Here, you will explicitly define where the style applies and where it does not, linking to individual ADRs as appropriate. Figure 24-20 shows an example of this section.

```
35   ## Scope <!-- optional -->
36
37   [What is the scope of this style? Where MUST it be applied, where SHOULD it be applied,
     Are there alternatives? If so, for whom?]
38
```

Figure 24-20. *Architectural Style Scope Section*

High-Level Overview

Here, you will provide a high-level description of the architectural style. It can sometimes be helpful to include architectural diagrams (see below) or link to ADRs, requirements, and other resources as needed. When providing diagrams, highlight how the various constraints factor in. Figure 24-21 shows an example of this section.

```
39   ## High-Level Overview
40
41   [Describe this architecture at a high level, what does implementation look like?
     Diagrams are useful here.]
42
```

Figure 24-21. *Architectural Style Overview Section*

Links

The final section of this document is a links section to provide helpful resources for implementation teams. These may be training, tutorials, reference implementations, or other relevant documents not previously linked. Figure 24-22 shows an example of this section.

```
43    ## Links <!-- optional -->
44
45    * [Link to anything relevant not already linked]
46    * … <!-- numbers of links can vary -->
47
```

Figure 24-22. *Example Links Section*

Diagramming and Visualizing Architecture

Although the documents described above will capture much of the essence of the architecture you have created, diagrams help bring the gap between architectural style and implementation. Here, you are no longer simply enumerating the architectural constraints that define the style but also what the system that should adopt this style will look like.

You have, no doubt, heard the adage *"a picture is worth 1000 words."* A picture of the architecture alongside your architecture documentation will save readers the effort of trying to visualize the architecture based on hundreds of thousands of words of documentation. A diagram will also reduce the risk of conflicting interpretations as, between documents and diagrams, little is left to the imagination. This assumes, of course, that the architect responsible for producing the diagram is a skilled visual communicator.

> *Ask somebody in the building industry to visually communicate the architecture of a building and you'll be presented with site plans, floor plans, elevation views, cross-section views and detail drawings. In contrast, ask a software developer to communicate the software architecture of a software system using diagrams and you'll likely get a confused mess of boxes and*

> *lines ... inconsistent notation (color coding, shapes, line styles, etc.), ambiguous naming, unlabeled relationships, generic terminology, missing technology choices, mixed abstractions, etc.*
>
> —Simon Brown[3]

The challenges in effectively visualizing a system's architecture and the diversity of notational systems and tools led to the creation of the Unified Modeling Language (UML) by Rational Software in 1994[4] to facilitate a shared understanding of a system (not necessarily a *software* system), which was later adopted by the Object Management Group (OMG) as a formal standard in 1997. As UML grew in scope, complexity in its use grew in proportion. In the early 2000s, SysML was created as a lighter weight dialect of UML, led in part by OMG, to define and extend a subset of UML 2.0 that is purely focused on system design and engineering. In 2006, software architect Simon Brown began work on the C4 model as an alternative lightweight modeling technique for software architecture that, like SysML, has roots in UML. Although not yet a formal standard, C4 (the focus of this section) is gaining traction in the architecture community.

Many architects eschew formal modeling techniques and proscriptive notation in favor of the friendlier and flexible drag-and-drop diagramming tools (e.g., LucidChart, OmniGraffle, Microsoft Visio, and others). Although these tools do not share the learning curve of formal modeling notations, there is value in the clear, unambiguous semantics of the latter. Tools like LucidChart offer a large library of existing shapes to satisfy various scenarios. However, those shapes do not share the precise semantics of UML (and its derivatives) which can lead to miscommunication. It is always important to include a legend of symbols in your diagrams, even when using formal graphical notations like C4. This can aid the reader in correctly interpreting the diagrams you produce.

The formal modeling notations are also more prescriptive than their "blank canvas" counterparts as to how to create various views of a system. Whether you use formal or informal visual notations, the guidance from the C4 model can be helpful. The entire C4 model is Creative Commons licensed, and a helpful portion is reproduced below.

[3] Brown, S. *The C4 model for visualizing software architecture.* Retrieved from `https://c4model.com`. Licensed under CC BY 4.0.

[4] Booch, G., Rumbaugh, J., Jacobson, I. (2005). *The Unified Modeling Language User Guide 2nd Edition.* Addison-Wesley Professional

C4 Abstractions

In order to create these maps of your code, we first need a common set of abstractions to create a ubiquitous language that we can use to describe the static structure of a software system. A **software system** is made up of one or more **containers** (applications and data stores), each of which contains one or more **components**, which in turn are implemented by one or more **code elements** (classes, interfaces, objects, functions, etc.). And **people** may use the software systems that we build. The people interacting with the software system forms the **context**. An example visualization of C4 abstractions is shown in Figure 24-23.

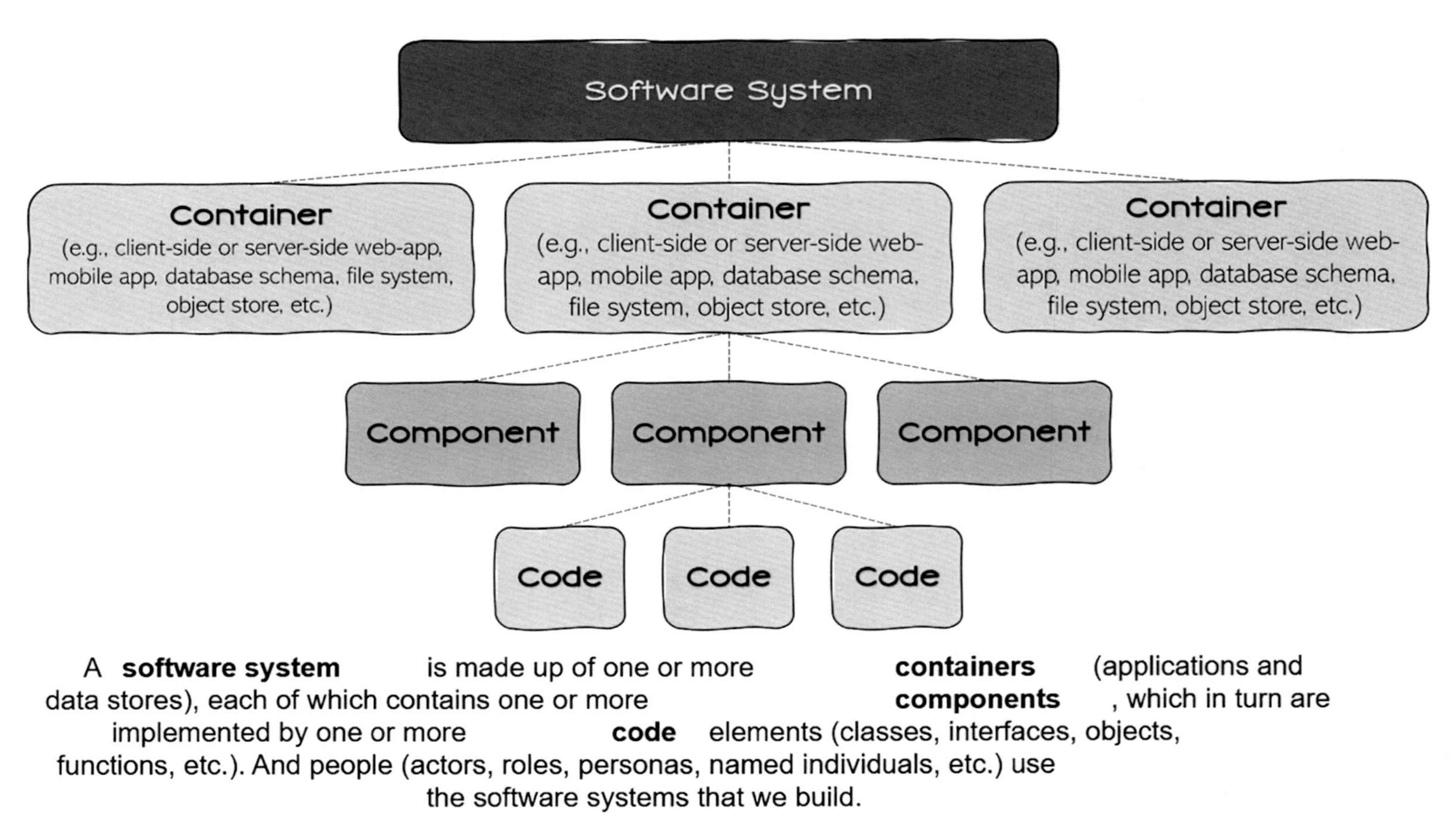

Figure 24-23. *C4 Abstractions*

Person

A person represents one of the human users of your software system (e.g., actors, roles, personas, etc.).

Software System

A software system is the highest level of abstraction and describes something that delivers value to its users, whether they are human or not. This includes the software system you are modeling, and the other software systems upon which your software system depends (or vice versa).

Unfortunately, the term “software system” is the hardest of the C4 model abstractions to define, and this is not helped by the fact that each organization will also have their own terminology for describing the same thing, typically using terms such as “application,” “product,” “service,” etc. One way to think about it is that a software system is something a single software development team is building, owns, has responsibility for, and can see the internal implementation details of. Perhaps the code for that software system resides in a single source code repository, and anybody on the team is entitled to modify it. In many cases, the boundary of a software system will correspond to the boundary of a single team. It may also be the case that everything inside the boundary of a software system is deployed at the same time.

Container

Not Docker! In the C4 model, a container represents an **application** or a **data store**. A container is something that needs to be running in order for the overall software system to work. In real terms, a container is something like

- **Server-Side Web Application**: A Java EE web application running on Apache Tomcat, an ASP.NET MVC application running on Microsoft IIS, a Ruby on Rails application running on WEBrick, a Node.js application, etc.
- **Client-Side Web Application**: A JavaScript application running in a web browser using Angular, Backbone.js, jQuery, etc.

- **Client-Side Desktop Application**: A Windows desktop application written using WPF, an OS X desktop application written using Swift or Objective-C, a cross-platform desktop application written using JavaFX, etc.
- **Mobile App**: An Apple iOS app, an Android app, a Microsoft Windows Phone app, etc.
- **Server-Side Console Application**: A standalone (e.g., "public static void main") application, a batch process, etc.
- **Serverless Function**: A single serverless function (e.g., Amazon Lambda, Azure Function, etc.)
- **Database**: A schema or database in a relational database management system, document store, graph database, etc., such as MySQL, Microsoft SQL Server, Oracle Database, MongoDB, Riak, Cassandra, Neo4j, etc.
- **Blob or Content Store**: A blob store (e.g., Amazon S3, Microsoft Azure Blob Storage, etc.) or content delivery network (e.g., Akamai, Amazon CloudFront, etc.)
- **File System**: A full local file system or a portion of a larger networked file system (e.g., SAN, NAS, etc.)
- **Shell Script**: A single shell script written in Bash, etc.
- **Etc.**

Component

The word "component" is a hugely overloaded term in the software development industry, but in this context a component is a grouping of related functionality encapsulated behind a well-defined interface. If you are using a language like Java or C#, the simplest way to think of a component is that it is a collection of implementation classes behind an interface. Aspects such as how those components are packaged (e.g., one component vs. many components per JAR file, DLL, shared library, etc.) are separate and orthogonal concerns.

An important point to note here is that all components inside a container typically execute in the same process space. **In the C4 model, components are not separately deployable units.**

C4 Diagrams

The C4 model prescribes different diagrams for different purposes. This guidance is helpful regardless of whether C4 is formally used. Each diagram provides a different perspective on the system that will be useful to different audiences.

System Context Diagram

A System Context diagram is a good starting point for diagramming and documenting a software system, allowing you to step back and see the big picture. Draw a diagram showing your system as a box in the center, surrounded by its users and the other systems that it interacts with.

Detail is not important here as this is your zoomed out view showing a big picture of the system landscape. The focus should be on people (actors, roles, personas, etc.) and software systems rather than technologies, protocols, and other low-level details. It is the sort of diagram that you could show to nontechnical people. An example C4 system context diagram is shown in Figure 24-24.

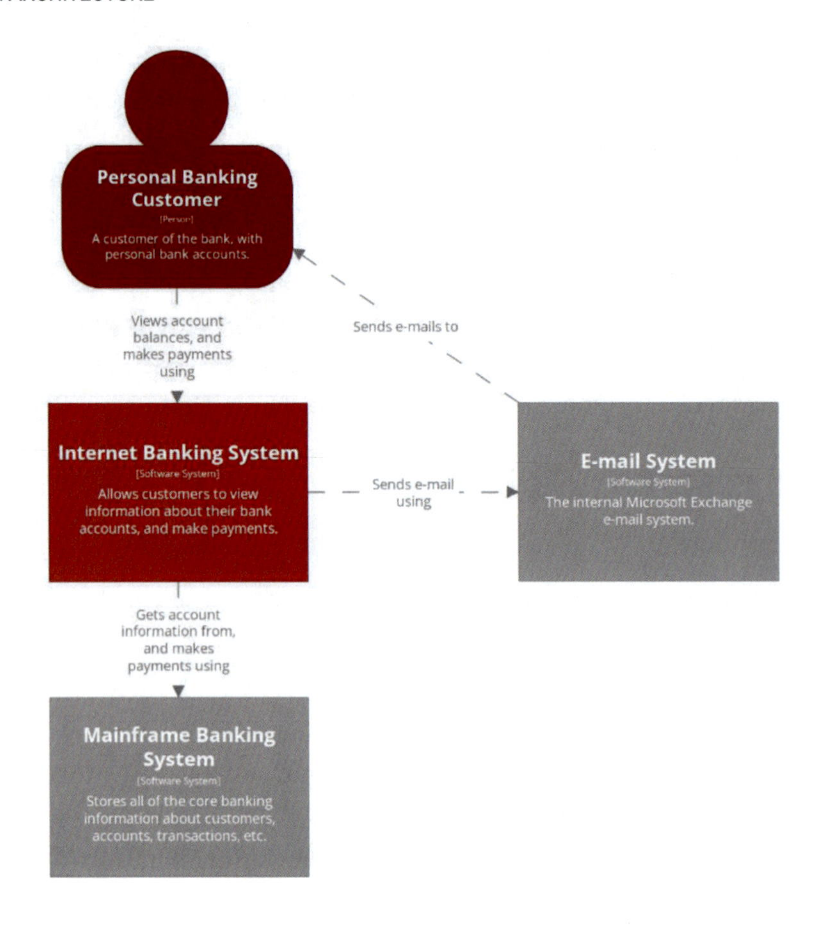

[System Context] Internet Banking System
The system context diagram for the Internet Banking System - diagram created with Structurizr.
Wednesday, March 22, 2023 at 8:16 AM Coordinated Universal Time

Figure 24-24. *A C4 System Context Diagram*

Scope: A single software system.

Primary elements: The software system in scope.**Supporting elements**: People (e.g., users, actors, roles, or personas) and software systems (external dependencies) that are directly connected to the software system in scope. Typically, these other software systems sit outside the scope or boundary of your own software system, and you do not have responsibility or ownership of them.

Intended audience: Everybody, both technical and nontechnical people, inside and outside of the software development team.

Recommended for most teams: Yes.

Container Diagram

Once you understand how your system fits into the overall IT environment, a really useful next step is to zoom in to the system boundary with a Container diagram. A "container" is something like a server-side web application, single-page application, desktop application, mobile app, database schema, file system, etc. Essentially, a container is a separately runnable/deployable unit (e.g., a separate process space) that executes code or stores data.

The Container diagram shows the high-level shape of the software architecture and how responsibilities are distributed across it. It also shows the major technological choices and how the containers communicate with one another. It is a simple, high-level technology-focused diagram that is useful for software developers and support/ operations staff alike. An example C4 Container diagram is shown in Figure 24-25.

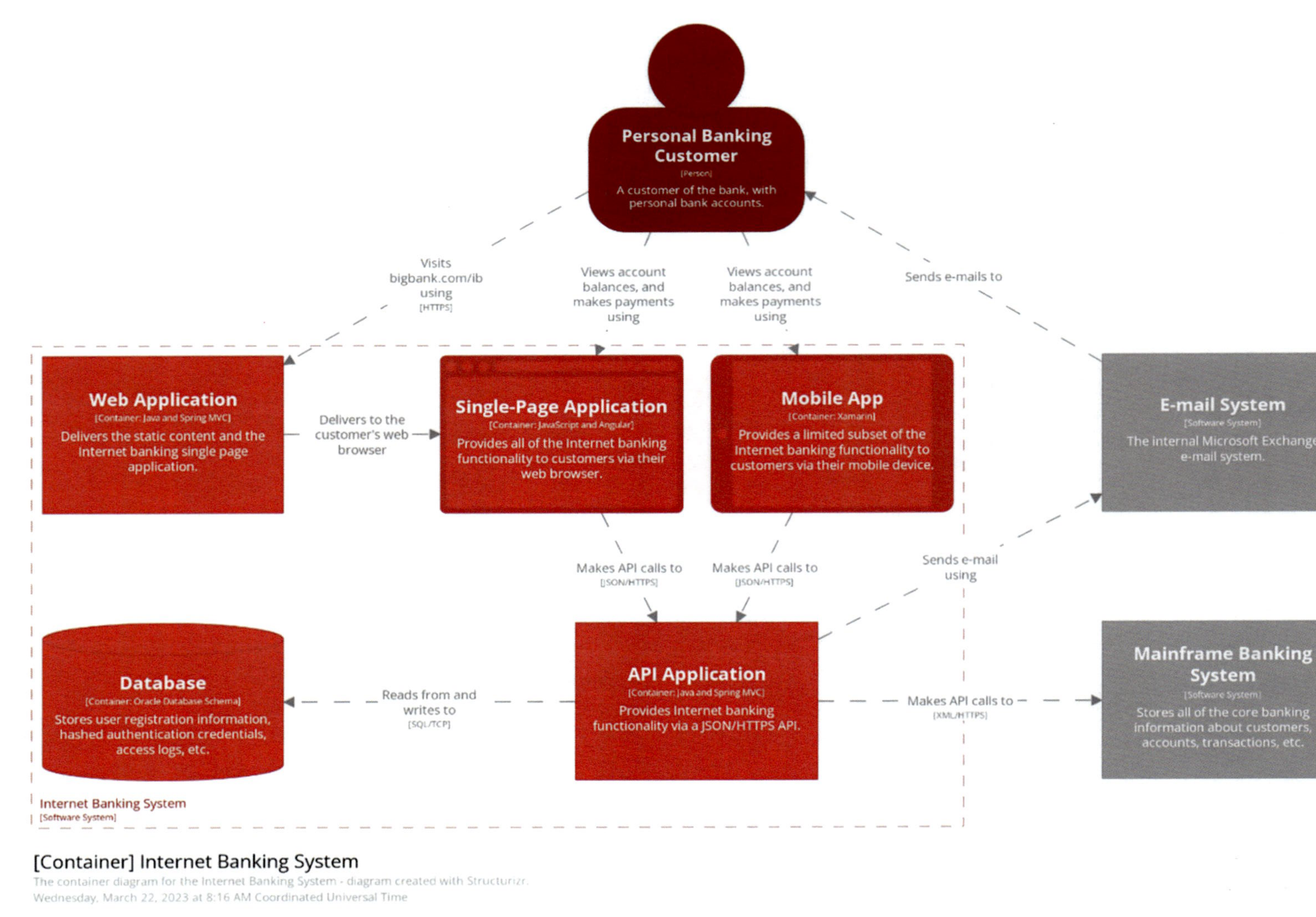

Figure 24-25. *A C4 Container Diagram*

Scope: A single software system.

Primary elements: Containers within the software system in scope.**Supporting elements**: People and software systems directly connected to the containers.

Intended audience: Technical people inside and outside of the software development team, including software architects, developers, and operations/support staff.

Recommended for most teams: Yes.

Notes: This diagram says nothing about clustering, load balancers, replication, failover, etc. because it will likely vary across different environments (e.g., production, staging, development, etc.). This information is better captured via one or more deployment diagrams.

Component Diagram

Next, you can zoom in and decompose each container further to identify the major structural building blocks and their interactions.

The Component diagram shows how a container is made up of a number of "components," what each of those components are, their responsibilities, and the technology/implementation details. An example C4 Component diagram is shown in Figure 24-26.

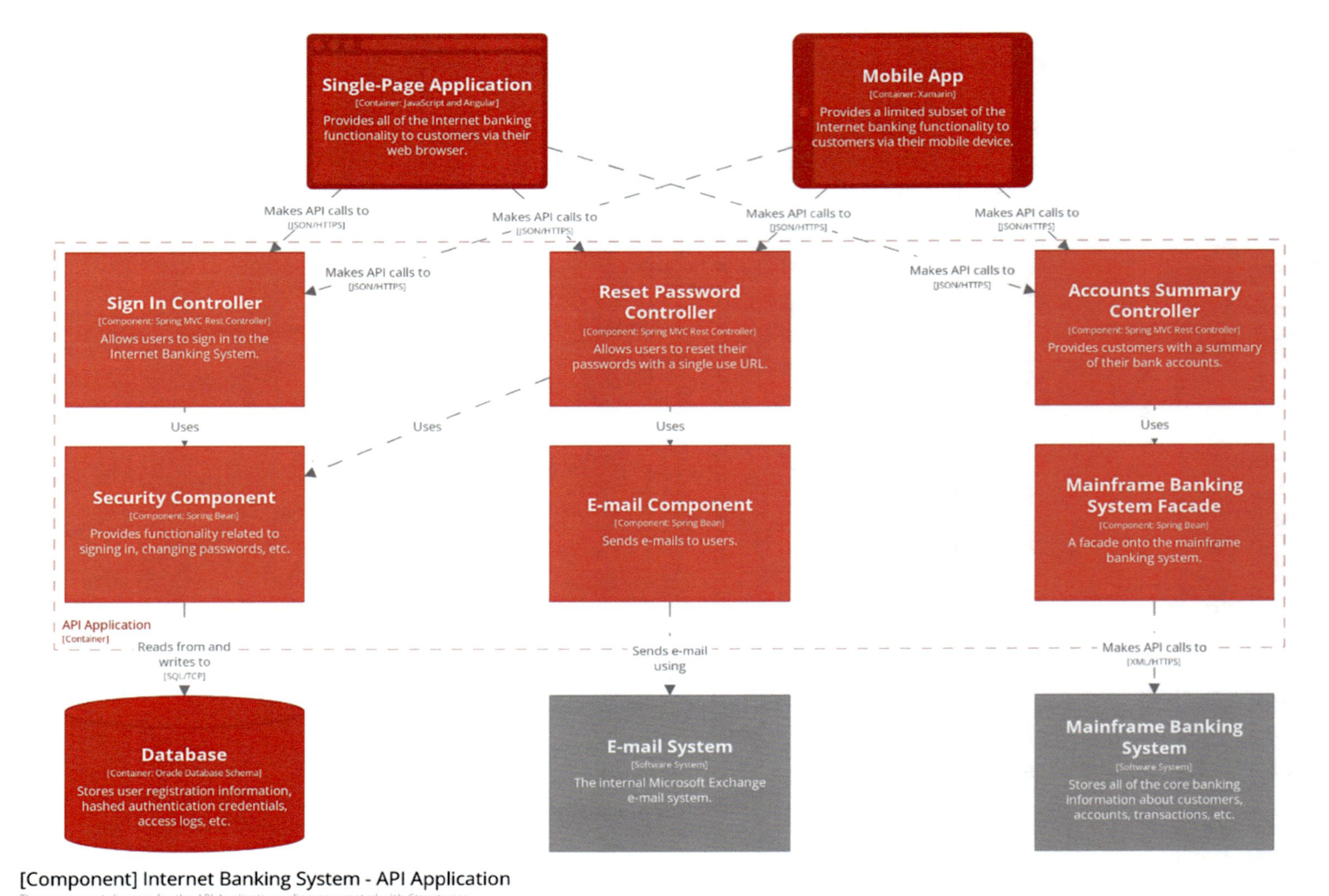

***Figure 24-26.** A C4 Component Diagram*

Scope: A single container.

Primary elements: Components within the container in scope.**Supporting elements**: Containers (within the software system in scope) plus people and software systems directly connected to the components.

Intended audience: Software architects and developers.

Recommended for most teams: No, only create component diagrams if you feel they add value and consider automating their creation for long-lived documentation.

Code Diagram

Finally, you can zoom in to each component to show how it is implemented as code, using UML class diagrams, entity relationship diagrams, or similar.

This is an optional level of detail and is often available on demand from tooling such as IDEs. Ideally, this diagram would be automatically generated using tooling (e.g., an IDE or UML modeling tool), and you should consider showing only those attributes and methods that allow you to tell the story that you want to tell. This level of detail is not recommended for anything but the most important or complex components. An example code diagram is shown in Figure 24-27.

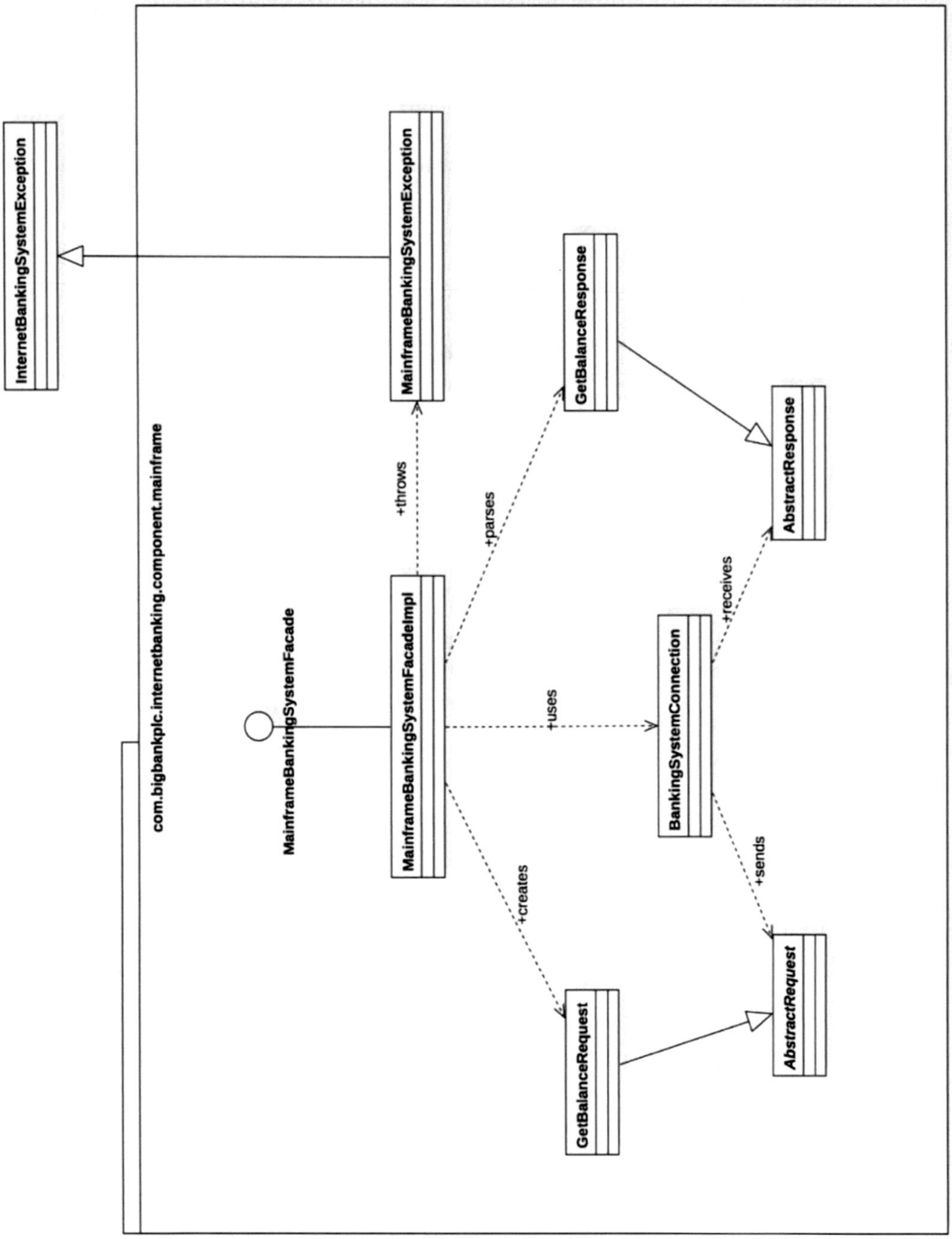

***Figure 24-27.** A C4 Code Diagram*

Scope: A single component.

Primary elements: Code elements (e.g., classes, interfaces, objects, functions, database tables, etc.) within the component in scope.

Intended audience: Software architects and developers.

Recommended for most teams: No, particularly for long-lived documentation because most IDEs can generate this level of detail on demand.

System Landscape Diagram

The C4 model provides a static view of a **single software system**, but, in the real world, software systems never live in isolation. For this reason, and particularly if you are responsible for a collection/portfolio of software systems, it is often useful to understand how all of these software systems fit together within a given enterprise, organization, department, etc. Essentially, this is a map of the software systems within the chosen scope, with a C4 drill-down for each software system of interest.

From a practical perspective, a system landscape diagram is really just a system context diagram without a specific focus on a particular software system. An example C4 system landscape diagram is shown in Figure 24-28.

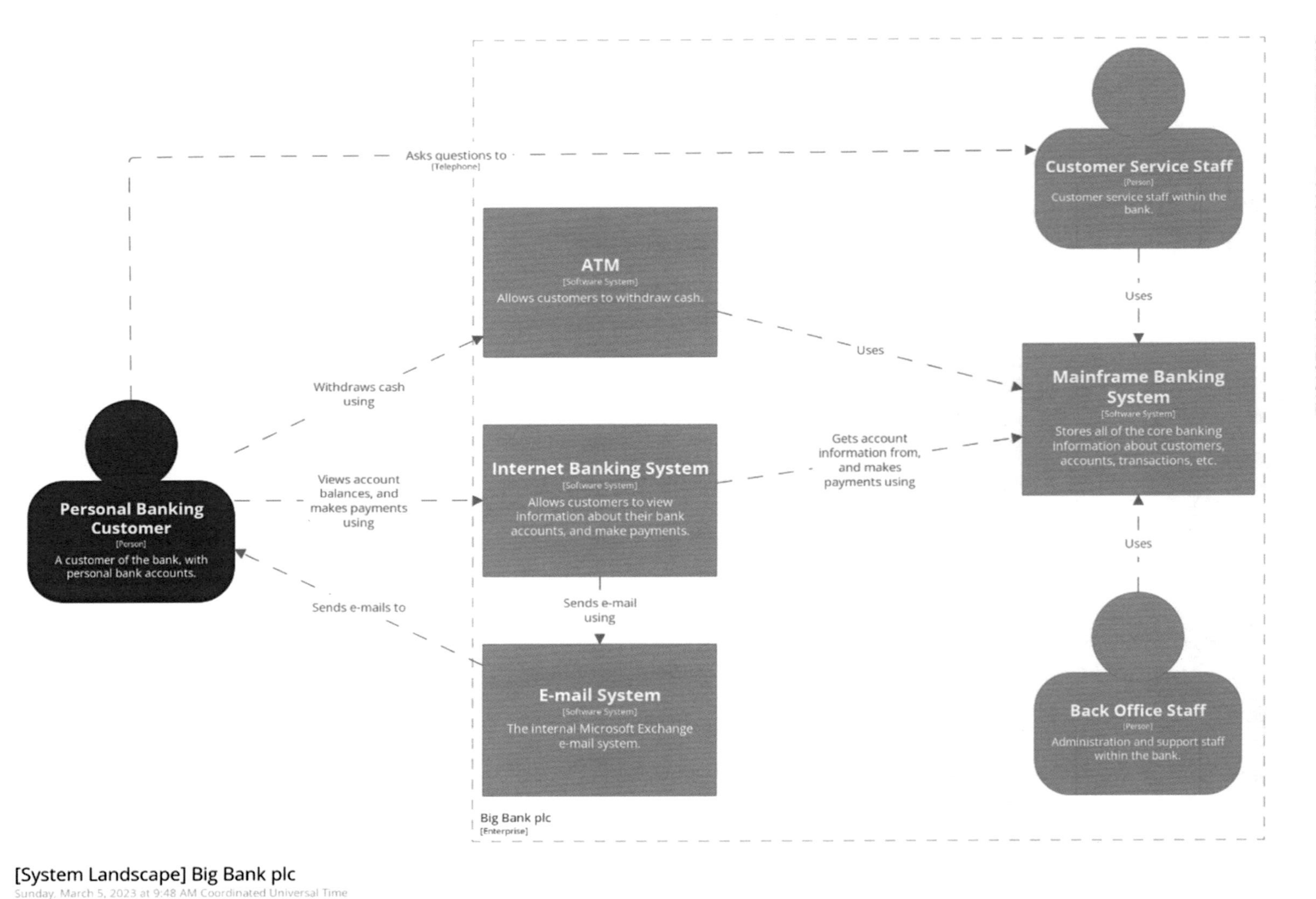

Figure 24-28. *A C4 System Landscape Diagram*

Scope: An enterprise/organization/department/etc.

Primary elements: People and software systems related to the chosen scope.

Intended audience: Technical and nontechnical people, inside and outside of the software development team.

Dynamic Diagram

A dynamic diagram can be useful when you want to show how elements in the static model collaborate at runtime to implement a user story, use case, feature, etc. This dynamic diagram is based upon a UML communication diagram (previously known as a "UML collaboration diagram"). It is similar to a UML sequence diagram although it allows a free-form arrangement of diagram elements with numbered interactions to indicate ordering. An example dynamic diagram is shown in Figure 24-29.

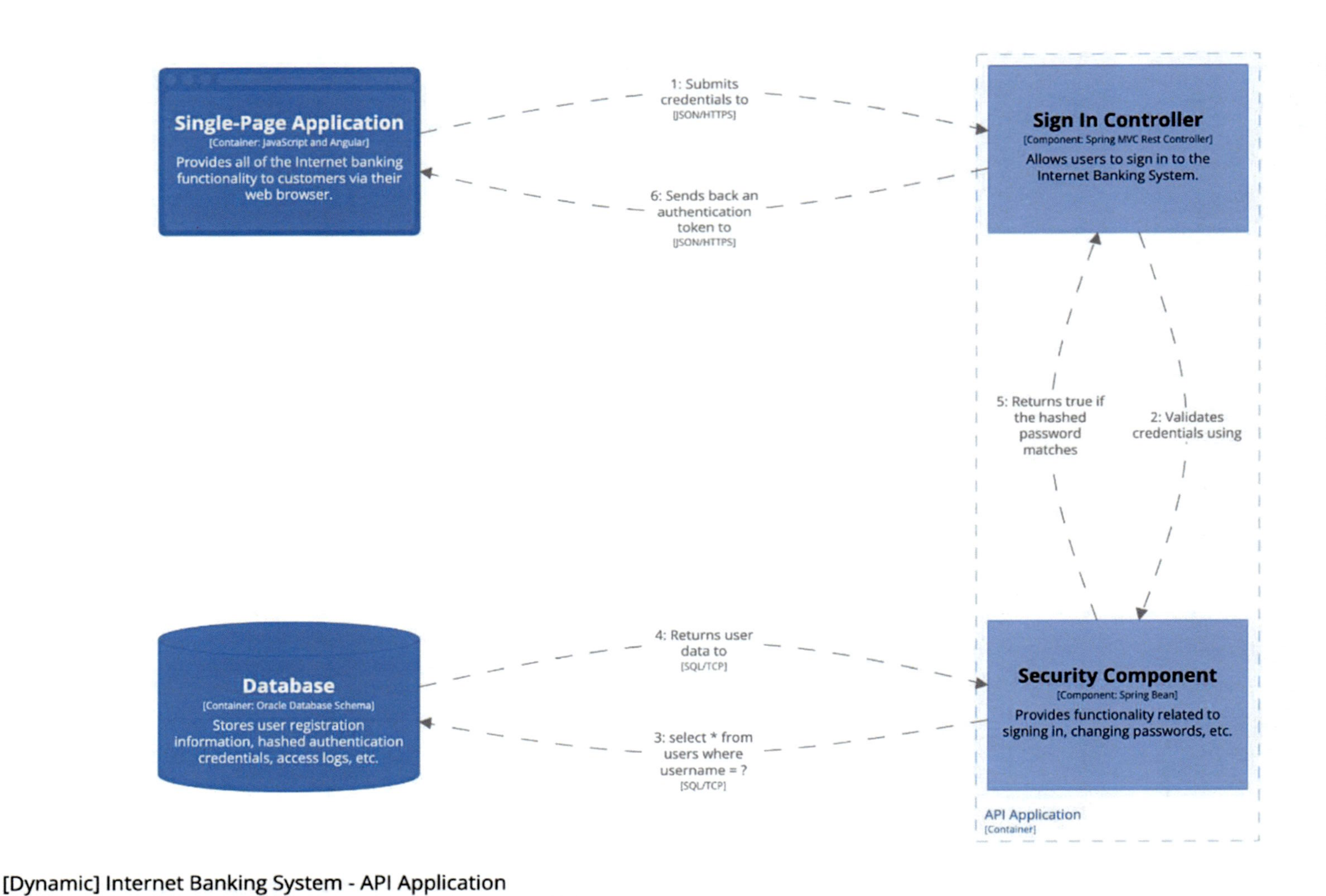

Figure 24-29. *A C4 Dynamic Diagram*

Scope: A particular feature, story, use case, etc.

Primary and supporting elements: Your choice—you can show software systems, containers, or components interacting at runtime.

Intended audience: Technical and nontechnical people, inside and outside of the software development team.

Notes: Feel free to use a UML sequence diagram if you prefer that visual style.

Deployment Diagram

A deployment diagram allows you to illustrate how instances of software systems and/or containers in the static model are deployed on to the infrastructure within a given **deployment environment** (e.g., production, staging, development, etc.). It is based upon a UML deployment diagram.

A **deployment node** represents where an instance of a software system/container is running; perhaps physical infrastructure (e.g., a physical server or device), virtualized infrastructure (e.g., IaaS, PaaS, a virtual machine), containerized infrastructure (e.g., a Docker container), an execution environment (e.g., a database server, Java EE web/application server, Microsoft IIS), etc. Deployment nodes can be nested.

You may also want to include **infrastructure nodes** such as DNS services, load balancers, firewalls, etc.

Feel free to use icons provided by Amazon Web Services, Azure, etc. to complement your deployment diagrams ... just make sure any icons you use are included in your diagram key/legend. An example deployment diagram is show in Figure 24-30.

Figure 24-30. *A C4 Deployment Diagram*

Scope: One or more software systems within a single deployment environment (e.g., production, staging, development, etc.).

Primary elements: Deployment nodes, software system instances, and container instances.

Supporting elements: Infrastructure nodes used in the deployment of the software system.

Intended audience: Technical people inside and outside of the software development team, including software architects, developers, infrastructure architects, and operations/support staff.

General Diagram Advice

To close this section, one final excerpt from the official C4 web page is reproduced for general advice that applies to any good software architecture diagram to ensure your diagram makes sense to the reader and can stand alone without you or another architect providing an external narrative. The C4 model makes the following recommendations:

Diagrams

- Every diagram should have a title describing the diagram type and scope (e.g., "System Context diagram for My Software System").
- Every diagram should have a key/legend explaining the notation being used (e.g., shapes, colors, border styles, line types, arrowheads, etc.).
- Acronyms and abbreviations (business/domain or technology) should be understandable by all audiences or explained in the diagram key/legend.

Elements

- The type of every element should be explicitly specified (e.g., Person, Software System, Container, or Component).
- Every element should have a short description, to provide an "at a glance" view of key responsibilities.
- Every container and component should have a technology explicitly specified.

Relationships

- Every line should represent a unidirectional relationship.
- Every line should be labeled, the label being consistent with the direction and intent of the relationship (e.g., dependency or data flow). Try to be as specific as possible with the label, ideally avoiding single words like "Uses."
- Relationships between containers (typically these represent inter-process communication) should have a technology/protocol explicitly labeled.

Summary

Effective documentation and communication are the bedrock of successful software architecture. As you have seen, capturing both the *what* and the *why* behind architectural decisions is not just a formality—it is a critical practice that ensures clarity, alignment, and continuity across teams and time. ADRs serve as the living memory of your project, providing a rigorous framework for decision-making, defending choices, and guiding future actions. By investing in meticulous documentation, you safeguard your architecture from misinterpretation and erosion, empowering both current and future teams to maintain, adapt, and evolve the system with confidence. The discipline of documenting and communicating your architecture is not merely about preserving the past; it is about securing the future of your project, your team, and your role as a software architect.

CHAPTER 25

Architectural Enforcement and Governance

> *Even systems with well-defined architectures are prone to structural erosion. The relentless onslaught of changing requirements that any successful system attracts can gradually undermine its structure. Systems that were once tidy become overgrown as PIECEMEAL GROWTH gradually allows elements of the system to sprawl in an uncontrolled fashion.*
>
> —Joseph Yoder and Brian Foote

Many well-designed architectures have failed to withstand the test of time. As the quote above notes, "*Even systems with well-defined architectures are prone to structural erosion.*"[1]

I want to stress that rarely is this the direct fault of developers. Should this type of decay occur over the course of your career, resist the temptation to assign blame. Llewellyn Falco, creator of strong-style pair programming and a leading exponent of the mob programming/teeming movement, advises teams to "*treat everyone with kindness, consideration, and respect.*" In his book on mob programming,[2] he continues with a valuable maxim:

> *We always assume that the person who wrote the code before us did the best they could with the knowledge and circumstances they were in at the time they wrote it.*

[1] Foote, B., & Yoder, J. (1997). *Big Ball of Mud*. Presented at the 4th Conference on Patterns, Languages of Programs (PLoP)

[2] Pyhäjärvi, M., Falco, L. (2015–2018). *Mob Programming Guidebook*. LeanPub. `https://www.mobprogrammingguidebook.com/`

M. Carducci, *Mastering Software Architecture*, https://doi.org/10.1007/979-8-8688-0410-6_25

This underscores a valuable truth that rarely (if ever) do the problems prevalent in decaying software system originate from maliciousness or a general disregard for architectural efforts; rather, these problems are a result of circumstances that are often outside the control of any single individual. This also means that such circumstances are also outside of our control. Our primary tool to combat structural erosion in a software system is to implement guardrails in the form of architectural governance and enforcement.

Architectural governance and enforcement are critical components of ensuring that an organization's software architecture aligns with its strategic goals, delivers value, and remains both aligned and sustainable over time. Proper governance helps to maintain the integrity of the architecture, while enforcement ensures adherence to standards, guidelines, and best practices.

Define Clear and Comprehensive Architectural Principles

As you have seen throughout this work, the prevalence of pattern-driven architecture often leads to misunderstanding and misalignment of vision when the architecture is defined by a broad pattern label. The Tailor-Made approach of deriving a unique architectural style that does not suffer from an overloaded label and is instead defined by architectural constraints will do much to reduce the risk of such misunderstandings. Broad understanding of an architectural style is, instead, limited by your documentation and communication efforts. The previous chapter offered extensive guidance on valuable practices that foster alignment and clear, unambiguous communication of both the *what* and the *why* of your architectural style.

In documenting your architectural style, its defining constraints, and other relevant paved roads and variances, you establish a set of clear, well-documented architectural principles that reflect the project or organization's strategic objectives, technical goals, and cultural values. Effort in capturing problem context, motivation, and decision drivers ensures that the architecture directly supports the organization's mission, vision, and operational goals.

Your documentation efforts should also comprehensively communicate well-defined architectural standards and guidelines that cover key aspects of software development, including technology selection, system design, data management, security, and deployment. Architecture diagrams also provide a *living reference* through which architecture and implementation teams may validate their work against to ensure ongoing alignment. *Living* is the operative word in this sentence. Regularly review and update these standards, diagrams, and architecture decisions to reflect new technological advancements, lessons learned from past projects, and changes in the business environment or underlying requirements.

It is critical that these resources are easily available to all concerned and should be published and updated in a specific location that is within convenient reach of teams. Beyond simply publishing documents, hosting regular tech talks, workshops, trainings, or architecture update meetings with development teams are effective ways to cascade and ensure everyone both understands the architectural standards and can apply them effectively. These efforts form part of the *ongoing support* that is crucial to avoid becoming an *ivory tower architect*.

Beyond communication with implementation teams, it is important that business stakeholders also understand the value of architecture. Often, structural decay is a consequence of shortsighted business decisions that put pressure on teams to cut corners and undermine the long-term viability of the overall architecture. Your detailed notes from the requirements analysis process (Chapter 4) will provide the business language to articulate to key stakeholders the long-term consequences of violating an important architectural principle for the sake of expediency. Do not expect this advice to be consistently dispositive and strive to trust that well-informed stakeholders are doing their best to balance short- and long-term needs.

Establishing a Governance Framework

The ADR template described in Chapter 24 includes the "deciders" in the Title and Metadata section. In the beginning, this might just be you or the architecture team. A more sustainable, long-term approach is to formalize the "deciders" by creating a formal governance structure that includes an architecture review board (ARB) or equivalent body. The ARB should be composed of senior architects, technical leads, and key stakeholders from across the organization.

Beyond sustainability, an ARB increases transparency and helps to further foster a culture of collaboration and shared ownership. For your ARB or other governance frameworks to operate smoothly, it is important to clearly define roles and responsibilities. This includes who is responsible for approving architectural decisions, managing variances, and enforcing standards.

This process democratizes decision-making. However, you should implement structured processes for decision-making, including the approval of architectural designs, technology stacks, and variances. Ensure that these processes are transparent, consistent, and efficient.

Within your governance framework, you must also establish a formal process for requesting and approving variances from architectural standards. This process should include a thorough evaluation of the proposed variance's impact on the overall architecture, including risks, benefits, and trade-offs/negative consequences. Ensure that every approved variance is documented in detail, including the rationale, scope, and conditions under which it was granted. This documentation should be easily accessible for future reference. You, or the governance body, should regularly review the implementation of variances to ensure teams applied these as intended. Conduct periodic reviews to assess whether variances are still necessary or if they should be phased out.

Design your governance framework to scale as the organization grows. This includes planning for the addition of new teams, technologies, and business units while maintaining architectural coherence. Also, ensure that your governance framework can adapt to new innovations and changes in the technology landscape. This might involve setting up innovation labs or "skunkworks" teams that can experiment with novel approaches outside the constraints of the standard governance model.

Architectural Enforcement Mechanisms

There are many avenues available for architectural enforcement. The most basic option is to perform periodic architecture or code reviews. This is especially important for critical projects or those involving complex or novel technologies. These reviews should assess compliance with established standards and identify any potential risks or deviations. Although simple, the primary challenge with this approach is one of scale. As the organization grows, this process can quickly place an untenable burden on the architecture team or otherwise cause architecture to become a bottleneck, undermining the value of your contributions to the project and the organization. This approach can also only identify deviations after they have happened. If the architecture is frequently ordering rework, this can foster an adversarial relationship between development and architecture.

As an alternative, consider that the easiest problem to fix is the one that never happened. W. Edwards Deming pioneered important improvements in the manufacturing sector with his Total Quality Management (TQM) strategy,[3] and his work continues to influence our modern DevOps movement. One of his famous *14 Points for Management* states the following:

> *Cease dependence on inspection to achieve quality. Eliminate the need for inspection on a mass basis by building quality into the product in the first place.*

A key component of Deming's theories around quality is to empower every individual on the factory floor to stop the entire line at any time as soon as they discover a problem. The modern equivalent of this is a continuous delivery pipeline that contains quality gates.

When we think about quality gates in software delivery, the emphasis is usually on automated testing and static analysis. Although these tools have immense value, code that is *behaviorally* correct is not necessarily *architecturally* correct.

In Chapter 14, you learned about the Modular Monolith Abstract Style. In this style, each domain module is implemented as a separate package or assembly, and all classes are scoped *internal* to enforce and maintain modularity and decoupling across components. When developers follow this practice, the structure of the system is maintained, even in a shared codebase. When the time comes to decompose that monolith into a Service-Based style, the process is trivial *if no developer ever decides to cut corners*. Consider the scenario where a team is coding down to the wire to prepare for that Friday night deployment that we prefer not to talk about. In the moment, it would seem to be such a trivial sin to, *just this one time*, couple two modules by violating the architecture's modularity constraints. This is where our CI/CD pipelines must "halt the assembly line" because it has detected a quality violation.

You can accomplish this by introducing *automated architectural enforcement*. My go-to tool for this purpose is Sonargraph (`https://www.hello2morrow.com/products/sonargraph`). Sonargraph is a powerful static code analyzer that allows you to monitor a software system for technical quality and enforce rules regarding software architecture, metrics, and other aspects in all stages of the development process. One aspect of Sonargraph is a DSL to describe software architecture, and, through this, we can define

[3] Deming, W. E. (1986). *Out of the Crisis*. MIT

rules that define permitted and prohibited interactions between modules. Integrated into a CI pipeline, Sonargraph will immediately detect a violation as soon as the build is triggered, halting the process and informing the developer of the violation.

Other tools in this vein include ArchUnit (`https://www.archunit.org/`), a free, simple, and extensible library for checking the architecture of your Java code using any plain Java unit test framework. ArchUnit's .NET counterpart is the C# fork of ArchUnit, ArchUnitNet, a free, simple library for checking the architecture of C# code. Another .NET alternative inspired by ArchUnit is NetArchTest (`https://github.com/BenMorris/NetArchTest`), which offers a fluent API for .NET Standard that can enforce architectural rules in unit tests. At the time of this writing, ArchUnitNet seems to be more active than NetArchTest.

When designing APIs that must conform to a standard, Spectral (`https://stoplight.io/open-source/spectral`) offers an open source API style guide enforcer and linter.

These tools and others aid in integrating architectural governance with DevOps practices to ensure that architecture standards are enforced throughout the software delivery lifecycle.

Empower Teams to Succeed

Invest in continuous education and training for architects and development teams to keep them updated on the latest architectural practices, tools, and technologies. Encourage open communication and collaboration between architects, developers, and other stakeholders. This can be facilitated through regular meetings, architecture workshops, and collaborative tools.

Also, consider creating communities of practice or guilds, where architects and developers can share knowledge, discuss challenges, and collaboratively solve problems. This fosters a sense of ownership and collective responsibility for architectural integrity.

Deming consistently focused on creating a culture of continuous improvement; I encourage all architects to do the same in collaboration with software development leadership. You should regularly hold retrospectives on architectural governance processes to identify what's working and what needs improvement. Involve a broad range of stakeholders in these discussions to get diverse perspectives.

Architectural governance can be disruptive initially. It is helpful to use pilot programs to test new approaches or tools before rolling them out across the organization. This allows you to identify potential issues and refine your approach based on real-world experience.

Finally, recognize that architectural governance is not static. Be willing to evolve your governance processes as the organization's needs change, technology advances, and new preferred practices emerge.

Summary

Architectural governance and enforcement are vital for ensuring that an organization's software architecture is aligned with its business goals, remains robust, and can adapt to changing needs. By defining clear principles, establishing a strong governance framework, and implementing both automated and manual enforcement mechanisms, you can maintain the integrity of your architecture while allowing for necessary flexibility. Managing variances, fostering a culture of excellence, and ensuring alignment with agile and DevOps practices are also crucial components of effective governance.

Moreover, by continuously measuring effectiveness, planning for evolution, and encouraging ongoing improvement, you can create a governance model that not only supports current operations but also positions the teams or organization for future success. In essence, effective architectural governance is about balancing control with flexibility, ensuring that innovation thrives within a well-defined and sustainable framework.

CHAPTER 26

The Art of Being an Architect

> *We are called to be architects of the future, not its victims.*
>
> —R. Buckminster Fuller

At this point, we have covered much of what it takes to master software architecture. You now have the broad foundation of knowledge necessary to design an architecture that is a holistic fit. Unfortunately, after analyzing requirements, deriving one or more candidate tailor-made architectures, evaluating said architectures, collaboratively selecting a single style, documenting it, designing a software system that adheres to the style, and communicating the design to the implementation teams, your work is just beginning. Architecture is more than simply solving problems, deriving styles, or designing systems; it is ultimately about stepping into a role of visionary technical leadership and effecting meaningful change within an organization. This is arguably the single most difficult aspect of software architecture. Your skills in effecting change will be the ultimate measure of success over the course of your career.

The Tailor-Made Architecture Model focuses on architecture design by constraint, and you have seen that several architectural styles presented in the previous section often require substantial change in technologies used, practices and behavior of teams, and even the entire organizational structure. Every organization has a finite tolerance for change that will necessarily temper our efforts. Although you may have a grand vision for the future of any given system or organization, it is important to remain pragmatic and balanced in your approach to change. This may require you to take a phased approach to architecture, where you limit your efforts to only a limited number of changes at a time. In truth, this is one of the most difficult realities to accept as an effective software architect.

M. Carducci, *Mastering Software Architecture*, https://doi.org/10.1007/979-8-8688-0410-6_26

There have been many attempts to systematize this process like the Architecture Tradeoff Analysis Method (ATAM)[1] process described in the book *Evaluating Software Architectures*, the techniques described in the book *Discussing Design*,[2] and the approach provided in the book *Articulating Design Decisions*;[3] however, many of them share certain elements. These were analyzed and combined with personal experience to provide an approach that will apply to most situations.

To systematize the process, you can break it down into the following stages:

1. Identify the problems that require change
2. Identify potential changes
3. Identify resources necessary to make the change
4. Plan to orchestrate the change
5. Execute the plan

This chapter will describe how to be effective in all those phases of effecting change.

Identify the Problems That Require Change

Before attempting to define the problem, you must understand both the problem and the environment surrounding the problem. The requirements analysis process described in Chapter 4 provides a useful starting point for identifying problems within the business domain. In this process, you should identify and define all the problems and then investigate potential solutions, keeping in mind that those solutions may impact the other problems and solutions for the project, company, customer, or user. Documenting the problems and solutions forces you to think through problems and solutions before presenting them to others. The more thought you and your team put into both the problems and solutions before communicating them, the more competent you will appear. One useful approach is to start by writing down each problem, without solutions, and break them down in the following way:

[1] Clements, P., Kazman, R., Klein, M (2012). *Evaluating Software Architectures: Methods and Case Studies*, Addison-Wesley

[2] Connor, A., Irizarry, A. (2015). *Discussing Design: Improving Communication and Collaboration Through Critique*, O'Reilly Media

[3] Greever, T. (2020). *Articulating Design Decisions: Communicate with Stakeholders, Keep Your Sanity, and Deliver the Best User Experience*, O'Reilly Media

1. State each of the problems, remembering to avoid specifying a solution, emotional or personal biases, or accusations. Also, remember to minimize the scope to only cover a single problem.

2. State the implications and impacts of the problem. Remember to document identifying measures or thresholds if possible.

3. State the best possible outcome that any solution to the problem could reasonably achieve.

Keep in mind that identifying and defining many problems like this will take time. If you are new to the team, you should spend a few months doing this process as you work on the project itself. For a new project (since there is no knowledge of what the existing problems are yet), it might make sense to use a predefined architectural style for a couple of months before making changes from prior experience.

Identify Potential Changes

Key factors for any proposed change are the costs and benefits to others as well as how others may respond to the potential solution, the relative advantage of your proposed change. There are a couple approaches to evaluating viable solutions and the approaches to apply those changes.

The Four-Way Test

When defining the problems and the solutions, evaluate how ethical or fair your evaluation of the problem is and, more importantly, how ethical or fair each alternative solution is. Instead of creating a mechanism from scratch, it is wise to draw from existing sources.

Rotary, an organization that helps business owners and operators, has created a simple rubric for making business decisions[4] which you may apply when defining alternative solutions. Rotary calls this rubric the "Four-Way Test" and defines it as follows:

> *... a nonpartisan and nonsectarian ethical guide for Rotarians to use for their personal and professional relationships.*

[4] Rotary.org. *Guiding Principles*. Retrieved from `https://my.rotary.org/en/guiding-principles`

The four questions to ask regarding these decisions are

1. Is it the TRUTH?
2. Is it FAIR to all concerned?
3. Will it build GOODWILL and BETTER FRIENDSHIPS?
4. Will it be BENEFICIAL to all concerned?

These rules are an excellent starting point when deciding if you should pursue the identified change.

Assertiveness vs. Cooperativeness

Cooperation is always more powerful than competition.

—Bob Proctor

Assessing how to achieve agreement on solutions and, occasionally, even on problem definitions is crucial. Some may not even view the identified problems as problems. This is particularly true for preventative solutions, speculative solutions, or technological and process improvements that bring gradual benefit over time. These can be a tough sell, particularly in the absence of a perceived need. Regrettably, sometimes the relative value of a potential solution can be difficult for others to see until the pain of the need is first felt.

There also exist many cases where one person's problem is viewed by others as a feature. For example, if it takes four months to bring someone up to speed on how the code works on a system because there is no documentation, no automated tests, and the code is not structured very well, some teammates might view the situation as beneficial for job security, and they may not want to fix the problems. However, another teammate may point out that the employee cannot go on a long vacation or may have to work long hours because they are the only person who can do the job, making the situation a problem rather than a benefit. From the project manager's perspective, code that many of the developers can maintain rather than only one or two is more valuable code because there is less inherent risk associated with that code.

One method for establishing a strategy for building consensus is known as the Assertiveness vs. Cooperativeness diagram, based on the Thomas-Kilmann conflict mode instrument[5] as shown in Figure 26-1.

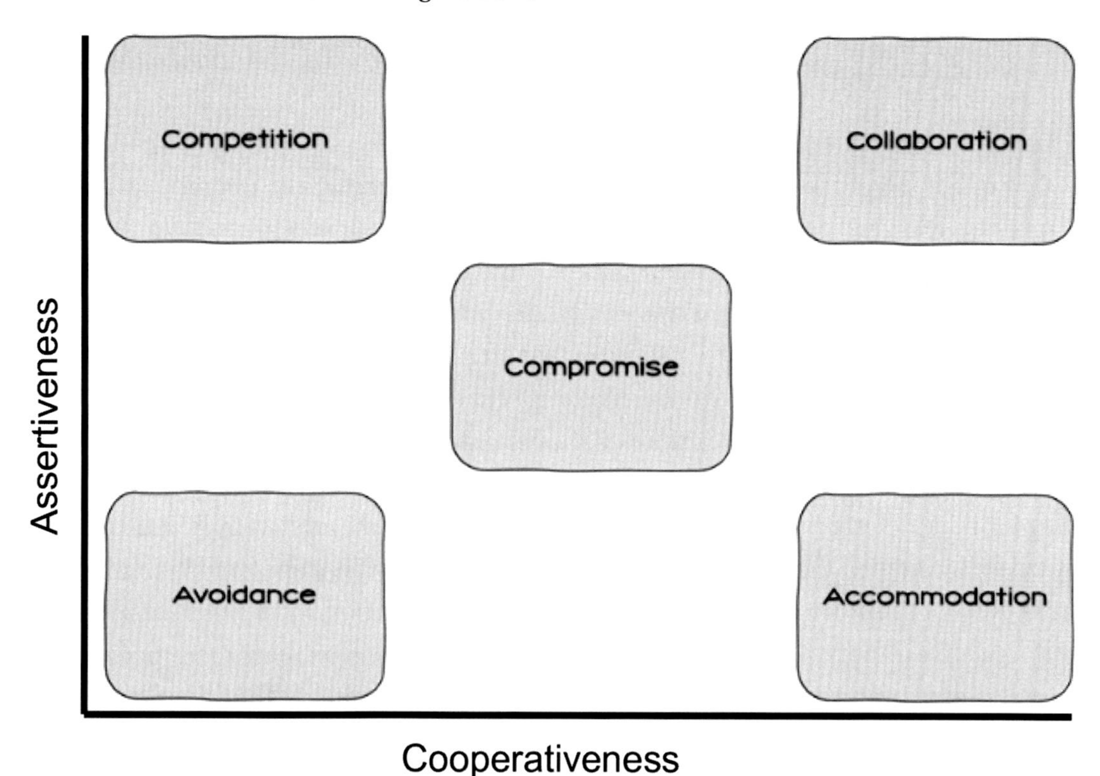

Figure 26-1. *The Assertiveness vs. Cooperativeness Diagram*

An architect's goal should be to work to present changes or solutions in such a way that one is as far to the upper right as is possible. Avoidance is bad. Competition, compromise, or accommodation is a little better, but collaboration is the ultimate goal. Not every situation will allow you to get the other parties all the way to the collaboration level. Your aim should be to prevent both avoidance for yourself and others while working collaboratively.

[5] Thomas, K., Kilmann, R. (1978). *Comparison of Four Instruments Measuring Conflict Behavior.* Psychological Reports, 42

The Weighted Decision Matrix

Once all the problems have been defined and all of the other parties' positions have been considered, it is time to identify solutions. Beware to avoid blanket solutions without defining alternatives such as "*this team should use scrum and all of their productivity problems would be solved*" or "*this team should use microservices because all their design problems would be solved.*"

As a rough target and an exercise in comprehensive thinking, aim to produce and *document* at least two or three alternative solutions for each identified problem. As you saw in Chapter 24, the architecture documentation process is a tool for both evaluation and communication. You may solicit solutions from others (e.g., the process in Chapter 22), but you should be careful to emphasize that architecture will consider multiple approaches, including, potentially, not making a change. Once you or your team have defined at least two solutions, it is time to evaluate each solution. Some use a weighted decision matrix (also known as Pugh matrix,[6] decision grid, solution matrix, criteria rating form, or criteria-based matrix). To create a decision matrix, start by identifying the criteria for evaluating the solutions on one side, and then list the different alternatives across the top. In any problem domain or context, each criterion will possess a different level of relative importance. Consequently, the weighted decision matrix approach prescribes assigning a relative weight to each criterion. The weights for the various criteria should add up to 100 as this forces you to rate them relative to one another. It is usually a bad sign if any two criteria possess the same weight. Most importantly, to maintain objectivity in this process, you should define these weights before evaluating any of the solution alternatives.

Once you have defined all the weights of the criteria, you are ready to take an impartial look at each of the alternatives and determine how well each addresses the various evaluation criteria. During this process, rank each solution using a value one to n where n is the number of alternatives. Higher values indicate how well the solution addresses a given criterion. It is important that none of them tie in any single criterion. Should this occur, it will take time to mindfully break ties if the two are extremely close.

During this process, a good test of objectivity is consistently scoring both the positive and the negatives that a potential solution brings for each criterion. Everything is a trade-off, and failure to identify trade-offs (e.g., one option is consistently positive, or one

[6] Pugh, S. (1981). *Concept selection: a method that works.* Proceedings International Conference on Engineering Design

option is consistently negative) is a sure sign of either bias or an error of omission. An example is shown in Figure 26-2.

	Solution Alternative 1	Solution Alternative 2	Solution Alternative 3
Criteria 1 (30)	1	3	2
Criteria 2 (25)	2	1	3
Criteria 3 (10)	2	1	3
Criteria 4 (15)	3	2	1
Criteria 5 (20)	1	2	3
Totals:	165	195	240

Figure 26-2. *A Completed Weighted Decision Matrix*

Some will make two passes through this process. The two-pass approach first focuses on considering the relative cost, and the second pass focuses on considering the relative benefit for each potential solution. While the two-pass approach takes longer, the additional exercise will lead you toward richer decisions.

This process is helpful to arriving at objective solutions; however, this is not merely an academic exercise, it is the first step toward leading change in the project or organization.

Another benefit of this process is its ability to help overcome a pro-innovation bias common in many software architects. Our breadth of knowledge and the diversity of contexts within which we tend to work commonly correlate with a trait of *techno-optimism*. The key to success (and building credibility over time) lies in the ability to connect a potential innovation to a genuine need within an organization. Change and innovation purely for change's sake is rarely a path to success and adoption. There must be a broad perception of value across both those individuals who have authority and influence to drive change and those who adopt it. The operative word here being *perception*. If we see value that others do not, we will not be successful; shaping perceptions is key.

Organizationally speaking, change equates to risk. Driving change requires clearly communicating that the risk of inaction outweighs the risk of action.

Understanding the Attributes of an Innovation

Another approach to evaluating potential solutions is to examine them through the lens of the core attributes of an innovation or solution. Everett Rogers' *Diffusion of Innovations*[7] formally defines the five key attributes of an innovation (Figure 26-3).

Attribute	Definition
Relative Advantage	The degree to which an innovation is perceived as better than the idea it supersedes.
Compatibility	The degree to which an innovation is perceived as being consistent with the existing values, past experience, and needs of potential adopters.
Complexity	The extent of the difficulty or friction adopters experience in attempting to adopt an innovation
Trialability	The degree to which an innovation may be experimented with on a limited basis.
Observability	The degree to which the results of an innovation are visible to others.

Figure 26-3. *Everett Rogers' Innovation Attributes*

Each of these attributes correlates either positively or negatively to the overall probability of success for a given solution and is common to virtually every innovation. Looking at any innovation through the lens of these variables can prove illuminating. Sometimes, the solution is not perceived as advantageous; sometimes, the advantages are clear, but teams are too set in their ways or can't make time for change. Sometimes, the change is simply too complex.

Use any or all the above tools to evaluate potential solutions and understand that the more effort you put into evaluating potential solutions, the better positioned you will be to effect meaningful change.

---

[7] Rogers, E. (2003). *Diffusion of Innovations, 5th Edition,* Free Press

Identify Resources Necessary to Make the Change

An architect position is a technical leadership position. Your efficacy in such a role depends on your ability to

- Communicate, guide, influence, and improve the outcome for others on the development teams, the management, the customer, and the user
- Identify things that you can, cannot, or should not influence
- Analyze your own influence, the influence of others within your organization, and your organization itself on the problem and the potential solutions

These factors are the measure that sets good and great architects apart from people who just have the title.

Some Terminology

Before moving forward, it is important to define several key terms: *processes, products, services, decisions,* and *evaluation.*

Processes

A process is a collection of planned tasks, events, and activities, usually arranged in a sequence, which allows the organization to meet their goals and objectives. Many organizational processes are informal, lacking documentation or strict enforcement. It is important to recognize that even informal processes may be just as important—and sometimes as hard—to effect change in as more well-documented processes that the organization enforces with rigor.

Products

A tangible or intangible item that the organization produces using labor. Sometimes, different departments will refer to company offerings as products, while another part of the organization will refer to them as services. Many accounting, marketing, or salespeople will refer to anything that the organization sells as a product. Others may define products as objects the organization sells, licenses, leases, or gives to another party. This semantic ambiguity underscores the value of tools like DDD that explicitly define domain vocabulary in the form of the *ubiquitous language*.

Notably, very few products exist in isolation and instead are often accompanied by services to either add value to the product, maintain the product, enhance the benefits of the product, or decrease the ongoing costs of the product.

Services

A business service is often an intangible asset that the organization provides for a fee, given as an incentive, or included as part of a broader offering. Services are sometimes tangible, or involve tangible assets, leading to challenges in differentiating services from products. Services provide a measurable, tangible, real-world change that may not reside on the customer or users' hardware.

Decisions

A conclusion or definition of action used in future activities. These may take the form of which product to pursue, what order to produce products, hiring, firing, technology usage, and many other actions that an organization makes. Whether you are making decisions such as picking technologies, architectural styles, or design processes or other collaborators (managers, users, customers, or developers) making decisions such as financial, acceptance of the product, implementation, or any one of many business decisions, the success or failure of an organization is influenced by many daily decisions made by you and your collaborators.

Evaluation

Any effort to analyze a situation or state concluding with an appraisal or assessment. You must learn to evaluate all the aspects of the situation to know what can be done and, more importantly, what cannot or should not be done. Some inputs for evaluation are

- The costs (financial costs, time costs, opportunity costs, etc.) and benefits for each evaluated option
- The organization, yourself, and the others involved before deciding to attempt to effect change

Formal evaluations may feel onerous at first, but after performing them a few times or over a certain period, you will become comfortable with all aspects of evaluating and find yourself immediately performing the analysis informally while in meetings or when reading emails. This process forms an integral part of your overall *architectural awareness* and is a key skill you will continue to utilize throughout your entire career.

Identify the Resources Necessary to Make the Change

Know the Entanglement, Environment, and Endurance of Change

There are three things to consider about any process, product, service, or decision that you must consider:

- How *entangled* is it with other aspects of the project?
- How *embedded* in the environment is it?
- How much *endurance* does the solution (and the organization) have? This is especially important in the case of solutions where the benefit of payoff of the effort comes later.

Entanglement

The decision of whether to pursue a change must include how entangled that change is with other aspects of the project. These entanglements may have direct or indirect impacts on the architecture and software development teams.

An example that has both direct and indirect entanglement is a decision to refactor a legacy project from using SOAP to RESTful interfaces.

Direct

- Communication efforts and meetings to convince both the customer and management that the change is justified
- Effort on the part of the team(s) necessary to create the new service interfaces

- Effort on the part of the team(s) to deprecate and later remove the legacy SOAP interfaces
- The effort involved in rigorous testing of the new interfaces as any failures will be far more politically damaging than defects introduced from new functionality

Indirect

- The consumers of the services will have to rewrite portions of their code.
- The schedule will be impacted by a delay in delivery of user functionality.
- The customers will have to pay for the changes both in development costs and in decreased value in the short term from pending user functionality.

Environment

The decision of whether to pursue a change must also include why that aspect originally occurred in the project, business, or customer that established the original process, product, service, or decision. When evaluating the environment within which you intend to make a change, a few questions should be asked:

- Why was the decision originally made the way that it was (are there existing ADRs or other decision documentation)?
- Would the same decision be made now as was made originally (has the problem context changed)?
- What has changed that should convince others to change it now?
- How will this impact all parties?
- How will all parties perceive this change?
- Is there a plan to phase in the new change?
- Is there a way to determine if it is working (or working better) or not?

Endurance

Finally, you should approach the decision of whether to pursue a change with more care and consideration than is typical among architects today. Consider how much effort is necessary to complete the change, including non-optimal paths to success, time impacts to the delivery schedule, risk of reputation damage if failure occurs, and risk of impact to the existing project's progress. Also, consider the ongoing costs post change and compare them to the costs of leaving things the same. Based on these factors, make a calculated choice to determine if you are willing to take on the change. Picking your battles is critical.

Know the Organization

Systematic Analysis

It is important for you to truly set aside any biases you may have when evaluating an organization. This part of the analysis may be best performed the first few times with a group of coworkers who possess both good judgment and good insight into the broader organization. You must strive to create an environment of candor, where participants feel comfortable being very honest about the organization, and it may need to be at least partially anonymous to encourage such candor. There are five categories that this group should evaluate.

Rigid/Flexible

Analyze how rigid the organizational structure is.

Alignment

Recognize whether your position lines up with the change that needs to occur and evaluate if the organization will allow one to effect change even if it pushes boundaries for an architect's typical job description.

Resources

Check to see if the change you want to make will be affordable both in the short and long term and/or if going without the change is affordable if the change is a potential cost savings.

Time

Evaluate if there is enough schedule to make changes and still meet deadlines.

Relationships

Determine how strong the relationship is between

- Business management and the customer
- The architect and the user
- Management and the team
- The architect and management
- Owners/stockholders and the management

Know Yourself and Your Place in the World

Systematic Analysis

Objective self-evaluation is rarely a skill that comes naturally. Consequently, you should initially perform this part of the analysis with the aid of a trustworthy and motivated colleague. Again, fostering an environment of trust and candor is essential; your colleague will need to feel comfortable being very honest.

This may be an uncomfortable experience at first. However, the good news is that your self-evaluation regarding various changes you hope to initiate will become easier to evaluate over time. It is also important to keep in mind that the answer will often be that you *should not* try to effect a given change for one or more of many reasons that will emerge during this analysis. Chapter 4 introduced five components that are necessary to effect change, namely:

- Authority
- Accountability
- Responsibility
- Knowledge
- Will

It is necessary to evaluate your position and role with respect to these five components.

Authority

Has anyone in the organization granted you authorization or authority over the problem or the solution? If so, is this authority recognized by others involved in the change effort?

Accountability

Are the outcomes, both positive and negative, directly impacting you, personally? Can you afford the consequences of a worst-case failure scenario?

Responsibility

Do you have an obligation to influence the thing you wish to change? Is this within the scope of your job description?

Knowledge (Know-How)

Do you know about the thing that you wish to change? Do you know what all the available alternatives are? Do you know what the result of an evaluation of the alternatives is? Do you know what the best and worst outcomes could be?

Will

Do you have the desire to overcome the challenges related to making the change you are proposing? In other words, are you prepared for the emotional, intellectual, and political investment required? Moreover, do you genuinely want to engage in leading the change?

There are tools later in this chapter that will take the results of this analysis and predict issues as well as identify remediation actions to help prevent the worst negative outcomes.

Also, it is unlikely that you will possess all five components necessary for change. Where gaps exist, you must identify your counterparts able to fill those gaps.

Truly Know Your Counterparts

Systematic Analysis

Consistent with the previous areas of analysis, to achieve objectivity this part of the analysis may be best performed the first few times with a colleague you trust to deliver an unvarnished perspective rather than simply agreeing with your assessment of the problem or a particular solution out of misplaced loyalty or friendship. As always, an environment of trust and candor is necessary as they need to feel comfortable being very honest about others. Likewise, you need to be in an environment where you can be honest about how you feel toward others while guarding against preconceptions that may cloud the evaluation of others. It is particularly important not to get into any gossiping or bad mouthing but instead be as factual, detached, and unbiased as possible to perform a proper evaluation.

Once again, it is important to keep in mind that the answer will often be that one should *not* try to effect the change for one or more of many reasons that will emerge in this analysis. We must evaluate our counterparts using the same five components to fill necessary gaps.

Authority

Do they possess authorization or authority over the problem or the solution? If so, is this authority recognized by others involved in the change effort?

Accountability

Are the outcomes, both positive and negative, directly impacting them, personally? Can they afford the consequences of a worst-case failure scenario?

Responsibility

Do they have an obligation to influence the thing you wish to change? Is this within the scope of their job description?

Knowledge

Do they know about the thing that you wish to change? Do they know what all the available alternatives are? Do they know what the result of an evaluation of the alternatives is? Do they know what the best and worst outcomes could be?

Will

Do they have the desire to overcome the challenges related to making the change you are proposing? Are they prepared for the emotional, intellectual, and political investment required? Moreover, do they genuinely want to engage in leading the change?

The Diagnostic Matrix

The following diagnostic matrix identifies the potential outcomes of pursuing a change. It specifies the worst-case outcome, but remember that the reality will probably be less absolute. When reviewing this matrix, do not become discouraged; instead, treat this as a tool to aid in identifying potential paths and outcomes you wish to avoid. **The *Diagnostic Matrix* will help you predict or understand where things are going wrong, while the *Approach Matrix* in the next section will help identify paths to success.**

To use the tool for predictions of possible negative outcomes, first evaluate yourself regarding the change you wish to make in the categories on the left side and then second evaluate your organization using the criteria across the top. Alternatively, it can be used to help identify the potential missing attributes for actors by reading the cells and seeing which scenarios apply to your situation and then see which organizational and individual attributes may be causing the issue. The diagnostic matrix is shown in Figure 26-4.

		Organization/Project				
Individual		Project Flexibility (Organization does not change with the requirements)	Structure Mismatch (project or company structure)	Funding (Tight or insufficient funding)	Schedule (Tight or insufficient time available)	Relationship Strength (Management to Customer, User, Team, and Owners)
	Authority (recognized as a person to make the final decision)	Delegation is not "real" and change cannot actually occur. Everything is a bureaucracy.	You do not have the authority to drive change so no one collaborates with you because other authorities have more pull than you.	You do not have the authority to get people funded to do work so the work never gets done. You cannot acquire the funding for tools so the work is not good enough or never gets done.	You are unable to move things around in the schedule. When something comes up and dependencies are inverted, there is no way for you to course correct.	No one listens to you. You are not able to effect change because you have not established authority in your relationships so passive aggressive behavior or passive disregard occurs.
	Accountability (One will get in trouble if it fails)	Nothing can change so you do nothing because nothing will happen to you and everything burns around you.	You do not have accountability. There are no consequences when you fail, so you stop being motivated to succeed.	You can spend money but you do not care if it is effective. You become wasteful, and someday someone realizes it and eliminates you.	Things that are late have no consequences for you. Eventually someone gets fed up, but it takes long enough that you destroy your reputation.	No one listens because no one will be hurt if they do not do things for you. They know there are no consequences and/or they do not care about you.

Figure 26-4. *The Diagnostic Matrix*

	Responsibility (Part of job description and recognized by others)	Nothing can change and you know that you will not be blamed because you "did your part." In the end you are associated with the organization's failures.	You do not have responsibility for the thing that is failing. You will either distance yourself or someone will try to make you accountable for it even though it is not yours.	You do not have the responsibility for the funds because someone else is responsible for the accounting, but you answer for it and malinvestment occurs.	You have no ability to affect the schedule and end up on a series of "death march" projects.	No one listens to you because you are trying to change something that is not your job. They have no personal stake in helping you because they know that you would not go above and beyond for them.
	Knowledge	You do not know how to fix things and there are no resources to learn. You watch as things fail, and you either give up and leave or you get burned out.	You cannot convey your knowledge to the correct people, or they will not accept it.	You will not learn how to fix it because they will not pay for your education.	You will not learn how to fix it because there is not time.	You do not know how to build and maintain relationships. You go from team to team being "that guy" that just complains but never identifies underlying issues or provides solutions to problems.
	Will	You do nothing because nothing will happen to you because you are not motivated to force change. You see what is happening and gradually either stop caring or get fed up.	You are not in the position to effect change. You become a pest to those to whom you talk about the problem. You get burned out trying to push the boulder up the hill.	The project will not get the resources needed to fix it.	It will not be fixed in time and the product will either be substandard or will never be fielded.	You do not care about other people. You do not invest in them so they are not inspired to invest in you.

Figure 26-4. *(continued)*

The Approach Matrix

Addressing what is learned from the *Diagnostic Matrix* is the hard part, but at least you now recognize the challenges ahead. Below is another tool that helps to identify what you need to add to the plan. To use the tool, identify the cells of the previous diagnostic matrix that apply to the situation and then find the corresponding cells on the approach matrix. Once you have located the cells where you are seeing issues in the previous diagnostic matrix, write them down the issue from the previous tool and the corresponding steps to help resolve the issue from the approach matrix below as inputs for the plan. Each generic procedure or alternative is just a starting point, and it is important to take each generic procedure and tailor it to your unique situation. The approach matrix is shown in Figure 26-5.

	Organization/Project					
Individual		Project Flexibility (Organization does not change with the requirements)	Structure Mismatch (project or company structure)	Funding (Tight or insufficient funding)	Schedule (Tight or insufficient time available)	Relationship Strength (Management to Customer, User, Team, and Owners)
	Authority (recognized as a person to make the final decision)	1. Identify and write down the person(s) who have the authority. 2. Find out what it would take to motivate them to collaborate. 3. Find out what processes all parties will need to execute. 4. Build the relationship.	1. Update your resume to reflect a position that would have that authority and look for a position on your team with those responsibilities. 5. Approach management about changing position/ responsibilities.	1. Find out who has the ability to approve the financial aspects and establish a relationship. 6. Then communicate the needed changes.	1. Find out who has the authority to approve updates to the schedule and establish a relationship. 7. Then communicate the needed changes.	1. Determine which relationships are the least well developed, most confrontational, or most counterproductive. 8. Work to develop your relationships with all of the parties (management, users, customers, teammates, and company ownership).
	Accountability (One will get in trouble if it fails)	1. Identify and write down the person(s) who are impacted by both the problem and the change. 2. Find out what it would take to motivate them to collaborate. 3. Build the relationship.	1. Update your resume to reflect a position that would have that authority and look for a position on your team with those responsibilities. 4. Approach management about changing position/ responsibilities. 5. Establish consequences for oneself (set a threshold that you will take actions on like leaving the program or restructuring the team if you have the authority).	1. Establish some thresholds for Return On Investment for your customer or businesses investments and use self-discipline to adhere to that threshold.	1. Establish what the task dependencies are. 6. Establish what the critical path is. 7. Establish some thresholds for late deliveries along the critical path items.	1. Establish better relationships so that they care about your success, and you care about their success. 2. Establish a more team focused environment.
	Responsibility (Part of job description and recognized by others)	1. Identify and write down the person(s) who usually would be involved in doing the work. 2. Find out what it would take to motivate them to collaborate with you. 3. Build the relationship.	1. Update your resume to reflect a position that would have that authority and look for a position on your team with those responsibilities. 4. Approach management about changing position/ responsibilities. 5. Establish consequences for oneself (set a threshold that you will take actions on like leaving the program or restructuring the team	1. Find out who knows how to have the funds allocated. 2. Work with those individuals to get it done.	1. Find out who knows how to adjust the schedule. 2. Work with those individuals to make the schedule changes	1. Show that you care about the outcome of the thing that you are changing. 2. Communicate how it impacts you and why you are taking the tasking on.

Figure 26-5. *The Approach Matrix*

			if you have the authority)			
	Knowledge	1. Identify what needs to be learned or ask others what needs to be learned. 2a. Request resources to address the lack of knowledge. 2b. If there are no resources, you may be able to take it on yourself.	1. Find out what you need to know and learn it. 2. Work on your communication skills (both written and verbal).	1. View it as an investment in your own career and buy books or pay for education on project cost estimation or accounting.	1. View it as an investment in your career as an architect and learn to use tools like Gantt charts, Work Breakdown Structures (WBS), Earned Value Management, etc. to help you interface with the rest of the organization.	1. Improve your communication skills. 2. Demonstrate that you can analyze the situation and the possible solutions.
	Will	1. Evaluate what is causing your lack of will. 2. Find a mentor or collaborator with experience with some aspect of the problem 3. Break problem down into manageable parts or steps if you are overwhelmed.	1. Motivate yourself to move into a position where you will be more engaged. 2. If you realize that you do not have the required will then it is important to either find someone else who does or evaluate if issue is actually the problem or if is just a nuisance that can be disregarded.	1. Determine why you are not motivated to allocate the resources using a cost benefit analysis or a product cost comparison.	1. Determine why you are not motivated to move the schedule to the right or reallocate resources to make it possible to work tasking in parallel.	1. Determine why you do not care about other people (personal apathy, no team spirit, or toxic team situation).

Figure 26-5. *(continued)*

Plan to Orchestrate the Change

> *An hour of planning can save ten hours of doing*
>
> —Dale Carnegie

After following this framework for identifying the problem, identifying the solution, identifying the path to success, identifying any barriers to that success, and committing yourself to the task, it is important to plan. One thing to remember is that your change effort might be more likely to succeed if you first pave the road to success before proceeding. This is accomplished by laying out how to address any potential issues before even advertising what the plan is. Most likely, the things you must do to be successful in this pursuit will be necessary for other pursuits, so it may make sense to invest in those actions or activities on their own. For example, you may discover that there is someone who needs to take a certain action to ensure the change is a success. That same individual will often be important to other future efforts. Building a solid relationship with them may be more rewarding in the long term than creating a shallow relationship that only satisfies the immediate need.

Packaging Your Solution

Often you will have a solution to a problem; however, even if your solution is well defined, the potential benefits are understood, and the formalized solution optimized for the organization, more work is necessary. Typically, some amount of effort is necessary to "package" the solution into a form that is ready for adoption. Often architects can be overly excited, with a fervent desire to unleash the solution on the world, but it is important to proceed carefully here. Every change invites some disruption, exemplified by the "J curve"[8] (Figure 26-6).

[8] Jellison, J. (2006). *Managing the Dynamics of Change.* McGraw-Hill

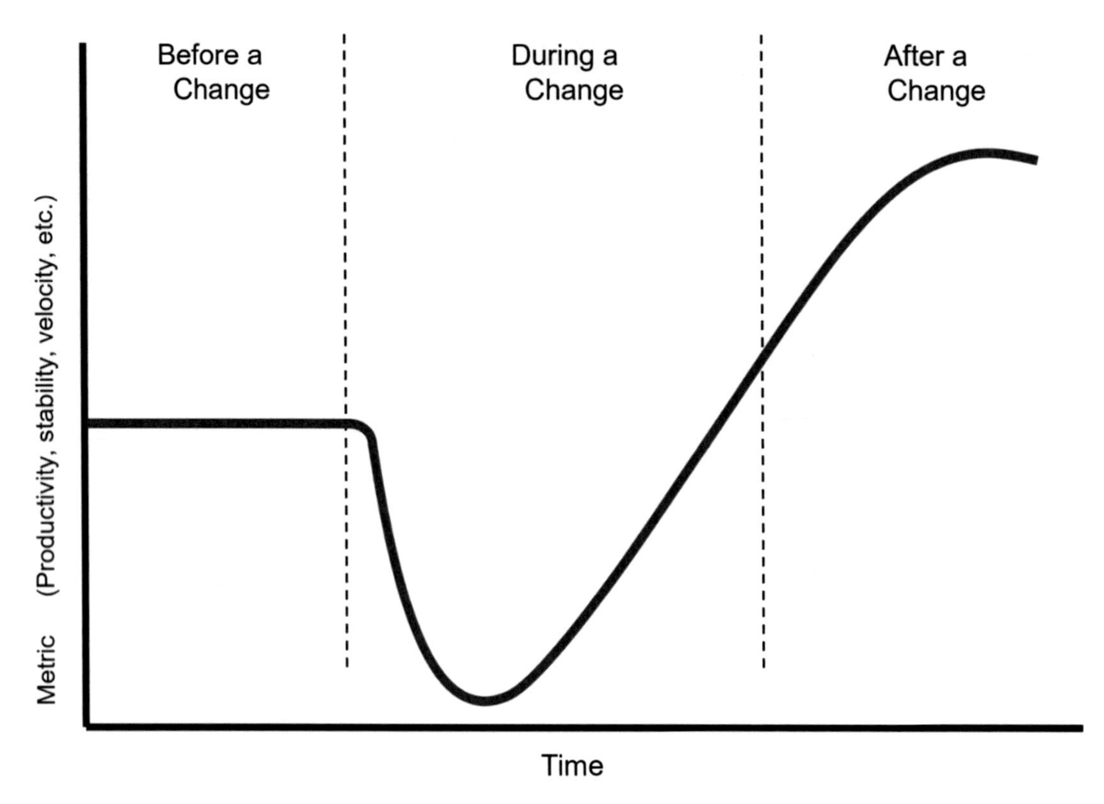

Figure 26-6. *The "J" Curve*

There is often an expectation and implicit assumption (by both architects and members of the organization) that the solution will trace a steady improvement over time, but, almost universally, changes introduce a striking initial disruption that must be overcome. Many promising solutions and architectural innovations are abandoned during the j-curve dip. Proper packaging of an innovation is a crucial step in reducing the potential disruption of a change. The less potential adopters must learn and the fewer ingrained behaviors/habits they need to change, the better the odds of success for the innovation.

Packaging is the process of removing as much initial adoption friction as possible. Packaging may involve building a POC, reference implementation, or tooling. It may involve training or coaching/mentoring. There is no one-size-fits-all approach.

Optimize Your Proposed Solution

If you examined your solution through the lens of Rogers' *Innovation Attributes*, the following would aid you in optimizing those variables.

Optimizing Relative Advantage

Obviously, the higher the perceived relative advantage of the innovation, the higher the likelihood of adoption. The degree of relative advantage may be measured in economic terms, but social prestige factors, convenience, and satisfaction are also important factors. Relative advantage, however, is always in the eye of the beholder. Savvy and adroit architects and change agents will look at relative advantage from multiple angles. When presenting the innovation to potential early adopters and champions, you must be able to succinctly communicate both what the innovation is and why *they* should care. The precise framing of this message will vary depending on the audience, and you should be able to articulate the value proposition of your solution to a wide variety of potential audiences.

Optimizing Compatibility

A strong belief in the benefits of a solution often leads us to assume that the practices our solution seeks to replace are so inferior they can be completely dismissed, yet history repeatedly shows the folly in this thinking. Adopters of your solution can only deal with a new idea within the context and basis of what is already familiar. You must ask yourself how compatible your solution is with the existing ways of working and existing mental models.

The truly revolutionary ideas and solutions simply cannot be introduced all at once. As Nikola Tesla's character in the 2006 film, *The Prestige*, says:

> *The world only tolerates one change at a time.*
>
> —*The Prestige*

Personally speaking, one of the hardest realities I have had to accept in my career is meaningful change often must take place in stages. On a case-by-case basis, the solution must be evaluated to determine if the big innovation can be broken down into smaller, more compatible changes that pave the way toward the final innovation.

Your solution must be ruthlessly examined to identify potential areas of flex or deferral. Perfection is the enemy of progress.

Optimizing Complexity

New ideas that are simpler to understand are adopted more rapidly than solutions that require potential adopters to develop new skills and understandings. Similar to how we must approach compatibility, ruthless examination must take place to identify where ideas can be simplified in the short term. We must look for every opportunity to reduce adoption complexity.

Taking time to create learning guilds, book clubs, or regular lunch-and-learn sessions are an ideal forum to gradually introduce ideas into the organization well before pitching them as solutions. This creates a foundation of fertile soil for future learning on a topic to take root and blossom.

It is also important to have "skin in the game." Taking the time to build POCs, tooling, reference implementations can aid greatly. Automation is another avenue to reduce friction points. Finally, consider a training strategy. You may possess the skill of building effective and engaging training, but also consider delegating so you may scale yourself.

Optimizing Trialability

To many stakeholders, change almost universally equates to risk. A solution that individuals can evaluate on a trial basis is one that carries significantly lower risk. The value of presenting a trial should not be underestimated.

Think carefully about the opportunities to trial your solution within a subset of the organization. First, the limited perceived scope of the risk will win over some who are skeptical, but also consider the trial as part of building your growing body of early adopters. Relatively earlier adopters of an innovation or solution perceive trialability as more important than do later adopters since we can see others' success later in the adoption process. For those later adopters, peers who perform early exploration of your solution amount to a vicarious trial.

Optimizing Observability

> *You can't improve what you don't measure.*
>
> —Peter Drucker

Think about ways to measure and demonstrate growing success over time. Your plan should consider how you might increasingly demonstrate that

- The innovation is successful.
- The problem is tractable.
- The benefits are materializing.
- This is better than the status quo.

The challenge for you lies in making this data visible. Based on what you have learned in Chapter 5, find metrics germane to various groups you wish to influence in the organization. The key is to figure out what you can measure and show to reduce uncertainty and then communicate this.

Write Down the Plan

Writing down your plan brings multiple benefits. First, the process will illuminate potential gaps and risks in strategy. Additionally, your plan will help you stay on track when things get tough.

As time goes by, it may be hard to stay motivated. Periodically looking back on what has been successful can aid in maintaining motivation and will. Each new problematic barrier or detour that occurs will seem easier to overcome when you shift your perspective by looking back on the series of successes that may have been hard fought or more circuitous than originally planned. Also, you will find that it is harder to give up when reflecting on what has already been invested and accomplished.

The plan should outline steps broken down into smaller tasks whenever possible, but the key is to determine the sequence and dependencies. The plan needs to remain adaptable, acknowledging that real-world events will not perfectly align with the planned activities.

The "happy path" your plan creates is only a starting point. Each step along the way should have an alternate route in case things do not work out as anticipated. Know that you cannot plan for every contingency. Invest more thought into the primary path to success, but do not neglect some amount of investment into alternative paths to success. Also, define points along the way where one can evaluate the cost of completion and sunk cost and decide if continuing the pursuit is worth it. The world is constantly changing, and you do not want to pursue something to completion if it will no longer bring material value.

Make sure to fully plan rigorously. If you only provide a simple road map without analyzing thoroughly and things go wrong that should have been easy to identify in advance, then you will lose credibility in your technical knowledge and leadership abilities.

Once you have written down the plan, it is time to begin communicating the idea for the change and even the plan to accomplish the change with the individuals that will be involved in and/or impacted by the change.

Execute the Plan

It is important to account for all the barriers and opportunities that have been identified and utilize these opportunities once execution of the plan begins.

Prepare for Change

Once an architect has identified a process, product, service, or decision that they wish to see changed and analyzed their influence, their counterparts' influence, and their organizational situation relative to the change that they wish to make, they can proceed to take action.

Prepare for Success

There will be a significantly higher likelihood of success once you grow accustomed to performing the analysis and using the resultant knowledge to help the organization effect change.

Summary

The Tailor-Made Architecture Model aims to bring the practice of designing systems closer to a science, but the soul of the role of architect may always be an art that develops over time with practice and patience. While mastering the technical aspects of software architecture provides the necessary foundation, your true value emerges in your ability to execute architecture and drive meaningful change within an organization. This chapter has equipped you with a systematic approach to identify, evaluate, and implement solutions. The lessons and guidance in this chapter are hard won that emerged out of many failures and frustration. I encourage you to profit from our past failures. Remember, it is not enough to design an elegant architecture; you must also skillfully navigate the complexities of organizational dynamics and change management. The ability to influence and lead others toward a shared vision is what will ultimately distinguish you as a truly effective software architect.

It has been a pleasure and an honor to join you on this phase of your journey. Although there is much more to learn and discover, this completes the book and what's next is up to you. How exciting!

I will bid you farewell for now, but you can contact me anytime at michael@magician.codes or view my travel schedule, speaking dates, and training classes at `https://magician.codes/`. I am grateful for our time together through these pages, and I hope our paths cross again in the future. I wish you joy, growth, and enlightenment for the many years and adventures to come.

Index

A

M. Carducci, *Mastering Software Architecture*, https://doi.org/10.1007/979-8-8688-0410-6

B

D

E

F

G

H

N

O

P

T

Printed in the United States
by Baker & Taylor Publisher Services